AF600443

THE AGON OF INTERPRETATIONS

The Agon of Interpretations

Towards a Critical Intercultural Hermeneutics

EDITED BY MING XIE

UNIVERSITY OF TORONTO PRESS
Toronto Buffalo London

Toronto Buffalo London
www.utppublishing.com

ISBN 978-1-4426-4353-6 (cloth)

Library and Archives Canada Cataloguing in Publication

The agon of interpretations : towards a critical intercultural hermeneutics / edited by Ming Xie.

Includes bibliographical references and index.
ISBN 978-1-4426-4353-6 (bound)

1. Hermeneutics. 2. Intercultural communication. I. Xie, Ming, 1958–, editor of compilation

BD241.A36 2014 121'.686 C2014-901327-2

University of Toronto Press acknowledges the financial assistance to its publishing program of the Canada Council for the Arts and the Ontario Arts Council, an agency of the Government of Ontario.

University of Toronto Press acknowledges the financial support of the Government of Canada through the Canada Book Fund for its publishing activities.

Contents

Part Two: Intercultural Complications and Problematics

Part Three: Expanding Horizons: Empathy, Dialogue, Critique, Wisdom

Acknowledgments

I want to express my sincere thanks to all the contributors to this volume for their support, engagement, and patience.

I am very grateful to Richard Ratzlaff, my editor at the University of Toronto Press, for supporting this project and for shepherding it through its various stages. I would also like to record my thanks to Barbara Porter at the press for her help and patience and to Matthew Kudelka for his copy editing.

The positive comments and helpful suggestions by the anonymous readers for the press are also gratefully acknowledged here.

MX, Toronto

THE AGON OF INTERPRETATIONS

Towards a Critical Intercultural Hermeneutics

MING XIE

We do not mistake ourselves without also being mistaken about others and our relations with them.

Paul Ricoeur[1]

In this introduction, as a first approximation, intercultural hermeneutics may be defined simply as the theory and practice of interpretation between cultures. As such, intercultural hermeneutics concerns the different modes of interpretation and understanding in and between different cultures. An example from my own experience may illustrate what I mean. Some years ago when I was teaching a graduate seminar on the translatability of cultures, one of the central issues I asked my students to ponder was the extent to which translation between languages and cultures presupposes interpretation and understanding, both of which in turn presuppose viewpoint and framework. "Suppose I am Chinese and say that ...": I was trying to pose a question about how a particular viewpoint may both affirm and transcend itself at the same time. Before I could finish my question, a student exclaimed, "But you *are* Chinese, aren't you?" To which I replied, "Yes, I *am* Chinese, but that's precisely *beside the point*!" Rather, my point was (and is) that in comparative intercultural inquiry a viewpoint or perspective is not bound by the person who holds it or by the location from which the viewpoint is asserted. The point is really about looking at an issue from a perspective different from one's habitual way of seeing. So my assuming a "Chinese" viewpoint did not mean that I was speaking *as* a Chinese person; rather, such a viewpoint can be made accessible and intelligible to anyone who is not or not merely Chinese. Indeed, assuming a "Chinese" viewpoint in this way would make it available not only for empathy or understanding, but also for examination and evaluation – in short, for critique.

To connect understanding with critical evaluation in intercultural situations inevitably raises questions about the basic assumptions of traditional hermeneutics. Hermeneutics has long been viewed as the art and science of interpretation and, through it, understanding. As such, hermeneutic theory has been concerned primarily with intracultural constructions of meaning. But in an increasingly globalized world in which intercultural concerns have risen to prominence, is hermeneutics still relevant? What is its potential, and what are its possibilities? These are questions about the nature of hermeneutic understanding. They are also about the implications that hermeneutics may have for intercultural inquiry. In this collection, a team of international scholars develop a critical intercultural hermeneutics by drawing on the strengths of traditional Western hermeneutic theory and, more importantly, by confronting that theory's limitations with the goal of transcending dichotomous Western/non-Western ways of thinking. The fourteen essays of this collection, which are interdisciplinary in approach and have been written especially for this volume, explore alternative positions and perspectives. They reflect on what is both strong and lacking in traditional hermeneutic theory, and on what hermeneutics might generate from within by freeing itself from the constraints of its primarily Western model of epistemological understanding. A hermeneutics reoriented and transformed in this way should offer us a heuristic structure for thinking both interculturally and transculturally.

A fundamental problem of intercultural hermeneutics is how to juxtapose and mutually evaluate two (or more) forms of life, systems of belief, or epistemes. Critical hermeneutics is intracultural and intercultural at the same time. These two dimensions cannot be neatly separated, although they may appear to be distinct. Often the intracultural can transform itself into the intercultural (as with the understanding of *sharia* or Islamic law and the ideological use of religion to further imperialist ends). It is in this sense that the critical comes to entail the testing and contesting of assumptions. Self-definition, self-critique, and self-revision are built into the internal dialectic of any given culture as its historical becoming and – more broadly in the intercultural context – as the continual articulation of the logic of relations between cultures, in terms of both commonalities and differences. This dialectic enables one to be more historically and critically self-reflexive towards one's own normative standards. Conversely, the epistemic logic of intercultural hermeneutics is one according to which our cognitive access to reality is both enabled and constrained by the modes of interpretation and understanding that individual cultures have devised. Interpretation and understanding have the power to transform so-called objective reality into truth, a truth that is lived intersubjectively and interculturally.

A central problem examined here is thus the very notion of a "critical" hermeneutics and its various connotations and implications, especially in the light of intercultural concerns.[2] What might "critical" mean in the context of intercultural hermeneutics? A guiding assumption of this collection is that if hermeneutics pertains not only to interpretation of one's own past or tradition, but also to interpretation of foreign traditions and cultures, in both cases hermeneutics has the potential for critique and self-critique. In this sense, to articulate the terms for critical intercultural hermeneutics is precisely to redress the limitations of traditional emphases in "the critical" or "critique," especially as practised in the West. In this collection, the critical is certainly not evoked as an exercise in fostering political contest or endorsing ideological power. To accentuate the critical function of hermeneutics for intercultural understanding is to reveal what is hidden or unconscious so as to render it available for understanding, examination, and transformation. Critique in these terms is primarily a philosophical reflection on, and a reconstructive transformation of, (self-)understanding. Critique might thus aim at intercultural stereotypes and prejudices and hence the habits of mind that underpin them, yet it would be more concerned with how it could compel us toward a self-reflexive awareness of our own historicity and contestability and hence our own creative capacity. Critique in this sense does not mean the negative or arrogant or even hostile criticism or denigration of what seem to be other cultures' faults or inadequacies or limitations. Critique is not dismantling or "debunking." Rather, critique consists in continually interrogating both the current and the long-held assumptions of one's own culture as well as those of a foreign one. Let us remember that "critique" is not an exclusively Western concept – the positive, peace-seeking meaning of "critique" has non-Western roots as well. In this non-Western sense, intercultural hermeneutics is critical because genuine understanding, dialogue, and exchange between cultures is not possible unless all of us *open up* our fundamental assumptions to interpretation, understanding, contestation, experimentation, and transformation. There can be no real exchange unless we consider different systems of assumptions. Without this opening up, intercultural dialogue may be reduced to outward tolerance or non-engagement. Critique in this productive sense could in fact be seen as indispensable in promoting intercultural exchange and harmony. Critical hermeneutics thus has huge international potential. Its goal is not the convergence of values and practices; rather, it is to keep alive an open-minded but critical spirit of intercultural inquiry.

This collection's main argument – that hermeneutics is vital for interculturality – also engages with issues that are shaping current debates about hermeneutics. Hermeneutics is often accused of being relativistic because it emphasizes the contextuality of knowledge and the resultant equivocality. Hermeneutics seems to risk being relativistic because, with its preoccupation with understanding, it often appears to support and justify the status quo of a given tradition and culture. Yet hermeneutics can just as easily be diagnostic in its explanatory understanding of traditions or cultures. Various cultures and traditions can communicate with and interpret one another without presupposing a universal consensus or uniform criteria. The perspective of a different or even rival culture or tradition cannot be neutral. Precisely in being defined by its own unique constraints as much as is one's own culture, a rival culture offers an alternative view. An alternative perspective becomes different only through its relevance to our own culture. The intrinsic value of such relations lies in the mutual revelation of both cultures, of what may otherwise remain unidentified or unidentifiable without a shift in perspective or conceptualization. This shift presupposes that we have somehow to suspend or overcome our original viewpoint so as to learn to appreciate and even inhabit another one. We gain a perspective on our own culture by getting inside another culture to some extent and in some ways. An inescapable question confronting intercultural hermeneutics seems to be whether the other can only ever be intelligible to us on our own terms. This is a question about translation. Translation in this particular sense is no longer concerned with making two views commensurable but with establishing new ways of thinking or conception that go beyond questions of commensurability. The act of translation as such would become the act of revealing and scrutinizing our own presuppositions and categories of understanding as well as those of a foreign culture. But when we take two views to be incommensurable, we are in fact measuring them in the light of our own conceptual framework. What we find lacking are shared terms or standards of understanding within this framework, not understanding of any degrees or kinds. Thus what is fundamentally incommensurable or untranslatable may still be understandable and translatable both in principle and in fact. When critiquing and evaluating our own culture – that is, at the level of built-in conceptual habits and cognitive categories – we may find an alien tradition indispensable. That alien culture may provide fundamental terms that enable us to ask vital questions. As the essays in this collection argue, internal evaluations need to be supplemented and complicated by evaluations that other traditions offer. This kind of mutual critique can overcome the dichotomous model of the "West" versus the "non-West."

On the other hand, critical intercultural hermeneutics is critical because it engages with the putative universality of communicative critical reason (as emphasized by Habermas, for example). Critical intercultural hermeneutics both draws on and differentiates itself from thinkers as diverse as Habermas, Gadamer, and Foucault. In this respect, while finding both hermeneutics and the critique of ideology valuable, critical intercultural hermeneutics consciously makes these two positions relevant to each other by setting them in mutual complication and enlightenment. This is to say that critical intercultural hermeneutics is both hermeneutical and critical, as well as intercultural. In this regard, Ricoeur is another important source. Two of his concepts – critical hermeneutics and poetic redescription – are particularly productive. Hermeneutics for Ricoeur needs to be self-critical because understanding is always limited. The effective distinction here is that hermeneutics seems to take meaning for granted and seeks to discover or decipher meaning, while poetics reflects on the dynamics and creation of meaning itself. The poetic function is thus concerned with imagining and creating new possibilities of, and alternatives to, hermeneutic thinking. Critical intercultural hermeneutics aims to articulate this poetic function in intercultural terms and to explore its potential for intercultural modes of thinking.

To integrate hermeneutical understanding with critical explanation and reflexivity as two interrelated approaches assumes that both are valid modes of interpretation and that each complements the other. One addresses precisely how we may see through our own perspectives what is similar to us, the other how we may account for traditions different from our own through their own perspectives. What enables such integration is the plural nature of interpretation. At a time when diverse systems of thinking have taken the place of an all-embracing paradigm of metaphysics, engaging with conflicts of interpretation becomes an immediate challenge. This is why incorporating reflexivity into an essentially non-analytical concept of interpretation may offer a possible step in this direction. If explanation as interpretation can also perform a critical function, then interpretation would benefit from reflexivity. Here we may recall Foucault's conception of "critique," defined in the sense of revealing and explaining the values and assumptions behind a certain social, political, or cultural practice. A critique is not (necessarily) an exposure of a system's flaws and imperfections. As Foucault formulates it: "A critique is not a matter of saying that things are not right as they are. It is a matter of pointing out on what kinds of assumptions, what kinds of familiar, unchallenged, unconsidered modes of thought the practices that we accept rest."[3] For Foucault, to be critical is to reveal how such practices are sustained and perpetuated by their underlying systems of values and assumptions. To be critical is to reflect on the conditions of experience. The plurality of interpretations allows *hermeneutic* interpretations to be combined with *critical* evaluation and reflexivity. Likewise, Ricoeur places great emphasis on exposing and explaining cultural codes. This should remind us that no comparison can contain something that is excluded from the schema of comparison. What may be called comparativity, or the awareness and activity of making and unmaking comparisons, means instead to break away from the fixed frames to which the indeterminacy of the world has been subjected.

Given the terms established here for a critical intercultural hermeneutics, to engage more specifically with current debates on intercultural exchange, we need to further explore and elaborate a number of crucial concepts and issues. For example, a distinction between limits and limitations can be brought to bear on our understanding of the concept of "horizon." As a vision, a horizon may be limited in its range. It may also be a constitutive part of a larger continuity or whole, as an "ampliative" way of extending the self – that is, extending or adding to that which is already known. Another sense of horizon could be that while the immediate present may present itself as intelligible and significant, this often becomes possible only when seen against the backdrop of more invisible customs and habits. In the same vein, a "fusion of horizons" may no longer mean simply an integration of more than one horizon. Any fusion itself calls for a larger fusion that would encompass it. In a fusion, particular horizons do not (necessarily) get "fused" together; rather, they are (often) kept in tension through mutual definition and revelation. It is through the constant maintenance of such a critical tension that our horizons are shaped or given as limits;

this would constitute a liminal field between accustomed and alternative (or even contrarian) habits of thinking. Thus limits and limitations are both related and transmutable. They are never stable but are constantly emerging by way of intercultural encounters.

The subject matter of the text, or the "matter" of the text, is another question that critical intercultural hermeneutics actively explores. The Gadamerian concept of the "subject matter" (*die Sache*) of the text should set us thinking more critically.[4] Critical intercultural hermeneutics actively engages with and develops this concept. According to Gadamer, it may be argued that without the subject matter (*Sache*), there will be no material basis for people from different cultures to have converging or even overlapping interests. Such a lack of commonality demonstrates what incommensurability is all about. Yet this view assumes that these different concerns would be about the same issue. The difference lies only in forms of seeing or articulating from one's own particular cultural tradition. The *Sache*, however, consists of more than just a common object for varied or different interpretations. No existing natural language can fully or completely exhaust its meaning. The concept of the *Sache* thus evokes what fundamentally cannot be exhausted by any one language. One has to transcend interpretations of a particular culture in order to understand the *Sache*. We may need to define the *Sache* further in terms of the notion of *magma* (as elaborated in the work of Cornelius Castoriadis, among others).[5] *Magma* highlights the irreducible and indefinite multiplicity of the real prior to interpretive access. *Magma* conceived in this way is about things that cannot be exhausted or even captured by interpretations. For example, the function of context in any given interpretation is paradoxical: an interpretation presupposes and is made possible by its context, but the context itself cannot be fully articulated by the interpretation. A given culture's own interpretations of itself are only self-interpretations and by their very nature cannot exhaust the reality and potential of this culture. Likewise, diverse modes of being, and diverse modes of making sense and understanding, are not subsumable under any single concept of being; hence plurality is an essential feature of a globalized intercultural world. In addition, precisely because different cultural views are derived from incommensurable perceptive scales, the multiplicity of *magma* is activated or becomes generative each time a specific interpretation is attempted. *Magma* thus points to the intrinsic need for intercultural interpretation or rather, defines the high stakes of such interpretation. To correlate or integrate the two concepts of the *Sache* and *magma* thus has important implications for reconceiving hermeneutics between cultures. This is to say that the matter or subject matter of understanding can be accessed only through the ways in which it in turn conditions understanding – that is, through seeing beyond the terms of understanding. Also important is that to access the matter of text through understanding is to appropriate and be disappropriated at the same time. Intercultural hermeneutics may thus identify for us a dual mode of distanciation as a fundamental approach to cultures. It would seem unlikely for different cultures to come up with an identical *Sache*. The likelihood of having different *Sachen* in dispute or at stake also points to the nature of what may be fundamentally contradictory or conflicting between different cultures and to the need for us to acknowledge, confront, and learn about different *Sachen* of different cultures.

Therefore, engaging genuinely with another culture or with the as yet undiscovered potential of one's own culture is about identifying alternative worlds and fulfilling new possibilities. Poetic redescriptions in Ricoeur's sense, for example, may help us imagine alternatives or alternative possibilities. It would be highly productive to extend Ricoeur's poetic sense from an intracultural proposal to an intercultural category. Intercultural hermeneutics, by imagining other worlds, moves beyond the confines of existing conceptual categories within a given culture. Hermeneutics is fundamentally about perceiving and imagining alternative possible worlds, recounting one another's imaginaries differently, and symbolically sharing the world-making resources of different cultures. Critical hermeneutics can thus be seen as an alternative to both arbitrary relativism (mere plurality of interpretations) and hierarchical foundationalism (ethnocentric Reason). It can also offer a poetics of creation through interpretation. In this sense, a creative and poetic capacity seems to be an inherent condition of hermeneutics itself. This transformative potential of poetic interpretation deserves more critical attention than has so far been given to it in the field of hermeneutics. To recognize and develop such a potential is to move beyond hermeneutics as traditionally conceived and practised. The multiplicity of interpretations remains open to the *magma* of significations, as this multiplicity is the only way to access and actualize such *magma*. This also means that interpretive recalcitrance is intrinsic to the *magma* of significations in intercultural exchanges. As this *magma* cannot be exhausted and will always yield a multiplicity of interpretations and their mutual contestation, one can no longer expect to identify the correct meaning of such *magma* and then unravel it. Critical intercultural hermeneutics foregrounds the opacity and recalcitrance in analysing a culture's self-understanding and its understanding of another culture. In short, critical intercultural hermeneutics foregrounds both the actuality and virtuality of a culture's imaginary significations.

Such virtuality is real even when it is yet to be actualized. To see such virtuality as both actual and not yet (fully) actualized is to acknowledge the contingency of our collective cultural identities and practices. This contingent nature does not detract from the reality of what is only virtually present. As Deleuze has shown, in contrast to what is possible, the virtual is always real.[6] Ultimately, critical intercultural hermeneutics promotes modes of thinking that may be called "speculative," in the sense that what is actual is only contingent and can be reactualized differently. The poetic function of hermeneutics is thus also about the emancipatory potential of critical intercultural hermeneutics. The poetic function of hermeneutics pertains to how we address the question of disclosure, or world-disclosure, in the sense of the capacity to articulate and engender different ways of looking at the world and different ways of acting in (and on) the world.

The complexity of all these issues seems to highlight that critical intercultural hermeneutics serves and validates both the historical continuity of individual cultures and their transformation. For this reason, critical intercultural hermeneutics consists in the process of continually articulating the logic of interculturally shared and differentiated values. There is a genuine and urgent issue of trying to move beyond a model of intercultural interaction as inscribed in a relationship of power and resistance, of domination and subordination, of authority and appropriation. Critical intercultural hermeneutics is predicated on the assumption that it is necessary to achieve a self-awareness of one's culture as discursive in nature – that is, on an awareness of how one's culture depends on an interpretation or understanding of the conditions and consequences of conceptual and socio-political norms within that culture. Critical intercultural hermeneutics should enable different cultures to regard other cultures as symbolic resources, with the result that many values are no longer narrowly ethnocultural in their application but become universal modes of thinking and being. Thus, the capacity to understand the thought of another culture is not only empathic but also has normative implications for the concept and practice of intercultural reason. We may clarify the normativity of intercultural reason by referring to Kant's discussion of taste or judgment, which he sees as a kind of universal "*sensus communis*," in the sense of a comparative judgment in which we compare our interpretations and understandings not with the actual but with the "possible judgments" of others, thereby "[putting] ourselves in the position of everyone else."[7] Intercultural hermeneutic reason concerns the normativity of intercultural truth, a normativity that is figured as a kind of rational ratification and self-modification on the part of a given culture. Intercultural truth has to do with the continual emergence of new relations and new modes of understanding, with the making common of something that emerges only in intercultural exchange and dialogue. Norms are thus not self-evident or taken-for-granted, but contingent, contestable, revisable ways of accessing and evaluating another's culture as well as one's own and of making these cultures mutually intelligible. On this view, intercultural reason pertains to the logic of articulating the modes of intelligibility between cultures. It is akin to the notion of immanent critique. The very possibility of disagreement is itself an essential function of communication, of intercultural reason. Thus the very concept of intercultural truth implies a normative horizon that transcends the occasions and instances of disagreement and even conflict. In other words, mere diversity of cultures is no guarantee of intercultural understanding or harmony. This is where intercultural hermeneutics is distinct from, albeit related to, the discourses of "multiculturalism." The normative function of critical intercultural hermeneutics lies in its commitment to articulating new cultural and intercultural norms and relations precisely by articulating and affirming both the validity of core intercultural values and the agency of individual cultures in contributing to such common values. The normativity of intercultural reason is, in the end, immanent in the very process of practising critical intercultural hermeneutics.

The essays in this collection take up a series of engrossing issues that bear on these challenges and possibilities of a critical intercultural hermeneutics. Instead of addressing the same issues from a range of angles, these chapters explore various issues and develop them in a cumulative way. Those issues range from current theories of phenomenology and hermeneutics as resources for critical intercultural hermeneutics, through the complications and problematics of articulating these theories in intercultural terms, to the implications that a critical intercultural hermeneutics may have for possibilities of empathy, dialogue, and wisdom. The aim is not only to investigate, without essentializing, the critical, constructive, and normative dimensions of hermeneutics by reconceptualizing it as an intercultural activity, but also to envision modes of intercultural inquiry that allow hermeneutics and critical theory to complement and complicate each other. The perspectives of these essays range widely, from literary and cultural criticism, through political science and sociology, to globalization studies and philosophy. Even just within philosophy, they approach questions not only from established perspectives such as phenomenology, philosophical hermeneutics, pragmatism, and moral philosophy, but also by deploying more recent and emergent models of thinking such as systems theory and object-oriented ontology. Combining philosophical orientation with historical and intellectual inquiry, the essays explore epistemological, methodological, and ethical problems in intercultural interpretation and understanding, by engaging with several cultural traditions (European, American, Chinese Confucian, Hindu, Islamic, etc.).

This book is divided into three parts that reflect the essays' shared interest in the conditions and issues of critical intercultural hermeneutics. Together, they help map out the terrain of critical intercultural hermeneutics and define it as a crucially important emergent field. Yet ultimately what the collection aims to offer is a forum for exploration. This means that the chapters do not necessarily agree with one another in their assumptions and conclusions. Instead, they set out to foster the practice of critical dialogue and exchange and may, therefore, mutually support or contest one another's assumptions.

The first part addresses the parameters and conditions of critical intercultural hermeneutics by locating it in a larger context of the critical resources of modern Western philosophy, especially Continental philosophy with its two main orientations: phenomenological and hermeneutical. The essays here raise central issues of intercultural critique through a rethinking of a number of established theoretical traditions and positions. The question of what happens when a tradition encounters its outside, for example, may be posed as one of both closure, through which a culture is constituted as such, and openness, by means of which a culture is revitalized. For Ian Angus, the crossing point of modern hermeneutics and phenomenology would approach intercultural encounters in contextual terms. Yet this is predicated on the imagining of a totalizing discursive knowledge similar to the universalism of modern scientific–technological reason. He thus argues for the need in intercultural exchange to distinguish conceptually between an "anthropological encounter" and a mediated encounter of cultures so as to preserve the difference of cultural values while establishing their comparability. Jean Grondin, by contrast, deplores the lack of exchange in current hermeneutical thinking between Gadamer and Ricoeur, two of the most eminent hermeneutic philosophers of the twentieth century. Examining the differences and convergences between their sources, methodologies, and impacts on modes of thinking, Grondin sees an urgent need for making these two approaches speak to each other. Such an exchange should be highly productive at a time when our own contemporary age has been turned into a "hermeneutic age of reason." But this scepticism towards the totality of reason should not cancel out the value of further exploration of "sociality" and "world" as a trans-subjective rather than intersubjective horizons of meaning. For Suzi Adams, this overarching world-horizon is intrinsically a phenomenological–hermeneutical problematic that can provide us with fresh terms for assessing cultural theories of leading thinkers such as Castoriadis, Arnason, and Patočka. Moving beyond Husserl and Heidegger, Adams offers an emergent position of an "a-subjective phenomenologically sensitive philosophy that offers a non-substantialist approach" to traditions that differ but may overlap ontologically and epistemologically. Bernhard Waldenfels, on the other hand, goes back to a historical tradition of conceiving comparison in the West (e.g., via Kant, Nietzsche, Hume, Rousseau). He argues that the idea of the "phenomenology of the Other" is strongly premised on an examination of intercultural comparison as a critical category. By underscoring both what precedes comparison ("the *intercultural* intertwining") and what exceeds all comparison ("a *transcultural* surplus"), we may guard against a sense of complacency that typifies an unduly normalizing and universalizing discourse of cultural comparison. In this sense, comparison can dislodge and liberate one from one's self-centric and self-satisfied normality. The self-centred locus is again scrutinized in Radhakrishnan's contribution as both Western-centric and anthropocentric. Addressing in general terms Indian politics and more specifically the case of Gandhi, Radhakrishnan rethinks the ideas of Heidegger and Maurice Merleau-Ponty. His critique unravels a double bind of hermeneutics as both epistemology and ideology. He recognizes a pressing need for a radical dislodging of human self-centredness in the field of post-colonial and planetary rethinking, for this would bring into sharp focus the politics of naming the world and of diverse ways of thinking about it.

The second part of this book focuses mainly on the complications and problematics that arise when we take intercultural critical thinking as a hermeneutic way of thinking. Further developing the multifarious but pivotal connections between the intercultural and the critical, the essays in this part focus more specifically on the hermeneutic functions of "cultural difference," a problematic notion that is often compromised and limited by entrenched positions in politics and ideology. The essays, however, remain confident about the possibility of reconceptualizing these issues and about the heuristic value and potential of critique as an important category of intercultural hermeneutics. In this respect, object-oriented ontology, as an emergent movement in contemporary philosophy, questions our deeply entrenched anthropocentric assumptions of human–world correlation – that is, the assumption that human–object relations are primary, to the exclusion of the relations between objects. As Graham Harman here argues, an object-oriented ontological approach sees the essence of objects, including cultural objects, as fundamentally mysterious and withdrawn. One can interpret objects of another culture, but one can never do so fully or adequately or exhaust the meaning or essence of such objects. This object-oriented approach to hermeneutics has profound implications for rethinking human self-reflexivity, for our concept of the world, and for our ways of thinking "about" the world. It is also a way of transcending the stagnant model of reality that, while denying objects any power of resistance to, even withdrawal from, human interpretive and appropriative access and hence denying them any intrinsic capacity for surprising us or making us wonder, converts objects into representations of cultural essentialism and exoticism. For Zhang Longxi, the hermeneutical act as such is always a mediated hermeneutic circle or an act of critique, both for self-examination and for understanding an alien culture in one's own terms. Examining several Western misconceptions about China, especially in the French exoticist Orientalist scholarly tradition, Zhang goes back to the history of China's encounters with Europe to argue against a hermeneutics of East–West relations as a rigid dichotomy of differentials or opposites. This often misplaced emphasis on China as alterity amounts to a projection of covert stereotypical thinking that challenges any emergent intercultural hermeneutics that addresses questions of truth, knowledge, and communication. From a different angle, Hans-Georg Moeller tackles the issue of whether rationality is universal or fraught with cultural relativity. Drawing on Niklas Luhmann's systems theory, Moeller's "Luhmannian deconstruction of the universalism–relativism debate" finds the distinction between universalism and relativism not only unsustainable but false. Rather, they are but *"two complementary kinds of semantic reactions to social changes in modernity"* (original emphasis). We may even say that cultural difference in a hermeneutic context exists only as a product of the very framework of interpretive distinctions deployed by the interpreter. For David B. Wong, moral understanding and judgment in intercultural terms may render the methodology of analytical philosophy meaningful, but it also tests the boundaries of its established form of reflexivity, as the diverse and plural configurations of the sources of moral value demand sustained, complex, flexible forms of cooperation. For this reason, the central issue of hermeneutics is how to know the other through our own terms while at the same time opening ourselves to the other. Wong explores this particular point in his discussion of how the West may read Chinese philosophy in Chinese terms. Bringing together distinct notions of Confucian ethics (rights in particular) and the Gadamerian fusion of horizons, he explains the significance of points of contact in hermeneutic "translation" by arguing that what each side gets from the fusion is not necessarily the same.

The essays in the third part of this book further broaden the terms of critical intercultural hermeneutics. They consider how a critical intercultural hermeneutics may be conceived through categories that have developed into general issues for contemporary humanities studies – categories such as affect, translation, pragmatism, and wisdom of communication – thus linking hermeneutics to other strands of discussion in current critical debates. From a variety of angles, the essays in this last part also explore how these broader categories may help chart a critical intercultural hermeneutics, leaving for further exploration its future horizons and possibilities. These are also questions about the geopolitical confines of a critical methodology – whether, for example, critique is necessarily or primarily Western, and whether non-Western critique is different only in degree or in kind. For Mihai Spariosu, it is in such questions about the uses and abuses of critical thinking and critical theory that we may see the necessity of being truly intercultural – that is, truly moving beyond the West and thereby becoming genuinely global. Commenting on the debate between Cardinal Ratzinger and Habermas, Spariosu sees the major conflict today as between the secular rationalist tradition and Christianity. Intercultural hermeneutics is an intensive and extensive dialogue between and among cultures, one that should help us reconceive the terms of a new science of interpretation, proper to a global reference frame, so as to reconstruct a new science of humanism. In particular, Spariosu offers a fluid model for intercultural hermeneutics, "moving back and forth between local and global reference frames," "adopt[ing] non-linear cognitive models and methods," in order to "help remap existing knowledge and create new cognitive forms from a global perspective." Spariosu's discussion of the Western practice of critique is continued in the essays that follow. The critical methodological dimensions of hermeneutics are explored by Lawrence K. Schmidt as a procedural act. He extends Gadamer's notion of the preconception of completion, or *a priori* conditions such as prejudgments and tradition, into the cross-cultural domain. Drawing on his experience of teaching Confucius to American students, Schmidt sees translation as an act of practical application of the work by the translator, an act that is inevitably worked on by her individual set of prejudgments in an "event of truth," or a process of reaching truth. There is thus the need to move beyond one's inherited prejudgment. A legitimate or adequate prejudgment is an agreed-upon judgment unforeseen at the beginning of a hermeneutic conversation. In this sense, translation is tantamount to critique. In it lies the critical potential of hermeneutic conversation. The convergences and differences between philosophical hermeneutics and pragmatism in the intercultural domain are taken up by Richard Shusterman and Wojciech Małecki in their collaborative essay. Their focus is on how meaning or meaningfulness is incorporated not only into written texts but also into actions, affects, and performances. That is, interpretations are for them events of understanding. A "coherent understanding" thus "exceeds the limits of the work itself." Addressing the political reception of pragmatism in France, Germany, and China, they argue that making sense of a text or culture across time and space requires us to attend to the contingent nature of cultural translation and exchange and to accept the fallibility of hermeneutics. Here, context is of paramount importance – for example, contexts of reception and misunderstanding. But coming to such an awareness can be at the same time a process of trying to calibrate and finesse our ideas of the critical function of interpretation that is "neither totally free nor ... arbitrary." The importance of context in practices of critique is elaborated in the chapter by Lorenzo C. Simpson, whose concern is also the normative rationality of intercultural hermeneutics. In response to Waldenfels's conception of a third-person position on which the self and the other would converge, and in reaction against the postmodern tendency to essentialize cultural difference, Simpson proposes instead "a dialogical or postmetaphysical humanism" or "a non-relativistic but hermeneutic version of critical rationality" against relative claims of pluralism. Recognizing the potential that this critical rationality may have for "non-parochial questioning of the other," Simpson sets out to "give difference its due without abandoning critical standards," which depends on the formation of "situated metalanguages." By evoking the complexity of Islamic identity, he promotes this critical rationality in terms of a "cosmopolitan humanism," a "hermeneutic charity" that would lead to a transcultural "second-order rationality," or the "*internal* normative pressure" that would enable us to analyse "intercultural normative disagreements ... as *intracultural* conflicts" and a "counterfactual narrative critique." This more expansive notion of rationality would reconsider the cultural scope delineated in the theories of Habermas and Gadamer through its firm belief in the transcultural self-critical capacity of cultures. Thus questions are raised as to whether the plurality of interpretations could serve as the primary enabling condition for the politics of the normative, or the politics of intercultural reason. In his contribution, Hans-Herbert Kögler is similarly concerned with rendering the other "intelligible" on our own terms and sees in this the potential for self-estrangement and defamiliarization. Analysing the perspective taking of female excision or genital mutilation in certain African cultures, he takes us through how the political influence on meaning may have a predominant cognitive influence on our existing modes of epistemology, as in the hermeneutic methodology based on empathy, dialogue, or ideological critique. He thus calls for a "normative project of reflexive self-determination" or "dialogic perspective taking." This would be a practical but critical intervention into "a symbolic–practical order without losing sight of the implied power relations and then applying the same perspectives to ourselves." It is a reciprocal hermeneutic circle that offers a more holistic form of normative agency and a more transformative sense of "critique."

The essays in this collection are intended to generate a sustained and cutting-edge exploration of the possibilities of, and challenges facing, critical intercultural hermeneutics as a newly established field. The essays thus move towards an open-ended model of critical intercultural hermeneutics that will have important and profound implications for an increasingly globalized world of cultures.

NOTES

1 Ricoeur, *The Course of Recognition*, trans. David Pellauer (Cambridge, MA: Harvard University Press, 2005), 257.

2 Two pioneering studies on critical hermeneutics have focused on its intercultural implications: Hans Herbert Kögler, *The Power of Dialogue: Critical Hermeneutics after Gadamer and Foucault*, trans. Paul Hendrickson (Cambridge, MA: MIT Press, 1996); and Lorenzo C. Simpson, *The Unfinished Project: Toward a Postmetaphysical Humanism* (New York: Routledge, 2001).

3 Michel Foucault, "Practicing Criticism," in *Politics, Philosophy, Culture: Interviews and Other Writings 1977–1984* (London and New York: Routledge, 1988), 154–5.

4 See Gadamer, *Truth and Method*, 2nd revised edition, trans. Joel Weinsheimer and D.G. Marshall (New York: Continuum, 2004).

5 See Castoriadis, *The Imaginary Institution of Society*, trans. Kathleen Blamey (Cambridge, MA: MIT Press, 1987).

6 Gilles Deleuze, *Difference and Repetition*, trans. Paul Patton (London: Athlone, 1994), 211.

7 Immanuel Kant, *Critique of Judgment*, trans. Werner S. Pluhar (Indianapolis: Hackett, 1987), 160.

PART ONE

Resources of Phenomenology and Hermeneutics

Chapter One

The Intercultural Horizon of Contemporary Understanding

IAN ANGUS

Hermeneutic understanding operates within a tradition, whereas phenomenological philosophy investigates the constitution of traditions and the collection of traditions that forms a culture. In this essay I seek to define the planetary event that motivates intercultural understanding. This event can be understood through a double horizon: the planetary character of scientific–technological civilization defines the context of the interaction of cultures, and the interaction of cultures defines the context for the planetary expansion of scientific–technological civilization. This is the motivating event for critique of traditions and of the collection of traditions that constitutes a culture. It is the experiential ground for a transcendental history of intercultural understanding.

1. The Temporal Structure of Hermeneutic Interpretation

The original situation of hermeneutical interpretation is the confrontation of a reader by a text that is readable in a basic or minimal sense but whose meaning in a more extended sense is opaque. The minimal conditions for the reading of a text are that it be preserved in a medium of some sort (preservation and legibility), that it be in a language that is understood by the reader (linguistic competence), and that it be constructed in such a way as to be read (composed of units of meaning, or sentences, that are not too fragmentary). A reader who is sufficiently able to read minimally such a text may confront a higher-level difficulty in understanding the text in a deeper or more extended fashion insofar as it contains aspects of structure, allusion, metaphorical description, reference, and so on whose significance for an understanding of the text is not clear to the reader. Such higher-level understanding is the object of hermeneutical interpretation. The reader is confronted with a text that is not doubted to be a text, to express a meaning, and to be in principle understandable, but that is not interpretable by the reader as a unity superseding problematic aspects of higher-level meaning. The purpose of hermeneutic interpretation is thus to remove these barriers to a unified, higher-level understanding by interpreting the problematic aspects based on a methodology that removes their obscurity, establishes their significance, and grounds their connection in a unified understanding.

The historical origins of this original hermeneutical situation in European intellectual history are in specific, localized issues in modern biblical interpretation, classical philology, and law; but what Hans-Georg Gadamer calls the "universalization of the hermeneutical problem" has turned hermeneutic understanding into a general approach to the social sciences and humanities because, as Paul Ricoeur says, "all *regional* hermeneutics are incorporated into one *general* hermeneutics"[1] The key element in the universalization of hermeneutic understanding was Martin Heidegger's description of human being as essentially self-interpretive. "Understanding is the existential being of the ownmost possibility of being of Da-sein in such a way that this being discloses in itself what its very being is about."[2] Interpretation is thus not primarily of texts but of the manner of human being itself. All regional interpretations thus become founded on this universal problem of self-understanding. Interpretation is only secondarily a matter of knowing and primarily a matter of being. Textual interpretation is thus founded on self-interpretation, and the specific projects of the social sciences and humanities are folded into the philosophical task of knowing oneself. Although developed with written texts in mind, with appropriate modifications hermeneutic methodology can be applied to the interpretation of musical works, dance, oral and gestural works, and social-historical events (to the extent that hermeneutic methodology can encompass the structural, demographic, and empirical elements of the social sciences without rejecting those elements).

The tradition stitched together by hermeneutical understanding is a form of life passed down through history to be recovered and renewed towards a projected future. It need not be self-enclosed in the sense of being impervious to outside influences, but such influences are brought inside by incorporation into the form of life. Hermeneutic interpretation is a recovery of meaning, a moment of renewal and carrying-forward within a tradition as it faces its future. Hermeneutic understanding is a project of recovery of lost meaning. It begins with a guess about what is the meaning of the whole text,[3] the higher-level meaning, and proceeds to refine this guess by dialectically relating specific parts to the whole. Such refinement of understanding works through a logic of better-or-worse, more-or-less, rather than a logic of true–false or yes–no. It thus involves appropriation by the interpreter in relation to the contemporary situation, which the interpreter must define in its actuality and future possibility through an analysis of identity-and-difference in relation to the situation of the text. This requires both cultivation by the interpreter and an increasing approximation to the whole of the text and its role in cultural history. The hermeneutical interpreter is a latecomer within a tradition that is no longer self-evident but is not (yet) exhausted whose activity of interpretation stitches the cultural tradition together to hold sway across time.

The temporal stitching constructed by hermeneutical interpretation occurs through linking the horizon of the reader with the horizon of the text. For example, if I read Plato, Cicero, or Montaigne on friendship, I bring my own prejudgments, prejudices, about the phenomenon of friendship and the scale of values that it organizes to the statements made by the author in question. Comparing these statements with each other, and putting them into relationship with my prejudices, I gain an understanding of where my view of friendship differs from that of the author – I might assume that friendship is a purely personal relation without implications for whole families, generations, or politics, for example. Scrutinizing individual statements of the author, I can determine places where such assumptions are not operative in the text, and by collecting these together I form an idea of both prejudices and articulations of friendship in the text. In the process, the text questions my prejudices about friendship and a dialogue is constructed between reader and text. Gadamer referred to this dialogue as a "fusing of horizons," which in the case of historical understanding "means that as the historical horizon is projected, it is simultaneously removed."[4] Concretely, as I understand that Plato's exploration of friendship occurs within the horizon of the search for knowledge, or philosophy, I realize that my assumptions, shared by many in the world of my time and place and perhaps taken over uncritically, tend to associate friendship more with intimacy than with a passion for truth. Nevertheless, in this very thought the possibility arises for me that the passion for truth is a more fitting horizon for the phenomenon of friendship. I am at the very least drawn into a dialogue between truth and intimacy as potential horizons.

It is a matter for argument within hermeneutic theory the extent to which fusing occurs or – perhaps better phrased – the extent to which difference is maintained within the unity constructed by dialogue between horizons. Ricoeur claims that "we exist neither in closed horizons, nor within a horizon that is unique,"[5] suggesting that the fusing cannot create an absolute horizon in the form of Hegel's absolute knowledge, nor can it remain in the radical incommunicability of Nietzsche's pluralism. The critical point in this discussion is his claim that Gadamer's conception of fusing tends in the direction of a Hegelian, or Leibnizian, unified horizon even though the terminology of horizon and the phenomenon itself make such a conception impossible. It remains debatable between these authors to what extent horizons fuse or there remains a difference. Thus the theme of friendship is known through the dialogue between, or fusing of, horizons, which, as an act of understanding, creates a temporal unity that can place both past text and present interpreter within a tradition. The dialogue between horizons illuminates the theme, even though the prior identity – or perhaps one should say more cautiously the "similarity" – of the theme is necessary for the interpreter to know that the phenomenon being interpreted is friendship – and not alliance, or kinship, or neighbourliness, or the commonality that one has with a fellow citizen. This is the meaning of hermeneutic interpretation as a latecomer within a tradition: there has to be already enough temporal continuity for there to be a unity of theme in order for the interpretation to get going, but there has to be enough of a break that the text is not immediately clear. It is this break that requires the dialogue between horizons as a means to understanding the text. This final understanding is a new unity to the extent that the horizons become actually fused, and contains an irreducible remnant of difference to the extent that there remains, in Ricoeur's words, a "contrast in virtue of which one point of view stands out against the backcloth of others."[6] It is such a dialectic of identity and difference that defines the latecomer's task of stitching together the tradition across time and allows it to occur in two modes: a restoration of unbroken tradition characteristic of Gadamer's hermeneutics, or a remnant of difference in the present horizon that can ground critique of that tradition, which Ricoeur wants to defend. Immanent critique inhabits tradition as the inability to fully stitch together temporal difference. On this model of immanence hermeneutic philosophy cannot address the issue of intercultural understanding.

2. Constitution of a Tradition

Hermeneutic understanding functions as a stitching-together and carrying-forward of a culture from within that culture by means of self-interpretation grounded in a form of life and encompassing its expressive and knowledge-forms. Insofar as it claims universality, hermeneutical understanding binds philosophy to a culture as the highest expression of its self-understanding and in productive dialogue with its other scientific, artistic, and other expressions. Let us begin by noticing two elements of the concept of tradition that cannot be understood on the basis of hermeneutical understanding: the inception, or institution (*Urstiftung*), of a tradition; and its destitution, or completion (*Endstiftung*). Since philosophical reflection in the hermeneutic mode is enclosed within, and acts within, a tradition, it cannot reflect upon, nor can it therefore understand sufficiently, how a tradition begins and how it ends. The constitution of a tradition as such is outside the realm of hermeneutic universality since it requires reflection upon the binding-together process that makes a tradition from the standpoint of its inception and destitution.

Phenomenology encountered the issue of the constitution of a tradition when Husserl inquired into the formation of science in the Galilean style as a tradition centrally constitutive of modernity. The formation of rationality by the "mathematical substruction of nature" in Galilean science understood the real, or primary, characteristics of nature to be mathematical and therefore the secondary, qualitative characteristics to be the "merely subjective" projections of human beings.[7] As a consequence, modernity has since been haunted by the association of reason with mathematical formalism and by the consequent derogation of qualitative characteristics of phenomena as irrational projections. Husserl asked: "Scientific, objective truth is exclusively a matter of establishing what the world, the physical as well as the spiritual world, is in fact. But can the world, and human existence in it, truthfully have a meaning if the sciences recognize as true only what is objectively established in this fashion, and if history has nothing more to teach us than that all the shapes of the spiritual world, all the conditions of life, ideals, norms upon which man relies, form and dissolve themselves like fleeting waves [...]?"[8] In investigating the origin of the tradition of objective-scientific truth, Husserl encountered the question of history, not simply as contingent, empirical history, but as the transcendental history that is constitutive of traditions.

In order to understand the constitution of the tradition of Galilean science, it is necessary to understand the original formation and perdurance of the structures that pre-form subsequent experiences. In *The Crisis of European Sciences and Transcendental Phenomenology*, Husserl placed great emphasis on Galilean science, but also on modern psychology and on the ancient origins of geometry, and there is no reason to believe that these constitute an exhaustive set. It is in the context of clarifying the sense in which Galileo established the new science that Husserl introduces the term *Urstiftung* – which can be translated as "primal establishment" in the sense of "inauguration," but which I will translate mainly as "institution."[9] The advantage of the term "institution" is that it can be used in two senses, both of which are relevant to the concept here. A tradition is "instituted" in the sense of being brought into being and is an "institution" in the sense of being an organized set of human relationships within which intersubjective and material relations are organized. It is mainly a temporal structure in the sense that it is different to be born after the introduction of compulsory public schooling than before it, but it contains a spatial dimension in the sense that such an introduction begins in some places before others; the consequent "uneven development" then exerts an interactive "push and pull" between those places. One can direct attention to the primal establishment or inauguration of an institution in order to point to its coming into being and therefore to the original temporality that it institutes. One can direct attention to its character as a social–cultural institution in order to point to the continuing shaping that it exerts over subsequent experience.

Transcendental history is thus concerned with the temporal inscription of the life-world such that subsequent empirical history as instantiated in traditions and their transformations takes a different form after than before its inauguration. The process of inauguration may be drawn out in empirical history, but from the viewpoint of transcendental history it constitutes one historical event. During this event of institution, its full implications and consequences are not yet evident. Similarly, certain elements enter into the institution, whose origin is simply passed over and whose validity is simply taken for granted due to its prior sedimentation in tradition. Thus, more is given in the instituting event than is visible at the time. An event in transcendental history will thus often require considerable empirical history for its institution to become a question worth investigation, let alone be completely clarified. Such was the case with the mathematization of nature by Galileo, which Husserl began to investigate within transcendental history due to the problem that the contemporary crisis of the sciences posed for the relation of science and philosophy to human life in the natural world. Husserl was well aware of a circle here. "The historical reflections we embarked upon ... demanded clarity concerning the origin of the modern spirit and ... the origin of these sciences. That is to say: clarity concerning the original motivation and movement of thought which led to the conceiving of their idea of nature, and from there to the movement of its realization in the actual development of natural science itself."[10] This intertwining of empirical and transcendental history does not eradicate their difference; rather, for Husserl, it demands that the investigation "proceed back and forth in a zigzag pattern" from contemporary breakdown to original institution and back again.[11]

This inquiry takes a particular form determined by its object and by the historical event of crisis that Husserl called "dismantling," or "unbuilding" (*Abbau*). This term arose in connection with Husserl's investigations into "Genetic Logic" in about 1921 and surfaced afterwards whenever it was an issue of the constitution of objectivities whose form was built upon prior achievements so that the objectivities could only be understood as founded not only in a layered, archaeological fashion but also in a temporal one (in the sense that temporally prior achievements formed the starting point for later superstructural constitutions). The genetic constitution of the predicative logical judgments from pre-predicative experience was the major theme of genetic logic.[12] The zigzag pattern of presentation that an investigation into the institution of modern science demands is based on a form of inquiry in which the instituted object – in this case the tradition of Galilean science – is dismantled into its components and the constitution of its originary form is clarified.[13] A genetic inquiry into a historical institution thus requires (1) an instituted tradition (*Urstiftung*) such as Galilean science, (2) a tracing back (*Rückgang*) of the sedimentations of instituted meaning whereby instituted meaning has gained its historical "weight," or "solidity," to this meaning's pre-predicative origin, (3) a dismantling (*Abbau*) of this pre-predicative experience itself, (4) a zigzag pattern of presentation that goes back and forth between the originary institution and the contemporary situation, and (5) a notion of completion, or final establishment (*Endstiftung*), of the tradition that may not yet be given in empirical history but that is present in transcendental history in the mode of being "assigned as a task."[14] The completion of a tradition is thus co-constituted in the dismantling of the institution.

In this way, phenomenology inquires into the beginning and ending of an institution in transcendental history. Whereas hermeneutic philosophy operated as a component of culture to carry forward a tradition, phenomenological philosophy requires the critique of tradition through a tracing back of its institution that allows the presentation of its completion in the mode of a task. Hermeneutic "immanent criticism" relies on the meanings inherent in a tradition to carry that tradition forward beyond its actual limitations. Immanent criticism obtains its effect precisely to the extent that it builds upon an already accepted basis and speaks to those for whom it contains an already established significance. Phenomenological critique of a tradition, however, criticizes the institution/completion dyad that constitutes tradition as such.[15]

3. Tradition and the Problem of Intercultural Understanding

Hermeneutic philosophy can ground immanent critique of a tradition – that is to say, its reformation/restoration dialectic in carrying itself both backward to its origin and forward towards completion – because a tradition carries within itself a *telos* that assigns a task to those who inherit it. It inhabits the task of completion that is given in the present. Phenomenological philosophy, by investigating the constitution of a tradition as such through its institution/completion, clarifies the constitution of what is given as being "assigned as a task" that is the active form in which a tradition is carried forward. The task is assigned as a value to the inheritor of a tradition, and hermeneutic philosophy in this sense occupies the position of an inheritor. The value of the task can only be inquired into, the character of the assignation can only be uncovered, if the constitution of the tradition becomes questionable as such.

The five components of Husserl's investigation of the tradition of Galilean science all rest on the thesis of the crisis of the European sciences itself, which is a contemporary event that motivates the inquiry. This event consists, most generally, in a dislocation between predicative and pre-predicative judgments or a crisis in the forming of life-world experience by formal knowledge-systems. Such dislocation defines the sense in which, from a phenomenological perspective, a tradition is formed through the forgetting of original, immediate evidence[16] that generates the "loss of meaning" of science for human culture and value. The phenomenological critique of a historical institution thus rests on an immediate, or intuitive, givenness of crisis of the tradition in question. This evidence is given in an event of dislocation between the pertinent knowledge-form and the pre-predicative judgments. It is this event that motivates a phenomenological critique that is not immanent criticism but rather *criticism of immanence* – criticism of the immanence constructed by a tradition as its inside.

The problem of intercultural understanding must then be addressed beginning from the motivating event within the life-world that gives rise to a critique of tradition. A culture can be defined phenomenologically as a collection of traditions. Collection takes the form of organization, in some respects super- and sub-ordination, albeit within an indefinite horizon in the sense that the relation between traditions is often not thematic for the actors within a culture. For example, I may inherit belonging in a tradition of education that assigns formal education such as a university degree a positive value. I may also inherit a tradition that values deep involvement in a place, a place in which perhaps "my people" have a long history. I may live for a long time without ever having to address thematically the relative values assigned within these two traditions, even though a critical event may at any time occur that requires me to choose between these two values and thus to pose exactly this issue. At the point at which the issue is posed, through my determination of the relative values, I become not only an inheritor but also a definer of the culture, one who not only carries out an assigned task but also defines the task that is assigned.[17]

Intercultural understanding implies an understanding of another collection of traditions. Such an understanding would begin from a critical event that dislocates or disrupts the established relation between knowledge-form and experience, or pre-predicative judgment. Before addressing the event of dislocation, it is first necessary to discuss empirical-historical forms of intercultural interaction, at least in a schematic manner. Perhaps one should begin with a zero-degree of cultural interaction in which several independent cultures exist in the world but there is no interaction between them. Without contact of some sort, intercultural understanding is obviously impossible and intercultural critique similarly so. The historical starting point is thus that any form of intercultural understanding requires a constituting cultural interaction as its experiential ground. A first form was developed through traveller's stories and reached its apogee in anthropological accounts. In this form, a person reaches maturity within a given culture and then moves outward to encounter another culture that is itself, in an identical manner, given as independent. Cultures are understood in this way to be self-enclosed and self-subsistent, so that the relation between them is a kind of "travelling" in which one culture is left in order for another to be entered. Encounter with an alien culture in this form can have two consequences. The first is that the alien culture can be denigrated as less human, or less civilized, so that a hierarchical relation between cultures can be posited. Often this is done by thrusting the alien culture into the past so that it is seen as an earlier form of human society doomed to pass away.[18] Denigration leads to the conception that a culture is not only alien but also inferior. The opposite alternative is also possible and has some, albeit fewer, historical precedents: the alien culture may be seen as superior and as a basis for the critique of one's own culture. A classic literary example of the latter form of intercultural critique is Montesquieu's *Persian Letters*. A more sophisticated possibility is that the existence of a coherent alien culture can motivate a self-reflection that understands one's own culture as a specific form of culture (and not simply as the given form of humanity as such) – perhaps a specific form that requires its own immanent criticism. This is actually how Montesquieu's *Letters* should be understood: they constitute a self-reflective immanent criticism masquerading for imaginative reasons as the voice of a superior alien culture, and they do so ironically, for political reasons, in the voice of a culture generally considered inferior. To simplify, we can say that when cultures exist largely separately and are connected by the external relations established by travellers, their relationship is of the us–them variety in a mode of curiosity about the alien: Isn't it strange, interesting, repugnant, or enlightening that they do not do things the way we do? The empirical-historical scheme could be continued at much greater length. Cultures have come into relation in a number of ways: through travellers and explorers, colonialism and imperialism, treaty and federation, immigration and exile, to name a few. Indeed, one can argue that the very concept of culture, used in this anthropological sense, is necessarily linked to a plurality of cultures, since one's own culture could not become visible without comparison to another.

Leaving the empirical-historical scheme to one side for the moment, let us investigate the motivating event in our own life-world from which emerges the possibility of a critique of traditions and therefore cultural forms. This event is pointed to by Husserl's critique of Galilean science: the horizon of scientific–technological civilization that proffers an abyss for the rational foundation of meaning, culture, and value. It is also pointed to by the question of the possibility of intercultural understanding itself: the interaction between cultures within scientific-technological planetary civilization occurs within the horizon of the difficulty of articulating a rationality of meaning and value that could sustain a culture. It is this that gives rise to a persistent anxiety concerning cultural homogenization.[19] These two horizons are mutually defining insofar as the planetary character of scientific–technological civilization defines the context for interaction of cultures and interaction of cultures defines the context for the planetary expansion of scientific–technological civilization. This is the motivating event for critique of traditions and the collection of traditions that constitute a culture. It is the experiential ground for a transcendental history of intercultural understanding.

The next two sections will take up in turn each of these mutually defining horizons of the contemporary planetary event.

4. The Horizon of Scientific–Technological Civilization

Scientific–technological reason constitutes a tradition that can be incorporated into different cultures. Its planetary reach defines the horizon within which different cultures come into contact. Philosophy, when it is understood in hermeneutic form as the carrying-forward of a tradition, will either carry forward the scientific–technological tradition directly itself or encounter the scientific–technological tradition as the horizon of the tradition that it does carry forward. Insofar as the scientific–technological tradition is the horizon for the encounter of different traditions and their collections into cultures, its universality tends to render such other traditions and cultures as merely local and particular. Phenomenological philosophy, since it reaches outside a tradition to its originary and completing moments, is capable not only of encountering the horizon of scientific–technological tradition but also of laying bare its constitution. One immediate empirical-historical consequence of this transcendental history is that there is no universal language that could encompass the relation of philosophy to the different cultures. The values expressed in traditions and cultures are not capable of discursive totalization.

The transcendental history through which the phenomenological philosopher surveys cultures and their horizon of connection in scientific–technological reason returns us to the point in Plato's *Republic* where Socrates asks Glaucon to survey "as from a tower" the many political forms in which human virtue struggles for its clarity. Stanley Rosen comments on this passage that here Plato discovers the Nietzschean perspective – which he claims is the truly philosophical one – that "the philosopher surveys the whole and in so doing stands beyond or outside of nature."[20] But, as Rosen himself notes, Plato says: "now that we have come to this height of argument I seem to see as from a point of outlook that there is one form of excellence, and that the forms of evil are infinite."[21] If only one of the forms is good, then it is not a Nietzschean perspective "beyond good and evil" as Rosen claims,[22] but a location from which the many forms can be ordered and the temporal succession of regimes resolved into a coming-towards or falling-away from the good – which amounts in the end to an ordering of cultures from a virtue/value that subtends them all. There is neither chaos nor abyss here but an order based in a unique intuition that subtends the many forms of human politics and culture. We are returned to the hermeneutic perspective from which philosophy carries forward a given tradition on the condition of being barred from investigating its constitution. Without such a unique intuition of the good it might seem that there is no alternative to the Nietzschean abyss – pure plurality not only of cultures but also of virtues/values in which any ordering is a pure positing based on nothing more than the power of the one who posits the leading value. But the perspective of transcendental history described here opens another possibility.

The relationship between pure plurality of values and the groundless positing of a leading value becomes clearer when it is set against another, apparently contradictory, statement of Nietzsche's that "the value of life cannot be estimated. Not by a living man, because he is a party to the dispute, indeed its object, and not the judge of it; not by a dead one, for another reason."[23] Where would one stand to estimate the value of life? Nietzsche asserts that one can stand neither inside life, without simply assuming that the values one lives are the reigning values *tout court*, nor outside life because the question is no longer a live one. From the perspective of a "philosophy of life" (*Lebensphilosophie*), Nietzsche concludes that the value of the whole of life, a value that would subtend all cultural worlds and their differences, cannot be *estimated* or *judged*. But he does not say that this value cannot be asserted, and this is what the one higher than mere humans does. The Nietzschean choice is only between passive and active nihilism. It is at exactly this point that phenomenological philosophy through its critique of traditions and their collection into cultures demands a "view from the tower," one that maintains the plurality of cultural forms and values at the same time that it undermines their externality through the horizon of scientific–technological reason.

It is necessary to distinguish between the view of the totality "as from a tower" that philosophy requires and the "fact" that there is no universal discursive language that could encompass the relation of philosophy to the different cultures. The discursive expression of philosophy is necessarily split by the plurality of cultures even though the view from the tower is itself enabled by the plurality of discursive forms in which it can be expressed. This paradox is an empirical-historical consequence of the transcendental history motivated by the mutually defining horizons of the contemporary planetary event. The values expressed in traditions and cultures are not capable of discursive totalization but they are capable of intuitive survey.[24] It is such intuitive survey that grounds dialogue between the necessary plurality of languages in which such intuition must be expressed.

The philosophical concept of totality is necessarily understood by phenomenological philosophers attending to the constitution of traditions in various cultural forms. Expressed in religious terms, one might say that even if there is one God, humans necessarily interpret God in various ways. For an individual, this means that one's conception of "all that is" must take a certain determinate form. Nevertheless, this concept is accompanied by the awareness that the determinate form is not itself ultimate but is one of many expressions of the ultimate. In this way a certain distance is introduced between the ultimate itself and the language in which it is expressed. At the same time, the condition for recognizing the legitimacy of other expressions of the ultimate is satisfied.

If philosophy could be expressed as a pure unsituated universality in a formal logic, it would contain no reference to the cultural specificity of the philosopher. However, in order for philosophy to form human conduct through reason, it must engage with the cultural, historical, and traditional parameters that the philosopher shares with others. The collection of traditions that constitutes a culture is the ground from which philosophy begins, and that ground can be neither erased nor entirely incorporated in the practice of philosophy. This is what I mean by saying that philosophy has no universal language by which its relation to cultures can be expressed. This phenomenon is a consequence of the universality of scientific–technological reason because the form of that reason abstracts from cultural contents yet requires such contents for its planetary reach. While phenomenological philosophy need not imagine, as does scientific–technological reason, that cultural contents are merely particular and local, it does need to accept that there is no straightforwardly universal but still encultured language *à la* Hegel that can express the relation between philosophical reason and its situated origin and effect. In short, it is necessary that there be many languages of philosophy.

Humans are constituted in such a way that they do not know automatically how to live, as we may presume other animals do. A presumptive answer to the philosophical question "How should humans live?" is contained in the institutions of a cultural form. The necessary fact that there are many languages of philosophy means that that there is no discursive knowledge of the whole from which the question of the true cultural–political virtues/values – the good for humans – could be definitively decided. There may be intuitive knowledge of the whole, but its political expression must enter into discourse and thus be compatible with more than one form of expression. This may be called a sceptical truth as long as it is clear that it does not deny the possibility of a philosophical answer to the question of how humans should live but only of a fully discursive answer to the question that could finally incorporate or cancel cultural contents. To deny this sceptical truth one would have to assert the validity of a discursive conception of the whole, like that proposed by Hegel, in which the discursive articulation of the forms of experience culminates in a conception of the whole that can be displayed as a material logic. By contrast, an intuitive account of totality such as that of Plato requires recourse to mythical expression precisely because it is not amenable to discursive presentation. For phenomenology, Plato's myth is now dispersed among the planet's many cultures and languages.

Philosophy's search for truth cannot replace the way of life inherent in a cultural form, nor can it legitimate a specific form as against all others. Thus, philosophy is always dependent on a form of life outside itself for its own existence. That there is a plurality of forms of expression of the truth – even if they were several forms of the same truth – means that a plurality of cultural forms is compatible with the same truth. Caught in this situation, each of us must ask which cultural form best incorporates a given value, but since each form is not total and therefore in some respect is lacking in other values, rational disagreement will occur regarding the respective merits of cultural forms. It is at this point, which grounds both intercultural learning and intercultural criticism, that intercultural understanding can genuinely begin. It must occur in this rational inquiry that different aspects of the best form of life are highlighted by different cultural forms. The plurality and diversity of multiculturalism in our contemporary world is for this reason basic and not merely a matter of accommodation to minorities. These multiple forms could themselves be articulated as a political–ethical theory only if a rigorous (discursive) account could be given of their relationship. Such an ordering would reduce the dispersed multiplicity to a pattern whose form could establish the superiority of one order. In this respect, the sceptical truth of philosophy takes the form in philosophy of an evaluation of the superiority of Socrates's inconclusiveness over Plato's theory of the whole.[25]

The sceptical truth of transcendental history thus has two dimensions: an anti-Hegelian one based on the distinction between intuitive and discursive accounts of the whole, and an anti-Platonic one based on the impossibility of ordering the necessary multiplicity of forms. But neither of these two aspects of the sceptical truth implies that there is no true answer to the question about how humans should live that could be expressed in philosophy, so that the descent into Nietzsche's abyss is rather a failure of philosophy, not its completion for the phenomenological investigation of the horizon of scientific–technological civilization.

5. The Horizon of Intercultural Understanding

Through a double horizon, scientific–technological civilization defines the context of the interaction of cultures and the interaction of cultures defines the context for the planetary expansion of scientific–technological civilization. A second immediate empirical-historical implication of this transcendental history is that the interaction of cultures can no longer be based on the traveller's model as an us–them relationship between independent and self-enclosed cultures established by movement in space.[26] Rather, a culture must be seen as existing from the start in relationship with other cultures, as constituted at least in part by what it brings inside from other cultures to make its own, and as continued as much by its productive effect on other cultures as by maintaining the same form. The success of a culture may well be constituted less by its ability to continue in the same form than by its ability to translate its traditions into other cultural forms. The possibility of intercultural understanding will depend on this possibility of translation.

This is the key question: *How is translation of values between cultures possible, or, how is a value from a different culture to be understood?* For something foreign to be understood, one must translate it by some means into the particular cultural form that one inhabits. Moreover, one must translate it in such a manner that the difference of that value is preserved and is not reduced to being measured simply by one's own criteria. The first condition, as described in the previous section, opens a distance between one's own ultimate values and ultimate values themselves; that distance then grounds the possibility of such translation. In addition, in order for translation of values to occur we need to consider two cases. First, if there is nothing even remotely comparable to the value requiring translation, then translation is obviously impossible. While such a case cannot be ruled out in principle, it would require the further condition that the *telos* of universality-in-difference be abandoned and therefore that the whole attempt at intercultural critique end in failure. For there to be a comparable value that is not identical, such that translation can overcome foreignness while maintaining difference, as we might phrase it, there must be some common element, but that common element must not have the same place, or role, within each cultural form.

Here it is useful to recall that when Claude Lévi-Strauss argued that Western scientific thought was not the only scientific form and that there were two different and equally valid forms, he made this comparison by reference to the French experience of the *bricoleur* – or, as we might say, the handyman – in contrast to the *engineer*, who stood for the mode of knowing of Western science. "Unlike the engineer, he does not subordinate each of them to the availability of raw materials and tools conceived and procured for the purpose of the project."[27] Rather, the *bricoleur*'s "universe of instruments is closed and the rules of the game are always to make do with 'whatever is at hand,' that is to say, with a set of tools and materials which is always finite and is also heterogeneous because what it contains bears no relation to the current project ... but is the contingent result of all the occasions there have been to renew or enrich the stock or to maintain it."[28] Through this contrast, Lévi-Strauss sought to accomplish two things: open a distance between Western science and science in other possible forms, and show that the people of his anthropological studies had such another form of science. The example of the *bricoleur* already existed and was comprehensible within French culture, but it had not previously been viewed as comparable to science. By analogizing the mytho-poetical (as it had been called) thought of non-Western people to French *bricolage*, it was possible to understand that thought as a form of rationality comparable to Western science; furthermore, it should be noted, *bricolage* within French culture could be understood as a rational form whose subordination had been achieved by the very same Western science that denigrated the "mytho-poetic thought" of non-Western people as non-scientific. This is a logic of the centre–periphery: by bringing a concept from the periphery of French culture to its centre, the rational content of both French *bricolage* and non-Western science could be understood. This is the logic of translation between cultural values such that their difference is preserved even while their comparability is established. It performs a critique of Western science by showing that it is only one form of reason in the same moment that it allows a revaluation of both *bricolage* and mytho-poetic thought.

The condition of cultural plurality that gives rise to the problem of identity and difference can issue in intercultural understanding through translation by means of centre–periphery comparisons. It is not an *immanent criticism* but a *criticism of immanence* that is possible, since cultures and their value-forms are not non-communicating vessels but remain open to the creative act of comparison. The key to hermeneutical understanding of another culture has thus been shown to consist in the nature of the closure whereby a culture is constituted as such: the first, "traveller's" stage consists primarily of "spatial" closure through temporal revitalization; whereas the second, "multicultural" stage consists in "spatial" openness (cultural borrowing, hybridity, etc.) through temporal forgetting. Since any such closure can only be temporary and partly effective, translation may well be, as Ricoeur suggests,[29] a model for all hermeneutical understanding – even that within a given tradition – but it could be so only through an investigation of the constitution of the tradition itself, including the manner of its closure. To this extent, the empirical-historical forms of intercultural contact set the framework within which the motivating event for transcendental history emerges.

Whereas hermeneutic interpretation carries forward the understanding imbedded in a tradition, phenomenology investigates the constitution of traditions and can thereby address intercultural understanding through a centre–periphery logic that, by displacing the assumptions inherent in one's own culture as a collection of traditions, opens one up to the potential centrality of assumptions rooted in another culture.

NOTES

1 Hans-Georg Gadamer, "The Universality of the Hermeneutical Problem," in *Philosophical Hermeneutics*, trans. and ed. David E. Linge (Berkeley: University of California Press, 1977); Paul Ricoeur, "The Task of Hermeneutics," in *Hermeneutics and the Human Sciences*, trans. and ed. John B. Thompson (Cambridge: Cambridge University Press, 1981), 43–4.
2 Martin Heidegger, *Being and Time*, trans. Joan Stambaugh (Albany: SUNY Press, 1996), 135.
3 Paul Ricoeur, *Interpretation Theory: Discourse and the Surplus of Meaning* (Fort Worth: Texas Christian University Press, 1976), 75–9.
4 Hans-Georg Gadamer, *Truth and Method* (New York: Crossroad, 1975), 273.
5 Paul Ricoeur, "Hermeneutics and Critique of Ideology," in *Hermeneutics and the Human Sciences*, trans. and ed. John B. Thompson (Cambridge: Cambridge University Press, 1981), 75.
6 Ibid.
7 Edmund Husserl, *The Crisis of European Sciences and Transcendental Phenomenology*, trans. David Carr (Evanston: Northwestern University Press, 1970), section 9.
8 Ibid., 6–7.
9 Ibid., section 16.
10 Ibid., 57.
11 Ibid., 58.
12 Ludwig Landgrebe, "Editor's Foreword to the 1948 Edition," in Edmund Husserl, *Experience and Judgment*, trans. James S. Churchill and Karl Ameriks (Evanston: Northwestern University Press, 1973), 5.
13 Such a dismantling, Husserl notes, has a double aspect of "going back," or regressive inquiry (*Rückgang*). It involves a going back from the pregiven world and its sedimentations of meaning to the "original life-world," and it further requires a going back from the original life-world to investigate the constitution of the life-world itself. In other words, predicative judgments must be traced back to the forming of pre-predicative experience that they accomplish, and then this pre-predicative experience itself must be dismantled (Husserl, *Experience and Judgment*, 50).
14 Husserl, *Crisis*, 72.

15 This sentence slides over an important question that requires separate investigation: To what extent does Husserl simply assume that phenomenology completes the tradition? For the tradition fundamentally in question for him is Western rationalism (as carried forward by mathematical science), and indeed, phenomenology continues and attempts to complete this. "This final establishment is accomplished when the task is brought to consummate clarity and thus to an apodictic method which, in every step of achievement, is a constant avenue to new steps having the character of absolute success … At this point philosophy, as an infinite task, would have arrived at its apodictic beginning, its horizon of apodictic forward movement" (Husserl, *Crisis*, 72). My presentation attempts to illuminate, albeit briefly, that even if Husserl himself makes this assumption, the logic of the phenomenon requires that critique of tradition extend to its completion – even to the completion of the tradition of reason.

16 Husserl, *Crisis*, 355.

17 This short description is indebted to Max Scheler's conception of "the relative natural conception of the world," which refers to the ordering of values within the domains of a cultural form by an overriding principle that defines the cultural form itself (Scheler, *Die Wissenformen und die Gesellschaft, Gesammelte Werke, Band 8* [Bern und Munchen: Francke Verlag, 1960], 60–3; Alfred Schutz, "Equality and the Meaning-Structure of the World," in *Collected Papers*, vol. II: *Studies in Social Theory* [The Hague: Martinus Nijhoff, 1971], 242). However, my description seeks to recognize that the notion that a culture is defined by a single overarching value is not tenable and that the relations among the values that comprise a culture are not always thematically clarified (Alfred Schutz and Thomas Luckmann, *Structures of the Life-World*, trans. Richard M. Zaner and Tristram Engelhardt, Jr. [London: Heinemann, 1974], 8).

18 Johannes Fabian, *Time and the Other: How Anthropology Makes Its Object* (New York: Columbia University Press, 1983).

19 Ian Angus, "The Anxiety Concerning Cultural Homogenization," in *Rescuing Difference: The Problem of Homogenisation in Architectural Form*, ed. Modjtaba Sadria (Geneva: Aga Khan Award for Architecture, 2013).

20 Stanley Rosen, *The Question of Being: A Reversal of Heidegger* (New Haven: Yale University Press, 1993), 132.

21 Plato, *The Republic*, trans. Paul Shorey, in *Collected Dialogues*, ed. Edith Hamilton and Huntington Cairns (New York: Pantheon, 1961), 445c.

22 Rosen, *The Question of Being*, 132.

23 Friedrich Nietzsche, *Twilight of the Idols*. In *Twilight of the Idols / The Anti-Christ*, trans. R.J. Hollingdale (Harmondsworth: Penguin, 1968), 30.

24 The ground of this assertion is an acceptance of Eugen Fink's revision of the consequences of late Husserl's conception of the transcendental reduction. If "language stands ready as *anticipatory ontological grasp,* as an *antecedent preinterpretation of being,*" then one must ask whether "the *antecedent grasp* is a *definitive* interpretation, or one that is annulled or modifiable" in getting back to "the forgotten *protosituation*" that motivates understanding (Fink, quoted in Ronald Bruzina, *Edmund Husserl and Eugen Fink: Beginning and Ends in Phenomenology 1928–1938* [New Haven: Yale University Press, 2004], 455). Language is formed by living-in and -toward Being and thus must be used differently within the phenomenological reduction that sets aside Being in order to investigate its constitution. The current presentation need not decide on the difference between Husserl's recognition of the "doubleness" of linguistic meaning and Fink's stronger sense of its "transformation" (Bruzina, *Edmund Husserl and Eugen Fink,* 576–81), since it relies only on the basic point that the discursive knowledge available in cultural forms cannot be the basis for the intuition of the plurality of cultural forms themselves. This is the significance of my use of the term "discursive" in the text to mark this difference.

25 Angus, "Socrates and the Critique of Metaphysics," *European Legacy* 10, no. 4 (2005).

26 Exploring the implications of replacing of a traveller's us–them model with a multicultural us–we one has been a major component of my work and is based in the Canadian experience of multiculturalism (Angus, *A Border Within: National Identity, Cultural Plurality, and Wilderness* [Montreal and Kingston: McGill–Queen's University Press, 1997], chapter 6; Angus, *Identity and Justice* [Toronto: University of Toronto Press, 2008], 78–82).

27 Claude Lévi-Strauss, *The Savage Mind* (London: Weidenfeld and Nicolson, 1966), 17.

28 Ibid.

29 Paul Ricoeur, *On Translation,* trans. Eileen Brennan (London: Routledge, 2006), 23–9.

Chapter Two

Do Gadamer and Ricoeur Have the Same Understanding of Hermeneutics?

JEAN GRONDIN

It is one of the most vital tasks of hermeneutics to build bridges and foster dialogue between cultures. Important hermeneutical thinkers like Gadamer and Ricoeur rightfully stressed this in their writings. But what about the dialogue between Gadamer and Ricoeur themselves? There is little doubt that these two are the leading figures in contemporary hermeneutics. They knew of each other, of course: they met at the Castelli conferences in Rome in the early 1960s and regularly encountered each other in North America and Europe when they participated in the same conferences. But there was, unfortunately, little dialogue between them.[1] This is mostly true of Gadamer: there is in his work no meaningful discussion of Ricoeur. As for Ricoeur, he did engage Gadamer's philosophy, but only relatively late – not until the 1970s.

Gadamer and Ricoeur, then, are the leading figures in hermeneutics. But do they have the same understanding of it? And if they do, to what extent? As far as I can tell, this question has too seldom been asked. This has to do perhaps with the fact that Gadamer and Ricoeur developed different "schools." One cannot really speak of "schools" in any doctrinaire sense; even so, there is no escaping that Gadamerians rarely discuss Ricoeur, and the same often holds for Ricoeur specialists regarding Gadamer. The various pupils and descendants of the two seem to have developed hermeneutical "niches," which at times tend to be condescending towards each other. There are thankful exceptions, but this attitude is, one can fear, widespread. Gadamerians and Heideggerians are at times dismissive of Ricoeur, associating him with some hidden "theological" agenda, whereas some Ricoeurians downplay Gadamer's importance, as I have often observed in France.

This common ignorance is unproductive and vain. My hope is to help overcome it and to contribute to a hermeneutics that takes into account the contributions of both. My contention is that Gadamer and Ricoeur share certain convictions, which are precious, but also differences, which are also important and need to be sorted out if we are to benefit from the contributions of both to hermeneutics. One can compare and contrast Gadamer and Ricoeur in a variety of ways, since both have worked on similar subjects: on practical philosophy and literature, on understanding and metaphor, and on ethics, not to mention the many thinkers that both have written about (Dilthey, Hegel, Heidegger, Husserl, etc.). A recent example of an effort to examine both is a book by Daniel Frey that compares their understandings of reading.[2] Frey's book is a valuable one, but still, little attempt has been made so far to sort out the differences and similarities in their understanding of hermeneutics. This essay is an attempt to begin doing so.

How Did Gadamer and Ricoeur Come to Hermeneutics?

It is a basic conviction of hermeneutics and of human reason that one can understand something when one knows a little bit about its genesis. So it is with Gadamer and Ricoeur as hermeneuticians. It is striking that both men came to the field relatively late. Gadamer published *Truth and Method* in 1960, when he was sixty. Before that, he had not really spoken of hermeneutics in his work, most of which was devoted to the Greeks and Hegel. As for Ricoeur, his early interests were Gabriel Marcel, Karl Jaspers, and the life-absorbing project of a philosophy of the will, whose first volume was published in 1950, and in which hermeneutics is at least nominally absent. He too only began to speak of hermeneutics – the coincidence is flabbergasting – in 1960, in his *Symbolics of Evil*, the second part of the second volume of his *Philosophy of Will*. He was then forty-seven. This is perhaps not very old, but still, hermeneutics was a late development in both men's careers, which in both cases turned out to be lengthy, most advantageously for hermeneutics. There are no psychological consequences to be drawn from this (say, "hermeneutics is for old people ..."). It is, however, noteworthy that both came to hermeneutics in the same year, 1960, for it excludes the possibility that one could have been influenced by the other in any meaningful way. There is no reference to Ricoeur in *Truth and Method*, and none to Gadamer in Ricoeur's work of 1960, nor indeed in his two other major works of the 1960s, *On Interpretation* and *The Conflict of*

Interpretations. This last observation is a little more surprising, but not all that much since Gadamer did not immediately become a major reference in the 1960s. *Truth and Method* was a "sleeper" that took time to become recognized as a classic.[3]

So it is safe to say that Ricoeur and Gadamer developed their hermeneutics independently of each other. This explains many of the differences between their hermeneutical projects, as well as the lack of dialogue between them: their motivations were different, but so were their sources and adversaries. Ricoeur and Gadamer may have situated themselves in the hermeneutic tradition of Schleiermacher, Dilthey, Heidegger, and Bultmann, but they did so to varying degrees and with different emphases.

Let us start with Gadamer's understanding of hermeneutics, since it offers the convenience of having been presented in a single seminal work, one that has dominated the momentous reception of his thought. In that work, under the rubric of hermeneutics, Gadamer's expressed aim is to develop a philosophical reflection that does justice to the truth experience of the humanities. His basic claim is that this truth cannot be understood solely out of the notion of method that defines modern science. That is why he breaks with Dilthey and his methodological understanding of hermeneutics. Gadamer's criticism of Dilthey is certainly influenced by Heidegger, his master and main inspiration, even if he by no means takes up the latter's hermeneutics of *Dasein* as such:[4] Gadamer does not strive to understand *Dasein* out of its possible authenticity in the confrontation with his mortality, nor is it his intention to deconstruct the bulk of the ontological tradition. What Gadamer learned from Heidegger was rather that understanding and interpretation are not primarily the "methods" of the human sciences; rather, they are the fundamental mode of Being of existence: our disquieted self seeks orientation through projects of understanding that have everything to do with our situation and historical condition. It is this quest for understanding, Gadamer argues in his work, that gives life to the human sciences: in history, literature, art, philosophy, theology, or jurisprudence, one is always seeking to learn and find meaning. So it is normal that the human scientist is "interested" by his or her object. This interest in the subject matter has been anathema for modern methodical consciousness. This is wrongheaded, Gadamer contends, since it blinds us to the humanists' unique contribution to knowledge. This leads Gadamer to emphasize the productive role of prejudices and historicity in understanding: the interpreter is always taken by what she is interpreting in what Gadamer famously calls a "fusion of horizons" between the interpreter and her object, which is also a fusion of the past with the present. Since this fusion is basically the achievement of language, Gadamer's hermeneutics takes the form of a universal philosophy of our linguistic and historical experience of the world. In stating that all understanding is framed and carried by language, Gadamer is raising a claim to universality, which enables him to leave behind the methodological understanding of hermeneutics. This is the ambitious project that Gadamer set forth in *Truth and Method*, and it has been at the centre of most hermeneutical debates ever since. It has sparked epic confrontations with heavyweights like Habermas, Betti, Derrida, and Hans-Robert Jauss and has been forcefully debated in North America by Richard Rorty, Charles Taylor, Richard Bernstein, and a few others.

By contrast, it is difficult to speak of a single conception of hermeneutics in Ricoeur, since his understanding of hermeneutics, by his own account, evolved considerably over the years.[5] This makes it difficult to compare him with Gadamer, whose conception of it can be identified with *Truth and Method*. When one compares Gadamer's hermeneutics with Ricoeur's, one has to ask: With *which* hermeneutics of Ricoeur? The hermeneutics of symbols in his *Symbolics of Evil*, or the one that grows out of the conflict between the hermeneutics of suspicion and those of trust in *On Interpretation* and *The Conflict of Interpretation*? The hermeneutics of semantic innovation in *La métaphore vive* or the hermeneutics of understanding and explaining of the 1970s (say, in the essays that make up *Du texte à l'action*)? In the 1980s and 1990s, Ricoeur offered yet another new hermeneutics – of time and narrative – as well as a philosophy of the "capable self," which he also referred to as hermeneutic. There are, to be sure, common concerns among these projects, but it is hard to maintain that Ricoeur's understanding of hermeneutics stayed the same over fifty years. This has made it difficult for his readers to identify Ricoeur with a distinct understanding of hermeneutics, which could then be contrasted with Gadamer's. Gadamer set forth his conception of hermeneutics in a "seminal book," whereas Ricoeur's conception is spread out over a dozen books, which all happen to be rather thick. This is an embarrassment of riches – one, however, that makes it a challenge to draw out his unique understanding of hermeneutics.

Yet for all its variety, indeed richness, Ricoeur's hermeneutic path does not lack coherence. That coherence can be found, as Ricoeur himself often suggested, in his starting point, which was French reflective philosophy. He did not start off with Dilthey or Heidegger, as Gadamer did, but with philosophers such as Maine de Biran, Lachelier, and

Ravaisson. Ricoeur encountered their tradition through authors like Nabert, Marcel, and Mounier, with whom he had close contact and to whom he often expressed his gratitude. (These authors had no impact whatsoever on Gadamer.) The regrettably forgotten tradition of reflective philosophy, which was founded on the self-reflection of the *ego*, led Ricoeur very early on to the figure of Karl Jaspers, to whom Ricoeur devoted his first books of 1947 and 1948 (and who was, incidentally, Gadamer's predecessor in Heidelberg). At the time, Ricoeur was also attracted by Husserl's phenomenology, not because of its search for an ultimate foundation (*Letztbegründung*), but rather because it explored the intentionality of consciousness, which he sought to apply to the phenomenon of the will.

As we have seen, hermeneutics is absent from Ricoeur's early work. But it emerges with a vengeance in the *Symbolics of Evil* (1960), especially in that book's conclusion, "Symbol Gives Rise to Thought," in which he sketches out the guiding principles of a "philosophical hermeneutics" (he uses that term, the same as Gadamer, no less than three times in a few pages[6]). He anticipated developing that version of hermeneutics in the *Poetics of Evil*, the projected third volume of his trilogy on the will. However, he never published that volume.

What is the task of hermeneutics in "Symbol Gives Rise to Thought"? If one believes the *later* explanations that Ricoeur provided of his "hermeneutical turn," his basic conviction is that the *ego* can only know itself by means of a detour through expressions, symbols, and myths, by means of which it tries to comprehend and express its experience. It follows that hermeneutics is the *voie royale* (royal road) of a reflective philosophy – a philosophy, that is, that recognizes that the *ego*'s self-knowledge develops not through introspection but rather through the patient interpretation of symbols. But when one reads more closely the work of 1960, a slightly different picture emerges: the task of hermeneutics appears far more ambitious than the later Ricoeur was willing to admit when he looked back on his first hermeneutical breakthrough. His hermeneutics of 1960 has to do with our relation to the sacred as it is expressed in myths and symbols. As the children of Enlightenment and historical consciousness, Ricoeur argues, we seem today no longer to be immediately moved by expressions of the sacred. But can we really, he asks, speak about the expressions of the sacred without being addressed (*interpelé*) by them? His main reference in this context is Bultmann's conviction that an interpreter always stands in the "aura" of the meaning she is interpreting and to which she has a vital relation.[7] It is fascinating that Bultmann expressed this idea in a pioneering article of 1950 entitled "The Problem of Hermeneutics." That article probably had a decisive impact on Ricoeur's hermeneutic turn, given that it is the most often quoted piece in the concluding section of his 1960 book.[8] And indeed, Ricoeur draws far-reaching conclusions from Bultmann's core hermeneutical insights. His conviction is that hermeneutics, as a product of historical consciousness, can help us communicate anew with the experience of the sacred in that it recalls – at least in its Bultmannian version – that interpretation is always challenged and touched by what it seeks to understand. Hermeneutics can thus reopen language for the experience of the sacred. At the same time, hermeneutics appears to be the expression of and the remedy for the loss of the sacred that defines our modernity ("expression de la détresse de la modernité et remède à cette détresse").[9] Although Ricoeur would later regret the term, he states that this hermeneutics is "restorative" (*restauratrice*, 482), in that it can foster a "*seconde naïveté* in our relation to the sacred."[10]

Ricoeur would later distance himself from the "restorative" nature of his early hermeneutical project, but one can argue it remained present – perhaps more discreetly – in his later hermeneutical work. What we know is that Ricoeur intended to develop this insight about the restorative nature in the third volume of his trilogy, which was to be devoted to the "poetics of the will." Why that volume was never published is an important matter for Ricoeur studies, but perhaps it had something to do with the rather contradictory predicament of a "second naivety." Be that as it may, Ricoeur did not abandon the theme of interpretation, as is evident in the title of his 1965 work, *De l'interprétation*. That 1965 volume, which he published instead of *Poetics of the Will*, was largely about Freud, even if it rested on an elaborate hermeneutic theory, developed in its first seventy pages. What he singles out in Freud is a peculiar *type* of hermeneutics, one that he would refer to more and more often as a hermeneutics of suspicion. While Ricoeur's instincts situated him more in the line of a hermeneutics of trust, he displays tremendous patience in his discussion of Freud. His basic argument, which he previewed in the *Symbolics of Evil*, is that a reflective philosophy can only benefit from a sceptical reading of symbols, since that approach can free us from some of the illusions of the *ego*, namely those of transparence and self-mastery. As his hermeneutics continued to develop, Ricoeur would become increasingly fascinated by the "conflict of hermeneutics" between suspicion and trust, a conflict about which he would conduct an impressive mediation. That meditation would lead him in the 1970s to emphasize the importance – indeed the necessity – of structuralist interpretations of language. His hermeneutics would from now on – that is, after 1970 – rest on the conviction that the arc of interpretation rests on the patient dialectic between moments of objectifying explanation and those of comprehensive appropriation.

In this, he is both very close to and miles away from Gadamer's understanding and practice of hermeneutics. He is close in that he believes that our self-understanding is always in play in any interpretation. Both have learned from Bultmann, and from Heidegger, that we are personally involved in the process of interpretation, which implies what Gadamer calls an application and Ricoeur an appropriation. There is a nuance, however: whereas for Gadamer understanding and application *coalesce* to the point of forming the same thing (in the fusion of horizons), for Ricoeur appropriation constitutes the *end point* of the arc of interpretation, which must start with structuralist explaining. That is, the emphasis on the belongingness of the interpreter to the interpretation process cements their fundamental hermeneutic solidarity. However, Ricoeur and Gadamer differ in their understanding of what hermeneutical philosophy should be about: Gadamer often states that he is not directly interested in the methods of interpretation, but rather in what happens with us, and to us, in interpretation, whereas Ricoeur is most attentive to the varied and indeed conflicting methods of interpretation, between which his philosophy hopes to mediate.

To put it differently: if Gadamer's question is, basically, "What *happens* to us when we understand?," Ricoeur's is "How should we interpret, which methods should we follow, if we want to understand ourselves better?" This leads Ricoeur to his famous distinction between the approaches of suspicion and trust, which Gadamer does not distinguish (for him, presumably, both are involved in any understanding). One would expect Ricoeur, coming as he does from the tradition of reflective philosophy, to be much closer to the hermeneutics of trust, but that is not really the case. Actually, he devoted more attention to and wrote more extensively on the hermeneutics of suspicion that he found in Freud and the structuralism of Lévi-Strauss, both of which, needless to say, amounted massive criticisms of reflective philosophy. In what could perhaps be described a philosophical variant of the "Stockholm syndrome," Ricoeur seems astonishingly ready to learn from schools that humiliate the self-reflection of the *ego*. Ricoeur's point is that the fractured and humbled *ego* that emerges from the cold shower of suspicion is an *ego* that understands itself better. He thus draws reflective gain from the suspicious destruction of self-reflection. This hermeneutics of the fractured self that emerges out of reflective philosophy and its debates with the philosophies of suspicion has, at first glance, little to do with the hermeneutics of Gadamer. These two hermeneutics answer different questions.

Different Adversaries and Different Allies

Every philosophy, and thus every hermeneutics, is indeed an answer to a provocation. The provocations that are answered by the hermeneutics of Gadamer and Ricoeur are not really the same, and this helps account for these two men's different understandings of hermeneutics. At the risk of simplifying, one can say that Gadamer's "enemy" in *Truth and Method* is what one could term "methodological consciousness," which views understanding and interpretation as operations whose validity depends solely on the observance of scientific rules. Gadamer does not dismiss scientific rules as such, and he repeatedly recognizes that there are rules of interpretation, but he contends that the scientific ideal of objectivity fails to account for the basic hermeneutic experience of understanding, where an interpreter is taken up, captivated by what he or she is understanding. Understanding appears less as the following of stringent rules than as the event of a fusion of horizons, between the interpreter and the *interpretandum*. The methodical perspective arrives too late, he argues, to describe the specificity of the hermeneutic experience of which *Truth and Method* offers the theory. Gadamer's adversary here is "Dilthey" (in spite of his genuine respect for his work) and what he represents – that is, all the merely methodological approaches of hermeneutics, the ones that have everything to do with our scientific age but little to do with the event of understanding they hope to domesticate.

Ricoeur's adversary is different, which is one reason why it is dangerous to speak of a common understanding of hermeneutics in Gadamer and Ricoeur. His enemy is by no means Dilthey, or methodology; indeed, Dilthey is mostly an ally of Ricoeur. Gadamer certainly believed that Ricoeur never succeeded in freeing himself from Dilthey, whom he claimed to have overcome. (This probably did not smooth the dialogue between the two.) Ricoeur presupposes Dilthey's methodological understanding of hermeneutics as a matter of course, perhaps not seeing that it was a *criticism* of Dilthey that Bultmann presented in his

1950 essay "The Problem of Hermeneutics." His problem is that there are very different methods of interpreting, most prominently those of trust and suspicion. If the hermeneutics of trust accepts meaning as it presents itself, the hermeneutics of suspicion calls into question this evidence of meaning, for it can abuse consciousness and induce a "false consciousness," for which Nietzsche, Marx, and Freud offer a hermeneutics of depths.

Notwithstanding his affinity with Dilthey, Ricoeur displays here a certain proximity to Gadamer in that he believes that the evidence of meaning is irrecusable. When one reads him closely, his adversaries are indeed the "anti-hermeneuts," who don't believe in meaning at all and who readily derive meaning from an economics of unconscious drives, needs, and will to power. Ricoeur generously claims that there is much to learn from these schools, but he also rejects their contention that meaning and consciousness can be reduced to a mechanics of hidden drives. His strategy in his debates with Freud and Lévi-Strauss is to show *ad hominem* that these anti-hermeneutics also presuppose this evidence of meaning and consciousness, whether they acknowledge it or not – after all, why would they propose a destruction of consciousness if not to enlarge and "heal" it?[11] In this, he is again close to Gadamer, since for him too the hermeneutic experience goes hand in hand with a transformation and indeed with a more modest understanding of consciousness.

In his debates of the 1970s and 1980s, in the same spirit, Ricoeur would defend the evidence of meaning and reference against structuralist theories that wished to explain it away. In what he characterized in 1989 as the essential "hermeneutical" thesis, he stated:

> The hermeneutical thesis, which is diametrically opposed to the structuralist thesis – but not to the structuralist method, nor to structuralist research – is that the difference between speaking [*parole*] and writing [*écriture*] cannot abolish the fundamental function of discourse [...] Discourse occurs when someone says something to somebody about something. "About something": therein lies the inalienable referential function of discourse.[12]

Here Ricoeur shows his true colours as a hermeneutician: one can learn a great deal from the structuralist understanding of language, he contends, but one has to resist its postulate – indeed, its ideology – that language would be fenced in within itself without referring to the world.

This structuralist exclusion of meaning and reference is absolutely fatal for Ricoeur, and many of his debates in *The Conflict of Interpretations* consist in defending the obvious referential nature of language. This debate is not at all crucial for Gadamer. He only encountered it in his discussion with Derrida, long after *Truth and Method*. It is safe to say that Gadamer never read Lévi-Strauss or considered structuralism and its challenge to the evidence of meaning.

Nonetheless, Gadamer did argue in *Truth and Method* that language is all about Being, and he insisted specifically on the porous openness of language to any Being that can be understood. Here, Gadamer and Ricoeur shared the view that language is essentially open and of an essentially ontological character.

In spite of their solidarity on this matter, the adversaries against which they defend their views are seldom the same. Whereas Ricoeur defends a hermeneutical view of language – that is, an ontological and open one – against the structuralist negation of reference, Gadamer calls into question the instrumental understanding of language, which views it a conventional construction, because it fails to grasp the primordial rootedness of language in Being. In this opposition to the instrumental and objectifying conceptions of language, Gadamer could have perhaps warned Ricoeur against the seduction of the structuralist view of language, which Ricoeur did not always resist (in spite of what he said in the text just quoted about the hermeneutical thesis being "diametrically opposed to structuralism"). This has perhaps something to do with the fact that Ricoeur does not relinquish the methodological understanding of hermeneutics, which is Gadamer's adversary. If Gadamer criticizes Dilthey, Ricoeur mostly views him as an ally (Ricoeur only resists the psychological orientation of Dilthey's "romantic" hermeneutics,[13] an opposition he shares with Gadamer). This different relation to Dilthey has for its part everything to do with their attitude towards Heidegger.

A Different Relation to Heidegger and the Human Sciences: The Long and Short Way of Hermeneutics

In a ground-breaking essay of 1965, "Existence and Hermeneutics," which opens *The Conflict of Intepretation*, Ricoeur famously distinguished between a short and a long way for hermeneutics.[14] According to him, the first way – the short or direct way – is that of Heidegger with his ontology of understanding. It is a short way in that it immediately locates understanding in the mode of being of a *Dasein* who is a question for himself. Under the heading of hermeneutics, Heidegger would thus offer an analysis of this being who is in the world through understanding and interpretation. This approach is characterized by its break with all the methodical debates surrounding hermeneutics, which Ricoeur, for his part, does not want to give up. "To the question: how can a subject understand a text or history? One [i.e., Heidegger] substitutes the question: what is the being of a being whose being consists in understanding?"[15] Heidegger's short way would lose sight of and dissolve all the epistemological problems of classical hermeneutics, which Ricoeur describes as the following, at least in 1965: "How, we must ask, can we provide an *organon* to exegesis, that is to the interpretation of texts? How can we ground the historical sciences vis-à-vis the exact sciences of nature? How to adjudicate the conflict between rival interpretations?"[16] Ricoeur further faults Heidegger in this context for failing to account for the linguistic character of interpretation and understanding.

The long way of hermeneutics – favoured by Ricoeur and always cherished by him – wants to continue the dialogue with the human sciences, initiated by Dilthey, in order to solve its epistemological issues. This way also takes into full account the new theories of language offered by linguistics and the human sciences. It would be interesting to inquire whether Ricoeur does justice to Heidegger, but our focus here has to be on Gadamer. Where should one locate Gadamer in this distinction between a long and a short way of hermeneutics? When the distinction was first presented in 1965, Gadamer was not named, perhaps because Ricoeur did not know him well enough, or because his hermeneutics had not yet become a classical reference of hermeneutics (although as we shall see, Gadamer was perhaps not entirely absent from his mind). One might think that Gadamer's distance to Dilthey's methodological approach would put him in the vicinity of Heidegger's "short way" of an ontology of understanding. But things are not that simple. If Gadamer repeatedly draws on Heidegger, he does not really retake his direct hermeneutics of *Dasein*. His intention is not to spell out the existentials of understanding, interpretation, fall, and so on, like Heidegger does. What complicates Ricoeur's distinction further is that Gadamer does follow Dilthey's lead, despite his criticism, in that he takes up again the dialogue with the human sciences. However, he does not do so to solve their methodological issues, but rather to free them from their methodological straightjacket (or, more cautiously, from their obsession with it). His purpose is to show that the methodological model, which seeks to ascertain a truth independent from the interpreter, is not up to the truth experience of the humanities. What Gadamer offers is thus a phenomenological hermeneutics of the event of understanding in the human sciences, with the aim of establishing that those sciences are not in dire need of a philosophical methodology if one wants to account for their truth experience. Is this the short or the long way of hermeneutics? It is the long way, in that Gadamer starts off with the human sciences, but it ends up retaking Heidegger's criticism and overcoming of Dilthey. Furthermore, one can hardly accuse Gadamer – as Ricoeur does with Heidegger – of ignoring the linguistic nature of language.

In the essay of 1965, there is however a nameless but revealing allusion to Gadamer (there are indeed two of them). Ricoeur writes that when we take up "the long way initiated by the analyses of language we remain in contact with the disciplines which practice interpretation in a methodical manner and can thus resist the temptation to separate the *truth* characteristic of understanding from the *method* put in practice by the exegetical disciplines."[17] It is Ricoeur who underscores in this passage the notions of truth and method. It could be a mere coincidence, but the fact that he repeats the very same claim four pages later[18] would seem to suggest it is not. Breaking with his customary conscientiousness, Ricoeur does not bother to name Gadamer in this context. Why is that so? This first allusion to the dichotomy of truth and method could be a reflection of his first and presumably rather hostile reading of *Truth and Method* in 1965, and of his belief that Gadamer stood in the footsteps of Heidegger. In that, he was not all that wrong, but as I have suggested, it is not clear that Gadamer's way of hermeneutics is necessarily a short one, or for that matter one that shies away from the theme of language.

A Different Kind of Hermeneutical Phenomenology

Both Ricoeur and Gadamer presented their projects as phenomenological hermeneutics. But they did so with different emphases and intentions. If I read them correctly, Ricoeur mostly speaks of a hermeneutic phenomenology and Gadamer of a phenomenological hermeneutics. This is not just a play on words, for it reveals something about the different approaches of those two readers of Husserl and Heidegger.

Gadamer's idea of a "phenomenological hermeneutics" can be understood by examining the important chapter of *Truth and Method* that aims to "overcome the epistemological question [which Ricoeur does not want to relinquish] through phenomenological research."[19] Indeed, this is a decisive chapter given that it is located just before Gadamer presents the outlines of his hermeneutical theory in the second section of *Truth and Method*. The idea of a *phenomenological* hermeneutics is here opposed to a mere *epistemological* hermeneutics, which would ground truth in a particular theory of scientific knowledge, as is or would be the case in Dilthey. Gadamer's idea, influenced by Yorck, Husserl, and Heidegger, is that a hermeneutical reflection on historical knowledge and experience doesn't necessarily have a specific methodology to offer the human sciences. It can be content with a description of the truth experience that distinguishes these sciences. Instead of being epistemological, this hermeneutics is phenomenological in that it returns to the basic phenomena of understanding and interpretation as we encounter them in the humanities. Gadamer maintains the notion of hermeneutics to describe a phenomenological reflection on the humanities. Given that he wants to offer a philosophical reflection on the humanities, he settles on the title of a "*philosophical* hermeneutics," whose intent, however, is phenomenological and not epistemological.

Ricoeur also uses here and there, and as early as his *Symbolics of Evil*, the term "philosophical hermeneutics," but the characterization he finally chose was "hermeneutic phenomenology."[20] His fundamental philosophical task was to offer a phenomenological account of the basic phenomenon of our "striving to be," our "*effort pour exister*."[21] This would culminate in his phenomenology of our capable being (*homme capable*). It is this appropriation by the *ego* of its striving to be that Ricoeur consistently sought to carry further and practice, in the tradition of French reflective philosophy. Yet, as became clearer and clearer to him, mostly in the 1960s, this *ego* cannot know itself through introspection, but only through the symbols and works of culture in which its "effort to be" finds its expression. Interpretation appears here as a "detour" for the *ego*, but this longer road is not really an inconvenience, since there is no other way to self-understanding. Hermeneutic thus becomes the byword of phenomenology, or philosophy as a whole for that matter.

This is why Ricoeur first and famously spoke of a grafting of hermeneutics onto phenomenology. His starting point remains phenomenological, but his way of practising phenomenology is hermeneutical: "contrary to the tradition of the Cogito and the subject's claim to know itself directly through immediate intuition, one has to say that we only understand ourselves through the long detour of the signs of humanity expressed in the works of culture."[22]

Thus, in the case of Ricoeur, one can speak of a *hermeneutical turn of phenomenology*. As for Gadamer's project of a phenomenological hermeneutics, it is more accurate to speak of a *phenomenological turn of hermeneutics*, which aims to free it from it methodological self-understanding.

As we have seen, Ricoeur does not jettison this methodological understanding. But one can ask whether he has delivered on his promise to provide such a methodological hermeneutics. He repeatedly faults Heidegger (and indirectly Gadamer) for having abandoned the epistemological concerns of hermeneutics, which are for him the following, as we have seen in the text quoted above: "How, we must ask, can we provide an *organon* to exegesis, that is to the interpretation of texts? How can we ground the historical sciences vis-à-vis the exact sciences of nature? How to adjudicate the conflict between rival interpretations?" Did Ricoeur ever offer a methodological solution to these problems? It is not all that clear. His hermeneutics thus turn out to be more phenomenological than methodological – at least, less methodological than he readily admitted, which is not necessarily a catastrophe.

Different Answers to the Challenge of Historicity: From Historically Effectuated Consciousness to the Initiative of the Capable Self

There is no doubt that the phenomenological hermeneutics of Ricoeur and Gadamer are marked by and can be seen as the answer to the challenge of historicism or historical consciousness. The term "historicism" evokes a host of experiences. In its more extreme form, historicity conjures up the spectre of relativism or nihilism, often raised by Nietzsche, the great ancestor of the universality of philosophical hermeneutics with his notion that there are no facts, only interpretations. In light of this historical and interpretative character of every world view, it appears difficult to speak of truth as a correspondence with reality or of a binding ethics. Are truth and ethical norms nothing but historical constructions, as has become fashionable to say?

On this all-important issue of hermeneutics, there are a few interesting similarities between Gadamer and Ricoeur. Both are well aware of the spectre of historicism; nonetheless, they continue to speak of truth as well as of a binding ethics. Both acknowledge the historical condition of our knowledge, yet they seldom discuss the general issue of relativism or nihilism. They also have relatively little to say about Nietzsche, who so fascinated Heidegger and the generation that came of age after Ricoeur and Gadamer. Ricoeur rightfully places Nietzsche among the masters of suspicion but devotes far more attention to other masters such as Freud and Marx. For the generation of the great humanists that are Gadamer and Ricoeur, Nietzsche remained somewhat on the fringes.

Regarding the challenge of relativism, both Gadamer and Ricoeur turned the tables on the spectre of historicism: instead of viewing historicity as an "impediment" to knowledge, they tended to view it as a unique opportunity for self-understanding. First of all, we seek to understand *because* we are historical beings (not in spite of it). Furthermore, history provides us with answers and orientation in our quest for meaning since we understand ourselves better through history.

Gadamer goes as far as to elevate history to the rank of a hermeneutical principle.[23] His aim, aside from the provocation entailed by this promotion, is to establish that the model of a non-historical knowledge borrowed from the exact sciences, which would be independent of the interpreter and its time, cannot be applied to the human sciences (indeed, one could ask whether it even applies to the exact sciences; following Thomas Kuhn, one can doubt that it does). There is for Gadamer no such thing as non-historical knowledge. It is far more important for him to recognize that historicity is the driving force of understanding: if we seek to understand, it is *because* we are agitated by questions and uncertainties that have everything to do with our historical condition and situated nature, but also because we are supported by a tradition. There is no need to exclude our historical pre-understandings ("prejudices") or tradition itself in the hermeneutic process, since the dialogue that is understanding is nourished and sustained by them. But we are not bound by them either, since prejudices are constantly revised through interpretation. Tradition also helps sort out productive prejudices from ineffective ones, and it contributes to the establishment of classical works that serve as references and guideposts for our understanding. What would we be without the orientation provided by those references? Gadamer's conviction is that effective history (*Wirkungsgeschichte*) can sort out and eliminate the prejudices that hamper understanding.

This historical and Hegelian optimism is, to say the least, somewhat tempered in the work of Ricoeur, who has reflected intensely on forgetfulness in history and on the power of ideology. Nonetheless, he, like Gadamer, prefers to insist that history is a *magistra vitae*, through which we acquire a proper knowledge of ourselves. To know oneself and to know oneself as a historical being is to recognize that insight is only possible through the major works of culture produced by history. Gadamer and Ricoeur share this humanism.

But there is more in Ricoeur. Even if history determines our being through and through, the individual remains endowed with an important margin of initiative. Ricoeur can rely here on his personalist roots, namely, Mounier's teaching that the individual is always engaged in society (and not only in History writ large), where he can resist the injustices that surround him. In this regard, it is important to note that Ricoeur constantly returns in his work to the theme of evil, which remains for all intents and purposes absent from Gadamer's philosophy. According to Ricoeur, evil is ultimately incomprehensible on a theoretical level (an idea Ricoeur took up very early on from Lachelier),[24] but it can be resisted on the practical level through the practical initiative of the subject. This initiative is limited, to be sure, but it is nonetheless real: "evil is a category of action, not of theory; evil is that against which one fights when one has given up on explaining it."[25] For Ricoeur, the historical determination of consciousness does more than mark the limit of a philosophy of reflection, as is the case in Gadamer; it also calls forth the initiative of which the individual remains capable. I see here one of the most precious contributions of his phenomenology of the "capable human" compared to Gadamer's more subdued understanding of the individual's role in the historical process. *Truth and Method* insists on our being-affected-by-history, whereas Ricoeur recognizes more readily that the subject can also, albeit to a modest degree, affect its course. To be sure, this capacity for initiative also includes a fair share of passivity (I can suffer, I am the inheritor of tradition, I must suffer mortality), but it is inhabited by an undeniable spontaneity, which can be summarized in this short sentence, which Gadamer probably would not have written: "I can change things."

A Reflective Philosophy versus a Criticism of the Philosophies of Reflection

Through this notion of initiative, Ricoeur safeguards the promise of autonomy, however fickle it may be in practice. This is essential to a reflective philosophy. This ideal of an autonomous subject is minimized in Gadamer's hermeneutics. One of the most telling chapters of his *Truth and Method* is "The Limits of a Philosophy of Reflection."[26]

In that text, Gadamer's criticism finds its most dramatic expression where he states that the "focus of subjectivity" is a "distorting mirror," since "the self-awareness of the individual is only a flickering light in the closed circuit of historical life," so that "the prejudices of the individual, far more than his judgments, constitute the historical reality of his being."[27]

Having read Freud, Ricoeur is well aware that subjectivity can be a distorting mirror and that self-reflection amounts to a flickering candle in the wind of historical life. It is, nevertheless, a light and the source of insight. Like Gadamer, Ricoeur is attuned to the incomplete character (*inachèvement*) of reflection for a being of finitude, yet his philosophy does not lead to any fatalism: one can always learn from history and in some cases – rare perhaps – affect its course, at least the course of one's own life. Although both insist on the historical and situated nature of our understanding, those accents positively distinguish Ricoeur's hermeneutics from that of Gadamer: for Ricoeur, initiative, distance, and reflective appropriation always remain possible and desirable in front of the Moloch of history.

The difference is also visible in the field of political philosophy. Ricoeur always engaged in it, theoretically and practically, whereas Gadamer kept a safe distance from all things political, perhaps because he had been warned off politics by the horrendous errors of his masters. One of his late texts is even entitled "On the Political Incompetence of Philosophy."[28] Ricoeur never shared this resignation.

In fairness to Gadamer, he did allude in his later writings to the political implications of his philosophy of dialogue and his sense of *phronesis* (shared by Ricoeur), which tend to attenuate the fatalism that is so prevalent in *Truth and Method*. In this he was perhaps influenced by Heidegger's views on the "destiny of being," which Ricoeur always resisted. The late Gadamer often presented himself as the defender of personal liberty and human judgment against the threats posed to them by our culture of experts.[29] Many of his followers, mostly in North America, such as Richard Palmer, Charles Taylor, and Richard Rorty, saw in this a consequence of his rehabilitation of the virtue of *sensus communis* at the beginning of *Truth and Method*.

The Last Horizon of an Ontology

There is a last significant zone of encounter between Ricoeur and Gadamer that needs to be sketched out here. It is that both men's hermeneutics promise to lead to an ontology. Both lean towards announcing as much at the end of their respective works, although in each case their ontological perspective always remains somewhat allusive. In the final section of *Truth and Method*, Gadamer alludes to an "ontological shift of hermeneutics under the guidance of language." This finds its strongest expression in the famous dictum "Being that can be understood is language," which must be read as a thesis on understanding as well as on being.[30] On understanding, in that it argues that we only understand through language (negatively put: there is no understanding that would not be oriented towards language). One must also see in this a powerful thesis on being: it is through language, and only through language, that the meaning, essence, and intelligibility of being can be deployed. Language appears as a presentation (*Darstellung*) of being in the powerful sense. Gadamer recognizes this idea of presentation in his analysis of art, in which he shows that the artwork enables the being of things to appear as if for the first time.[31] As the presentation if not the present of being, language enjoys the same ontological bearing: it is through language that the being of things presents itself and reveals itself to understanding.

As far as I know, Ricoeur did not comment directly on Gadamer's famous dictum, but he would have agreed with many of its tenets. He has no difficulty recognizing that we can only understand through signs. (Gadamer, for his part, speaks less of signs, since language provides us with such a powerful and immediate presence of being that signs disappear behind what they allow to appear.) Ricoeur would certainly agree that our understanding is basically linguistic. He would also stress that it is being that we understand, since our language is always about something that in and of itself is not language. So, they would concur that language is about being and that our experience of being is linguistic, while at the same time arguing against a wholesale reduction of reality to the world of signs.

But where Gadamer draws from this the outlines of a universal ontology ("Being that can be understood is language"), Ricoeur is after another ontology. The one he hopes to develop is rather an ontology of the capable human; such an ontology could do justice to our striving to be (*effort d'être*), even if this effort is unthinkable without language ("I *can* talk and narrate"). This ontology wishes to fight against the substantialist ontology of being which would have dominated our ontological tradition, but which could not account for the dimension of our effort to live. Here, Ricoeur rejoins Heidegger's critique of *Vorhandenheit*. But instead of confronting "Western metaphysics" as a whole – a settling of accounts that is at odds with his generous and conciliatory hermeneutics – Ricoeur draws on another understanding of the intelligence of being, one to which Aristotle and a few of his modern followers allude – that is, an understanding of being as potentiality and act, or, in the language of Spinoza and Leibniz, of *conatus*, that is, of effort, appetite, and desire.

It goes without saying that these "ontological" categories take on an anthropological meaning in his thinking, since man's toil to live that can find in them its stammering vocabulary. To this extent, Ricoeur's hermeneutical phenomenology leads to an anthropology, which he surprisingly often describes as a "fundamental ontology," again following the not always acknowledged lead of Heidegger.[32]

In this manner, Ricoeur's long way of hermeneutics hopes to lead to the promised land of ontology, instead of starting from it (as Heidegger supposedly did). But if this ontology is truly "fundamental," it is legitimate to see in it a starting point. Its inclination is basically anthropological and humanist since Ricoeur is always seeking to develop an ontology of our striving *cogito*. To be sure, we are dealing with a fragile, decentralized, and broken *cogito*, one that is nevertheless capable and endowed with initiative. This more or less "personalist" underpinning to an ontology of the capable self is rather foreign to Gadamer's ontological outlook. *Ego* having been removed from the centre in his hermeneutics, it is effective history that occupies this centre. As in Ricoeur, the subject is invited to draw from this lessons of modesty, humility, and openness to alterity. Gadamer's ontology, for its part, rests on the universality of being: it is only in language that being presents itself. To the extent that this language remains ours, one can say that this ontology is also basically humanist. Some postmodern readers of Gadamer – Vattimo, for example – have drawn relativistic consequences from this: being reduces itself to the multiple interpretations that our cultural languages can offer of it. But this leads to a nihilistic relativism that is foreign to both Gadamer and Ricoeur. The time has perhaps come to outline a more radically ontological understanding of hermeneutics, one in which the various interpretations can be traced back to being, which is also capable of invalidating them. Of this, hermeneutics is perhaps capable.

Conclusion

Can we speak of a common understanding of hermeneutics in Gadamer and Ricoeur? Even though they often share themes (understanding, history, language) and references (Bultmann, Dilthey, Heidegger), it would be imprudent to readily assert that they do. Their starting points are quite different, as are their enemies and even allies. Ricoeur maintains the methodological focus of hermeneutics and sees in it a continuation of reflective philosophy. Gadamer does not follow him in this. But they share some core convictions – on language, history, and practical wisdom – that enable us to bridge their understandings of hermeneutics. That is why the dialogue between the two, which barely occurred when both men were alive, can only be beneficial today. Incidentally, both stressed the importance of dialogue in this hermeneutical age of reason. If the later Gadamer acknowledged that "the soul of hermeneutics consists in recognizing that the other might be right,"[33] then there is no doubt that is a hermeneutics Ricoeur practised throughout his work. So we must resist choosing between Gadamer and Ricoeur. No, the way of the future for hermeneutics – even if this answer is perhaps more Ricoeurian than Gadamerian – is Gadamer *and* Ricoeur, if one wishes to grasp the full extent of the hermeneutic arc and, thus, its universality.

NOTES

1 This finds confirmation in one of the rare public debates between Gadamer and Ricoeur that has been published: "The Conflict of Interpretations," in R. Bruzina and B. Wilshire, *Phenomenology: Dialogues and Bridges* (Albany: SUNY Press, 1982), 299–320.
2 D. Frey, *L'interprétation et la lecture chez Ricœur et Gadamer* (Paris: PUF, 2008). See, more recently, M.-A. Vallée, *Gadamer et Ricœur. La conception herméneutique du langage* (Rennes: Presses universitaires de Rennes, 2012); and F.J. Mootz III and G. Taylor, eds., *Gadamer and Ricoeur: Critical Horizons for Contemporary Hermeneutics* (New York and London: Continuum, 2011) (published after this chapter was written).
3 On this, see my essay "El milagro del éxito de *Verdad y método*" (The miracle of the Success of *Truth and Method*), in A *cinquenta años de Verdad y método: Balance y perspectivas*, ed. R. Cúnsulo et al. (Tucumán: Editorial Unsta, 2011), 77–86.
4 See my "Le passage de l'herméneutique de Heidegger à celle de Gadamer," in *Le tournant herméneutique de la phénoménologie* (Paris: PUF, 2003), 57–83.
5 See the self-interpretation he offered of his own hermeneutical path, in *Réflexion faite* (Paris: Esprit, 1995). It is also less obvious that the *entire* philosophy of Ricoeur can be summed up under the heading of hermeneutics. For instance, his long restrospective dialogue with Ricoeur in *La critique et*

la conviction (Paris: Calmann-Lévy, 1995) focuses very little on hermeneutics, perhaps because that subject was less familiar to those who conducted the interview with Ricoeur.

6 Ricoeur, *Philosophie de la volonté 3. Finitude et culpabilité* (1960) (Paris: Aubier, 1988), 484, 485, 486. Cited in the text as *FC*.

7 Ibid., 483.

8 On the impact of this Bultmann essay on Gadamer, see my *Herméneutique*, 3rd ed. (Paris: PUF, "Que sais-je?," 2011), 43–7; in German: *Hermeneutik* (Göttingen: UTB, 2009), 45–9.

9 See the presentation of Ricoeur's path to hermeneutics in my *Paul Ricoeur* (Paris: PUF, "Que sais-je?," 2013).

10 *FC*, 482: "Mais si nous ne pouvons plus vivre, selon la croyance originaire, les grandes symboliques du sacré, nous pouvons, nous modernes, dans et par la critique, tendre vers une seconde naïveté. Bref, c'est en *interprétant* que nous pouvons à nouveau *entendre;* ainsi est-ce dans l'herméneutique que se noue la donation de sens par le symbole et l'initiative intelligible du déchiffrage."

11 Ricoeur, *De l'interprétation. Essai sur Freud* (Paris: Seuil, 1965), 43.

12 Ricoeur, *Lectures 3* (Paris: Seuil, 1994), 285: "La thèse herméneutique, diamétralement opposée à la thèse structuraliste – non à la méthode et aux recherches structurales –, est que la différence entre la parole et l'écriture ne saurait abolir la fonction fondamentale du discours [...] Le discours consiste en ceci que quelqu'un dit quelque chose à quelqu'un sur quelque chose. 'Sur quelque chose': voilà l'inaliénable fonction référentielle du discours."

13 Ricoeur, *Du texte à l'action* (Paris: Seuil, 1986), 83ff.

14 Ricoeur, *Le conflit des interprétations* (Paris: Seuil, 1969), 10–15.

15 Ibid., 10.

16 Ibid., 14 ("Comment, demandions-nous, donner un organon à l'exégèse, c'est-à-dire à l'intelligence des textes? comment fonder les sciences historiques face aux sciences de la nature? Comment arbitrer le conflit des interprétations rivales?").

17 Ibid., 15.

18 Ibid., 19: "L'approche sémantique maintient l'herméneutique au contact des méthodologies effectivement pratiquées et ne court pas le risque de séparer son concept de vérité du concept de méthode."

19 H.-G. Gadamer, *Truth and Method*, 2nd rev. ed. (New York: Crossroad, 1989), 242–64: "Overcoming the Epistemological Problem through Phenomenological Research."

20 Most clearly in a text of 1973, "Pour une phénoménologie herméneutique," in *Du texte à l'action*, 55–75.

21 Ricoeur, *Le conflit des interprétations*, 324.
22 Ricoeur, *Du texte à l'action*, 116.
23 Gadamer, *Truth and Method*, 265: "The elevation of the historicity of understanding to the status of a hermeneutical principle."
24 See Ricoeur, *Philosophie de la volonté*, vol. I: *Le volontaire et l'involontaire* (1950) (Paris: Seuil-Points, 2009), 45.
25 Ricoeur, "Le scandale du mal" (1989), in *Anthologie* (Paris: Seuil, 2007), 281.
26 Gadamer, *Truth and Method*, 341–46f.
27 Ibid., 276–7.
28 In Gadamer, *Hermeneutische Entwürfe* (Tübingen: Mohr Siebeck, 2000), 35–41; English translation: "On the Political Incompetence of Philosophy," in *Diogenes* 46, no. 182 (June 1998): 3–11.
29 See, for example, Gadamer's essays such as "Théorie, technique et pratique," in *Langage et vérité* (1972) (Paris: Gallimard, 1995), 254–83; "Les limites de l'expert" (1989), in *L'héritage de l'Europe* (Paris: Rivages, 1996), 121–39; and "Humanisme et révolution industrielle" (1988), in *Esquisses herméneutiques* (Paris: Vrin, 2004), 43–52.
30 See my "La thèse de l'herméneutique sur l'être," *Revue de métaphysique et de morale* 4 (2006): 469–81.
31 See my "L'art comme présentation chez Gadamer. Portée et limites d'un concept," *Études Germaniques* 62 (2007): 343–55.
32 Ricoeur, *La mémoire, l'histoire, l'oubli* (Paris: Seuil, 2000), 639. See also Ricoeur, *Finitude et culpabilité*, 13 ("ontologie fondamentale de la réalité humaine"); and *Le conflit des interprétations*, 23.
33 See "Un entretien avec Hans-Georg Gadamer," *Le Monde* (3 janvier 1995); *L'héritage de L'Europe* (Paris: Rivages, 1996), 141.

Chapter Three

The Commonality of the World and the Intercultural Element: Meaning, Culture, and *Chora*

SUZI ADAMS

Recent debates on "intercultural hermeneutics" – or, more broadly, "intercultural studies" – have been particularly heterogeneous. Generally the emphasis has been on an "intercultural hermeneutics" understood as an interaction between – or the exchanges made between – different cultures (or different cultural actors). Many approaches seem to reduce "intercultural hermeneutics" to some form of intercultural communication or dialogue understood as the intersubjective interactions between subjects of different cultures; here the enhancement of mutual understanding appears as the ultimate aim. An "intercultural hermeneutics," however, also presumes a "hermeneutics of the intercultural." A philosophy of "the intercultural" seeks to elucidate the intercultural element of the human condition in-the-world. Always configured in a dynamic interplay, these two aspects are nonetheless irreducible to the other. This essay focuses on the second aspect and begins to sketch a hermeneutics of "the intercultural element." But rather than going directly to the question of the "intercultural element," it takes a hermeneutical detour to focus on the commonality of the world horizon to the human condition. In so doing, it argues that the world as a shared *and* intercultural horizon forms the very *precondition* of encounters and interactions among cultures, civilizations, and cultural actors, and thus forms a precondition for greater mutual understanding. The essay begins by reconsidering the interlocking questions of "culture," "world" and the "phenomenal field" to gain greater insight into the common foundation of *anthropos* underlying its cultural (and civilizational) varieties. Here it takes its cue from the Czech phenomenologist Jan Patočka, who argues that "as long as this foundation, shared by all forms of humanity, no matter how diverse, is not exhumed from its long obscurity, no real dialogue between 'cultures' and 'peoples' will be possible."[1] For Patočka the elemental commonality of the human condition lies in the "mystery of the world." It is only after we have elucidated the world as the shared ground of humanity that intercultural variety can be addressed. Although the present writer agrees with Patočka concerning the world as the primordial ground of human commonality, this essay sketches the onto-phenomenological preconditions of the intercultural element, instead of following Patočka to exhume a "care for the soul" as the basis for his anthropology of a "moral" order common to humanity.[2]

The essay focuses on the *phenomenological* problematic of the world as the basis of any *(inter)cultural hermeneutics*. Indeed, from Heidegger onward, phenomenology and hermeneutics have been in constant interplay. The achievement of phenomenology and hermeneutics has been to highlight the centrality of meaning to the human condition, on the one hand, while showing that meaning is always already situated within a world horizon that is socially and historically instituted, on the other. The argument to be elaborated here insists that cultural meaning emerges first at the properly "social" or "trans-subjective" level (not at the "intersubjective" level), and, moreover, appears as a plurality of cultural worlds each of which encounters, interprets, and articulates the world as an overarching and undetermined horizon. The point will be to problematize the possibility of the conditions of existence of a plurality of cultural worlds; the possibility of their commonality and difference with other cultural worlds; the ontological – and culturological – status of the relative closure or openness of these cultural worlds; and the possibility for encounters with a variety of cultural worlds. The essay is structured primarily around a discussion of three thinkers and their respective contributions to the world as an intercultural horizon. After a brief contextualization of the problematic of "culture," "world," and "meaning," it turns to the work of Cornelius Castoriadis – in particular, to his elucidation of social imaginary significations; then it takes up Johann P. Arnason's phenomenology of the world as a shared horizon and his cultural hermeneutics; after that, it summarizes key elements of Jan Patočka's *a-subjective* phenomenology and his later approach to the world as a "field of manifestation." Finally, the essay argues that reconsideration of Plato's *chora* would enrich elaborations of the trans-subjective field; this concluding section briefly considers the significance of Nishida Kitaro's concept of *basho*.

When we speak of culture, three overlapping aspects require elucidation: meaning, sociality, and world relation. First, the phenomenon of "meaning" is necessarily foregrounded when the question of culture arises (whether in terms of symbolic practices, cultural narratives, cultural significance, or cultural institutions and artefacts). For present purposes we will focus on an elaboration of "culture" as an autonomous element within the social world that other social spheres (e.g., economic, political, or aesthetic) in turn articulate/institute in concrete form. Furthermore, "cultural" meaning is understood to emerge at the "social" level, which itself becomes an explicit point of interrogation. To argue for a specifically "social" or "cultural" level of meaning is to critique the more common emphasis on "sociality" as reduced to the *intersubjective* (or *dialogical*) level of reality. Approaches that take the "intersubjective" as their basis have confused the "intersubjective" – which still analytically takes "the subject" as its core – with the distinctive "sociality" and "anonymous collective" of the social world. Such an approach is reductive, for "meaning" and "signification," rather like "language," first emerge at what might be variously termed the "social," "a-subjective," "trans-subjective," or "cultural" level of reality, and as such form the very *precondition* for intersubjective contexts of interaction, dialogue, and mutual understanding. The final aspect of "culture" is its "world relation." The question of the "world" has always been part of phenomenological discussion, but the world as a "horizon of horizons" – that is, as no longer reducible to the "lifeworld" as articulated by Husserl in his later thought – first becomes a problematic in its own right with third-generation phenomenology. This phase, as evident especially in the work of Fink, Merleau-Ponty, Levinas, and, of course, Patočka, is characterized by the search for new approaches to the relation between *anthropos* and the world that would simultaneously go beyond the limitations of Husserl and Heidegger. "Being-in-the-world" and "articulations of the world" as an "overarching horizon" comprise different aspects of the trans-subjective field of the world's human – that is, cultural – manifestation and articulation.

Perhaps more than any other twentieth-century thinker, Cornelius Castoriadis has continually drawn our attention to the centrality of *the imaginary element* to the human condition.[3] He does so chiefly through his elucidation of the social-historical, on the one hand, and the creative imagination, on the other. Each is fundamental to the mode of being of "human creation"; that mode, and the elucidation of the "project of autonomy," form the axis around which his thought revolves.

On Castoriadis's account, "human creation" occurs *ex nihilo*. Human creation refers to the creation of new ontological forms that cannot be understood on the basis of determinist logic-ontologies; new socio-political forms can neither be *reduced to* nor *produced from* any antecedents. As such, Castoriadis's account of creation is a critique of what he calls "inherited thought" and its long-held convention of conceptualizing "being" as "being-determined." Absent from such accounts, claims Castoriadis, is the capacity to grasp modes of being that are characterized not by "determinacy" but rather by "*self-creation*." In this context, Castoriadis refers to human modes of being in particular, which for him incorporate the ontological regions of the social-historical and the psyche.[4] To illustrate his point about the human capacity for ontological creation, Castoriadis analyses the founding of democracy in ancient Greece. Amidst a sea of monarchies, the ancient Greeks brought a new political form into being – democracy – that had no precedent elsewhere.[5] As a form new to the human condition, it brought with it ontological novelty as the creation of "*otherness*." This provides Castoriadis with an important critique of conventional accounts that reduce ontological novelty to its antecedents; as such they can only articulate the "production" or "reproduction" of the "same" form as *predicated on* that which came before (such as "causalist" accounts of history). These accounts are caught within "identity" – or, more precisely for Castoriadis, *ensemblistic–identitarian* thought. A "new" form, such as democracy, on the other hand, cannot be explained by way of its antecedents; it comes "out of nothing," whence Castoriadis's insistence on human creation as *creatio ex nihilo*.[6]

Underlying the ancient Greek creation of democracy, however, was a further creation, one more fundamental for our present purposes: *the autonomist imaginary*. For Castoriadis, the creation of the autonomist imaginary forms the *precondition* for the creation of democracy, and "democracy" as instituted by the ancient Greeks emerges as a particular cultural interpretation and institution of it.[7] On Castoriadis's account, the autonomist imaginary is a central *social imaginary signification* for both the ancient Greek world and the modern one, and it is such core social imaginary significations that form the basis of the social world that is created by the social-historical *ex nihilo*. For Castoriadis, the creation of a world is always that of a world of meaning (at the basis of which are the social imaginary significations). One of the most innovative aspects of Castoriadis's elucidation to meaning is its link to the creative imagination.

The *creative imagination* is Castoriadis's generic term for the imagination in its threefold aspect of the *corporeal imagination* of the living being, the *radical imagination* of the psyche, and the *radical imaginary* of the social-historical.[8] Meaning in the strict sense occurs at the level of the social-historical as/through social imaginary significations. Like language, meaning is trans-subjective and a product of what Castoriadis calls the *anonymous collective*. Cultural meaning at this level is latent but is made concrete through the articulation of institutions and the subsequent interpretations and actions of subjects.[9] Castoriadis tells us that

> the imaginary of which I speak is not an image *of*. It is the unceasing and essentially undetermined (social-historical and psychical) creation of figures/forms/images, on the basis of which alone there can ever be a question *of* "something." What we call "reality" and "rationality" are its works.[10]

Castoriadis's most systematic discussion of social imaginary significations is to be found in the final chapter of *The Imaginary Institution of Society* (hereafter *IIS*). The chapter itself is less systematic than the previous three chapters of the 1975 section, but no less interesting for that.[11] Castoriadis approaches his discussion of social imaginary significations through ontology: he is more interested in their mode of being than in their phenomenological and hermeneutical significance. In fact, he rejects any suggestion of a hermeneutical aspect to social imaginary significations (I return to this).[12] Social imaginary significations create or self-institute a "world of significations"; as such, social-historical worlds are characterized by "significance" where everything must be put into meaning, and society can only exist in continuing reference to the world of meaning that it has self-created. After elucidating what he calls "second-order" significations – that is, those that "lean on" the proto-institutions of *legein* and *teukhein*[13] – Castoriadis turns to address core social imaginary significations.[14] These core (or *nuclear*) social imaginary significations cannot be said to "lean on" the first natural stratum in any way whatsoever; instead they create a purely "social reality."[15] In Castoriadis's view, they are wholly generative and radically creative. These significations, such as "autonomy" or "God" or "rational mastery," are definitive for the particular society in question and shape its "reality" and its "identity" as well as constellations of its socio-political world at the nuclear level that give the society in question its particular form. The "radical imaginary," the creative force of social imaginary significations and their world-creative capacity, manifests at the trans-subjective level of social reality and can no longer be regarded as a "human faculty" located in an individual person that we associate with the "imagination."

However, as mentioned above, these social imaginary significations, this world of meaning, must be further articulated as a variety of concrete institutions – from the *autonomist imaginary* to the political institution of *democracy*, for example. As mentioned, at this level of meaning the core layer of social imaginary significations must be understood as latent and can be interpreted and articulated in a variety of ways. To take the *autonomist imaginary* as an example, again, historically there were a plurality of "democratic forms" articulated by the various ancient Greek cities: Athens, Sparta, and Corinth, to name the best-known three. That is, the example of ancient Greek democracy shows *intra*cultural variety, while its historical expansion (e.g., modern Indian, Canadian, French, or Australian democracies) shows *inter*cultural variety. Because of his polarization of "autonomy" and "heteronomy," Castoriadis could not fully grasp this aspect of the "autonomist imaginary," and this partial blindness blocked openings in his thought onto recognition of intercultural varieties of political autonomy. His emphasis on the radical aspects of creation led to a neglect of the interpretive element of the human condition – and of the interpretative element to autonomy.

Castoriadis's thought gives us deeper insight into the imaginary element of meaning and its sociality but is less helpful for thinking through the hermeneutic aspect of the overarching horizon that central social imaginary significations institute. This highlights his relative neglect of the phenomenological problematic of the world as an *intercultural* horizon. For Castoriadis, the world was something that the social-historical radically and immanently created as singular and unique, and this blinded him to both its common and its intercultural aspects. To help us understand this aspect better, we turn to the thought of Johann P. Arnason.

Johann P. Arnason (1940–), an Icelandic sociologist and philosopher, is best known for his social theory and historical sociology of "multiple modernities" and for his comparative civilizational analyses of the Axial Age and beyond. Generally, however, his contribution to phenomenology and hermeneutics has received much less attention.[16] Yet his reconfiguration of key phenomenological problematics deserves greater attention. His work is especially pertinent for present purposes because he explicitly tries to do justice not only to the sociality and world relation of cultural meaning at the trans-subjective level, but also to the world as an intercultural horizon. What is distinctive about Arnason's approach is the centrality it gives to the interplay of the "world horizon" and "culture"; ultimately, they cannot be separated in his thought – one presumes the other.

First, it is important to clarify the scope and domain of "culture" (and "world") for Arnason. "Culture" and "world" inhabit the *trans-subjective* (and trans-objective) domain of human collective existence, which is irreducible to intersubjective analysis. The phenomenon of language as created by the *collective anonymous* of society provides a good example of trans-subjective phenomena; symbols, too, operate at this trans-subjective level. *Cultural meaning*, however, is embedded in both and reducible to neither. Unlike the vast majority of philosophical anthropological approaches – especially in the phenomenological tradition – Arnason's anthropology does not focus on the "individual person" or the "human self" per se; as a sociologist, Arnason knows full well that we can only become "human" within the fabric of society – or, more precisely, following Aristotle, within the political institution of society.[17] Culture, in the sense that Arnason uses it most often, refers to varieties of cultural meaning; this is similar to Castoriadis's notion of social imaginary significations (while Arnason prefers the term "cultural patterns"), although generally, social imaginary significations are more concrete for Arnason than for Castoriadis.[18]

Although Arnason agrees with Castoriadis that central social imaginary significations shape the social world (or broader civilizational worlds), there is a fundamental disparity in their approaches that lies in their varying treatments of the problematic of *interpretation*.[19] In turn, the basis of this disagreement is found in their differing approaches to "culture" and "world." Arnason argues that social imaginary significations are as much world interpreting as they are world creating, whereas, as we have seen, Castoriadis maintains that core social imaginary significations are purely generative, purely creative. Arnason's approach in effect reconfigures Merleau-Ponty's famous statement in the Preface to *The Phenomenology of Perception* that "because we are in the world *we are condemned to meaning*":[20] on Arnason's account, however, because we are in the world we are condemned not only to *meaning* but also to *interpretation*. Here Ricoeur is also an important intellectual source for Arnason; both argue that our hermeneutical mode of being in the world is not characterized primarily by "understanding" but rather by "interpretation" and the concomitant "conflict of interpretations."[21] Herewith Arnason emphasizes that meaning – as cultural articulations of the world horizon – is underdetermined and contextual and that a plurality of interpretations is always already involved.

Arnason understands "culture" as the "relationship between man and world."[22] As such, in that it goes beyond the limitations imposed by more conventional accounts of culture as socio-centric, his approach offers an important breakthrough for the theorization of culture (and society). A socio-centric basis is evident in philosophical, anthropological, and sociological currents, from Durkheim to Lévi-Strauss to Ram Adhar Mall. Socio-centric accounts of culture/society take many forms but are rarely questioned. Yet it is only with a decentred approach to culture that the intercultural element of the world can become clear. Arnason elaborates a middle way between "social constructivism" and "determinism," one that allows for historical trajectories and for the shaping – but not determining – force of overarching cultural orientations and civilizational patterns. Arnason's decentred approach to "culture" is evident in his work as early as 1982; this essay of Arnason's, addressing Max Weber's social theory, can be seen as the earliest prefiguration of his later hermeneutical turn.[23] Arnason develops his cultural-hermeneutical phenomenology through a reconstruction of Weber and Merleau-Ponty, later enriching it by engaging with Castoriadis's elaboration of social imaginary significations and by making connections between the imaginary element and cultural meaning. Both Arnason and Castoriadis work in the wake of Merleau-Ponty, but whereas Castoriadis turned to ontology, with the hermeneutical element remaining implicit, Arnason turned to history and cultural hermeneutics, thereby sidestepping ontological considerations. Arnason's deepening of the entwined problematics of "culture" and "world," with the explicit aim of giving the intercultural element of the human condition its due, saw him emphasize the world as a "shared horizon." This shared, or intercultural, horizon of the world common to the human condition is articulated variously along civilizational lines. Arnason's reactivation of the comparative analysis of civilizations sees him broadening the "culture" problematic to emphasize that the "cultural orientations" of a specific society might also be part of a broader civilizational pattern shared among a "family of societies." His resolute "macro-phenomenology" and focus on the "Objective Spirit" instead of everyday life brings the *trans-subjective* sphere into relief, while his articulation of the unfinished hermeneutical turn does much to focus our attention at that level of reality, by elaborating (inter)cultural patterns of rationality and social imaginaries, thereby liberating our gaze that has been for so long fixed on the human faculties of the individual person.[24]

In brief, for the purposes of this essay, Arnason's mature phenomenology of the world can be characterized by a fivefold hermeneutical movement. First, the emphasis on the world requires, in the first instance, a hermeneutics of culture – or, more precisely, a comparative hermeneutics of the cultural articulation of civilizational worlds. Second, the world as a shared cultural horizon is an intercultural "unity in plurality," where overarching cultural patterns of meaning, such as "the autonomist imaginary," are culturally interpreted and instituted in a variety of ways.[25] Third, in that *anthropos* is always "world articulating," Arnason's conception of culture finds a middle path between overly *constructivist* and overly *determinist* approaches to cultural worlds – a path that goes beyond the limitations of a socio-centric approach. Fourth, Arnason draws on a hermeneutical notion of creation as *creative interpretation* (or *interpretative creation*). In contradistinction to Castoriadis, Arnason argues that creation is not *ex nihilo*, but historically contextual, in that it draws on, reactivates, and reconfigures the latent reservoirs of meaning in existing or historical social imaginary significations that form *cultural* – and civilizational – *orientations*.

Arnason's thought offers an approach to culture that does justice to the world as an intercultural horizon. In turn, the world as a shared and intercultural horizon emerges as a "unity in plurality." Taking the example of "modernity," an overarching horizon of "the modern" emerges that has been culturally articulated and instituted in a variety of ways (such as Japanese, Chinese, and Western European modernities). Although Arnason's approach balances these two, overall his comparative historical studies have emphasized the need for a greater appreciation of human *diversity* rather than commonality. To gain further insight into the commonality of the world and to deepen our understanding of the shared phenomenal field of trans-subjective reality, we turn to the thought of Jan Patočka.

Jan Patočka (1907–77) is now recognized as the most important Czech phenomenologist of the twentieth century. A Czech dissident long banned from university teaching, and co-author of Charta 77, Patočka died in 1977 after a prolonged police interrogation. He was one of the last of Husserl's students as well as a pupil of Heidegger, and his work demonstrates a lifelong engagement with each of them. As with Merleau-Ponty, Patočka's phenomenological path can be situated within post-transcendental currents; each in his own way made "the world horizon" a central theme to his philosophical itinerary, and their contributions were significant in clarifying the world horizon as a question in its own right within phenomenological thought. Indeed, Domenico Jervolino has written that "the world is the great speculative theme of Patočka's thought."[26]

Patočka's early work critically expands the Husserlian program while remaining within a transcendental approach. His *Habilitation* thesis (1938), published in French in 1976 as *Le monde naturel comme problème philosophique* (*The Natural World as a Philosophical Problem*), is perhaps his best-known work.[27] It was, in some sense, also a work-in-progress, as attested by his lengthy postscript to the second Czech edition (1970), his afterword to the French translation (1976), and a slightly earlier essay with a very similar title.[28] Noteworthy in the present context, during his "middle period," as part of an unfinished project, Patočka composed his essay "Negative Platonism" (1953), which was his attempt to both overcome and retrieve the kernel of the metaphysical dimension. Although he did not pursue this line of inquiry further, some commentators have read it as a complementary approach to his maturing phenomenology of the world and a-subjective phenomenology.[29] Patočka's interest in Plato was long-standing, and it was in dialogue with Plato's thought that he developed his distinctive understanding of "care for the soul" as part of his "three movements of human existence" – a phase in his thought that is related to but also distinct from his a-subjective phenomenology and his philosophy of history.[30]

Patočka's *a-subjective* phenomenology is of most interest here. Its problematic emerged late in his trajectory (after 1970), and he did not systematically pursue it; thus it remained more a promise than a program. It emerges as one of several parallel movements towards an expanded elaboration of the world; these include his earlier attempt at *Negative Platonism* (1953), as well as his later philosophy of history and the three movements of human existence. Two of his papers in particular directly address the a-subjective problematic: "Der Subjektivismus der Husserlschen und die Möglichkeit einer 'asubjektiven' Phänomenologie" and "Der Subjektivismus der Husserlschen und die Forderung einer asubjektiven Phänomenologie."[31] Central to his a-subjective phenomenology was his conviction that phenomenology had confused its central question, identifying it with "what appears" – that is, with "entities" (*Seiende*) – rather than with "appearance as such."[32] As mentioned,

Patočka wrote only two essays in which the term "a-subjective phenomenology" features in the title (written in reference to Husserl); the remainder of his a-subjective writings are scattered among a number of essays and seminars.[33] As his a-subjective phenomenology is neither clearly nor extensively developed, it is open to a number of interpretations. One track of thought views Patočka's a-subjective phenomenology as in line with a shift towards a focus on the embodied subject as a way of criticizing the philosophy of consciousness. This interpretation is often also linked to Patočka's overlapping but distinct line of thought in "Three Movements of Human Existence."[34] As should be apparent, however, the present essay focuses on a-subjectivity as the trans-subjective field of cultural articulations, where the world is always already an *intercultural* horizon. In each case, however, it should be emphasized that in moving away from the limitations of an anthropocentric view of the phenomenological field, Patočka sought to elucidate the situation of the world and its *proto-movement* in relation to appearance *as such*.

Although the two a-subjective essays were explicitly critiques of Husserl, a critical encounter with Heidegger was also central to his a-subjective approach. Patočka criticizes what he thinks of as the two "subjectivist" approaches of Husserl and Heidegger. With Husserl, the focus of his criticism is transcendental subjectivity, and with that, "intentionality," the "reduction," and concomitantly the realm of *givenness* as an absolute realm of self-given immanence. That is, he critiques the idea that the transcendental subject is the source of the "appearance." He critiques Heidegger (of the *Being and Time* period) for reducing "appearance" and its possibilities to a characteristic of *Dasein*, by excluding the world.[35] In contrast, Patočka's project of an a-subjective phenomenology seeks to theorize the structure of "appearance as such" as an a-subjective – or trans-subjective – modality. Following Karfík,[36] the structure of appearance consists of three moments: that which shows itself as something; that which shows itself to someone; and the way in which it shows itself, although none of these moments are reducible to the others. Importantly, that which shows itself and the self to whom it shows itself have the same source. The "projection" (*Entwerfung*) from possibilities does not emerge from *Dasein*, but rather from the "field of possibilities" in which it is always already "thrown"; *Dasein* does not conjure up the possibilities; rather, those possibilities are given to it. That is, an understanding of the level of "phenomena" is not to be found within "the subject" but within "manifestation as such" and its own, particular a-subjective structure, otherwise known as "the field of manifestation." The field of manifestation, as the world, is the *a priori*, in the sense of the precondition of all appearances.[37] The horizon of the world makes possible the various possibilities of *Dasein*'s existence; that is, it *opens* the field of possibilities for us. For Patočka, the world itself does not *have* "being," and neither is it *a* "being" (in the Heideggerian sense of Being/beings), and in that sense it has no "positive reality." Unlike Husserl's notion of the world as a "horizon of horizons," Patočka's elaboration takes it in the direction of articulating it as a "field of possibilities."[38] In Patočka's a-subjective thought, the world is an open and dynamic field of possibilities, on the one hand, and the ground of possibility for the phenomena to appear, on the other. Thus the world for Patočka forms the precondition of appearances and is as such to be considered "pre-ontological," which perhaps might be better interpreted as "me-ontological."[39] The world not only is the precondition of appearance as such, but also is slightly reconfigured in Patočka's thought as the "field of manifestation"; and in a further reworking, it re-emerges in his late work as a dynamic "field of possibilities." These are of course interrelated: the world is the *a priori* of manifestation as such, and the field of manifestation is one of the key aspects of the (human) appearance of the world and its possibilities. Patočka's last phase, according to Karel Novotny, results in a hermeneutical ontology of the world through phenomenological means.[40] On this reading, Patočka's thought could bridge Arnason's culturological with Castoriadis's ontological account of the trans-subjective horizon of the world.

It also brings Patočka's a-subjective phenomenology into contact with another Platonic problematic: the *chora*. The mysterious *chora*, the "spatial receptacle" or "midwife" found in Plato's cosmology of the *Timaeus*, finds itself midway between the intelligible and the sensible realms. When viewed as part of a Negative Platonism, however, it can be said to be not only a precondition for appearance in the sensible realm, but also, more precisely, *that which allows the phenomenalization of the world as a field of possibilities*. Like the "world," the *chora* is a metaphysical element not reducible to Being/beings; a "third kind," it makes the phenomenal field possible, yet its significance for a phenomenology of *appearance as such* has not been raised so far. Patočka himself does not link his a-subjective phenomenology to the *chora*, but he does discuss it in an important essay from a slightly earlier period, "Der Raum und seine Problematik."[41] In his discussion of ancient Greek philosophical and mythical articulations of forms of spatiality, he discusses the *chora*/receptacle as central to Plato's theory of space. Here Plato represents a transitional figure in the history of philosophy. The *chora* is the midwife to geometrical forms.[42] Patočka sums it up thus: "This mythic-sensible space is not a space of geometric forms and their eternal regularity, but originally a dynamic space of chaotic movement and forces."[43]

While it might be going too far to argue that Plato's *chora* has become a theme in its own right within phenomenological circles, there is no doubt that it has received significant recent attention. The *chora* has appeared intermittently in phenomenological debates, especially among those thinkers who are also interested in ontology. Significant in this context is Heidegger and his elucidation of "*Lichtung*," but significant as well are Fink and, implicitly, Merleau-Ponty and his notion of "Flesh." Recent years have seen a return of the question of the *chora* within phenomenology, with the debate between John Sallis and Jacques Derrida emerging as the most significant.[44] Up until the past few years, a surprising absence in this phenomenological literature has been Nishida Kitaro and his concept of *basho* (place), but this is slowly changing.[45]

Nishida Kitaro (1870–1945) was Japan's most significant twentieth-century philosopher and founder of the Kyoto School. His late thought was characterized by an elaboration of the "logic of *basho*," usually translated as "place."[46] It can be understood as an early version of a-subjective phenomenologically sensitive philosophy that offers a non-substantialist approach to the metaphysical stratum, with overlapping epistemological and ontological dimensions. His critical dialogue focused not on Husserl, however, but rather on Kant and the subjectivist approach. Kitaro's logic was accompanied by an ontology of "absolute nothingness."[47] "To be" for Kitaro means "to be within," and the "absolute nothingness" is thus not an absence of being; rather, it comprises a field of dynamic, creative, active movement that is world creative (here, links to Castoriadis's articulation of chaos and creation seem apparent). Indeed, each of the three thinkers considered in this essay provides an implicit opening onto the *chora*. With his trenchant critique of Plato's *chora*, Castoriadis[48] would seemingly be the least amenable to such a reconstruction; nonetheless, hermeneutic reconstruction shows that his work provides insights into the chaotic residue of the *chora* and thus a dynamic notion of place/space necessary when elaborating the field of manifestation. Arnason draws implicitly on Heidegger's notion of the *Lichtung* (clearing), although he would prefer the sense of "cultural clearing" rather than an ontologically conceived *Lichtung*, as the field where the world as a shared horizon converges on the shared problematics of the human condition and on the plurality of responses that are historically articulated.[49] Finally, as discussed, Patočka's long essay "Space" begins to develop a notion of non-spatial spatiality that can be linked to his a-subjective phenomenology and the field of manifestation.[50]

This essay argued that an indirect route is required to make sense of the intercultural element of the world. It took the enigma of "the world" as the pre-ontological ground of human commonality in order to elucidate a conception of culture that goes beyond socio-centric confines and that can do justice to the human condition in both its unity and its diversity. Only a decentred approach to culture can make full sense of the intercultural world. This essay focused on three thinkers – Castoriadis, Arnason and Patočka – each of whom deepened our insights into various aspects of the trans-subjective field: meaning, culture, world, and/or the phenomenal field of appearance as such. It argued that further consideration of Plato's *chora* can expand our insights into the trans-subjective field, especially in light of Patočka's openings towards its imaginary and not just its mathematical content. One hermeneutical circle opens onto another; the essay concluded its argument for a "hermeneutics of the intercultural" by drawing on an "intercultural hermeneutics" in relation to Plato's *chora*. It highlighted the importance of Nishida Kitaro's onto-epistemological philosophy of *basho* for current phenomenological discussions of the elemental field of human commonality, and, ultimately, for elucidating the dimensions of human diversity.

NOTES

1 Jan Patočka, "Die Selbstbesinnung Europas," *Perspektiven der Philosophie* 20 (1994): 272.

2 This interpretation of Patočka's anthropology leans on Kwok-Ying Lau's excellent essay, in which he seeks to bring Patočka into intercultural dialogue with Chinese cultural forms. See Lau, "Patočka's Concept of Europe: An Intercultural Consideration," in *Jan Patočka and the Heritage of Phenomenology: Centenary Papers*, ed. Ivan Chvatik and Erika Abrams (New York, London: Springer, 2010).

3 *The Imaginary Element* (*L'element imaginaire*) is the title of an unfinished work by Castoriadis, first mentioned in the preface to *The Imaginary Institution of Society* (Cambridge: Polity, 1987) in 1975.

4 For Castoriadis the opposition between "society" and the "individual" is a fallacy, for the individual is always already socially shaped. Rather, the true opposition is to be found between "society" (or, in Castoriadian terms, the social-historical) and the psyche.

5 For a discussion of this, see Johann P. Arnason and Peter Murphy, eds., *Agon, Logos, Polis: The Greek Achievement and Its Aftermath* (Stuttgart: Franz Steiner, 2001).

6 In his later thought (i.e., in the 1980s), Castoriadis qualified his strong statement about *creatio ex nihilo* by explaining that this did not mean it was also *cum* and *in nihilo* (Castoriadis, "Fait et à faire," in *Revue européenne des sciences sociales: Pour une philosophie militante de la démocratie* 27, ed. Giovanni Busino (Geneva: Librairie Droz, 1989), 86.

7 Each aspect occurs in interplay with the other, with the "autonomist imaginary" more indeterminate and the "democracy" a concrete manifestation of it in socio-political life.

8 Although the creative imagination is indeed threefold, generally speaking, when Castoriadis writes of the "creative imagination" he is referring to the imagination in the human realm – that is, the radical imagination and the radical imaginary – and not to the corporeal imagination of the living being. In addition, the corporeal imagination is not yet the "radical" – that is, *defunctionalized* – imagination of the human condition, for the corporeal imagination operates within functional closure.

9 Generally, Castoriadis speaks of meaning at both the psychical level and the social-historical level, with the level of the social-historical (i.e., social imaginary) significations the most important. Underdeveloped in this context is the place of what he calls the "social individual."

10 Castoriadis, *The Imaginary Institution of Society*, 3.

11 *The Imaginary Institution of Society* is a heterogeneous text. It has two parts. The first, in which Castoriadis develops his critique of Marx, consists of three essays first published in *Socialisme ou Barbarie* in 1964–5; the second, which he wrote between 1970 and 1974, and which announces his ontological turn, consists of four chapters on different aspects of the human condition: ontological, epistemological, anthropological, and hermeneutical.

12 See Castoriadis, "Fait et à faire"; Johann P. Arnason, "The Imaginary Constitution of Modernity," in Busino, ed., *Revue européenne des sciences sociales*; Arnason, "Culture and Imaginary Significations," *Thesis Eleven* 22 (1989): 25–45; and Suzi Adams, "Arnason and Castoriadis' Unfinished Dialogue: Articulating the World," *European Journal of Social Theory* 14, no. 1 (2011): 71–88.

13 For a detailed discussion of these aspects, see Adams, *Castoriadis's Ontology: Being and Creation* (New York: Fordham University Press, 2011), esp. chapters 2 and 4.

14 Castoriadis, *The Imaginary Institution*, 355.

15 Ibid., 355.

16 But see Wolfgang Knöbl, "In Praise of Philosophy: Johann Arnason's Long but Successful Journey Toward a Theory of Modernity," *Thesis Eleven* 61 (2000): 1–23; Suzi Adams, "The Intercultural Horizons of Johann P. Arnason's Phenomenology of the World," *Journal of Intercultural Studies* 30, no. 3 (2009): 249–66; and Adams, "Arnason and Castoriadis' Unfinished Dialogue."
17 Arnason, *Praxis und Interpretation: Sozialphilosophische Studien* (Frankfurt am Main: Suhrkamp, 1988); Arnason, "Culture and Imaginary Significations"; Arnason, "Merleau-Ponty and Max Weber: An Unfinished Dialogue," *Thesis Eleven* 36 (1993): 82–98.
18 Arnason, "The Imaginary Constitution"; Arnason, *Civilizations in Dispute* (Leiden and Boston: Brill, 2003). In chapter 4 of *Civilizations in Dispute*, Arnason uses the term "culture" in two ways but does not always clarify in which sense he means it.
19 Arnason, "The Imaginary Constitution."
20 Maurice Merleau-Ponty, *Phenomenology of Perception* (London and New York: Routledge 1962), xix; emphasis in original.
21 Arnason, "Culture and Imaginary Significations"; Arnason, *Civilizations in Dispute*. The conflict of interpretations is central to Arnason's hermeneutic of modernity as a field of tensions (Arnason, "Die Moderne als Projekt und Spannungsfeld," in *Kommunikatives Handeln*, ed. Axel Honneth and Hans Joas, [Frankfurt am Main: Suhrkamp, 1986], 278–326.
22 Arnason, "Rationalisation and Modernity: Towards a Culturalist Reading of Max Weber," in *Sociology Papers* (Melbourne: La Trobe University, 1982), 3.
23 Arnason, *Praxis und Interpretation*. It can be said that the "later" phase of Arnason's thought emerged with his hermeneutical turn, as announced in *Praxis und Interpretation*. In a recent interview, however, he noted that his engagement with the "world" problematic had been continuous throughout his intellectual trajectory (Arnason and Suzi Adams, "Interview with Johann Arnason: Sociological Contexts and Philosophical Problematics," in Adams, *The World Horizon between Phenomenology and Ontology: Essays on Cornelius Castoriadis and Johann P. Arnason* [Traugott-Bautz: Nordhausen, forthcoming]). Arnason deepened his hermeneutical turn through his rediscovery of the importance of civilizational analysis. For a detailed discussion of the significance of Arnason's thought for a phenomenology of the intercultural world, see Adams, "The Intercultural Horizons."
24 Arnason does not discount the problem of "universals" in human life; he does, though, argue that Merleau-Ponty's approach of "lateral universals" – that is, comparisons of human diversity – is the only way to uncover them.

25 For a detailed discussion of this aspect of Arnason's thought, see Adams, "Arnason and Castoriadis' Unfinished Dialogue"; Adams, "The Intercultural Horizons."
26 D. Jervolino, "Langage et phénoménologie chez Patočka," *Études Phénoménologiques* 15, nos. 29–30 (1999): 59–78 at 62.
27 There is not yet an English version of this book; I have referred here to the French edition. By "natural world," Patočka means "lifeworld" in the Husserlian sense, although for Patočka it meant the 'pre-historical' world; "natural world" was a term that Husserl used in his early lectures.
28 Patočka, "The 'Natural World' and Phenomenology" in *Jan Patočka: Philosophy and Selected Writings*, ed. E.V. Kohak (Chicago: University of Chicago Press, 1989).
29 For example, Arnason, "Negative Platonism"; and Tamas Ullmann, "Negative Platonism and the Appearance-Problem" in Chvatik and Abrams, eds., *Jan Patočka and the Heritage of Phenomenology*.
30 These emerged as overlapping but distinct aspects of his later thought.
31 Patočka, "Der Subjektivismus der Husserlschen und die Möglichkeit einer 'asubjektiven' Phänomenologie," and "Der Subjektivismus der Husserlschen und die Forderung einer asubjektiven Phänomenologie," both in *Die Bewegung der menschlichen Existenz* (Stuttgart: Klett-Cotta, 1991).
32 Patočka, "Der Subjektivismus der Husserlschen und die Möglichkeit."
33 Although it is clearly in gestation in his long postscript to the second edition of the Czech publication of *The Natural World as Philosophical Problem*. See Patočka, *Le monde naturel comme problème philosophique* (The Hague: Martinus Nijhoff,1976).
34 For example, Renaud Barbaras, *Le mouvement de l'existence. Études sur la phénoménologie de Jan Patočka* (Chatou: Éditions de la Transparence, 2007).
35 Filip Karfik, *Unendlichwerden durch die Endlichkeit: eine Lektüre der Philosophie Jan Patočkas* (Würzburg: Königshausen und Neumann, 2008), 57.
36 Karfik, *Unenlichwerden*, 57.
37 Patočka, *Vom Erscheinen als Solchem: Texte aus dem Nachlaß* (Freiburg: Karl Alber, 2000).
38 See also Karfik, *Unenlichwerden*.
39 Karel Novotny detects a tension in Patočka's asubjective approach in that in elaborating the sense of "manifestation as such" as an open field, he substitutes the "metaphysical closure" of the world as the ground of the world (Novotny, "L'ouverture du champs phénoménal: la donation ou l'interprétation? Sur le problème de l'apparaître comme tel chez Jan Patočka," in *Phenomenology 2005: Selected Essays from Northern Europe*, ed. H.R. Sepp and I. Coperu [Bucharest: Zeta Books, 2005]). A central aim of

Patočka's asubjective phenomenology was to emancipate the field of appearances from the "metaphysical closure" of (Husserlian) transcendental subjectivity. This move led him to elaborate the field of manifestation in conjunction with a deepening of his phenomenology of the world.

40 Novotny, "L'ouverture."

41 Patočka, "Der Raum und sein Problematik," in *Die Bewegung der menschlichen Existenz* (Stuttgart: Klett-Cotta, 1991).

42 Although it is to be noted that they are radically separated from "space" (p. 112) to form the intelligible "supra-spatial" domain of the Forms – while retaining aspects of the mythic-sensible (i.e., irrational) space of meaning and signification, as the phenomenal field. The geometrical forms are the precursor to mathematical space as we know it today.

43 Patočka, "Der Raum und sein Problematik," 113, my translation.

44 John Sallis, *Chorology: On Beginning in Plato's Timaeus* (Bloomington: Indiana University Press, 1999).

45 See, for example, Klaus Held, "World, Emptiness, Nothingness: A Phenomenological Approach to the Religious Tradition of Japan," *Human Studies* 20 (1997): 153–67; John W.M. Krummel, "The Originary Wherein: Heidegger and Nishida on the Sacred and the Religious," *Research in Phenomenology* 40, no. 3 (2011): 278–407.

46 Kitaro Nishida, "The Logic of *Topos* and the Religious Worldview," trans. Michiko Yusa, *The Eastern Buddhist* 19, no. 2 (1986): 1–29 & 20, no. 1 (1986): 81–119.

47 Nishida, *Last Writings: Nothingness and the Religious Worldview*, trans. David Dilworth (Honolulu: University of Hawai'i Press, 1987).

48 Castoriadis, *The Imaginary Institution of Society*.

49 Arnason, *Civilizations in Dispute*.

50 Patočka, "Der Raum und sein Problematik."

Chapter Four

Comparing the Incomparable: Crossing Intercultural Borders*

BERNHARD WALDENFELS

I. The Dilemma of Comparing

Over the past two centuries we have come to accept the existence of diverse languages, customs, and cultures; in doing so, however, we run the risk of going from one extreme to the other. Sometimes we emphasize foreignness to the point that life-worlds and culture-worlds close up like clams in their shells, sealing themselves into their own meanings and norms; other times we play down foreignness by allowing it to become blurred by an ethos of general humanity, by entrusting it to global regimes, or by offering it as a cultural good in the world market. The former tendency amounts to culturalism, which continues the "blind collection mania" of historicism on a larger scale;[1] the latter promotes cultural projection whereby specific processes of globalization – whose productive potential cannot be doubted – are deemed to be saturated with the West's imperial designs. In both cases, it is not so much a matter of interculturality as of a happening-in-between, within which various cultures fertilize and eventually conflict with one another. Intercultural foreignness does not coincide with intercultural enmity, yet foreignness runs the risk of turning into enmity. There is a grain of truth in the term *clash of civilizations*.[2]

The general problem underlying the culturalization of foreignness can be couched in Levinasian terms. He refers to justice, which is not only entrusted to the judge but also demanded from every one of us in relation to all others, as a "comparing of the incomparable thing (or persons)."[3] Here, in effect, he is expressing a special kind of dilemma: when what is *not* the same is *made* the same, complete justice cannot be given to the singular thing. This dilemma arises wherever appears the singular thing, when that singular thing is understood neither as part of a complete whole nor as a case of general law. This dilemma also appears on the level of regional or national cultures and on the level of world cultures. One can read Levinas's terminology of justice in different ways by emphasizing either the comparable or the incomparable, but the peculiar characteristics of intercultural experience disappear when these two are kept apart. The crux lies in the paradoxical tension of a comparing of what is and remains incomparable, but what turns out to be incomparable only in the comparing. Nietzsche has this tension in mind, when in *On Truth and Lies in a Nonmoral Sense* he traces every term back to an "equating of non-equal things," insofar as he exceeds the limit of momentary impression.[4] The "leaving-out of the unequal," which makes comparing possible, and the "overlooking of the individual characters," with which the comparison is redeemed, does not mean cultural decline but rather belongs to the basic conditions of culture. But this insight is not self-evident. The "unconsciousness," with which the equating goes, and the "forgetting," in which it used to wrap itself, together feed the illusion of a true culture, which covers over its own limitations. We consider it to be true that which has proved its pragmatic worth. Thus Nietzsche. The question is simply this: How we can counter this forgetting without falling into new illusions? Considerations like these prompt me to grasp the foreign as something extraordinary, something that goes beyond the limits of the changing order but at the same time makes those limits visible. From the Ordinary – that which makes comparisons possible – springs the Extraordinary in its incomparableness, and this is equally true in the field of interculturality.[5]

II. The Process of Comparing

We begin with the process of comparing. Comparisons are essential when it comes to developing personal and collective characteristics, or discovering oneself and other people. I am I, as I am different from you; we are we, as we are different from you. The use of personal pronouns already indicates that every self-reference accompanies a difference, and one's own name – which a child repeats from adults – shows already how much the Foreign goes through the Own. The condition of absence of comparisons that Rousseau in the *Second Discourse* ascribes to the Savage is based on the assumption that the Savage, who wanders the woods, might live a totally unsociable life all by himself, and only the civilized human being may live out of himself and be spurred to make comparisons (*comparaisons*) and to have preferences (*sentiments de préférence*) through the proximity of other people.[6] But the assumption of an initial indifference and indolence is part of the backward wish-projection, which allows us to seek a lost unity and to feel any difference as blemish. If there is something incomparable, then it is only on the other side, not on this side of the comparison. Comparison does not spring from a history of degeneration; rather, it forms the essence of an intra- and inter-personal, as well as an intra- and inter-cultural, history of discovery. In the process of comparing – a process stemming from a movement of *détachement* and *dépaysement* – we learn to see ourselves and our own character with foreign eyes. Although he flirted with the idea of an unsullied, precultural nature, Rousseau was also aware of this, when he uncovered the shady sides of civilizational progress without denying progress itself. It is not for nothing that Claude Lévi-Strauss is called the forerunner of cultural anthropology and ethnology.[7]

But how are comparisons made? Every act of comparing requires one to unravel certain threads from the weave of a life-form or life-world. Experiences, statements, and decisions being far too superficial, we stick to generalities whose meanings, rules, and structures repeat themselves; these could be language rules, lawbooks, constitutions, or social formations, which appear at different places and different times and can be detached from their specific contexts. The ordering of specific cultures is reflected in such generalities; at the same time, cultures are differentiated by their world views and artefacts. Thus we encounter in Odysseus a sly flexibility that enables him to overcome both literal and figurative obstacles along his return home; Michael Kohlhaas, for his part, is unafraid to act unscrupulously in his efforts to seek justice. In this sense, style, which shapes conduct, is often more powerful than content (i.e., the ideal that is sought). Thus every intercultural comparison can be only a partial one. To compare cultures or languages in their entirety would be a hopeless task, for the site of comparison seldom coincides with the place compared, just as the site of the measurement in physics is not the same as the place being measured. Cultural exchange between source and target cultures operates in the same way as linguistic translation between source and target languages. Comparing occurs on the horizon of a certain culture and not in a transcultural "nowhere." Temporal, spatial, and thematic horizons (which Nietzsche and Husserl discussed in detail) are borderlines of experience that, like our own shadows, walk with us. They cannot be grasped conceptually, yet their loss would have a powerful impact on us, as was the case with Peter Schlemihl, who lost part of himself with his shadow. Those who fail to recognize this and who go on comparing the Germans with the French, or medieval societies with modern societies, or white people with black people, are refusing to acknowledge this. "National psychology" generates cultural images of friend and enemy; the resulting overdrawn comparisons amount to clichés.

Comparing requires not only something comparable, but also a vantage point of comparison, what is referred to as a *tertium comparationis*. Something or somebody can be compared with other somethings or somebodies only in certain respects; otherwise we would have duplicates in front of us, and every comparison would thus be deprived of its objects. We would have to make do with two Cratyluses by the perfectly finished image of Cratylus.[8] Similarity in this respect is never simply given. It is not enough to say, with Hume, that we *choose* something similar;[9] this is valid only for normal experience, during which what we encounter reminds us of something familiar. We see in every new type of experience something *similar*. This "seeing-as," which plays a central part in Husserl's description of intentional acts and in Wittgenstein's description of language games, also marks the search for similarities. That *as* serves as an adaptable hinge, one that makes a change of aspect possible. In the finding of in-between parts, which makes a connection possible, lies a fictive and also creative moment, one that takes the close image-form of an original and live metaphor for linguistic comparison.[10] Similarity, which has been a basic form of association since Hume, not only makes links possible but also creates new contexts, even against our will – for example, when we are surprised by a joke or encounter the free play of associations (e.g., in Freudian psychoanalysis).

The selectivity of comparison also entails that one point of view is preferred to another. The linguistic form of comparative acts already serves as a comparison-form, in that a *standard of comparison* is provided. At the same time, we can distinguish between a tracery, which is embodied in the structures and shapes of things and can be known together with them, and a formal standard, which resembles a folding rule or a surveyor's pole, in order to subject the experience to firm rules.[11] The figures and laws of *comparison* have their traditional place in disciplines such as rhetoric, linguistics, theory of knowledge, logic, deontology, and mathematics. But *comparing* – which is to be distinguished from comparison in much the same way as saying from what is said – is never purely cognitive; comparing has what I call pathos and response, its involvement. Something strikes us as similar because it looks like or sounds like ... like something that touches us,[12] something to which we respond with questions, suppositions, or statements or simply with explicit comparisons. What a thing does and what piques our interest are never purely determined by that thing. A preference inevitably sneaks into the difference. It comes to light when comparison serves evaluation and *standards of value* are established, so that one is rated higher, the other lower. Otherness itself is linked with an Over-Order and an Under-Order. One is not only more important than the other but also better than the other. To that – what Hume calls the *gentle force* of the connections of ideas[13] – belongs the effort to protect differences that are important for us, by developing a hierarchy out of indifferences. Once the variety of cultures, peoples, languages, races, sciences, arts, occupations, religions – or simply the difference between right and left – enters the field of vision, there is the tendency to replace the attribute "different from" with "better or worse than" or (slightly more moderately) "more important than." But this is highly problematic. The standard, which forms and also changes itself in the act of comparison, is then transferred to the things compared, and the standard thus appears as naturally given, God-given, reasonable, or evolutionarily advantageous.

Clearly, comparing the Own with the Foreign has a special part to play. Robert Musil, who witnessed the downfall of the Austrian multiethnic state, discusses this problem, with his usual sceptical irony, at the beginning of his great novel *Der Mann ohne Eigenschaften* (*The Man without Qualities*). Ulrich, the man without qualities, dissociates himself from that state's raging patriotism; in an article in a school newspaper on the topic of patriotism, he notes "that a serious friend of the fatherland might never consider his fatherland as the best." The Own will not be denied, but the equating of the Own with the best will be denied him. But how can one keep the Native from nationalistic excesses? The young Ulrich now adds a second controversial sentence to the first: "that probably God also would speak about his world rather in *conjunctivus potentialis* [in the potential mood] [...], since God makes the world and thinks at the same time, it could just be something else." The Austrian school administration cannot be certain whether this double denial is a blasphemy against the fatherland or a blasphemy against God. The father, angered by the shame his son has brought on him, exiles him to a Belgian education institute. The education Ulrich receives there has problematic consequences: "There Ulrich learned to extend internationally his disregard of the ideals of others."[14] In his *Anthropology*,[15] Kant, who had no opportunity to witness the later excesses of nationalism, helped dampen the praise of European national characters by enumerating their characteristic faults. He credits the Italian for the "freedom that the gondolier and Lazzaroni are allowed to have opposite the noble ones," but also faults him that his "conversazioni" are similar to a bourse, where news is exchanged at the same time as meals, but without the joviality. The Frenchman is blessed with a "spirit of freedom" but then overshoots the target "by also probably drawing the reason itself into [...] play." To the Germans, Kant concedes honesty and domesticity, "which anyway are not exactly sparkling qualities," and in addition to this, a mild tendency to emigrate, an ability to learn foreign languages, to get on well everywhere in the world and as "wholesalers of scholarship" to blaze trails that will subsequently be used by others with fanfare." Conversely, Germans are reproached for being "addicted to method" and for having a weakness for titles, with the result that "somebody who has no business, and also no title, is nothing." Kant ends this discussion by pointing to the immaturity of Europe's peripheral nations: the Russians have not yet achieved a character capable of development; the Poles no longer show such character; and the European Turks have never had and never will have what is necessary for a national character. This general reason fits well with the faults and deviations of even "the most civilized peoples on earth," which here means the English and the French, and it resigns itself to the fact that the rule of reason on the peripheries of Europe shows signs of strain also within the European heartlands, to say nothing of those who greet us in the "wilderness" of strange continents.[16] As a German, Kant takes care not to place the Germans in the highest rank, to ensure that praise doesn't degenerate into self-praise.[17] Yet he sees no problem in the fact that Europeans praise Europeans, because this praise covers itself with the praise of reason, when praise is actually unnecessary.

The convergence of the Own with the Universal makes for what is called Eurocentrism.[18] The only preference that ultimately counts is reason – and the preference of those who speak in the name of reason. Raw ethnocentrism, which clings to the Own, is replaced by an enlightened ethnocentrism, which relies on a universal *logos*. One might be tempted to take the sting out of the logocentric opposition between civilization and wildness, or out of the civilizational differences between Occident and Orient, merely by letting the differences be regarded without preference. The *tertium comparationis* would change peculiarity and foreignness as formal communication-structures into mere variants. That already points in the direction of practice: East is not non-West, West is non-East, and so on. I distinguish between something foreign, from which the singular claims arise, and the third, who as neutral observer or as judge subjugates the Own and the foreign to the usual points of views or rules. It is easy to understand that there would be no order – which also means no culture – without the role of the third. Whoever undermines this role approaches chaos. But the legitimate third, who *interferes* with comparing and mediating in the foreign experience, transforms itself into a usurpatory third, which *supersedes* the difference between the Foreign and the Own when comparing gets the upper hand. Comparative studies would then lose their methodological innocence. I call this the structuralist or universalist temptation. If one gives in to this temptation, one holds up a universal cultural grid, which is managed by culture specialists and guarantees a *universal comparability*. But with the rest of the Own we would also abolish the Foreign. Only dashes of colour would remain out of the incomparable, which is what gives the cultures their colour.

But here an objection raises itself: Have we fallen into cultural relativism, which reduces the normative contrast of right and wrong, of good and evil, to mere shadings of otherness? We can take several examples that challenge our statement: slavery was practised by the Greeks as well as by Christians and Muslims; and women have long been suppressed through traditional family structures. In addition to these, torture, terrorism, and war crimes are still widely practised, and criminal para-institutions like the Mafia and the Camorra continue to thrive. Some situations are apparently incorrigible, in the sense that they will never correct themselves and can only be eradicated. In such extreme cases, should we establish universal standards through human rights laws and international courts of justice? My answer is that we must distinguish between a relativism of validities and the unavoidable relativity of conditions of validities.[19] In the cases described, there is also a comparing of the incomparable, because crimes perpetuated collectively have their breeding ground in a given culture. Crimes against humanity are not committed by mankind as a whole, but by human beings who belong to a certain culture. Just as there are idioms of thinking, so there are idioms of cruelty and violence: "Der Tod ist ein Meister aus Deutschland sein Auge ist blau [death is a master from Germany his eye is blue]" (Paul Celan). If genocides against Jews, Indians, or

Armenians were totally incomparable, then it would not be enough to condemn – we would also have to fight against such actions; if they were completely comparable, then specific parts of each of the offending cultures would have to be annulled. What exceeds each culture, though, belongs to that culture only in some way.

III. What Precedes Comparison

Let us take a step back. To what extent can the Own be separated from the foreign at all? If we reject the untenable assumption that cultures fall fully formed from heaven or grow out of the soil, then we must start from a process of differentiation, which has no clear beginning or end. Also, cultures cannot be catalogued as if they were a list of chemicals, and even here there are elective affinities governed by powers of attraction and repulsion. Intercultural experience requires that the cultures concerned relate to one another. Cultures are not separate worlds; they comprise a net of life-worlds; so we must start from an *in-one-another-ness* [*Ineinander*] of different cultures. Cultures are interwoven with and chained to one another; they engage in exchanges and disputes. They *seep into* one another and are not separate from one another like independent entities. The idea that there are pure, unmixed cultures, to which Kant pays homage in his *Anthropologie*,[20] is highly dubious but still widely held, when in fact, every culture stumbles across the tracks of other cultures. This is valid for world-open, border-rich, and history-pregnant Europe, just as it is for the Ibero-American countries, whose native cultures overlap with cultures imported or imposed from the outside, and for the countries of Africa, whose population was decimated through the slave trade and whose traditional cultures became estranged from themselves and thoroughly remade as a consequence of colonialism. Wherever foreign violence has brought native cultures to the brink of death, what is needed is not hermeneutic reflection, but rather a radical form of rewriting, which takes place in a "third space" of the in-between.[21] In general it can be said that a reciprocal spillover of cultures can be brought about by peaceful exchange, as well as by agonistic confrontations, and if it goes well, our agonist partner transforms us by demanding new powers from ourselves. According to Tacitus, the Romans regarded the Teutons as the antithesis of a less effeminate culture. When Japan cut itself off for centuries against foreign influences, this lent their own culture a fortified character of a special kind. Anti-Occidentalism is just as stamped by its opponent as anti-Orientalism.

This in-one-another-ness produces *border zones* where cultural exchange becomes especially dense. This has long been true of sea coasts such as that of Asia Minor, and of border regions like Galicia, Armenia, Georgia, and some parts in the Rhineland. In times of nationalist fervour the Rhine was referred to as the "German river, not German border." All border zones risk turning a foreign country into an enemy one. "Why do you kill me? – Why? Don't you live on the other side of the river?" Whoever lives on the other shore becomes literally a "rival." According to Pascal, it was possible that the Pyrenees formed a moral watershed, with the French side right and the Spanish side wrong – or the other way round. Similarly, border zones can become death zones when we try to flee across them, as happened to Walter Benjamin and countless other political refugees. And how about the Alps? Does the Brenner Pass mark the border between Austria and Italy, or is it not really a pass, but a sign of passage between North and South? A city that calls itself Lwiw in Ukrainian, Lwow in Russian, Lwów in Polish, and Lemberg in German is betraying that it belongs to nowhere exactly. Even the geopolitical standardization of place names equates what is not plainly equal. Yet just as history has its high tides and low tides, intercultural interweaving and condensation may increase or decrease over time. A term like "German-Roman" can be reversed to "Roman-German." Such terms do not name mixed beings, but rather figures in which something new comes into being out of the interweaving. This something new does not lend itself to being distributed evenly onto national cultures. The fact that we have to thank the Italians for producing the great Nietzsche edition shows how much the threads run to and fro. When we cross borders, we see, hear, and read with other eyes and ears. I myself discovered Husserl in Paris and then made a plan to trace and continue *German–French trains of thought*. The foreign begins in the Own, without ending in the Own. We can speak of biculturality just as we can of bilinguality. The unity of Europe draws its strength from bilateral relations, whose selective variety does not include the Other in a general order. Nor is the ambivalence, which is inherent in all boundaries, abolished.

Finally, the *interpenetration* of cultures can be conducted *more or less* narrowly, depending on the degree of kinship and proximity. Again, the linguistic relations are revealing. Dutch is closer to German than Polish is; Spanish is closer to Italian than Slovenian. Moreover, without inner polyphony, with its linguistic hybrids, Bakhtin's polylog resembles only an enlarged orchestra.[22] But cultural proximity or distance does not stop at the language; it continues in bodily situatedness and spatial mobility. The excesses of geopolitics, which in the Third Reich found the support of a "German geography" that betrayed an all scientific ethos, should not tempt us to sacrifice geopolitical and (indeed) geo-moral perspectives for the directives of a world politics and a universal morality. For us Germans, Poland is a neighbouring country of a special kind. In his border novel *Levins Mühle* (*Levin's Mill*), Johannes Bobrowski relates how there were Germans in Mazury who called themselves Kaminski, Tomaschewski, or Kossakowski, while there were Poles who called themselves Lebrecht or Germann. There is much crossover. Close proximity does not preclude enmity such as we find within families; and elective enmities can run out of control and become as powerful as elective affinities. Remember that the Greek "ethos" points back to an accustomed place, and that a point of spatial proximity is also inherent in the biblical neighbour, even when the ethical *proximité*, as Emmanuel Levinas insistently emphasizes, breaks the frame of the accustomed things. These are factors of social proximity and distance that no vision of a *global village* will redeem. The media cannot easily obscure the fact that there are near-worlds and far-worlds. Today we tend to smile when in Goethe's *Faust*, during the Easter procession, the citizens comfortably believe themselves to be safe from the noises of the battles in the far distance: "On Sun- and holidays, there is no better fun, / Than chattering of wars and warlike fray, / When off in Turkey, far away, / One people beats the other one."[23] For us, distance is inherent to the mass media, but it is linked to the danger that as passers-by we will allow a nearby act of violence on the street to affect us just like a television program. Looking away and "listening away" correspond to switching off, even when the gaps in our experience remain open and we do not entirely succeed in forgetting differences. The differentiation of the life-world into near- and far-worlds, home and foreign worlds, which Husserl has made familiar for us, has not been invalidated. When we are here, we are always also somewhere else. That is true today, but even more intensely so, and it would be important to reconcile the development of global communication spaces with on-the-spot obligatory participation in one's own locale.

Whoever therefore believes that he can begin with pure comparing is aiming too high. What precede the exploratory process are overlayerings and overlappings of the Own and the foreign. The process of comparing sets in motion imperceptible shifts or sudden rejections, which provoke comparisons. The same is also true of border conflicts. Experiences of equality are awakened, as something suggests itself as similar or dissimilar, even before we begin our comparisons. Circles of similarity, regarding which, following Hume, Husserl speaks in *Logische Untersuchungen*,[24] widen like ripples after a stone falls in the water. The *becoming the same* has the character of an experiential event and goes beyond every instance of *making the same*. All comparing is therefore open downwards; it comes out of an experience, which following Husserl's pre-predicative experience we can call the *pre-comparative* one.

IV. What Goes Beyond Comparison

However, a further step is required. The act of comparing opens not only downwards but also upwards, and the two are connected to each other. There is something *incomparable* that eludes intercultural comparison, because this cannot be based on separate elements of a carefully measured quantity; instead, it springs out of an intercultural network. But this is not the only reason. There are also *transcultural* surpluses, in which every culture goes beyond itself.[25]

In what follows, however, we must take care not to fall into a culturalistic extreme by inscribing the incomparability of cultures as such. What turn out to be incomparable are not culturally immanent works and values, in which each culture is precisely embodied. Unlike what the advocate of a newly resurgent philosophy of culture imagines, the foreign world does not allow itself to be transported into a "work-world," which is reduced to a "certificate of human mastery of existence" and to a "concrete manifestation of culture." If the "correlation of human being and world … is accepted as an uncircumventable given," and if philosophy is considered merely as "part of culture," then culture revolves around itself; philosophy is then nothing more than an ideology-prone expression of each culture. I call this culturalism. The case is no better when the spirit of the age is invoked to mediate between contingent history and universal reason, because the borders of the prevailing monoculture will then be unnecessary, but not exceeded. For a human world, which "has nothing outside itself," our own foreign world is reduced to a caricature of an "external foreign world." The vague project of a "humanization of the world," which, as Michel Foucault has demonstrated, involves us in the aporias of a self-humanization, could shrink interculturality to unquestionable culturality if it succeeds.[26]

So let us return to the question about incomparability. As the hermeneutic tradition unanimously acknowledges, there is no point in relating Dante and Shakespeare, Leonardo and Cézanne, Rodin and Brancusi, or the Pantheon and the Ryoanji Temple, to each other, as if we had some possible ranking lists at hand. The same applies to everyday life, for example, street life in Rome and Tokyo or Viennese classical music and classic jazz. Today's popular ranking, which culminates in Centers of Excellence, fails here, but why? Not somehow because the respective points of comparison would be absolutely different from one another. Of course one can measure Dante and Shakespeare with each other, as T.S. Eliot actually did in one of his literary theoretical essays. In just the same way, one can compare the traffic density in Tokyo with that in Rome, without reference to the peculiarities of the cities' urban system. Elmar Holenstein points out, with many apt examples, that intracultural and intercultural hermeneutics are already closely imbricated in each other, because many intercultural varieties find parallels in intracultural varieties.[27] Thus some intercultural experiences of revelation, which are experienced as surprised by a "total Other" as by an extraworldly revelation, are actually based on a simple ignorance of one's own culture. Incomparability can also mean that something has simply shut itself up against a comparison, but it can very well mean that *in the course of comparing*, something withdraws itself from the comparison. That incomparable then corresponds with the dissimilar thing we have talked about; we can find it in equating and nowhere else.

There are several reasons for this problem. The place of foreignness does not lend itself to being grasped with the binary contrast of inside and outside, because the foreign is neither absolutely inside, nor absolutely outside, nor is it both at once. It is, rather, a threshold phenomenon. We fall into the foreign, without living there. In order to intimate this threshold-character, I speak of radical foreignness as something extra-ordinary, that goes beyond the border of each cultural order. At first, the *extra-ordinal foreignness* differs from the *exotic foreignness* that simply moves to the outside and therefore determines itself totally through the contrast to the inside. When the foreign is valid only as not-Own, then it is stuck, furthermore, with all threads in the Own, just as the not-I is also still an offshoot of that I. It opens here a field for projections, flight movements, and reversals that does not leave its own terrain. And it is relatively indifferent whether the place of refuge lies in the South Pacific, at the North Pole, or in an imaginary landscape of the soul. If the foreign were really absolutely outside, then it would be so only by way of a cultural brainwashing or in order to obtain the prize of a cultural schizophrenia. However, the brokenness of the experience, without which there would not be any foreign experience, approaches a breach of experience, when the traumatized person remains fixated on a traumatic happening, as on a foreign body, so that *nearly* every answer can be taken out of his mouth. Here we stumble upon limit processes, which can be attributed to a pathology of the foreign and in which the incomparability emerges *almost* as naked as the incomparability of a violation, of a violent act.[28] And furthermore, extraordinary foreignness differs from *normal foreignness*, which remains as *intra-ordinal foreignness* within an order and whose foreignness is therefore only comparative. The singular is therefore not to be confused with the particular, with the individual variants of a hair colour, of a genome, of a habit of language, or of an unusual crime; all of these find their places within a general structure of sense or system of rules, if necessary with the help of meaning-extensions, rule-adaptations, or additional hypotheses. However, the singular does not belong to a higher world either, as if it were a *supra-ordinal foreignness* that was revealed to an overcultural, as Kant said, an effusive experience that ends in any case. It is obvious how particularly foreign cultures promote an esotericism, which does not put the existing rationality in question, but simply jumps over it. If we dispense with "friction with reality," then we confuse the thinking that grows out of the foreignness of astonishment with what we imagine at our discretion.

What is left for us then when we consistently want to apprehend the foreign in its incomparability? My answer is: the incomparable foreign is comprehensible not in a direct, but only in an indirect way, namely, as a *surplus* that goes beyond the normal standard, as a *deviation* that brings an existing normative system or value system out of the frame, as *something un-conditional* and *something im-possible* that breaks up the frame of the conditions of possibility. What is foreign breaks open or infiltrates; its effect precedes its making possible. It allows us to live, feel, see, hear, think, and act differently than before. In all fields of culture, in science and technology, in politics and law, in morality and religion, and also in our personal lives, we encounter singular foundational events that "would not be forgotten," as Kant said about the French Revolution. Forgetting them means that we forget ourselves. Such a forgetting is possible, but only as a form of repression, because that forgotten thing also remains effective under the surface and comes again on occasion. Intracultural and intercultural foreignness carries traits of an unconscious that, like all foreignness, afflicts us in our own house. A productive forgetfulness remains opposite to a reactive forgetfulness, which hangs on to the past. With productive forgetfulness the old things are not repressed but are changed into new things. Shifts in the structure of order, which also changes with the outside of the order, open the way for unexpected challenges and risks. As that which is excluded by each existing order does not simply disappear, history must always be rewritten, and the atlas must always be redrawn. Intracultural and intercultural constellations are always on the move.

Translated from German by Yu Gu and Ming Xie

NOTES

* Originally published in *Hyperphänomene* (Berlin: Suhrkamp, 2012), chapter 12. English translation permission by courtesy of Suhrkamp Verlag GmbH und Co. KG.

1 See Nietzsche's presentation of the antiquarian art of history in the second "Untimely Meditation": *Vom Nutzen und Nachteil der Historie für das Leben* [On the Use and Abuse of History for Life] (KSA 1, 268). KSA (*Kritische Studienausgabe*) is the abbreviation for the critical study edition edited by G. Colli and M. Montinari (Berlin: Walter de Gruyter, 1980).

2 See my "Fremdheit, Gastfreundschaft und Feindschaft [Strangeness, Hospitality and Hostility]," *Hyperphänomene* (Berlin: Suhrkamp, 2012), chapter 10.

3 E. Levinas, *Jenseits des Seins oder anders als Sein geschieht* [Beyond Being or Otherwise than Being], trans. Th. Wiemer (Freiburg and München: Alber Karl, 1992), 344f.; see also my "Hyperbolic Justice," in *Idiome des Denkens* [Idioms of Thinking] (Frankfurt am Main: Suhrkamp, 2005).

4 Nietzsche, *Über Wahrheit und Lüge im außermoralischen Sinn* [On Truth and Lies in a Nonmoral Sense] (KSA 1, 880f.).

5 See my *Ordnung im Zwielicht* (Frankfurt am Main: Suhrkamp, 1987). English edition: *Order in the Twilight*, trans. D.J. Parent (Athens:Ohio University Press, 1996). This book contains the seeds for my later studies on strangeness (*Fremdheitsstudien*), in which the comparison of the incomparable plays a leading role. The basis of what is developed there can be found in *Grundmotive einer Phänomenologie des Fremden* (Frankfurt am Main: Suhrkamp, 2006), English edition: *Phenomenology of the Alien: Basic Concepts*, trans. A. Kozin and T. Stähler (Evanston: Northwestern University Press, 2011); see esp. the final chapter, "Between Cultures."

6 See J.-J. Rousseau, *Schriften zur Kulturkritik* [Writings on Cultural Criticism], trans. K. Weigand (Hamburg: Meiner, 1978), 20–5, 264f.

7 Cf. Claude Lévi-Strauss, *Strukturale Anthropologie* [Structural Anthropology], vol. II (Frankfurt am Main: Suhrkamp, 1974), chapter 2. Here is a significant area of proximity between phenomenology and ethnology. See my *Topographie des Fremden* [Topography of Strangeness] (Frankfurt am

Main: Suhrkamp, 1997), chapter 4: "Phänomenologie als Xenologie [Phenomenology as Xenology]." See also Iris Därmann's book *Fremde Monde der Vernunft* [Strange Moons of Reason] (München: Fink, 2005).

8 See Plato, *Cratylus* 432 c, trans. C.D.C. Reeve, reprinted in *Plato: Complete Works*, ed. J.M. Cooper (Indianapolis: Hackett, 1997), 148.

9 Hume, *A Treatise of Human Nature*, ed. L.A. Selby-Bigge (Oxford: Clarendon, 1960), 24 (I.1.7).

10 The phrase "to transfer well" (literally: to metaphorize) comes from Aristotle and means "to see the same" (*Poetics* 1459 a 7 f.). See Birgit Griesecke's overview of the problem, *Japan dicht beschreiben. Produktive Fiktionalität in der ethnographischen Forschung* [A Thick Description of Japan: Productive Fictionality in Ethnographic Research] (München: Fink, 2001). Applying the descriptive practices of Geertz, Husserl, Wittgenstein, and Ricoeur, and on the basis of the Japanese as a prime example of the Culture of Shame, State of Theaters and Wrapping Culture, this author provides a productive comparison at the ethnographic level.

11 See my *Ordnung im Zwielicht*, chapter E.4.

12 Hume wrote: "the word […] touches the soul," but in turn the genesis of the similarity is so greatly limited that the word "revives" in us an idea and a corresponding habit (*Treatise*, 20).

13 Hume, *Treatise*, 14 (I.1.4).

14 Robert Musil, *Der Mann ohne Eigenschaften* [The Man without Qualities] (Reinbek: Rowohlt, 1978), 18f.

15 Immanuel Kant, "Anthropologie in pragmatischer Hinsicht," *Schriften zur Anthropologie*, ed. Wilhelm Weischedel (Frankfurt: Suhrkamp, 1977), Bd. VI, 662–71.

16 Within the people who are united under the law into the civil whole of a nation, there is for Kant the lawless "wild crowd," the mob; the extra-cultural wilderness matches, so to speak, an intercultural one (see Kant, "Anthropologie in pragmatischer Hinsicht," *Schriften zur Anthropologie*, ed. Wilhelm Weischedel, 658).

17 Ibid., 659.

18 For more details, see my *Topographie des Fremden*, chapter 6, "Europa angesichts des Fremden [Europe in the Face of the Strangers]" and chapter 7, "Nationalismus als Surrogat [Nationalism as Surrogate]." It goes without saying that cultural centrism can also take other forms, such as pan-Slavism or Japan-Centrism. See relevant studies: Irmela Hijiya-Kirschnereit, ed., *Überwindung der Moderne? Japan am Ende des zwanzigsten Jahrhunderts* [Overcoming of Modernity? Japan at the End of 20th Century] (Frankfurt am Main: Suhrkamp, 1996), or Dagmar Herrmann and Mechthild Keller, eds., *Zauber und Abwehr. Zur Kulturgeschichte der deutsch-russischen*

Beziehungen [Magic and Defense. On the Cultural History of German–Russian Relationship] (München: 2003).

19 See my *Ordnung im Zwielicht*, chapter E.8.

20 See Kant, "Anthropologie in pragmatischer Hinsicht," 671.

21 This applies to post-colonial literatures with their own writing culture. See Monika Reif-Hülser, *Fremde Texte als Spiegel des Eigenen. Postkoloniale Literaturen und ihre Auseinandersetzung mit dem kulturellen Kanon* [Foreign Texts as a Mirror of One's Own. Post-Colonial Literatures and Their Contestation of the Cultural Canon] (München: Fink, 2006), 61–89.

22 See my *Vielstimmigkeit der Rede* [Polyphony of Speech] (Frankfurt am Main: Suhrkamp, 1999).

23 Walter Kaufmann, trans., *Goethe's Faust: The Original German and A New Translation and Introduction* (New York: Anchor, 1990), 129.

24 See Edmund Husserl, "Investigation II: The Ideal Unity of the Species and Modern Theories of Abstraction," §§34–7, in *Logical Investigations*, trans. J.N. Findlay, 2 vols. (London: Routledge, 1970), I:291–300.

25 Binding to the here and now differentiates transcultural surplus from transcultural universals and constants.

26 All quotations come from the introductory theses of Ralf Konersmann's essay collection *Kulturelle Tatsachen* [Cultural Facts] (Frankfurt am Main: Suhrkamp, 2006), 44, 52–9. Following the steps of Vico, Simmel, Cassirer, and Blumenberg, the author explores a path from the "Socratic distance to the world" to the "ineluctability" of the human world. But does the ineluctability also mean "uncrossability"? It seems to me that the specific cultural analysis that the author presents in rich abundance does not require a culturalist amplification at all. For my critique of culturalism, see *Verfremdung der Moderne* [Alienation of the Modern] (Göttingen: Wallstein, 2001), chapter 4: "Genealogie der Kultur [Genealogy of Culture]."

27 See E. Holenstein, *Menschliches Selbstverständnis* [Human Self-Understanding] (Frankfurt am Main: Suhrkamp, 1985) and *Kulturphilosophische Perspektiven* [Cultural-Philosophical Perspectives] (Frankfurt am Main: Suhrkamp, 1998). The emphasis of these insightful studies, however, is on understandable comparison, which is content with a relative strangeness.

28 I am speaking of "almost," because were the answer completely absent and the connotation totally erased, man could probably only talk about the lost but not the pain of a patient. Regarding the interplay of intercultural and pathological alienation, I refer the reader to my article "Doubled Otherness in Ethnopsychiatry," *World Culture Psychiatry Research Review* 2, nos. 2–3 (2007): 69–79. On the singularity of brutal actions such as genocide, see my clarification in *Schattenrisse der Moral* [Silhouettes of Morality] (Frankfurt am Main: Suhrkamp, 2006), chapters 6 and 7.

Chapter Five

World, Home, and Hermeneutic Phenomenology

R. RADHAKRISHNAN

I begin this essay with a reference to Mohandas Gandhi's famous description of India as a house with open windows all around so that the winds of influence may flow in from wherever. But I add this strong caveat: the house itself must not be blown away by the forces of change. As Gandhi added sternly, even threateningly, he would not be left a beggar in his own house. Remarkable about Gandhi's manifesto is its measured tone – it emerges from a purely ontological perspective, even while it addresses the turmoil of India's immediate political situation. Gandhi's exhortation – which he is making to himself as well as to the emerging Indian collectivity – is phenomenologically free and proactive and unconditional, yet at the same time reactive, belligerent, and paranoid in the colonial context. It expresses a yearning for an intransitive, autonomous, and Utopian "freedom towards" but also a rigorous commitment to a determinate, heteronomous, and politically conditioned "freedom from" the poverty caused by colonialism.[1]

Gandhi provides an opportune point of entry into this collection of essays, which probes this important question: Is a hermeneutically inflected phenomenological ontology viable simultaneously both as a way of being and a way of knowing, both as an overall philosophical horizon for the staging of political praxis and as the actual ideological content of such a praxis? Like the great ontological thinkers – those who had the courage to base their thinking on Being with a capital B even as they honoured the ontico-ontological continuum – Gandhi examined ethics, epistemology, radical oppositional politics, and ontology, and all of these simultaneously. Much like Martin Heidegger, he insisted on a nuanced ontico-ontological difference even while adamantly refusing to sanitize the ontological by stripping away its ontic contamination (and here I maintain that his politics were more "worldly" than those of Heidegger). Like Heidegger, and also like Emmanuel Levinas, Gandhi embraced alterity and practised ethics as an inviolable first philosophy; unlike his philosophical counterparts, however, he did not allow the ethical to be twisted by the political. He dwelt with much more "conscience" than Levinas and Heidegger in the hyphen that animates the space between the ethical and the political in the "ethico-political."

Now for a brief discussion of Gandhi's thought, before I proceed to the main subjects of this essay, Heidegger and Maurice Merleau-Ponty. India is commonly viewed as both a home and a contested political terrain. Yet to be at home in the world cannot be reduced either to pure ontological speculation or to the polemically political. Home is not natural (if by natural we mean something primordial or unconstructed), but neither is it simply an artefact of opportunistic convenience that erases questions of one's own relevance and integrity. Home is both bounded and unbounded – it is anchored but not autochthonous – and I hope to connect this point to notions of the worlding of the world in Heidegger's thought, as well as to the world as described by Merleau-Ponty, which we share both with nature and with "other" humans. One might have asked Gandhi this question: What would be so deplorable if the winds of change were to de- and re-territorialize India? Where in that would be the calamity? If home is the world, and if the world is the basic value of which home is after all contingent instantiation and localization, why not give the world the authority as well as the sovereignty to uproot the latitude and the longitude of the home, which is a mere political construct? What purpose does it serve to protect India, the home as nation-state, so fiercely? What is the root of the visceral anger, the *ressentiment,* in the words "a beggar in my own home?" If home belongs to all as the world (the *Visva-Bharathi* cherished by Rabindranath Tagore), then why is so much vehemence attached to the words "my home"?[2]

How, then, are we to balance phenomenological openness in the name of all Being, or Being with a capital B, with the need to protect ourselves against hermeneutic aggression or violence? The problem Gandhi is facing head on, unflinchingly and without ethically overdetermined piety, relates to the asymmetry between absolute ethical vulnerability to the Other and a compelling need, in a world structured by dominance, to defend one's political integrity against hostile hermeneutic takeover. How wise is it to submit to the demands of ontological thinking in a situation where it is not at all clear that ontology has earned, historically speaking, the right to speak for or represent the political? To be more specific with reference to the project at hand, when is it the proper time to insist on the ontico-ontological difference, what are the consequences of doing so, and when is it the proper time to read the Being–History relationship as a continuum? And in the context of hermeneutics, when and how are we to distinguish between inter- and intra-cultural exchanges and negotiations? For we must not forget, both in Heidegger's context and even more in Hans-Georg Gadamer's, that hermeneutic openness does not happen in a vacuum. The horizon within which it occurs is never namelessly universal; it is always named and nameable as a specific tradition. That precisely is Gandhi's concern: there can be no hermeneutic openness between the reality of the colonized as a text and the hermeneutic gaze of the colonizer. In such a context, all talk of ontological thinking – with Being as the subject, even if that Being is the Heideggerian *Dasein* – is indefensible and plain wrong. The loss of meaning here is the active and intended result of a calculated epistemic impoverishment, and it is that reduction to beggary that Gandhi is aware of and that he sharply condemns. In other words, the openness of hermeneutics is not a *fait accompli:* it all depends on historical context and circumstances. The other important complication for us to be aware of (and more on this later in the essay) is that in an incompletely universalized world, the politics of an intracultural hermeneutics are not inevitably covalent with the values and trajectories of an intercultural hermeneutics. The conundrum that arises when we juxtapose the Gandhian problematic with phenomenological hermeneutics is this: How is the human subject, the self-reflexive *cogito,* to negotiate the reality that there are many unequal but coeval worlds within the same world? That is the question this essay addresses.

There is a clear reason why the past few years have seen a return to "post-phenomenological phenomenology," much of which has turned into ontological thinking, not as a form of self-indulgent nostalgia for lost origins, but as a way of reinventing the political as such. Thinkers in this vein have included Alan Badiou, Slavoj Žižek, Jacques Rancière, Jean-Luc Nancy, and Philippe Lacou-Labarthe. Disaffection with politics – with its tricks, lies, and scheming – has been so total that the need has arisen to entirely re-create the political. The challenge has been to actualize this ontological interrogation of the political as an immanent critique rather than as a gesture of utopian transcendence. It is as though the ontic has been too much with us, so that the time is now ripe to emphasize the theme of ontico-ontological difference and to rescue the question of a universal Being, or the be-ing of such a universal being to arise from the reigning hypocrisies of all political regimes. The problem, as much methodological as axiological and epistemological, is one of location: From what site is such a critique to be launched? There is no question that disaffection with the political has become ubiquitous and that condemnation of today's politics is approaching the universal across all ontic locations – which itself is a symptom of the failure of the political. Yet there is a real problem with establishing a location from which – and in the name of what emerging subject – a re-energized ontological thinking might be launched (for example, would such a subject be singular, plural, heterogeneous, hybrid, normative, sovereign, or non-sovereign?). Because true universality is lacking, each site of disaffection is suspicious of the politics of representation and wishes to preserve the right to impose its own general ontology. The task of the reinventing a general ontology – one that cannot be reduced to ontic imperatives and sovereignties – is inseparable from the project of conceptualizing a universality to come (*avenir*) out of the historical-phenomenological perspective of a flawed universality. As Jacques Derrida and Ashis Nandy have pointed out, each in his own context and tradition, the very attempt to reimagine amounts inevitably to a *pharmakon* whose historical traces are indelible and can at best be remembered differently than they actually were.[3]

Back, then, to the question of the many worlds within the same world and of the many historicities that constitute our human temporality: How does the world "world," and how should the human *cogito* register the worlding of the world and bear witness to it? Hermeneutic phenomenology suggests itself as the most useful resource in this regard, for two reasons. First, phenomenology is a way of knowing precisely because it is also a way of doing or acting, and furthermore, as a historically aware modality of "returning to things themselves," it can be practised as a "return to that world which precedes knowledge, of which knowledge always *speaks*, and in relation to which every scientific schematization is an abstract and derivative sign-language, as is geography in relation to the country-side in which we have learnt beforehand what a forest, a prairie or a river is." It is easy to see how such a project of reconnecting with the world of experience can be crucial to the task of reimagining politics, which in the final analysis is no more and no less than a regime that speaks to and for the realm of experience. Second, hermeneutics complicates phenomenology by insisting that there can be no innocent descriptive return to things, to experience, or to life for that matter; and that all returns are deeply interpretive and therefore part of certain pre-established traditions that both constrain and enable novelty and transgression. In the context of a post-phenomenological hermeneutic phenomenology, the question of the historical becoming of an ontology that is not reducible to the merely ontic can be posed as truly world-historical, which is to say, as nothing but fallibly perspectival. In the relationship between phenomenology and hermeneutics, the former would be obliged to open the world up as the openness of perspective, and the latter would be committed to incessantly pointing out that the very "open," in the Heideggerian sense of the term, cannot be a nameless "open"; rather, it must be a specific tradition of the open, such as the Hellenic, or the secular, or the Judaic, or the Christian. What a hermeneutic phenomenology enables is a renewed political dialogue between names and namelessness.[4]

I next ask two reciprocal questions: Is politics phenomenological? And is phenomenology political? Any responsible answer to these questions would involve some tacit theory of "interest" and "interestedness," for clearly, neither phenomenology nor politics is or can be disinterested. What is the difference between a political and an epistemological deployment of interest? The basic complaint levelled at political knowledge is that it has become relentlessly and unrelievedly *interested*. And here is the double edge of interest. Any respectable phenomenologist would argue that the world, in all its given objectivity, precedes human interest. It already exists, and with it and in it we as human beings exist, but with this difference: we do not belong to or inhere in the Real without making secondary ripples. The Cartesian *cogito, ergo sum* thematizes that philosophical or cognitive reflexivity through which the human *cogito* both appropriates and loses the world. The I in the "I am" and the I in the "I think" are forever philosophically separated from each other, and what ensues is a necessary and chronic dualism. Epistemology and existence find it difficult, after that point, to come together harmoniously, and a variety of phenomenologies have tried valiantly to close this rupture without resorting to mysticism or to the fallacy of numinous Gnosticism. The classic question for phenomenology has been this: How can the world be experienced and understood both as the function of and as transcending human interest? Another version of the same dilemma has been the phenomenological struggle or negotiation with "givenness." Givenness is both objectively given and perspectivally reappropriated by the human subject as its own. Once givenness bears the signature of the human, it is not truly given any more; yet to be human is to insist on that signature.

It is in this context that Merleau-Ponty, as a Marxist phenomenologist, maintains that as human beings we are constrained to do violence to Being as a prerequisite for our own anthropocentric valence. Yet he also holds out possibilities for the "pre-personal one" whose gaze is coextensive and consubstantial with the world. In much the same vein, he argues that as humans we are condemned to meaning (for this, he was harshly criticized by Michel Foucault). Yet in *Humanism and Terror*, Merleau-Ponty accepts responsibility for a form of post-Stalinist leftist accountability. He fine-tunes an important distinction that Edmund Husserl makes between two forms of intentionality: one of these is human and ego- or interest-driven, and the other inscribes the human as part of its givenness within the phenomenological order of Being. And here is Merleau-Ponty's critical appreciation of Husserl on intentionality:

> This is why Husserl distinguishes between intentionality of act, which is that of our judgments and of those occasions when we voluntarily take up a position – the only intentionality discussed in the *Critique of Pure Reason* – and operative intentionality (*fungieren Intentionalitat*), or that which produces the natural and antepredicative unity of the world and of our life, being apparent in our desires, our evaluations and in the landscape we see, more clearly than in objective knowledge, and furnishing the text which our knowledge tries to translate into precise language. Our relationship to the world, as it is untiringly enunciated within us, is not a thing which can be any further clarified by analysis: philosophy can only place it once more before our eyes and present it for our ratification.[5]

I will take up the issue of our human rectification of nature a little later in this essay in the context of self and nature and other selves and the human world, but for now I am interested in how intentionality, interest, and the production of knowledge all relate to one another. My question here is: How could a hermeneutic phenomenology revolutionize the very meaning of the political without at the same time severing the relationship between politics and "interest"? Another way of asking the same question would be: How are we to rescue politics from a bad kind of interestedness and imbue it with a good kind?

Let us take, for example, Disraeli's (in)famous statement that Edward Said uses so tellingly as an epigraph in his *Orientalism*: "The East is a career." Said demonstrated brilliantly that Orientalism was the result of the violent and non-dialogic professionalization and objectification of the East by the West. When the phenomenologist declares her passion for the world, does the world then automatically become a career for the phenomenological philosopher? What sorts of relationships are imaginable here? Let the world be (*Gelassenheit*)? Let the world be actively or passively? Let the world be from the world's point of view? Or let the world be from one's own unavoidably anthropocentric point of view, with the human being as the hegemon? The issue here involves more than the basic dualism that is intrinsic to the *cogito;* it also concerns the relationship between the knower and the object of knowledge. The term "career" as Disraeli applies it indicates a strong professionalism that leads to this question: Who is a professional, and how and what does she profess? Is a profession a mere objectifying knowledge that generates mercenary opportunism; or does it "profess" a strong world view, an ethical philosophy, a set of beliefs and convictions in the context of the world that is waiting to be objectively known, recognized, and honoured?

This last question is highly salient for the phenomenological philosopher. Is a phenomenologist a "professional of the world," or a "lover of the world" in the Barthesian sense of the term? For all his philosophical rigour and conceptual complexity, Merleau-Ponty would insist that phenomenology is a way of being in the world. In other words, philosophizing, though it cannot be avoided, is not "where it is at" for the simple reason that the world is already there as object and subject of knowledge: both as ontology (Being) and as domain (the epistemological subject of knowing, given to the *cogito* to be realized as human knowledge of the world). That is precisely why Merleau-Ponty was able to declare that "our relationship to the world, as it is untiringly enunciated within us, is not a thing which can be further clarified by analysis: philosophy can only place it once more before our eyes for our ratification." This is a far cry from Cartesian, Enlightenment, or any kind of professional philosophy. In one wise yet radical move, Merleau-Ponty is both valorizing and deprofessionalizing or decelebrating philosophy as autonomous professional practice. He is recasting the very autonomy of philosophy as profoundly heteronomous in relationship to the world. The world is not the autochthonous native – like the Orient, like the colonized – waiting to play the role of the dumb informant *vis-à-vis* the learned professional from the advanced and all-knowing West.

Merleau-Ponty's brilliantly sophisticated formulation of the human *cogito* as double and dilemmatic braids two epistemological strands together. The *cogito* must address two forms of alterity, both of which are already objectively "there" and waiting to be known. There is the alterity of the natural world, that which according to Heidegger we already know but have moved away from, of which we are a part. Unlike, say, mysticism or Zen or Shankara's *Advaita*, Merleau-Ponty does not recommend that the human subject become one with the universe; what he does insist on, notwithstanding the autonomy of philosophic activity, is a certain pre-existing relationship between the human and the world, a relationship that is "untiringly enunciated within us." Merleau-Ponty works against the unilateralism of the human hegemon, insisting at all times that such a hegemon is already in place within a bilateral configuration that is as much ontological as it is epistemological. His phenomenological concern is that this constitutive bilateralism not be abused by the human hegemon in the name of its own philosophical professionalism. The message is clear: bilateral arrangements cannot be put in place unilaterally. So, is the phenomenologist as philosopher a professional, a lover, an empathizer of Being, a producer of new meaning, a sympathetic and attentive re-presenter of a meaning already in place awaiting discovery or a Heideggerian kind of "unconcealment"?[6] And what is the nature of the phenomenologist's interest in reality? Is this interest the same thing as perspective, and if it *is* perspective, is such a perspective similar to the Marxian definition of class as a perspective whose obligation is not to describe reality but change it?

Phenomenology of the Merleau-Ponty variety is caught in a dilemma: whether to shore up the process of knowing as representational of reality or as an interested production of reality. His is a double-voiced epistemology. The double register on the one hand is solicitous of the priority of Being to thought; on the other, it takes great pains to assert a fundamental human role in the production of knowledge. There are two pitfalls to be avoided: the fallacy of primordialism, and the hubris of anthropocentrism. In the final analysis, Merleau-Ponty's epistemology represents knowledge neither as pre-discursive nor as the exclusive function of anthropocentric discourse. It focuses on the relationship of the human to the natural world. It is within this primal, not primordial, horizonal network of given significations that human meaning-making occurs. As Merleau-Ponty put it in his master work, *Phenomenology of Perception*:

> The phenomenological world is not the bringing to explicit consciousness of a pre-existing being, but the laying down of being. Philosophy is not the reflection of a pre-existing truth, but, like art, the act of bringing truth into being. One may well ask how this creation is *possible*, and if it does not recapture in things a pre-existing Reason. The answer is that the only pre-existing Logos is the world itself, and that the philosophy which brings it into visible existence does not begin by being *possible*; it is actual or real like the world of which it is a part, and no explanatory hypothesis is clearer than the act whereby we take up the unfinished world in an effort to complete and conceive it.[7]

Merleau-Ponty would want the best of both worlds. In the first, he would acknowledge the inevitability of human epistemic violence as it produces normativity by taking on the hegemonic (Heidegger would want to gloss this as "custodial") assignment of "the laying down" of being. In the second, this very laying down would be aestheticized as the act of "bringing truth into being." Does this phenomenological act work? Is it even in good faith? Is it persuasive as a genuine intellectual balancing act? The problem that Merleau-Ponty is facing is the problem of naming the *imprimatur* in the name of which all philosophic activity is being sanctioned. Clearly, Merleau-Ponty, unlike Heidegger or Husserl, is a painstakingly immanent thinker. He is, in Said's sense of the term, a thoroughly secular humanist.[8] This is at the level of the political, and there is no greater testimony to this than his *Humanism and Terror*.[9] Yet into his epistemology there does creep in a certain need for transcendence: transcendence renamed and toned down as the given realm of primal significations. Like Derrida, who in his late works would talk about "religiosity without religion," Merleau-Ponty dabbles with transcendence without naming it as such.[10]

What makes Merleau-Ponty's work so compelling is its unflinching focus on human accountability. In the name of what or whom does the human being act? He is intensely aware that while in the heat of any action, the act itself and the principle it applies to justify itself seem instantaneous, there is actually a lag. The only way this lag can be erased is through a leap of faith, a tacit submission to transcendence. The principle or supreme value *in the name of which* the action is being performed – say, the act of killing a foreign soldier in the name of one's nation – is indeed elsewhere, present as an *a priori* that is ratified by faith and faith alone. The otherwise abhorrent act of killing a human being is in this way sanitized, hallowed, and given meaning from elsewhere. The mere fact of one's nationality is alchemized into an irrefutable idea that produces authority, comfort, and certitude. Through the sheer act of willing it so, the principle becomes manifest as *imprimatur*. The most eloquent (and to my mind, problematic) example of an action that begins with the utmost scepticism and lack of conviction (the protagonist is literally in a state of immense sadness and debilitating melancholy) and, thanks to divine intervention, arrives at a muscular resolve to prosecute war and kill, is the story of Arjuna in the *Mahabharatha*. The message of the *Bhagavad Gita* and of Lord Krishna to Arjuna the reluctant warrior is that of absolution: sublimate one's individual ethical responsibility in the name of a higher authority – do your stuff and leave the responsibility to me. That is Krishna's transcendent message to Arjuna, who is told that it would be hubris on his part to claim the action in his name. Action can be ratified only on the basis of surrender to a higher *imprimatur*. When a soldier kills spontaneously and unflinchingly in the name of his nation, he is voiding his individual conscience and leaving it to his nation to absolve and ratify his action. Needless to say, this primordial faith is not open to secular grammatological verification: it exists as pure pre-script, as primal signification by which we have already been interpellated.

There is a reason why I am dwelling this long on the principle of justification and ratification. The principle of ratification is caught up in a double bind: the separation of "what we know" from "what we know *in the name of*" needs to be honoured in the name of due immanent process; but at the same time, the authority that underwrites the ratification process must be accorded the privilege of an *a priori*. In other words, the ratification process must proudly proclaim its role as constitutive of the *imprimatur*, yet at the same time it must make-believe that it already knows in some primal fashion what it will come to know historically. It is as though there are two knowledges and "knowings" at stake here: one primal, the other secular. Within his phenomenological model, Merleau-Ponty does all he can to do double justice to the measure of the human: (1) its prior and primal implication and constitution, at the level of primal significations, with the natural world made available to the human being as the perceptual world; and (2) its own history, its secular measure and historicity, which could not have been fully scripted within the text of primal significations. Should human historicity recuperate what it already knows, or should it perform as the dangerous Derridean *supplement*? A reductive but legitimate way to confront Merleau-Ponty would be to ask him the following: How would you, as the phenomenological thinker committed to the pre-existing *logos* of the world, derive from that *logos* the truth of Marxism or the truth of the anti-colonial struggle? Or would you, in the name of what *is,* derive Hitler, Stalin, and colonialism and the histories thereof from the pre-existing *logos* of the world? Where in this gaping chasm between what *is* and what *ought to be* is the human "laying down of being"? Where is the sanction for producing normativity in a relationship that is constrained to repeat, or bring the truth into being? How is historicity to be arrived at truthfully from the givenness of temporality? How would you ratify secular historicity in the name of a primal temporality? Can such a process even be sane, unless schizophrenically sane? Where, in short, is the human measure, its range, scale, wavelength, register, bandwidth between nature and culture, between nature as cultural or first culture, between culture as natural or as second nature?

Two important linked questions need to be asked of the phenomenological enterprise and its double dance with temporality and historicity. First, what exactly is the link between truth content and the principle in the name of which truth is ratified as content? And second, what is a relationship – or to put it in a hermeneutic register, how should a relationship be honoured in good faith? This second question could be analysed further into the following micro-questions: Is the logic of a relationship thematic or procedural? Is it possible to predict, anticipate, and even annul a relationship – as in, say, divorce – in the spirit of the truth of the relationship? In other words, does the primal, given, or filial sanctity of a relationship permit a fundamental, axiological deconstruction; and if the answer is yes, with the deconstruction, does the *imprimatur* change as well? To the first question, then, with the help of an example, again from Gandhi: What exactly am I doing when I identify and honour an untouchable as a *harijan* (a person of Hari or Vishnu, the Hindu god), or a poor man, a beggar, as *daridra narayan* (as a deity of poverty)? Is this renaming a political move, an ethical move, an epistemological sleight of hand? Why not valorize the untouchable as untouchable without making her a god's being? Is the logic here that of a veiled theodicy? Is it a matter of rendering the untouchable eloquent at the expense of his material historicity? If, indeed, a casteist Hinduism is what made the untouchable an untouchable, isn't it downright duplicitous to invoke the same religion to endow the untouchable with equal humanity? Is the guilt of Hinduism being laundered here subtly but surely? Does such a move not depoliticize the very context of the untouchable, render her unfit as an agent of her own revolution, and at the same time rechristen her as the beneficiary of a Hindu god? Where was that same god when the untouchable was forced into untouchability? The same questions can be asked of the term *daridra Narayan*, where too an abject and ignoble reality is ennobled through a reference to a transcendent principle that is not in evidence empirically, historically. My point here is that the "fallen historicities" of the untouchable and the beggar are being redeemed by an alien and transcendent temporality that is now being claimed by Gandhi as the source of benign succour. Ambedkar, Gandhi's eminent adversary in caste issues, contended vigorously that there was something unjust and crazily lopsided about Gandhi's positive interpretation of the same Hinduism that spawned untouchability in the first place. My point is that the category "in the name of" could be understood as an immanent rule of accountability, or as a safe alibi for evacuating immanent secular responsibility.

The concept that gives Merleau-Ponty all kinds of headaches is "human nature." Unlike Foucault, Merleau-Ponty cannot laugh off "human nature" as an oxymoron. Sure enough, the term "nature" attaches itself to the "human" in a non-essentialist, non-given, non-filiative mode; if there is a human nature at all, it can only be the set of ongoing possibilities created by human history acting on human history. Yet, and here is the rub, this brings me to the second issue: Merleau-Ponty cannot – and understandably so, for ecological and anti-anthropocentric reasons – abandon the human's primal relationship with the world and its perceptual *logos*, its ineradicable givenness in and for the human. So, what is a relationship and how binding is it? How normative is a relationship, and what is the statute of limitations for a relationship? Can a relationship be divorced, recanted in principle? *Mutatis mutandis*, both for the phenemenologist and for the hermeneutic philosopher, this relationship functions like a horizon that is neither expendable nor reducible to a specific item or detail in the landscape that is rendered visible in and by the horizon. With a strong and appreciative nod towards thinkers such as Luce Irigaray, Elizabeth Grosz, Sara Ahmed, and others who have kept Merleau-Ponty alive by having candid critical conversations with him, I would say there is something canonically and monogamously heteronormative about Merleau-Ponty's loyalty to our relationship to the world, a relationship that is not external but "is untiringly enunciated within us." It is like saying that human beings are genetically so, and genetically such and such: an inevitable "nature" is being precipitated and sedimented here. And who can or dare go against nature – that is, when something that is a mere description turns, by a sheer act of faith, into an irrefutable norm? A relationship – say conjugal, parental, fraternal, or national – in all its *a priori* authority enjoins a certain loyalty without any need to specify the actual terms of the loyalty. Whatever the human being does, she is obligated to evaluate that deed ethically, with respect to an "other," the other as adumbrated in the relationship: no acknowledgment of a relationship, then, no other. The "other" plays a shadowy role in the life of the self to the extent that all that the self can know of the other is that the self has been enunciated within by virtue of the relationship; yet it is not clear what the actual implications, consequences, and entailments are of such an enunciation within the relationship.

It is time now, in the context of this primal enunciation, to return to the braiding together of the two strands of thought in Merleau-Ponty that I referred to a few paragraphs ago. Those two thematic strands are – and these are subchapter headings in *Phenomenology of Perception* – "The Thing and the Natural World," and "Other Selves and the Human World." Perhaps it is now time to invite Heidegger in for a limited conversation. My big question here, for both philosophers, still keeping in mind the Gandhian polemic, is this: If Nature is Other, and so are other selves (i.e., both within one's culture and without), then how is alterity to be understood and parsed both "naturally" and "constructedly," both ontologically and historically, both perceptually and "perceptually" – which is to say, both descriptively and symptomatically, given that perception itself is culturally coded, sexually and racially distorted, and misdirected?

How does the theme of alterity work when the other is not the big other that is nature, the universe, or being, but other human selves who are human like us but who are products of other histories, cultures, and civilizations (the German other, the Nigerian other, the Arab other, the Jewish other, the lesbian other, the white other, the black other, the Third World other, the immigrant other, the nomad other, and so on)? And here we are back to that fuzzy relationship between temporality and historicity. Since we are in and of time, we are clearly temporal. We are then coeval with nature if nature is indeed temporal. Since we are in and of time as human beings, we are also historical or historically temporal, and we are coeval with other selves who are the subjects of other histories. Now, back to that internally enunciated and fateful relationship: Is our relationship to other selves within our own culture, be it national or civilizational or centrist in some other way, and our relationship with other selves outside "our fold," as much and as intimately and as undeniably and indelibly enunciated within us as our relationship to the world? What do we mean by the world here? Historical, ontological, physical, perceptual? Is nature/being/the universe enunciated within us in a relationship in much the same way that a Palestinian is enunciated within the Israeli, the French within the Algerian, the lesbian within a heteronormative gendered citizen? In the double-stranded theme of alterity, which is the driver and which the vehicle? Which is the point of entry, and which the scene?

This precisely is the problem that the hermeneutic philosopher poses herself. She then considers whether the other who is there but not yet known – who is real but not yet intelligible – is the other within or the other outside. Hermeneutic thought could be intercultural or intracultural, intertraditional or intratraditional, inter-identitarian or intra-identitarian. The issue here is simultaneously ontological and epistemological. How can Being be both real and knowable? And most crucially, how does "knowing" happen? Does it happen openly? Does it take place within or outside specific traditions, such as the European Enlightenment, Upanishadic thought, German Idealism, Biblical or secular hermeneutics, and so on? And to bring Gandhi and Disraeli back into the conversation, does knowledge make *home* happen or the *world* happen? In the context of knowledge and knowing, are home and world synonymous, mutually constitutive, or incommensurable? Is knowing to be undertaken as a career? Should knowledge be interested, disinterested, or interested perspectivally but in the name of the all? In the ongoing negotiations within and between histories, both intracultural and intercultural hermeneutics, how does knowledge stand with Being, with a big B? Would the hermeneutical phenomenologist define perspective one way when it comes to ontology with the big Being, the assumption being that the perspective here is generally and non-denominationally human; whereas at the level of history, interest rather than perspective would take over as the active proponent and agent of bias and partisanship?

Of great relevance here is Heidegger's famous "Letter on Humanism," which starts out as a critique of Sartre's equally well-known definition of existentialism as humanism.[11] Heidegger is quick to point out that existence is in fact a decentred ek-sistence and that the "being there" of *Dasein* is not to be reduced to the human subject. What is obviously at stake here is the "ontico-ontological difference." Heidegger tells us: "Ek-sistence, thought in terms of *ecstasies*, does not coincide with *existentia* in either form or content." Furthermore: "As ek-sisting, man sustains Da-sein in that he takes the *Da*, the lighting of Being, into 'care.' But Da-sein itself occurs essentially as 'thrown.' It unfolds essentially in the throw of Being as the fateful sending."

This disagreement between Sartre and Heidegger regarding the ontological or "being" status of the human goes to the very root of the problem. If the ontic is the human and the existential – in other words, if the ontic is what we live and experience – then on what non-experiential and non-empirical basis is *Dasein* to be validated? How do we even know that the *Dasein* is real, existential? How are we to initiate the conversation between the human and the post-human, the anthropocentric and the post-anthropocentric? Is anybody out there! Is there even an interlocutor there, except as a function of our creative hallucination? True, Heidegger provides a magnificent segue for the conversation by hyphenating ek-sistence. But is ek-sistence real except as a philosophical fiction, an ethical attitude? If no one is the *Dasein*, who is the *Dasein*? If no one can speak for the *Dasein*, what is the *Dasein* saying? What is intriguing in all this is Heidegger's incomprehensible investment in the *Dasein*. Sartre as a public intellectual and writer *engagé* is easy to read, and his ideological bias is transparent; it is not so easy, though, to see through Heidegger. Is Heidegger literally willing into belief and *ergo* into ek-sistence the thrownness of the *Dasein*? In whose interest is it (without invoking Heidegger's dabbling with Nazism and his later silence about his early career) that he instrumentalizes the thrownness of the *Dasein* in order to sideline the historically human, the human that is all-important to Sartre, the politically committed existentialst? Is Heidegger's "custodial" re-presentation of *Dasein* pure and disinterested; or is it an "authentic" ploy to divert attention from historical being towards a primordialism of Being that is only incidentally accountable to history?

I am not for a moment suggesting that a *Dasein*-oriented critique of anthropocentrism is any less viable or valuable than Sartre's existentialist or (later) Marxist humanism. My investigation has more to do with certifying an intellectual due diligence. What is the agenda? Why is it the agenda? What is behind the agenda? How is the agenda rendered viable by a certain expertise? Here, what concerns me is Heidegger's rationale for moving in the direction of *Dasein* rather than towards the Sartrean humanist, human-centred subject. By extension, my concern is with a range of similarly motivated contemporary attempts to ontologize the political. Is the ontological move a ruse, a decoy, a sly attempt to provide an alibi for the heavily contaminated historical subject? To put it simply, why bother with such a cosmically generalized critique of anthropocentrism when there is no shortage of historically grounded calamities and horrors to examine such as colonialism, Eurocentrism, global patriarchy and sexism, and predatory capitalism? Why is the ek-static thrownness of *Dasein* a nobler and more compelling focus of attention than the German sovereign national subject, the colonized Algerian subject, or the colonizing French subject? Given the sanctity of the ontico-ontological difference, is it even possible to articulate the thrown condition of *Dasein* in terms of the very determinate and the not so thrown predicament of a variety of historical subjects under a variety of repressive and non-egalitarian regimes? Assuming that *Dasein* can even be acted upon agentively and with intentionality, can *Dasein* be persuaded to take on a local habitation and a name and thereby be subjected to a double parsing?

In submitting the Heideggerian ontological project to a symptomatic reading, I focus on two aspects: the aesthetic, and the hermeneutic. I will be emphasizing the latter as I bring my essay towards tentative closure. Both in Merleau-Ponty and in Heidegger, the bringing into truth of Being is strongly identified as an aesthetic project. I will have more to say about this in a few of my forthcoming essays, but what I ask here is this: In the final analysis, is the phenomenological thinker an unapologetic aestheticizer of politics as such? The relationship of the aesthetic to the political, under fascism, cultural nationalism, German Marxism, and so on, is too deep and complicated an issue for me to broach here; suffice to say that the contemporary recourse to aesthetics, when it is persuasive – that is, when it is historically grounded and not just vapidly ethical and utopian, like the return to ontological thinking – has as its objective nothing less than the reimagining of the political. As Walter Benjamin's astute analysis tells us, the aesthetic can go either way: it can mystify, or it can inaugurate a second-order overhauling of politics altogether. Having said this tersely, let me turn to the role played by hermeneutics.

Heidegger's daunting and radical project of "de-structive hermeneutics," of reading the entire metaphysical, Western onto-theological tradition against the grain and placing it under erasure, is fundamentally hermeneutic in nature and intent. The questioner is placed within the question; hermeneutic circularity is opened up and embraced; pre-judice is unflinchingly acknowledged and endorsed as a precondition for the production of truth, as the underlying relationship between self and other, empowered as an epistemological dimension; and finally, truth itself is uncovered as *a-letheia*, as a form of unveiling of a possibility of the open and "the clearing" that has been covered over, misrecognized, and imperialized by a Platonic, onto-theological, metaphysical tradition: a tradition that has betrayed the be-ing of Being in the name of the inauthentic, the *das Man*, the vulgarly ontic. There is then in Heidegger a project, and a corresponding manual of action, as it were. Does the project entirely "antecede" that manual, or does the *how to* as process actually constitute the project? We will see. Is this project always already universal, given that *Dasein* is not intended to be German except in a provisional sort of way (i.e., *Dasein* in any other language would be the same); or does it seek universality through appropriate forms of persuasion, argumentation, and rhetorical strategies? Is the Heideggerian hermeneutic-ontological project acultural, intracultural with respect to Europe, comparatist, intercultural? Or is it Möbius-like in its perennial displacement of inside–outside distinctions based on historical habitation and determination? In being a resident at all, is one a resident of Germany/France/India/Japan/China/Algeria, and so on, *and* of Being? Is there reciprocal residence and habitation, both sovereign and non-sovereign, without excess or residue, all within the ontico-ontological dimensionality of the Möbius strip?

In celebrations of the Heideggerian openness of the fourfold and of the self-effacing generosity of *Gelassenheit* as methodology, often forgotten is the brute fact that, *a-letheia* or no *a-letheia*, Heidegger – and even more so his disciple Gadamer – is actively involved in the very act of de-struction, in the renewal of a tradition that has been covered over by the wrong kind of thinking. Something deeply ideological is at stake here, and the de-struction of onto-theology and Western metaphysics is really not as "nameless" as it would seem. A certain lost Greek proximity to Being is to be reclaimed, not as an aggressive act of epistemological procurement, but as a gentle move of "care" and "letting be." One can hear in this an anti-Heideggerian snort: Can anything be more full of hubris and more anthropocentric than that? In the name of the earth-world relationship of strife that Heidegger is solicitous of, who is Heidegger to let Being be, and who sanctioned the nostalgia for a pre-Socratic Hellenic accent that is so desperate to find the truth that has always been there and that awaits Heideggerian unconcealment? The basic point I am making is that the task of hermeneutic de-struction, in all its ontological openness, is also a historically specific project of rebuilding a very specific tradition. Rama, for all of Gandhi's declarations, remains the Hindu god Rama, Rama the seventh incarnation of Vishnu, the preserver; so too, in Heidegger's case, the temples of Being he refers to in the context of the Open, the fourfold, and the "clearing" are all irreducibly Greek temples: they are not Hindu temples or Jewish synagogues or Buddhist pagodas or Islamic mosques or Christian Cathedrals or Sikh gurdwaras or Zoroastrian fire temples. Greek is a proper noun and a name, and the tradition that Heidegger so insists on rescuing from imperial Rome and subsequent distortions is not a namelessly open or universal tradition: *au contraire*!

Notwithstanding my basic fellow-heartedness (a rough translation of useful Sanskrit word, *sahridayatva*) with Heidegger, I want to raise the red flag when it comes to certain Heideggerian assumptions, all the more so since they are tacitly ideological and potentially virulent. Whether or not he dabbled with the *Führer* and his regime, Heidegger's category of "authenticity" in the name of *Dasein* needs to be scrutinized rigorously – that is, historically – and along secular lines. Whether or not it is the result of the famous *Kehre* (the turn) in his philosophical trajectory, Heidegger's poetic project of synchronizing "the language of Being" with "the being of language" ought not to be given an ontological free hand. History may well have fallen on bad times; but the remedy to those bad times must be worked out historically and not through some ontological recourse to an unproven primordialism of Hellenic, Brahmanic, Zionist, or whatever provenance. The challenge here is to find history historically, and not just historically, but multi-historically – that is, to find history, through active perspectival revisionism, in all its multiple and heterogeneous manifestations. Such a hermeneutic must go beyond the intra- and inter-cultural dimensions of lived experience towards what Edward Said has termed "secular history" – that is, a history that by definition is already interpenetrated, counterpointed, thrown into relief, rendered multivocal and multi-linguistic and multilateral by the histories of others. It is only because we are confined ontologically by the binary regime of identity and difference that we are also constrained by the intra- and inter-structuration. Once history itself, and with it the progressive temporal generation of Being, is understood as secular, we are in the region of the contested and contestable "Open" or clearing where the world may be seen to "world" by the logic of a genuine phenomenological perspectivism whereby each perspective is joined not to its own limited truth but rather to an emerging narrative of multiple and multilateral counterpoints and versions. This is exactly the kind of world that is envisaged by Merleau-Ponty in some passages in *Phenomenology of Perception*: not the world versus perspectivism, but the world as perspectival, where the human subject/agent/hegemon carries in her being this very pre-script or obligation to be nothing but rigorously perspectival. The onus is on the human to realize historically the givenness of the world as perspective, with respect both to nature and to the other selves in the world.

With this last reference to Merleau-Ponty and perspectivism, I seem to have come full circle. I will complete that circle by returning to Gandhi. The same Gandhi who conceived of an open India argued that India had nothing to learn from the world (clearly, he was a frustratingly complex and contradictory thinker). So, what is his real message? Is it "at home in the world"? Or "at world in the home"? Or is it "to each being his or her provincial home, which she is free to magnify and universalize as the world"? Why would India have nothing to learn from the world? Clearly, it is the nostalgic, backward-looking Luddite Gandhi who will not be parsed and made sense of in a rapid and unstoppable emerging modernity based on global industrial capital, and who is taking a fierce stand on behalf of a primordial India. In a way, Gandhi is saying both substantively, as a proud primordial Hindu/Indian, and polemically, as a colonized subject who has been rendered a beggar in his own home, that his culture/history/civilization is the alpha and the omega, that his is the culture in which time stands still in its primordiality and is instantiated in every historical present as the hoary repetition of the origin. Hence there is no need to look elsewhere. The plenitude is already in its proper place; the breezes from elsewhere have already fertilized India as the microcosmos of the macrocosmos.

The tension between ontology and politics regarding what is and what should be, and anxiety about the past, its loss or recoverability, its relevance or lack thereof to the present moment: these issues point to history both as problem and as solution. No less a historian than Ranajit Guha has been registering in some of his recent work a profound and moving disillusionment with the realization of history in the disciplinary field known as "history." According to Guha, (1) the people haven't spoken in history, nor has the individual; (2) there is a deep schism between academic historiography and history as lived; and (3) as a kind of summing up, in what we call historical studies, "the existential does not tangle with the epistemological."[12] Guha's disillusionment is both phenomenological and anti-academic and anti-disciplinary; and surprise, surprise! he too turns to poetry (to Rabindranath Tagore in particular) as an antidote. Poetry is experientially real, vibrant, expressive, perhaps authentic; and in poetry, existence and epistemology begin to dance together. History lives thrillingly, memorably in poetry. Now, is this a romantic, elitist, bourgeois mystification?

I think in some ways it is; but this disillusionment, not its resolution through poetry, has much to say by way of critique. Fundamental to phenomenology and hermeneutic thinking is nostalgia for something lost, for something that could have been, that could have been otherwise, as well as deep regret for the betrayal of some rich and precious potentiality. History is to blame for having lost that potential en route, although of course it is in history that the potential is/was conceived in the first place. Is the potential a gerund, a present or past participle, an infinitive? Is it tensed or tenseless? Does nostalgia have an object? Is such an object real, imagined, present, absent? Is the hermeneutic project confronted by the need to "return to things themselves" in their own pristine, immaculate, eidetic temporality – to return to origins, an origin, the Origin? And this is exactly where what seems to be a harmless poetic exercise in wistfulness and nostalgia turns viciously political and centrist; for it cannot be forgotten that the revisionist creation of a tradition is also an attempt to create an authentic, authoritative, and pedagogically mystical synchronicity that unites past, present, and future within a seamless temporality of value parading as authenticity. The phenomenological-hermeneutic project of the worlding of the world along secular lines does not require the jargon of authenticity.[13]

NOTES

1 See *The Essential Gandhi*, ed. Louis Fischer (New York: Random House, 1962); and *The Cambridge Companion to Gandhi*, ed. Judith M. Brown and Parel Anthony (Cambridge: Cambridge University Press, 2011).

2 For more on the profound debate between Gandhi the *Mahatma* and Tagore the *Poet*, see my "Between Nation and World: Gandhi and Tagore," in *Forms of Knowledge: Critical Revaluations*, ed. Suresh Raval, G.M. Mehta, and Sitanshu Yashaschandra (Delhi: Pencraft International, 2008), 326–57.

3 See Jacques Derrida, "Plato's Pharmacy," in *Dissemination*, trans. Barbara Johnson (Chicago: University of Chicago Press, 1981), 63–171; and Ashis Nandy, "Towards a Third World Utopia," in *Traditions, Tyranny, and Utopias: Essays in the Politics of Awareness* (Delhi: Oxford University Press, 1992), 440–69.

4 See Martin Heidegger, "The Origin of the Work of Art," in *Basic Writings*, ed. David Farrell Krell, 2nd rev. ed. (San Francisco: Harper Perennial, 1993), 139–212.

5 Maurice Merleau-Ponty, *Phenomenology of Perception*, trans. Collin Smith (London: Routledge, 1962), xviii.

6 See Heidegger, "The Origin of the Work of Art."

7 Merleau-Ponty, *Phenomenology of Perception*, xx–xxi.

8 See Edward W. Said, *Humanism and Democratic Criticism* (New York: Columbia University Press, 2004).

9 See Merleau-Ponty, *Humanism and Terror: An Essay on the Communistic Problem*, trans. John O'Neill (Boston: Beacon, 1969).

10 See Derrida, *Acts of Religion*, ed. Gil Anidjar (New York: Routledge, 2002).

11 See Heidegger, "Letter on Humanism," in *Basic Writings*, 213–66; and Jean-Paul Sartre, *Existentialism and Humanism* (Brooklyn: Haskell House, 1977).

12 See Ranajit Guha, *History at the Limit of World-History* (New York: Columbia University Press, 2002).

13 See Theodor W. Adorno's *The Jargon of Authenticity*, trans. Knut Parnowski and Frederic Will (Evanston, IL: Northwestern University Press, 1973).

PART TWO

Intercultural Complications and Problematics

Chapter Six

Objects and Orientalism

GRAHAM HARMAN

This essay considers the possible vulnerability of object-oriented ontology (OOO) to charges of "Orientalism." Although the charge has not yet been made by any serious author,[1] there are reasons why it ought to be answered in advance. Object-oriented thought defends the mystery and exoticism of objects, describing them in poetic language that sometimes makes use of Oriental-sounding metaphors. It defends a version of realism and essentialism that might seem dangerous, from fear of the condescending manner in which an unchanging essence has often been ascribed to vast stretches of the non-Western world. Another point to consider is that for some, the very term "object" inherently promotes the objectification of human subjects beneath a haughty imperial gaze. Moreover, the object-oriented model downplays any historical approach to objects, and this may sound like a reactionary commitment to timeless and durable categories such as "European," "Levantine," or "Asiatic." Since all of these points might understandably give cause for political alarm, this essay will try to show that there is no connection between object-oriented philosophy and the concept of Orientalism criticized by Edward Said.[2] It will be shown that the object-oriented sense of mystery, exoticism, realism, essence, objects, and ahistorical entities has only an oblique connection with the traditional sense of these terms. More than this, I will argue that such concepts provide new resources for preventing or outright forbidding the reduction of cultural difference to totalizing surveillance by the Empire.

This essay has three sections. In the first, I outline the basic concepts of object-oriented philosophy, a term I coined myself in 1997.[3] In the second, I note the surface resemblance between some object-oriented concepts and the Orientalist strategies most denounced by Said: exoticism, reification, and an ahistorical ontology of objects. In the third and final section I claim that object-oriented ontology is better suited to defend the so-called subaltern realm from objectification than the now familiar brands of anti-realism and anti-essentialism defended by postmodern and post-colonial thought.

1. An Outline of Object-Oriented Realism and Essentialism

It will be helpful to summarize briefly the basic features of the object-oriented position, a stance represented not only by my own works but by those of such authors as Ian Bogost, Levi Bryant, and Timothy Morton as well.[4] If the following summary does not initially seem to be directly related to any potential critique of OOO by Said's followers, it should take only a few pages for its relevance to become clear.

The basic principles of object-oriented philosophy can be traced to Edmund Husserl and Martin Heidegger.[5] One of Husserl's guiding concerns was to protect philosophy from the rising tide of the natural sciences late in the nineteenth century, a situation in which philosophy was in danger of being replaced by experimental psychology. Like his teacher Franz Brentano before him,[6] Husserl noted that unlike the natural world dealt with by the sciences, there is a special realm of knowledge typified by *immanent objectivity*. Mental acts, unlike physical events, have *objects* as their *contents*. For Brentano this feature belongs to the realm of *psychology*, a term he views positively. For Husserl it is somewhat different, given his worry that a psychological approach would lead to a "psychologism" in which logical laws are reduced to mere laws of thought. Nonetheless, Husserl's *phenomenology* covers roughly the same terrain as Brentano's philosophical psychology. What is important for both thinkers is the realm of the immediately given. Before developing any theories about sound as the vibration of air leading to the disturbance of the eardrums and chemical signals then being sent through the nervous system, we must realize that these are merely *theories*. All such theories are grounded in the immediate evidence of phenomenal experience, and this must be described in minute detail to provide a foundation for the sciences. The exact subtleties of the human experience of sound must be carefully examined and catalogued, not merely explained away through physical theories of the behaviour of waves. In short, Husserl grounds his entire philosophy in the presence of phenomena to consciousness.

It is very different with Heidegger, who began as Husserl's star pupil but was later a heretic and a rebel against his teacher's phenomenology. Beginning in 1919,[7] as a twenty-nine-year-old lecturer, Heidegger began to challenge the basic principle of phenomenology. For the most part, we *do not* deal with the entities of the world in terms of their presence to consciousness. As I sit in a hotel room typing these words, my attention is focused on the computer screen, on the tactile sensation of my fingers striking the keyboard, on some minor discomfort in my sitting posture, and occasionally on some annoying laughter from the lobby below. But these conscious phenomena are a mere superficial crust in comparison with all the things constituting my environment at the moment. The solid floor beneath my feet supports me in a stable position some thirty feet above the earth, but might easily rot away over time or collapse in a sudden earthquake. Dozens of bodily organs keep me alive, but any of them could fail without prior notice, either killing me outright or causing sufficient pain that writing becomes impossible. Finally, I am also dependent on a relatively stable military truce here in Cyprus where I am writing; if the conflict of 1974 were to flare up again, events on the island would become too urgent and distressing for writing to be possible. The vast majority of entities in our environment are *not* present to us. Instead, they are silently relied upon as an invisible geography supporting our every action, and are generally noticed only when they fail. What we call tools or the ready-to-hand (*Zuhandenheit*) tend to withdraw invisibly into shadow, while what we call presence-at-hand (*Vorhandenheit*) is all that comes into conscious view. In this respect, the phenomenal realm that made up the whole of Husserl's philosophy is shown to be no better than half of reality; the other half is engaged in dark and silent labour, enabling the more explicit engagements that fill up consciousness.

The first thing that should be noted is that this so-called tool-analysis does not apply only to a special class of entities called "tools," as if it informed us only about hammers, saws, chisels, and airplanes but told us nothing about people, animals, and plants. The tool-analysis is not a taxonomical description of technical devices, but an ontology of entities in general. All things withdraw from our grasp and are never fully translatable into the terms through which we access them. The mountains themselves are never *quite* the mountains of geologists, who perpetually struggle to update their theories; the hammer itself is never *quite* the hammer that is now working very well in the hands of the labourer, since it may be riddled with unnoticed cracks and fissures that expand unnoticed by the worker. At the same time, all entities *can* be made the object of more explicit awareness, although such awareness will never exhaust the nature of the entities it describes. Now, Heidegger uses the word "object" solely in a pejorative sense; he means by it things as reduced to presence for an observer. But object-oriented philosophy does not follow him here. In order to unify Heidegger's tools with Husserl's intentional objects of consciousness, the object-oriented position uses "object" as a general term for all real and phenomenal entities alike. Some might complain that by using the word "object" for people as well as for inanimate things, we are "objectifying" humans and taking away their status as free individual subjects. This is not the case. There will still be important differences between humans, animals, vegetables, and minerals, but these differences will emerge at a later stage of the discussion rather than being built into the very foundations of philosophy, as has been the case since René Descartes's distinction between thinking and extended substance.

Yet the usual interpretation of Heidegger's tool-analysis takes a rather banal form that runs approximately as follows: "What Heidegger shows is that theory is grounded in praxis. Explicit theoretical concepts always emerge from an unthematic practical background." While true enough, this claim is in fact a dangerous platitude that risks overshadowing the basic feature of Heidegger's revolution in philosophy. For while it is true that our theoretical grasp of mountains, wasps, or music fails to do justice to the total depth of these realities, the same is just as true of our *practical* interaction with them. The mountaineer does not grasp the rich depths of Mount Everest any more than the geologist does. In short, the distortion of objects into present-at-hand caricatures of their full plenitude is not just the tragic fate of human thinking, for it haunts our unconscious practice as well. Here, too, objects are deeper than any relation with them can exhaust.

It can be argued that Heidegger himself already understood this further implication of his discovery. Yet there is no question that he failed to push his tool-analysis the additional step further that is needed to do it justice. Namely, not only do objects withdraw from human theory and practice: they withdraw *from one another* as well. When a meteor strikes Mount Everest, or when gusts of wind are blocked by its towering North Face, the meteor and the wind *also* encounter nothing but a painfully inadequate caricature of the mountain. Far from being a mere description of the pre-theoretical practices and moods of human *Dasein*, Heidegger's tool-analysis turns out to be a global theory of objects that withdraw from direct contact with one another. For this reason direct contact is completely impossible, to the extent that objects can affect one another only through a process that I have termed "vicarious causation."[8] But more to the point for the present essay, objects must always remain exotic for *one another* as well. It is certainly true that candied almonds, alluring water pipes, and decadent steam baths are able to charm the cynical imperialist who advances through the Old City of Damascus. But it is equally true that even the most soul-sucking Indianapolis strip mall harbours something exotic and mysterious for the fire that reduces it to cinders, since the fire is never able to grasp the veiled depths in which this horrendous and doomed entity withholds itself from total access.

One of the implications of this reading of the tool-analysis is a frank realism of the sort with which the speculative realist movement (including its object-oriented wing) has rightly been identified from the start.[9] It is not just that there is some dark residue lurking beyond any human attempt to know the world, as Immanuel Kant and even a number of phenomenologists have already noted. Rather, the point is that even human–world relations are haunted by such a residue, since they are not different *in kind* from object–object relations in which no humans are present. If Kant's so-called Copernican Revolution is defined by the privileged status it grants to the permanent correlation of human and world, the object-oriented branch of speculative realism treats the relation between wind and coconuts, or raindrops and wood, as being just as imprisoned in incomplete translation as even the most flawed sort of human cognition. A social and linguistic construction of reality does indeed take place, but there is already a reality there prior to any construction. Whatever Palestine, India, and China may be, if they are genuine units (and unlike Said I hold that they *might* be) they are not identical with the manner in which they are shaped by either scholars, activists, or imperial agents. Assuming that India actually exists as a unit (we can leave that question open for now) then there will indeed be a "true India" behind the multitude of interpretations of that entity, however inaccessible it remains to humans. What makes this different from Kant's noumena is that the noumenal India is not just a mysterious X withdrawing from all human access, but also one that cannot be directly encountered by the genuine Sri Lanka and Nepal, or even by the genuine Indian states and persons encompassed by India itself. Assuming India is real, then it is a unified object. And while it is certainly a reality that can be constructed and shaped both by imperial powers and by Indians themselves, it is by no means entirely under the control of these constructions. As we will see when discussing Said's reference to Giambattista Vico, it is simply *not* the case that humans master whatever they themselves create. If India as a unified nation has something to do with the ambitions of colonial power, it has also proven more appealing and more durable to its residents than might have been expected, and perhaps more real than its founding conditions made likely.

This brings us to a related tenet of object-oriented philosophy: the notion that there can be objects of many different sizes. One common objection to the reification of entire cultures would be to say "there is nothing in the world but countless individuals, and one cannot generalize and grant the status of individuals to such fuzzy notions as 'India' or 'France.'" Here, an ontological decision is being made to the effect that all that exists are individual people, and that any larger collectives to which they might belong are simply arbitrary linguistic categories having only a mental existence, whereas specific humans have a real existence. Ironically, even while this attitude hopes to exempt individual people from broad cultural stereotypes, it also risks making common cause with Lady Thatcher's infamous claim that "society does not exist," the neoliberal credo that individuals alone are decision-making agents and that they alone have ontological worth. The ostensibly liberating effort to forbid the reification of cultures also makes common cause with the most conservative principle of classical metaphysics: namely, a distinction between substance (natural flowers and horses) and aggregate (unnatural corporations, societies, and machines) as found most vividly in the worst moment of the otherwise wonderful Leibniz. Against this dreary traditional taxonomy, object-oriented philosophy holds that every real object is both substance and aggregate simultaneously. For instance, an atom of sulphur can be viewed as a unified thing with a reality that is not exhausted by any of its interactions with other things in the environment. But it is obvious that the sulphur atom can be decomposed into protons, neutrons, and electrons, that the protons and neutrons can be decomposed into quarks, and so forth. Likewise, the larger cloud of sulphorous vapour into which the individual atom vanishes is no less real than the atom itself. It is simply not the case that we can identify a privileged layer of individuals that alone is real, so that all collective gatherings of these individuals would be nothing more than creations of the mind. There is no reason to think that individual French soldiers are more real than the whole divisions of them that saw action at the Marne in 1914. But this does not mean that every object we can *imagine* is also a real object. "The Red-Headed League" investigated by Sherlock Holmes was a sheer fabrication designed merely to deceive. By the same token, it is possible that "Sub-Saharan Africa" refers to no genuine unit, quite probable that "the Monotheistic World" refers to no real entity, and almost a certainty that an even sloppier term such as "the Orient" refers to no collective reality at all. But it does not follow from this that only individual people are real, so that cultures as a whole would be reduced to merely fictional status.

It must also be noted that every reality necessarily has an *essence*. If a hammer is real apart from any current or even possible use of it, then that hammer has certain features that typify it that are not found in skyscrapers and zebras. Objects are not interchangeable, after all. Nor are objects reducible to the sum total of their current effects on other entities. The same holds true of me as a person. Over and above my sum total of current effects on all other people and things that interact with me, there is in fact a "real me" capable of certain additional actions and not others: if a saxophone were present in this room I could play it, but putting a guitar in the room instead would lead to no music of any sort, but simply careless and idle strumming. Deeper than the current expressions of my reality, there is a real me with numerous, currently unexpressed features. This is my essence. But what does not follow from this is the traditional assumption that this essence must be *eternal*. To say that an object (including an entire culture) has an essence is not to turn it into a timeless, unchanging entity. Italy was not always the land of painters, nor Germany the land of philosophers; these traits emerged over the course of time. But note that they emerged *from the prior reality of Italy and Germany*. If we cannot explain the whole of *quattrocento* paintings or German Idealist philosophy in terms of the prior cultural history of those nations, we would hardly be wrong in trying to shed light on these great revolutions by describing the background conditions that made them possible. In similar fashion, the advent of the First World War or of Islam may have been tremendous surprises to those who lived through them, but these events are not beyond all historical clarification as to why they happened when and where they did rather than at another time and place.

Let this suffice as a basic description of the principles of object-oriented philosophy. Already it should be clear why some readers of a post-colonialist bent might be uncomfortable with the basic concepts of OOP. Object-oriented thought is a realist philosophy that sets limits on what social construction is able to accomplish, at least in any given moment of time. It necessarily defends the idea that there are essences of things that are never fully expressed in any set of environmental effects or events. Under some circumstances it also defends the reification of collectives, in contrast with those who would claim that one cannot speak meaningfully of "India," "France," or "The Developing World" but only of a massive array of individuals whose basic features cannot be generalized. Nonetheless, I hold that all these features of object-oriented thought are not only politically harmless, but even politically beneficial.

2. Said's Anti-Realist Ontology

As is well known, the major theme of Said's *Orientalism* is the politics of the Middle East, and that is not one of the topics of the present article. He is interested in Orientalism not just as an isolated form of knowledge production, but as "a Western style for dominating, restructuring, and having authority over the Orient."[10] Due to this oppression, "the Orient was not (and is not) a free subject of thought or action."[11] And we remain blinded to this reality, insofar as "the literary-cultural establishment as a whole has declared the serious study of imperialism and culture off limits."[12] Indeed, "'East' has always signified danger and threat."[13] As for the Middle East, no one in the United States has wholeheartedly identified with the Arab cause except those who are viewed by Said as tainted with oil company involvement or religious conversion.[14] In what follows, I will not contest Said's claim that the Orient has been a site of Western domination, nor even that the very notion of a unified Orient has been constructed by the needs of imperialism. Instead, I will simply identify some objectionable aspects of the anti-realist and anti-essentialist ontology that Said employs in the course of his critique. Ultimately, I will claim that this typical sort of postmodernist ontology undercuts the very liberation of the oppressed that Said hopes to achieve. In sum, to strip oppressed entities of any autonomous reality or essence reduces them to nothing more than their current "subaltern" status. To speak of the mystery of the Orient, as of any other entity, need not be a sign of condescending exoticism, but may point to genuine depths in the things that are not masterable by the current Imperium or any possible future one. To explore this theme, let's briefly address four separate claims found in Said's ontology.

The first is his notion that the Orient is constructed by the West as its exotic "Other." As Said puts it early in the book, "European culture gained in strength and identity by setting itself off against the Orient as a sort of surrogate and even underground self."[15] It was a "difference between the familiar (Europe, the West, 'us') and the strange (the Orient, the East, 'them')."[16] This results in a marvellous litany of stock exotic Oriental characters, which Said here confines to those of the Middle East: "the Sphinx, Cleopatra, Eden, Troy, Sodom and Gomorrah, Astarte, Isis and Osiris, Sheba, Babylon, the Genii, the Magi, Nineveh, Prester John, Mahomet, and dozens more."[17] On the one hand this list evokes images of the Oriental as "a threatening, immoral debauchee,"[18] but on the other it is linked with an admiring enthusiasm for "the exotic, the mysterious, the profound, the seminal,"[19] or with a "cloistered intimacy *away* from the West, [a] perdurable exoticism."[20] In this way, the East was an irresistible summons to the West, as in "Casimir Leconte's observation that an eccentric life would develop significant originality in men, and from originality would come great and unusual exploits."[21]

But this Orient is not a *real* Orient for Said; instead, it is something merely constructed. While Said denies that this was part of some nefarious Western imperialist "plot," he does hold that it entailed a more insidious mode of domination in the Foucauldian manner: "a *distribution* of geopolitical awareness into aesthetic, scholarly, economic, sociological, historical, and philological texts."[22] But of course, "Europe was always in a position of strength, not to say domination. There is no way of putting this euphemistically ... Knowledge of the Orient, because generated out of strength, *creates* the Orient."[23] Said proceeds further with what is perhaps excessive praise of Vico's claim that since "men make their own history ... what they can know is what they have made."[24] This later turns into Said's somewhat stronger claim that "all things in history, like history itself, are made by men ... [and that for this reason] we will appreciate how possible it is for many objects or places or times to be assigned roles and given meanings that acquire objective validity only *after* the assignments are made."[25] Although this passage asserts only that all things in *history* are made by humans, there is little textual evidence that Said allows anything to exist outside the scope of historical construction, and in this way we begin to see how deep his anti-realism runs. But the main point here is that, having been constructed by a much more powerful West, the Orient was never allowed to speak for itself, as witnessed by Flaubert's position of dominance over a local courtesan described in his (highly offensive) letters from Egypt.[26] Said goes so far as to find this silencing of the East even in Aeschylus, though he was writing of a war with Persia during a time utterly devoid of Western dominance, in which Greece was victorious by a mere hair's breadth.[27] The supposed attitude of the West was this: "if the Orient could represent itself, it would; since it cannot, the representation does the job, for the West, and *faute de mieux*, for the poor Orient."[28]

For Said, the real problem with this forbidding of the Orient to speak is that its *novelty* is thereby suppressed. For example, Islam was constructed by the West in such a way that its *true* novelty was concealed: "The Orient at large, therefore, vacillates between the West's contempt for what is familiar and its shivers of delight in – or fear of – novelty."[29] Europeans feared Islam rather than learning from it. "Like Walter Scott's Saracens, the European representation of the Muslim, Ottoman, or Arab was always a way of controlling the redoubtable Orient."[30] Said admits briefly that "there is nothing especially controversial or reprehensible about such domestications of the exotic; they take place between all cultures, certainly, and between all men."[31] Nonetheless, for the West "empirical data about the Orient or about any of its parts count for very little; what matters and is decisive is what I have been calling the Orientalist vision, a vision by no means confined to the professional scholar, but rather the common possession of all who have thought about the Orient in the West."[32] To summarize, the East is treated as an exotic "Other," but at the same time this supposed Other is actually constructed by the Western mind. We are left unsure as to whether the Middle East is different from Europe or not. Apparently, either answer renders one equally guilty of Orientalism.

The second point is Said's oscillation between an extreme diversity of individual cultures and an extreme reluctance to view humans as differentiated in terms of cultures at all. For in the first place he complains about "'the Oriental' as a kind of ideal and unchanging abstraction,"[33] and about the process by which "Orientals" were treated "for all practical purposes [as] a Platonic essence, which any Orientalist (or ruler of Orientals) might examine, understand, and expose."[34] The Orientalist is confident "that *any* knowledge of the Orientals will confirm his views, which ... find the Oriental to be guilty."[35] Dante, for example, displays "an ahistorical vision" that treats all non-Christians as alike.[36] Here Said seems to regret that the rich diversity of the many Oriental cultures and individuals goes unrecognized. But at the same time he shows marked discomfort for this very requirement, going so far as to ask rhetorically: "Can one divide human reality, as indeed human reality seems to be genuinely divided, into clearly different cultures, histories, traditions, races, societies, even races, *and survive the consequences humanly*?"[37] In other words, Said's humanity leads him to resist distinct categories of humans at all, yet his dislike for generalization and abstraction in the historical field leads him to insist on a kind of particularism in which individual cultures and even individual people must be treated piecemeal, with a ban on sweeping generalizations about the larger categories to which they belong.

The third point worth mentioning is Said's *anti-realism*. At times he seems only to reject the thesis that a thing remains forever unchanging, while at other times he seems opposed to the notion that it has any inherent reality at all apart from its constructedness. Said is fond of theatrical metaphors when discussing the status of the Orient, as when he tells us that "the Orient is the stage on which the whole East is confined. On this stage will appear figures whose role it is to represent the larger whole from which they emanate."[38] Orientalism presents a series of tropes, and "these figures are to the actual Orient ... as stylized costumes are to characters in a play."[39] It remains unclear how far Said's constructionism goes. In his book we sometimes find cautious-sounding statements of the following sort: "It is perfectly possible to argue that *some* distinctive objects are made by the mind, and that these objects, while appearing to exist objectively, have only a fictional reality."[40] But since even the most ardent reactionary would not deny this fact for *some* objects, it seems that Said's "some" really means either "most" or "all." At the very least, he holds that what is added poetically by the mind is *more important* than the objective features of the world, as in his unexpected remarks on Gaston Bachelard's theory of space: "The objective space of a house – its corners, corridors, cellar, rooms – is far less important than what it is poetically endowed with, which is usually a quality with an imaginative or figurative value we can name and feel."[41] He also critiques the sort of knowledge that aims at the "ontological stability" of the supposed facts that it discusses.[42] Such stability is questionable, because "the Orient is not an inert fact of nature. It is not merely *there*, just as the Occident itself is not just *there* either,"[43] and this remark is followed by Said's hommage to Vico's theory that humans can know whatever they make. Elsewhere, Said makes a far vaster philosophical claim along the same lines:

> Philosophically, then, the kind of language, thought, and vision that I have been calling Orientalism very generally is a form of *radical realism*; anyone employing Orientalism, which is the habit for dealing with questions,

> objects, qualities, and regions deemed Oriental, will designate, name, point to, fix what he is talking or thinking about with a word or phrase, which then is considered either to have acquired, or more simply to be, reality.[44]

But once again, the status of this claim is ambiguous. Said does not go so far as to claim that reality does not exist outside human construction of it, but only to criticize those who think they can grasp the essence of a thing in a single word. He also criticizes Orientalism on the same page for categorizing and subdividing, which would merely seem to be the inevitable fate of all forms of knowledge. But Said adds further that "psychologically, Orientalism is a form of paranoia, knowledge *of another kind*, say, from ordinary historical knowledge."[45] What this paranoia leads to is the attitude of the British imperialists Balfour and Cromer, who "strip humanity down to … ruthless cultural and racial essences."[46]

Fourth and finally, Said criticizes what he calls "textualism," a bookish means of encounter with the Orient. This begins with further criticism of the mad wish to classify and codify, as when he strangely mocks the enthusiasm of the polymath William Jones for his diligent "course of personal study that was to gather in, to rope off, to domesticate the Orient and thereby turn it into a province of European learning … with an irresistible impulse always to codify, to subdue the infinite variety of the Orient to a 'complete digest' of laws, figures, customs, and works."[47] This is connected with Said's more general critique of the "textualism" of Orientalism: "the Orient studied was a textual universe by and large … rarely were Orientalists interested in anything except proving the validity of these musty 'truths' by applying them, without great success, to uncomprehending, hence degenerate, natives."[48] For example, Emperor Napoleon "saw the Orient only as it had been encoded first by classical texts and then by Orientalist experts, whose vision, based on classical texts, seemed a useful substitute for any actual encounter with the real Orient."[49] In Napoleon's case the authority was the Comte de Volmey, whose "work constituted a handbook for attenuating the human shock a European might feel as he directly experienced the Orient."[50] The present reality of the Orient was overshadowed by its classical period, preferred by the Europeans: "not to its modern realities, but to a series of valorized contacts it had had with a distant European past."[51] He later salutes both Voltaire and Cervantes for their apparent awareness, lacking among the Orientalists, "that it is a fallacy to assume that the swarming, unpredictable, and problematic mess in which human beings live can be understood on the basis of what books – texts – say; to apply what one learns out of a book literally to reality is to risk folly or ruin."[52] Said's distrust of texts goes hand in hand with his aforementioned anti-realism, as when he complains that "many writers of travel books compose them in order to say that a country *is* like this, or better, that it *is* colourful, expensive, interesting, and so forth,"[53] a lament that, if accurate, would have crippling consequences for the ability of humans to speak about anything at all.

3. Objects and Oppression

We have seen that the four main targets of Said's ontology are as follows: (1) the Orient constructed by the West as an exotic "Other"; (2) an attack on the reification of entire cultures, which are held by Said to be made only of diverse individual parts; (3) the realist view that things exist independently and timelessly outside the process of human construction; and (4) the textualist attitude that tries to understand other cultures through books rather than through direct contact. By contrast, object-oriented ontology (1) promotes an exotic conception of entities; (2) is willing to reify entire cultures in principle, although in practice it recognizes that not all cultures that are held to exist as units need actually exist ("Pennsylvania culture" may or may not be really distinct from that of New Jersey); (3) defends a realist ontology of mind-independent entities, although without viewing them as timeless; and (4) sees no particular evidence that direct empirical contact with the world is always more accurate in its conclusions than the kind that is mediated by written texts.

The response of object-oriented philosophy to Edward Said is simple and clear. The critique of Orientalism is right to fear a realist *epistemology*, but wrong to fear a realist *ontology*. Note that Said's main complaints run roughly as follows:

1. "The West views the Orient as exotic and 'Other,' but this is a false exoticism produced from the West's own biases, and *covers up a truly disturbing exoticism* in these cultures." Object-oriented thought stands firmly with Said on this point, holding that entities withdraw from *any possible grasp* by any sort of knowledge. Any exoticism of the East cannot be an exoticism circumscribable by the knowledge of the West, because it will always be something deeper and more

surprising than any mass of cultural clichés. And furthermore, object-oriented thought also finds an exotic dimension present in *all* entities: in Wal-Marts and Nike warehouses no less than in the snake charmers of Calcutta. If there is an "Orientalism" in the object-oriented position, then it pertains to a cosmic Orient not locatable anywhere in particular on an imperialist map of the planet.

2. The West makes sweeping generalizations about entire cultures, unaware that there is much individual variation within these cultures and that exceptions abound. While Said probably introduces this provision in order to protect individuals from the mechanisms of stereotype, the object-oriented view is that this is too high a price to pay. There is no more reason to think that individual humans are the sole concrete reality than to think that the individual hearts, kidneys, cells, or atoms in human bodies form the bedrock of all reality. From the fact that one must be very careful not to make triumphalistic generalizations about North Africa, the Japanese, or the city of Alexandria, it does not follow that to speak of these objects as real objects is automatically false. The object-oriented principle of the withdrawal of objects from human access already guarantees that all knowledge of objects must be regarded as highly tentative, and that stereotypes *are* therefore automatically false. But the falsity of stereotypes about Filipinos does not entail that Filipino culture does not exist. Quite the contrary: our ontology must take into account the possibility that it does, and that if real it will surely have strong retroactive effects on the individuals who inhabit and compose it.
3. For Said, realism is dangerous insofar as it promotes the notion that individual people and cultures embody timeless Platonic essences. Object-oriented philosophy agrees that the concept of timeless essences would be politically dangerous. To hold that the Malay or Vietnamese or Palestinian peoples have an essence that locks them into an eternal and unchanging pattern would certainly be a politically threatening doctrine. But it does not follow that any theory of essence must be committed to the *timelessness* of essence. "Essence" in the object-oriented version is not about the "timeless" at all. It simply means that an object is always more than its current relations with or effects upon the environment. Edward Said actually ought to salute such a doctrine, since it immediately makes room for his critical point that the exotic "Other" should be granted a permanent power to surprise, to overturn any imperialist categories by which the "Other" is silenced or enslaved. And furthermore, against the

usual view that "essence" is an inherently oppressive notion, object-oriented philosophy holds that the opposite is the case. For if we disdain all notion of realities concealed from view, and see the world instead as an immanent surface where everything is merely staged or performed without any secret back rooms (as is still fashionable today), then entities will hold nothing in reserve that can ever surprise us. Indochina would forever remain a colony of France, if not that something in its people resisted the slot it had been granted in what was once the present-day order of things. Any doctrine of post-colonial *resistance* requires some element outside the current gridwork of things that is *able* to resist, and such a dark fibre is woven into the very fabric of OOO.

4. Said also holds that the West always knew the Orient only through books, not through direct contact. But here it seems that Said lapses into what I have sometimes called "the taxonomic fallacy," taking a global ontological distinction and wrongly trying to embody it in two distinct *types* of entities. After all, the issue is not so much one of books versus direct experience: Said would surely admit that some exotic travel books are masterpieces of enlightened description, while some direct experience yields nothing more than the clumsy observations of prejudiced fools. The true distinction that occupies Said in his talk of textualism is that between the rigid categories of knowledge that format the Other in sterile fashion ("books") and a more flexible openness to shock and surprise from that same Other ("direct experience"). Stated differently, some reading is so valuable that it must count as direct experience, and some direct experience is so rigid and formalistic that it approaches what Said condemns as mere bookishness. And here again, object-oriented philosophy stands with him in endorsing the permanent value of shock and surprise in our encounters with the world.

If at first it seems that object-oriented thought defends the sort of exoticism, realism, and essentialism that Said most disdains, this turns out not to be the case at all. By globalizing the exotic to cover all corners of reality, the object-oriented philosopher removes the exotic from the realm of imperialistic thrill-seekers. And by defending a real and essential sphere beneath the current deployments of power, it infests the world with conspiratorial pockets of potential uprising. At the time of the French Revolution, social construction was a conservative doctrine, invoked to uphold the rights of gradually evolving classes and bloodlines over the abstract universal claims of reason. In the twentieth century the balance flipped: realism became viewed as the "conservative" doctrine, while the vision of reality as socially constructed was portrayed as progressive and liberating. It is my view that we are due for another reversal in this picture. For there is really no choice but to reverse it, given the stagnant model of reality that results if we deprive objects of any excess beyond their current place in the state of things.

NOTES

1 There have been a handful of wild attacks along these lines by pseudonymous and insincere bloggers, but it is well known that such people are ready to accuse anyone of anything.
2 Edward Said, *Orientalism* (New York: Vintage, 1979).
3 Recently I discovered an occurrence of "object-oriented philosophy" in notes made on my computer in 1997, despite my earlier recollection that the term dates from 1999. In any event, the term "object-oriented philosophy" was first introduced in public in a lecture of the same title at Brunel University near London on 11 September 1999. The lecture has since been published as chapter 6 of Graham Harman, *Towards Speculative Realism: Essays and Lectures* (Winchester: Zero, 2010), 93–104.
4 See Ian Bogost, *Alien Phenomenology* (Ann Arbor: Open Humanities Press, 2012); Levi Bryant, *The Democracy of Objects* (Ann Arbor: Open Humanities Press, 2012); and Timothy Morton, *Ecology without Nature: Rethinking Environmental Aesthetics* (Cambridge, MA: Harvard University Press, 2009).
5 The best introduction in any of my books can be found in the opening chapters of *The Quadruple Object* (Winchester: Zero, 2011).
6 See Franz Brentano, *Psychology from an Empirical Standpoint*, trans. Antos Rancurello et al. (London: Routledge, 1995).
7 See Martin Heidegger, *Towards the Definition of Philosophy*, trans. Ted Sadler (London: Continuum, 2008).
8 See Graham Harman, "On Vicarious Causation," *Collapse* 2 (2007): 171–205.
9 See Ray Brassier et al., "Speculative Realism: Ray Brassier, Iain Hamilton Grant, Graham Harman, Quentin Meillassoux," *Collapse* 3 (2007): 306–449.
10 Said, *Orientalism*, 3.
11 Ibid., 3.
12 Ibid., 13.
13 Ibid., 26.
14 Ibid., 27.

15 Ibid., 3.
16 Ibid., 43.
17 Ibid., 63.
18 Ibid., 66.
19 Ibid., 51.
20 Ibid., 92.
21 Ibid., 90.
22 Ibid., 12.
23 Ibid., 40.
24 Ibid., 5.
25 Ibid., 54.
26 Ibid., 6.
27 Ibid., 56.
28 Ibid., 21.
29 Ibid., 59.
30 Ibid., 60.
31 Ibid., 60.
32 Ibid., 69.
33 Ibid., 8.
34 Ibid., 38.
35 Ibid., 39.
36 Ibid., 69.
37 Ibid., 45; emphasis added.
38 Ibid., 63.
39 Ibid., 71.
40 Ibid., 54.
41 Ibid., 55.
42 Ibid., 32.
43 Ibid., 4.
44 Ibid., 72; emphasis added.
45 Ibid., 72.
46 Ibid., 36.
47 Ibid., 78.
48 Ibid., 52.
49 Ibid., 80.
50 Ibid., 81.
51 Ibid., 85.
52 Ibid., 93.
53 Ibid., 93.

Chapter Seven

Understanding, Misunderstanding, and the Critical Function of Hermeneutics in Cross-Cultural Studies

ZHANG LONGXI

1. Hermeneutics and the Validity of Interpretation

A few years after the first appearance of the original German edition of *Wahrheit und Methode* in 1960, E.D. Hirsch published *Validity in Interpretation*, in which he launched a strong critique of Gadamer's hermeneutics. Hirsch was concerned with the stability of meaning and the validity of interpretation, and he saw Gadamer as representing a dangerous tendency towards subjectivism, which tends to destabilize meaning and lead to the loss of certainty and all grounds for scholarly pursuit. "Validity requires a norm – a meaning that is stable and determinate no matter how broad its range of implication and application," says Hirsch. "A stable and determinate meaning requires an author's determining will, and it is sometimes important, therefore, to decide which author is the one being interpreted when we confront texts that have been spoken and respoken. All valid interpretation of every sort," he concludes, "is founded on the re-cognition of what an author meant."[1] Hirsch's theory of interpretation is completely predicated on the authorial meaning, which, he argues, is in principle reproducible. Drawing on Husserl's phenomenology, Hirsch argues that meaning is a repeatable and reproducible intentional object, for "*an unlimited number of different intentional acts can intend the same verbal meaning.*"[2] Interpretation is thus the recognition or reproduction of the same intentional object or verbal meaning as the author originally intended.

Hirsch's emphasis on authorial intention as the stable and reproducible meaning goes directly against Gadamer's argument for the historicity of understanding and the irrelevance of the authorial intention, as well as his famous statement that "we understand in *a different way, if we understand at all.*"[3] Difference in understanding comes from different subjectivities in different times and spaces – that is, from the ontological situation of *Dasein* that Heidegger brings into the discussion of hermeneutics. As each person exists in a different situation than the author or anyone else, and has a different horizon of expectations, it is impossible to reproduce exactly what the author or the other person intends. According to Gadamer, a phenomenological description of the hermeneutic process cannot ignore the historicity of understanding, the fact that we all start with what Heidegger calls the fore-structure of understanding, or what Gadamer deliberately calls our prejudices – that is, prejudgments and anticipations of what we are to understand. For Hirsch, however, to talk about historicity and differences of understanding would be to undermine the stability of meaning and the validity of interpretation. Of course he knows that different people may have different interpretations of the same text or event, but he brushes this aside by differentiating meaning (which does not change) from significance (which does change). Hirsch maintains:

> The meaning of a text is that which the author meant by his use of particular linguistic symbols. Being linguistic, this meaning is communal, that is, self-identical and reproducible in more than one consciousness. Being reproducible, it is the same whenever and wherever it is understood by another. However, each time this meaning is construed, its meaning to the construer (its significance) is different. Since his situation is different, so is the character of his relationship to the construed meaning.[4]

The differentiation of meaning (*Sinn*) from significance (*Bedeutung*) is not new – it was well established in nineteenth-century German hermeneutics – but it does nothing to address the real issue of the change of meaning each time a reader or interpreter construes meaning in a given hermeneutic situation. Hirsch's unchanging meaning is in fact something of an arbitrary postulate rather than a necessary given in understanding, for he admits, "no presently known normative concept other than the author's meaning has this universally compelling character. On purely practical grounds, therefore, it is preferable to agree that the meaning of a text is the author's meaning."[5] That is almost an acknowledgment that the unchanging meaning is a theoretical construct considered necessary "on purely practical grounds" despite the reality of interpretation, in which meaning and understanding are always changing and changeable. But how can we agree that the author's meaning is stable when in reality meaning exists only in interpretation and is always understood more or less differently by different readers and interpreters? Hirsch talks a lot about generic expectations that would constrain both what the author may mean and what the reader may construe, but those expectations are also the result of interpretation. In the case of an author like Shakespeare, for example, Hirsch argues that a Freudian interpretation of *Hamlet* is invalid because "we posited that such an implication did not belong to the type of meaning Shakespeare willed."[6] We may well agree that nothing in Shakespeare's play justifies the idea that Hamlet harbours a secret or unconscious desire to sleep with his mother, and therefore that the Freudian reading of *Hamlet* is a misinterpretation. From Hirsch's remarks above, however, it is also clear that what he calls the "type of meaning Shakespeare willed" is in fact not Shakespeare's, but what "we posited." That would completely undermine Hirsch's "objective criticism" based on the "authorial meaning," for ultimately it is the critic or interpreter who decides what the author may mean and intend.

Hirsch's fear of the loss of certainty is understandable, but does Gadamer's theory of hermeneutics really lead to subjectivism and relativism? Does his theory, with its emphasis on the historicity of understanding and its notion of "prejudice," lead to a position without a solid ground or a firm critical stance? The idea of the hermeneutic circle – that is, that understanding moves back and forth from the parts to the whole and from the whole to the parts – may easily be misunderstood as constituting a circular interpretation that only confirms one's subjective expectations and prejudices. But that is not what the hermeneutic circle is about. "The circle of understanding is not an orbit in which any random kind of knowledge may move," writes Heidegger. "It is the expression of the existential *fore-structure* of Dasein itself. It is not to be reduced to the level of vicious circle, or even of a circle which is merely tolerated. In the circle is hidden a positive possibility of the most primordial kind of knowing" (1962, 195). That is to say, Heidegger considers the fore-structure of understanding to be the starting point of a hermeneutic process, but "the point of Heidegger's hermeneutical reflection is not so much to prove that there is a circle as to show that this circle possesses an ontologically positive significance," Gadamer writes in explaining the significance of Heidegger's concept. "All correct interpretation must be on guard against arbitrary fancies and the limitations imposed by imperceptible habits of thought, and it must direct its gaze 'on the things themselves.'"[7] Thus the hermeneutic circle is not at all a means to legitimize the subjectivity of the interpreter; rather, it is the necessary means to reach adequate understanding by always modifying one's anticipations and expectations according to "the things themselves." Gadamer never loses sight of objectivity, although he emphasizes the interaction between the interpreter and the thing interpreted, and the change of meaning in various hermeneutic situations. Indeed, there is a crucial moment in *Truth and Method* that has not received sufficient attention in the debate: commenting on Paul Valéry's claim that his poetry has whatever meaning the reader attributes to it, Gadamer rejects this totally relativistic view as "an untenable hermeneutic nihilism."[8] For Gadamer, understanding is different in each case, but that does not mean that all understanding is equally valid, or that no criteria exist to assess the relative validity, adequacy, and legitimacy of different understandings and interpretations.

Gadamer tells us that the way we encounter a foreign language and require that it be translated is an "especially informative" case, one that proves the objectivity of the linguistic world:

> Here the translator must translate the meaning to be understood into the context in which the other speaker lives. This does not, of course, mean that he is at liberty to falsify the meaning of what the other person says. Rather, the meaning must be preserved, but since it must be understood within a new language world, it must establish its validity within it in a new way. Thus every translation is at the same time an interpretation. We can even say that the translation is the culmination of the interpretation that the translator has made of the words given him.[9]

The foreignness of a foreign language, its irrefutable otherness, the fact that one cannot "falsify the meaning of what the other person says," all point to limitations in one's ability to anticipate – to the fact that one's expectations, prejudices, and fore-structure of understanding cannot just subjectively and wilfully decide what meaning foreign words have. In a foreign language, one encounters an uncontrolled and uncontrollable alien system. For Gadamer, however, translation is mediation rather than real understanding. "Where there is understanding, there is not translation but speech. To understand a foreign language means that we do not need to translate it into our own … Every language can be learned so perfectly that using it no longer means translating from or into one's native tongue, but thinking in the foreign language."[10] Anyone who knows a foreign language well knows this is true, but to think in the foreign language also means to think in a way that is systematically different from one's native tongue, to think in a different vocabulary and according to a different set of grammatical and idiomatical rules. Learning a foreign language is indeed an experience of the foreign, of something out there, different from what is familiar and one's own.

The presence of the foreign and the possibility of understanding it, internalizing it, and making it one's own – those constitute the concept of *Bildung*. The presence of something that is alien and that does not always meet our expectations reveals the existence of an objective world *vis-à-vis* the subjectivity of the mind, a world the meaning of which is not simply what "we willed" or read into, but something to be understood with reference to "the things themselves." The process of understanding is thus one of constant revision of our own expectations or prejudices, and hermeneutics thus understood is not at all relativistic – rather, it insists on an objective basis for its operations. The idea of *Bildung*, however, encompasses not just the necessary acknowledgment of what is foreign and alien, but learning from the foreign to become a richer and more knowledgeable person. "To recognize one's own in the alien, to become at home in it, is the basic movement of spirit, whose being consists only in returning to itself from what is other," writes Gadamer in exploring the hermeneutic significance of Hegel's concept of *Bildung*. "Thus what constitutes the essence of *Bildung* is clearly not alienation as such, but the return to oneself – which presupposes alienation to be sure."[11] Therefore, the idea of *Bildung* presupposes both the presence of the foreign and the possibility of complete understanding of what is foreign, the going out to the "other" and the eventual return to the self.

The encounter with a foreign language and the possibility of learning it well can be seen as a special case as well as a model of cross-cultural understanding, in which we encounter an alien culture and try to learn and understand it adequately. The model of learning a foreign language also indicates clearly the presence of regulations and rules for judging adequacy or inadequacy in understanding, the possibility of "doing it right" or making mistakes, of understanding properly or failing miserably because of serious misunderstanding, even total incomprehension. It is a fact that each language has its own grammar, vocabulary, and structure and that one must make a great deal of effort to master these in order to function adequately in a particular language. In confronting a foreign language, one cannot wilfully decide what the foreign words mean; rather, one must accept the rules of an alien system in order to figure out what those words mean. To make a claim about a foreign language without deep understanding risks misunderstanding and misinterpretation and eventually leads to the collapse of communication. Yet at the same time, it is certainly possible to understand a foreign language so well that one becomes able to think in that language and to switch languages without difficulty. Casting this as an analogy, we may first assert the possibility and validity of cross-cultural understanding, but we may also see that misunderstanding and misinterpretation are problems in cross-cultural studies. So it is vital for intercultural hermeneutics to be critical of all mistakes and distortions in understanding different cultures. In cross-cultural studies – particularly for understanding across immense linguistic and cultural divides between East and West – the hermeneutic act is thus always an act of critique, one with a strongly critical function in both self-examination and in the critical scrutiny of misplaced emphasis on difference or the projection of one's own stereotypical preconceptions onto an alien culture. Debates about intercultural misconceptions and misunderstandings are integral to East–West cross-cultural studies and demonstrate the critical function of hermeneutics today.

2. East–West Studies: A Historical Perspective

Many of the misconceptions and false claims relating to East–West cross-cultural understanding can be traced back to the late sixteenth and the early seventeenth centuries, when European missionaries came across very different cultures and traditions in East Asia. A historical perspective is especially helpful here.[12] Marco Polo, in the thirteenth century, was one of the first Europeans to travel to China, yet the significance of his "discovery" of the East was not cultural – rather, as John Larner argues, it lay mainly in the observation and study "of the topography and human geography of Asia, of its customs and folklore, of, above all, the authority and court of the Great Khan, all seen from a Mongol point of view."[13] Because Marco Polo went to China as a trader and traveller (i.e., not as a scholar) during the Yuan dynasty, when China was under Mongol rule, he had little opportunity to observe "mainstream" Chinese culture, and this has led some scholars to question the veracity of his account.[14] Intellectual encounters with the Chinese tradition did not begin in earnest until several hundred years later, when the Jesuit missionary Matteo Ricci (1552–1610) travelled to China during the late

Ming dynasty and began to build a church in Beijing. The Jesuits found that China had such a long history, such a rich cultural tradition, and a society materially so well developed, that it would be quite impossible for them to tell the Chinese they were barbarian pagans to be civilized by a higher culture and religion. That simply would not work. The Jesuit missionaries realized that they wouldn't be able to turn millions of Chinese into Christians overnight by force or by proselytizing; so they adopted an "accommodation approach," arguing that the Chinese had already perfected morality with a natural religion and that they were ready to receive the light of Christianity as a revealed religion.

Ricci wrote in his journals that there were "traces of Christianity" in Chinese culture and their ancient books, and even some "evidences of the cross among the Chinese."[15] He adopted some Chinese terms from Confucian classics and used *tian zhu* to signify the Lord of Heaven, saying that the missionaries "could hardly have chosen a more appropriate expression" to translate the Christian God.[16] Applying such strategies and arguments, as well as what scientific knowledge and technological skills existed at the time, the Jesuits succeeded in converting quite a number of Chinese to Christianity, including high-ranking officials like Xu Guangqi (1562–1633), Li Zhizao (1565–1630), and Yang Tingyun (1557–1627) – the so-called three pillars of Chinese Catholicism in the late Ming dynasty. Together, Ricci and Xu translated the first six books of Euclid's *Elements* into Chinese, and many other scientific ideas and technologies were introduced to China by the Jesuits. These were appreciated not just by literati-officials but also by Emperor Kangxi himself in the early Qing dynasty. Commenting on the introduction of Euclid to China, Catherine Jami argues that "Euclidian geometry is just one of many instances that show that the changes that took place both in China and in Europe during the two centuries of Jesuit evangelisation in East Asia need to be taken into account in order to understand the interactions between the two civilisations, and that these interactions cannot be epitomised as a static encounter between two immutable entities."[17] Indeed, the introduction of European scientific ideas by the Jesuits to China must be seen as a significant part of cross-cultural interactions at that time, and the Jesuit accommodation can be seen as essentially an effort on the missionaries' part to come to a sympathetic understanding of a very different and alien culture.

On the Chinese side, the teachings of the philosopher Wang Yangming (1472–1529) were influential in the Ming dynasty, and Wang's iconoclastic tendency to reject the orthodoxy of Zhu Xi (1130–1200) had prepared – perhaps purely fortuitously – an openness of the mind among the Chinese literati with regard to receiving new ideas. "In the late sixteenth century," as the historian Zhu Weizheng remarks,

> Michel Ruggieri and Matteo Ricci arrived in China just at the time when the teachings of Wang Yangming were at the height of influence on the intellectual scene. Among the literati-officials, it was followers of Wang's teachings, such as Li Zhi and Xu Guangqi, who were the first to become interested in the European learning and religion Matteo Ricci tried to propagate, and who let themselves be converted to Catholicism without any sense of compunction. On the other hand, the authors who attacked the West and its religion in *Demolishing Heresies: A Collection of Essays from our Celestial Dynasty*, a book edited by Xu Changzhi at the end of the Ming, were for the most part self-appointed defenders of the orthodoxy and undistinguished epigones of Zhu Xi's teachings.[18]

It is a widely acknowledged fact, Zhu Weizheng goes on to say, that "the followers of Wang Yangming despised the tradition of rites and teachings handed down from the Song dynasty and thereby objectively created a cultural atmosphere in which Western learning as modern scholarship could gain a foothold in China."[19] The East–West encounter seemed off to a promising start, and it was more than serendipity that the Jesuits' light-handed approach enjoyed some success. Its ultimate religious motives and agenda notwithstanding, that approach can be viewed as an effort to acknowledge at least the existence of a very different cultural tradition and to make sense of it in terms of what was already known and familiar. Apparently, despite the huge gaps in languages, customs, and traditions, Ricci and his followers had no difficulty believing that cross-cultural understanding was both possible and valid. The Jesuits learned the Chinese language, and Ricci wrote his Christian doctrine, *Tianzhu shiyi* (*The True Meaning of the Lord of Heaven*), in Chinese. For them, translatability was not a problem, and linguistic and cultural differences were simply obstacles to be overcome in their effort at cross-cultural understanding – an act of intercultural hermeneutics.

As cultural mediators, the Jesuit missionaries not only brought European culture and knowledge to China, but also translated ancient Chinese texts into Latin and other European languages and introduced them to Europe. Through their letters, reports, and treatises, they made China and its social customs and institutions known in Europe, and their largely positive views exerted considerable influence on the way China and its culture were received in Europe at the time. Confucius became a well-known figure among the intellectual élites, and *chinoiserie* quickly became the rage in Europe, with porcelain, silk, wallpaper, and furniture gaining popularity in material culture. By the end of the seventeenth century, as Arthur Lovejoy remarks, "it had come to be widely accepted that the Chinese – by the light of nature alone – had surpassed Christian Europe both in the art of government and in ethics."[20] Enlightenment philosophers, notably Leibniz and Voltaire, deeply appreciated China and its social organization based on what they understood as secular reason. Leibniz's *Discours sur la théologie naturelle des Chinois* and Voltaire's *Essai sur les mœurs* are not simply textual evidence of the Chinese influence in Europe at the time, but part of the philosophical discourse on such essential concepts as reason, morality, secularism, and meritocracy, which these two philosophers related closely to China and the Chinese tradition.

This highly positive image of China created a problem within the Catholic Church. Other Catholic orders – particularly the Franciscans and the Dominicans – criticized the Jesuits for conceding too much to a pagan people and their culture, and they suggested the Chinese converts were practising idolatry in continuing to pay homage to their ancestors at home and to Confucius in temples dedicated to him. The Jesuits responded that the Chinese respect for ancestors and Confucius was an expression of moral sentiments, not religious rituals; the purists in the Church did not agree. They condemned these as heretic idolatry, and in 1704 and again in 1715, Pope Clement XI twice issued decrees that forbade Chinese rites and the use of Chinese terms for God on the grounds that the Chinese were pagans and that their language could not possibly express the spiritual truths of Christianity. In the Chinese rites controversy, the debate on Chinese terminology thus reached a philosophical level concerning the nature of language and thinking, with the purists insisting that the Chinese language and the Chinese "way of thinking" could not possibly transcend the materiality of things and form abstract concepts. Speaking of the Chinese, Ricci's successor and rival Niccolò Longobardi declared that "their secret philosophy is pure materialism" and that "the Chinese have never known any spiritual substance distinct from matter."[21] Similarly, the Franciscan Father Antonio de Caballero contended that the Chinese converts had no understanding at all of the real spiritual meaning of Christianity. "In the passages where they appear to speak of our God and his

Angels," wrote Caballero, "they are merely aping the Truth or, if you like, they resemble the peacock whose feet are a disgrace to its splendid rich plumage."[22] In this way, a rigid dichotomy was established in the Chinese rites controversy, one that insisted that China and Europe were fundamentally different in thinking, language, and culture. This dichotomous view of China and the West would have profound implications for later and modern times and for East–West cross-cultural understanding in our own.

3. Critical Hermeneutics and Cross-Cultural Studies

In his book discussing the failure of the Christian mission in China, Jacques Gernet almost takes the same view as Longobardi and other doctrinaire purists in seeing the Chinese as invariably and fundamentally different from Europeans not just in social customs and cultural traits, but also, as he puts it, in "mental categories and modes of thought."[23] Perhaps drawing on the sociologist Lucien Lévy-Bruhl's concept of "mentality," Gernet argues that the Chinese "mode of thought" differs fundamentally from the Greek or Western one, and he describes these fundamental differences as oppositions between transcendence and immanence, abstraction and concreteness, the spiritual and the material, and so on. Gernet views the Greek language and thinking as representative of the West and contrasts them in every way with their Chinese counterparts. "A comparison between the Chinese and Western situations confirms Benveniste's analysis," he writes. "The structure of Indo-European languages seems to have helped the Greek world – and thereafter the Christian one – to conceive the idea of realities that are transcendental and immutable as opposed to realities which are perceived by the senses and which are transitory."[24] Here transcendence and permanence belong to the Greek and Christian worlds, whereas the Chinese world is sensual, material, and transitory. Christian missionaries had difficulty getting their ideas across to the Chinese because – so Gernet writes in a controversial passage at the end of his book – the missionaries "found themselves in the presence of a different kind of humanity."[25] This last statement borders on denying the Chinese full humanity or attributing to them some kind of a diminished humanity. No one can deny that cultural differences exist between China and the West, but to set up such a strong and rigid dichotomy, while denying the cultural Other certain capacities (in this case, for transcendence, abstraction, spiritual understanding, and so on), comes dangerously close to an ethnocentrism, if not racism, and reflects a seriously biased Eurocentric misconception of a different, non-European culture.

Actually, it is not uncommon to find similar views about China and Chinese culture as the opposite to Greece or Europe and European culture. Currently perhaps the most persistent proponent of this dichotomy of China and Greece – or China and Europe and the West in general – is the French scholar François Jullien. In a large number of books and articles, Jullien has repeatedly made more or less the same argument: that China, as an ancient culture not in direct contact with Greece or Europe until modern times, can serve as a sort of magic mirror, in which the Westerner may find a clearer self-image by examining what he is *not*. Thus "the Western Sinologist can also be – quite legitimately – a discoverer of the West; and Sinological knowledge would then serve him as a new *organon*."[26] For Jullien, the purpose of studying China is to return to the Western self by way of a detour. In this process, one can find oneself through the experience of the "intercultural otherness [*l'altérité interculturelle*]," which makes the Western self clearly recognizable *vis-à-vis* its non-Western Other. In this peculiar attempt at *Bildung*, which in itself is perfectly reasonable, China becomes the most suitable symbol of difference, "a case study through which to contemplate Western thought from the outside."[27] The same idea and argument is expressed in the title of one of Jullien's books – *Penser d'un Dehors (la Chine)* or *Thinking from the Outside (China)*, which sums up pretty much all of his arguments about China in his various works. By constantly contrasting China as the outside and opposite of the European self, Jullien hopes to achieve a better self-understanding; expanding on Foucault's idea of non-Europe, he declares that "strictly speaking, *non-Europe* is China, and it cannot be anything else."[28] As Jean François Billeter points out, Jullien's work is "entirely based on the myth of the otherness of China."[29] Billeter refutes Jullien's distorting myth by discussing the issues of understanding China and of philosophy, and particularly by addressing the problem of transcendence and immanence. He traces the origin of Jullien's myth from more recent manifestations in Victor Segalen and Marcel Granet, back to Enlightenment philosophers like Leibniz and Voltaire, and from them to the Jesuit missionaries' first encounters with China in the late sixteenth and early seventeenth centuries. "The Jesuit fathers are the authors of this 'other' China," of which, says Billeter, "François Jullien has presented to us the latest reincarnation."[30] Indeed, Jullien follows most closely the Franciscan and Dominican purists as well as those few Jesuits who were opposed to Ricci, such as Longobardi. When we place Longobardi's comments on the Chinese language and thinking side by side with Jullien's, we see striking similarities.

Now what about the claims that Jullien has made about Greek and Chinese thinking and language? Are those dichotomies valid and sound, hermeneutically speaking? Can we measure them by "the things themselves" – that is, by testing them with real experience, historical knowledge, and textual evidence? Even in the eighteenth century, Voltaire realized that the doctrinaire purists in the Vatican were contradicting themselves in condemning the Chinese both for atheism and for idolatry, and he detected the root of the problem as the application of a European standard to judge non-European cultures. "We have slandered the Chinese just because their metaphysics is not ours," says Voltaire. "The great misunderstanding of Chinese rites comes from the fact that we have judged their customs by our own: for we would carry the prejudices of our contentious spirit to the very end of the world. A genuflection, which for them is but an ordinary act of reverence, we take it to be an act of adoration; we have taken a table for an altar: that's how we judge everything."[31] Voltaire's criticism of French or European arrogance is quite insightful, for that arrogance does indeed reflect an ethnocentrism that lurks behind the dichotomies and leads to fundamental misunderstanding. Jullien would have a list of concepts in two columns, one Greek and the other Chinese, with the two always directly opposed to each other. The Chinese are often said to lack a certain concept or notion that Jullien identifies as essential to the Greek and thus the European tradition. For example, he argues that Greek philosophers always tried to search for truth and that the Greek concept of truth was linked to their concept of being; whereas Chinese thinkers "did not conceive of the existential sense of being (the verb *to be*, in that sense, does not even exist in classical Chinese)." Therefore, says Jullien, in China there was "no concept of truth."[32] Again, the idea of "way" in the West leads to truth or a transcendental origin, whereas in China, he declares, "the way recommended by wisdom leads to nothing. No truth – revealed or discovered – constitutes its destination."[33] But to reduce different Greek views on truth to one related to being is a simplification, while to make a claim about the Chinese as without a concept of truth is astonishingly simplistic.

Let us take the question of truth as a case in point. We may say that the pre-Socratic philosopher Parmenides does relate things true to their existence when he says: "That which is there to be spoken and thought of must be. For it is possible for it to be, but not possible for nothing to be."[34] But the sophist Gorgias explicitly denies this proposition in his work entitled *On What Is Not*, in which he argues, first, that "nothing is: if [something] is, either what-is is or what-is-not [is], or both what-is and what-is-not are. But it is the case neither that what-is is, as he will show, nor that what-is-not is, as he will justify, nor that both what-is and what-is-not are, as he will teach this too. Therefore, it is not the case that anything is."[35] Then he goes on to argue that "even if something is, it is unknowable and inconceivable by humans," and, moreover, "even if it should be comprehended, it cannot be expressed to another."[36] As Robert Wardy comments, Gorgias's nihilistic argument "deliberately overturns Parmenides' denial that 'is not' is either sayable or thinkable." Wardy then asks a pertinent question, which we may borrow and put to Jullien: "Parmenides had argued that reality is single and changeless; when Gorgias maintains that reality is not, is he any less credible? If both thinkers marshal deductions to reach contradictory but equally incredible conclusions, what becomes of Parmenides' theme that conviction unfailingly accompanies truth?"[37] Obviously, we have here two Greek philosophical views on truth that are incompatible, and we cannot simply declare one to be *the* Greek view at the expense of the other. Add to this, there are yet other and different views held by Plato, Aristotle, and several other philosophers.

On the Chinese side, too, we have not one but several views about truth, knowledge, and communication. The intellectual scene more than 2,000 years ago, before the establishment of the first Chinese empire of Qin in 221 BC, was marked by lively debates and contentions among various philosophical schools, and it is impossible to single out one view as representative at the expense of other views. On the one hand, we find the Confucian philosopher Xunzi engaged in the "rectification of names," trying to make name and the thing named correspond to each other, saying that "that which man knows is called knowledge, and knowledge corresponding to things is called wisdom."[38] There we find a concept of truth as correspondence between the thing and the name with which one denotes reality. On the other hand, Taoist philosophers Laozi and Zhuangzi emphasize the futility of names and the uselessness of language, insisting that the profound concept of *tao* is impossible to know or express. Laozi begins his book on the concept of *tao* with the famous dictum that "the *tao* that can be spoken of is not the constant *tao;* the name that can be named is not the constant name."[39] Zhuangzi declares that "*tao* cannot be heard, what is heard is not it; *tao* cannot be seen, what is seen is not it; *tao* cannot be said, what is said is not it."[40] Yet, for Zhuangzi, the ineffability of *tao* does not mean that it does not exist, for it does, and it does everywhere, even in ants, in weeds, in broken pieces of pottery, in feces and urine.[41] As in ancient Greece, these are very different views and positions concerning the questions of truth, language, and knowledge, and it is impossible to single one out as *the* Chinese concept to be contrasted with its Greek counterpart.

Any philosophical and cultural tradition worth its name must have a great variety of different views, concepts, positions, and articulations, and it is only the most determined reductionist urge to find the "unique essence" of a tradition that would drastically simplify the richness and variety of realities in order to formulate a neat opposition between cultures and traditions. Unfortunately, such an urge seems rather strong and manifests itself from time to time, particularly in the West. In a fascinating study of European images of non-European people, Henri Baudet identifies a particular urge that "has reigned in the minds of [European] men," the urge to create imaginary images of the Other:

> Its domain is that of the imagination, of all sorts of images of non-Western people and worlds which have flourished in our culture – images derived not from observation, experience, and perceptible reality but from a psychological urge. That urge creates its own realities which are totally different from the political realities of the first category. But they are in no way subordinate in either strength or clarity since they have always possessed that absolute reality value so characteristic of the rule of the myth.[42]

Here perhaps is a clue to Jullien's constant emphasis on China's alterity, or what Billeter identifies as a "myth of the otherness of China." Billeter admits that "François Jullien has had a considerable influence, and therefore also a responsibility."[43] The popularity of Jullien's works, not just in France but elsewhere, offers evidence of the strength or appeal of such cultural myths; but at the same time, it highlights the need to demythologize, as well as the importance of critical hermeneutics in East–West cross-cultural studies. Adequate understanding does not naturally arise, but has to be gained through the painstaking effort at careful study, meticulous research, and tireless critique of misunderstandings and misinterpretations of every kind.

NOTES

1 E.D. Hirsch, Jr, *Validity in Interpretation* (New Haven: Yale University Press, 1967), 126.
2 Ibid., 38; original emphasis.
3 Hans-Georg Gadamer, *Truth and Method*, trans. Joel Weinsheimer and Donald G. Marshall, 2nd rev. ed. (New York: Crossroad, 1989), 297; original emphasis.
4 Hirsch, *Validity in Interpretation*, 255.
5 Ibid., 25.
6 Ibid., 124.
7 Gadamer, *Truth and Method*, 266–7.
8 Ibid., 95.
9 Ibid., 384.
10 Ibid., 384–5.
11 Ibid., 14.
12 Haun Saussy is perhaps the first to remind us of the historical connections between missionary work in China – particularly the so-called Chinese rites controversy in the seventeenth and the eighteenth centuries – and contemporary debates in Sinology or China studies. See Saussy, *The Problem of a Chinese Aesthetics* (Stanford: Stanford University Press, 1993), esp. 13–46.
13 John Larner, *Marco Polo and the Discovery of the World* (New Haven: Yale University Press, 1999), 85.
14 See, for example, Frances Wood, *Did Marco Polo Go to China?* (Boulder: Westview, 1996).
15 Matteo Ricci, *China in the Seventeenth Century: The Journals of Matthew Ricci: 1583–1610*, trans. Louis J. Gallagher (New York: Random House, 1953), 110, 111.
16 Ibid., 154.
17 Catherine Jami, "From Clavius to Pardies: The Geometry Transmitted to China by Jesuits (1607–1723)," in *Western Humanistic Culture Presented to China by Jesuit Missionaries (XVII–XVIII Centuries)*, ed. Federico Masini (Roma: Istituto Storico S.I., 2000), 195.
18 Zhu Weizheng, *Zouchu zhongshiji* [*Out of the Middle Ages*] (Shanghai: Shanghai renmin, 1987), 160.
19 Ibid., 162.
20 Arthur Lovejoy, *Essays in the History of Ideas* (Baltimore: Johns Hopkins University Press, 1848), 105.
21 Quoted in Jacques Gernet, *China and the Christian Impact: A Conflict of Cultures*, trans. Janet Lloyd (Cambridge: Cambridge University Press, 1985), 203.

22 Quoted in ibid., 33.
23 Ibid., 3.
24 Ibid., 244.
25 Ibid., 247.
26 François Jullien, *La valeur allusive: Des catégories originales de l'interprétation poétique dans la tradition chinoise (Contribution à une réflexion sur l'altérité interculturelle)* (Paris: École française d'Extrême-Orient, 1985), 8.
27 François Jullien, *Detour and Access: Strategies of Meaning in China and Greece*, trans. Sophie Hawkes (New York: Zone, 2000), 9.
28 François Jullien, with Thierry Marchaisse, *Penser d'un Dehors (la Chine): Entretiens d'Extrême-Occident* (Paris: Éditions du Seuil, 2000), 39.
29 Jean François Billeter, *Contre François Jullien* (Paris: Éditions Allia, 2000), 9.
30 Ibid., 14.
31 Voltaire, *Essai sur les Mœurs et l'Esprit des Nations* (Paris: Chez Treuttel et Würtz, 1835), 34–5.
32 Jullien, "Did Philosophers Have to Become Fixated on Truth?," trans. Janet Lloyd, *Critical Inquiry* 28, no. 4 (Summer 2002): 803–24 at 810.
33 Ibid., 820.
34 Patricia Curd, ed., *A Presocratic Reader: Selected Fragments and Testimonia*, trans. Richard D. McKirahan, Jr (Indianapolis: Hackett, 1996), 46.
35 Ibid., 99.
36 Ibid., 100 and 101.
37 Robert Wardy, "Rhetoric," in *The Greek Pursuit of Knowledge*, ed. Jacques Brunschwig and Geoffrey E.R. Lloyd, trans. under the direction of Catherine Porter (Cambridge, MA: Harvard University Press, 2003), 314–34 at 317.
38 Wang Xianqian (1842–1917), *Xunzi jijie* [*Xunzi with Collected Interpretations*], in *Zhuzi jicheng* [*Collection of Writings of the Masters*], 8 vols. (Beijing: Zhonghua, 1954), II:275.
39 Wang Bi (226–249), *Laozi zhu* [*Laozi with Annotations*], in *Zhuzi jicheng*, III:1.
40 Guo Qingfan (1844–95?), *Zhuangzi jishi* [*Variorum Edition of the Zhuangzi*], in *Zhuzi jicheng*, III:330.
41 Ibid., 326.
42 Henri Baudet, *Paradise on Earth: Some Thoughts on European Images of Non-European Man*, trans. Elizabeth Wentholt (Middletown: Wesleyan University Press, 1988), 6.
43 Billeter, *Contre François Jullien*, 7.

Chapter Eight

Universal Values or Cultural Relativity: A Pointless Question

HANS-GEORG MOELLER

I

"Orientalists" and comparative philosophers are often confronted with the question whether cultures or traditions are essentially distinct, or whether, at some basic level, all human beings are the same. Do "the Chinese think differently,"[1] or is rationality universal? The political and ideological issues here are obvious, which makes the question not only an academic one but also morally charged. Providing the "wrong" answer can threaten one's academic reputation and cause one's audience to withdraw its sympathy. So, the question can be considered dangerous – as well as, to a certain extent, academically pointless. Given all this, I intend to question the question as such by deconstructing the "ontological constructions" that it implies.

In the universalism–relativism debate in the humanities and social sciences in Germany, the (admittedly rather awkward) term *Selbstbehauptungsdiskurs* has been coined.[2] In English it can be translated as "self-assertion discourse." What it refers to are the efforts by non-Western intellectuals in colonial and post-colonial times to identify their respective cultures or traditions as substantially unique. Typically, these attempts have been responses to military, economic, political, and semantic–ideological expansion by Western imperial powers, which often claim that their own economic, political, and ideological concepts are universally valid. The conflict between these "self-assertion discourses" and universalisms has yet to be resolved; however, its focus has largely shifted from debates about "(East) Asian values" to those between Middle Eastern and Islamic self-assertions and Western universalisms.

I deliberately refer to both sides of this antagonism in the plural. Pluralism is self-evident with respect to self-assertion discourses since each such discourse tends to tend to highlight its uniqueness relative to others. With regard to universalisms, however, the plural sounds strange, given that by definition, the universal would seem to be singular. However, when we take a diachronic or synchronic perspective, a colourful multiplicity of universalisms becomes evident. In the nineteenth and early twentieth centuries, religious (more precisely, Christian) universalisms were *en vogue*, but even they were already split into various denominations. Christian universalisms are rather unpopular today, and Western politicians, in particular, take pains to appear religiously tolerant. Religious universalisms have been replaced by different and more secular ones, the most important of these being human rights and democracy. But again, there is a wide variety of "denominations" or schools of thought. Jürgen Habermas, for instance, advocates discourse ethics, and John Rawls fairness and justice.

The mere multiplicity of universalisms provides an argument against them: Which of the many is actually the right one? But something else speaks against them – namely, their style.[3] Universalisms often cloak themselves in formal, rational arguments, yet most of the time they rely quite heavily on normative demands and condemnations. They tend to present themselves as culturally and ideologically neutral and to accuse the self-assertion discourses of being partial, nationalistic, or intolerant. In this context, the term "fundamentalism" is often applied. Ironically, however, that word was coined by North American Christians as a positive term, which they applied to themselves. In other words, universalists originally applied this concept in reference to themselves. Which raises this question: Are the universalists perhaps just as fundamentalist as the cultural "self-assertionists"? Is it perhaps justified to speak of both Islamic fundamentalism and "human rights fundamentalism" – as Niklas Luhmann does?[4]

II

This leads me to my proper topic – namely, a Luhmannian deconstruction of the universalism–relativism debate. From the perspective of social systems theory, universalisms and relativisms are not that different at all, but rather appear as *two complementary kinds of semantic reactions to social changes in modernity*.

To explain this, I will first briefly describe how the concept of modernity can be defined in a Luhmannian way on the basis of three main criteria: (a) a shift toward functional differentiation, (b) the emergence of a world society, and (c) the emergence of the distinction inclusion/exclusion as a prominent social form of differentiation.

(a) The transition from stratified to functional differentiation that, according to Luhmann, occurred in Europe between the sixteenth and eighteenth centuries brought about the demise of classes or social strata as the main social divisions. In a stratified society, classes or strata are the primary form of social differentiation. This is not to say that no other differences matter, such as centre/periphery (Europe/Africa) or segmentary (Normans/Anglo-Saxons), but only that class distinctions, such as the difference between aristocrats and non-aristocrats, are structurally the most basic. What one is as a social being is largely determined by one's class and one's position within it, and only to a lesser degree by such characteristics as one's geographical location.

    In modernity, functional differentiation has replaced stratified differentiation as the most important structural feature in society. Autopoietic communication systems evolve: the legal system, the economy, politics, art, religion, science, the mass media, and so on all develop their respective codes, functions, and efficacies. In current social life, we communicate permanently within such systems. This very essay, when written or read, is communication within "science" (in the sense of the German term *Wissenschaft,* which includes not only the natural sciences but also the social sciences, the humanities, and so on). Perhaps a little earlier, I operated as a consumer in the economic system; perhaps in a little while, I will make a phone call to a relative within the intimate or personal communication system, after which I may watch the news and thus communicate in the mass media system.

(b) Functional systems are not geographically anchored. This is obvious with respect to the economy and the mass media, for instance. We sometimes have to change our money into a different currency when entering a foreign country, but when we do, economic communications continue to function in a similar way. We do not need to speak Japanese in order to buy a postcard in Japan. Different currencies do not mean different economies; rather, they enable specific transactions within a global economy. Similarly, the mass media spread the same information everywhere. We all know who the American president is, and we all know that Michael Jackson has died. In principle, we can assume that anyone who happens to be sitting next to us on an airplane shares this knowledge and can discuss it with us.

Even for the legal system and for politics, national boundaries are of secondary importance. The political code normally does not change when one crosses a political border. This does not mean there are no regional differences; obviously, the law and politics in the United States are not the same as the law and politics in Germany. Each communication in the legal system or in politics is as such unique. But there is, metaphorically speaking, a specific grammar (a continuously evolving one) that constitutes each respective system, so that one normally understands immediately and without any problem whether a communication is legal or political, no matter what country one is in. When I get legally punished for something in the United States that would have been legal in Germany, I still understand that I am operating in the context of the legal system. And I do not mistake the verdict of the judge for a political speech that tries to get my vote. Regional differences do not contradict global systemic identity. Indeed, the opposite is the case: an important feature of the global economy is that it enables people to speculate with different currencies, and the world system of science allows for communication about regionalism.

(c) The non-regional character of modern social functional systems is related to their tendency towards all-inclusion. Systems such as the economy, or politics, or education, or the mass media, address everyone. Everyone who has money can buy something. Everyone who possesses a TV set can switch it on. Politics includes not only the government but also the opposition. Election results include all votes equally, even those that were invalid.

Yet this indifference of communication systems towards the persons supposedly participating them is haunted by a paradox. In principle, everyone is "free" to communicate in the economy or in the mass media; but in practice, this not the case. Not everyone has money, and not everybody possesses a TV set. In reality, the "reckless" all-inclusiveness of the functional systems results in "reckless" exclusion. Mass inclusion and mass exclusion are simultaneous in global systems, which demonstrates that systems are not regionally rooted. Global capitalism does not equal increasing economical "democratization." The more persons are included, the more are excluded – and not only in Baghdad or Kinshasa, but also in Chicago or London.[5]

III

What systems theory finds problematic about universalisms is not so much their assertion that they are talking about something that is valid everywhere and all the time, but rather their *simplicity*. Universalisms assume that what is ultimately real is *one*. In fact, it seems, modern reality is much more complex than that – and thus also more contingent and paradoxical than the universalisms allow. There are three possible criticisms of the simplicities inherent in *uni*-versalist positions: (a) they insist on *uni*-versal principles (such as "human rights"); (b) they assume, too simplistically, that society is a *unit* (i.e., the sum of all individuals); and, in conjunction with this, (c) they tend to assume that *universal* all-inclusion is possible.

(a) Universalisms, especially those of Kantian and Habermasian varieties, tend to found the unity of a world society on a singular principle such as "universal reason" or "rationality." These can be combined with specific universal normative claims such as the claim that there are certain fundamental human rights. Rationality or human rights can then, to use a Luhmannian metaphor, be offered as a "monoculture."[6] Given the plurality of social systems, however, such a "monoculture" can hardly be viewed as a realistic basis for a functioning society. Modern social complexities cannot be reduced to a single foundational principle, because structural differences are inescapable. If human rights are supposed to play a meaningful role in society, then from a Luhmannian point of view, they will have this role within the legal system, and not in all other systems. To give a simple example: the sports system methodically "violates" gender equality by often barring women from competing in men's competitions. Sports could not function as "autopoietically" as it does if it was required to strictly apply the supposed universal human right of gender equality. From the perspective of systems theory, there is no hierarchical order of systems, nor is there a system capable of dominating all others and imposing its codes on them. In this way the theory of complex systems contradicts the idea of a transcendental order of society on the basis of a universal principle such as reason or rationality. Rationality is, according to

Luhmann, systems-rationality.[7] The rationality of the sports system is not the same as the rationality of the legal system.

(b) More recent universalisms still tend to assume that world society is constituted by all of the individual human beings who live in it. In this way, world society can be viewed as a sort of collective that ideally grants each member the same rights and responsibilities and thereby somehow reaches, or at least aspires to, a global consensus. Systems theory regards this as an illusion. First, it assumes that society consists of communication, rather than individuals. Second, it assumes that differentiation, not consensus, is what allows society to function. World society is thus not defined on the basis of what everyone can ultimately agree on, but on the basis of the incompatible "disagreements" that emerge within and between various social systems, such as politics, law, sports, and religion.

(c) Social systems theory finds it difficult to accept that all-inclusion is empirically possible. Indeed, social reality blatantly contradicts this assumption. Global systems generate not only more inclusion but also more *exclusion*. World society does not teleologically move towards more and more integration – it moves, rather, towards nothing in particular, constructing itself by means of ongoing differentiation. World society is a fact, but it is hard to see how universal rationality, universal human rights, and universal democracy are facts or may become facts. In other words, universalistic descriptions of a unified world society are much more an effect of the semantic heritage of the European Enlightenment than they are of actually existing and observable social realities.

IV

From the perspective of social systems theory, regionalist relativisms and self-assertion discourses are equally inadequate descriptions of world society. As was mentioned earlier, global functional differentiation does not imply the disappearance of regional peculiarities. One might even say the opposite – that world society has allowed regional identity constructions to flourish, as evidenced by a multitude of separatist and/or nationalist movements. These regional peculiarities, however, arise as phenomena within the mechanics of "globalization." Often they are simply aesthetic or nostalgic in character. It is somehow "nice" that there are still different coins in different countries, and to provide room for pleasant experiences of regionalism, Euro coins are minted in various "national" designs. Similarly, in the United States, each state is allowed to have its own regional 25-cent coin. It is undeniable that systemic reality looks different in different places. But at the same time, workers in China and Mexico and consumers in Europe and North America operate within the same economy.

The regionalisms of self-assertion discourses appear historically as a reaction to the globalization of functional systems. Yet they are unable to work functionally against globalization and can do so only rhetorically. When self-assertion discourses become visible in science or in the mass media – for instance, at academic conferences or on TV – they use the same codes, programs, and semantics as these global systems. Otherwise no one would notice them. *Regional self-assertion discourses can only be perceived within social systems that function globally.* They have to become a *discourse* before they can be *self-asserting*. Therefore they are, so to speak, *a priori* condemned to display a performative contradiction. They face a communicative dilemma: they intend to assert themselves, but in order to do so, they have to discursively switch sides and ally themselves with the forces against which they want to assert themselves. As soon as they succeed, they fall short of their goal.

Such a tragic role can be, as in novels or movies, attractive to external observers. So I cannot deny a certain personal sympathy for such discourses. In fact, their amalgamation into global discourses remains incomplete, and they function, so to speak, as the included excluded. As noted earlier, while universalisms tend to envision social development towards consensus, social systems theory does not. From its perspective, competition fuels business. Self-assertion discourses play an important role in global academic, mass media, and political communication. They contribute positions that allow for dissent and thus serve communicative autopoiesis. By their very existence, the proponents of Asian values or *sharia* law give global academics, journalists, and politicians something to talk about and thus an opportunity to differentiate themselves.

V

Seen in the light of such a system theoretical criticism, both universalisms and relativisms appear as semantic variations within globalization processes of autopoietic communication systems. Both can be viewed as semantic exercises that continue traditional discourses. Current universalisms that defend reason, rationality, human rights, or democracy, and that appear frequently within mass media, political, and academic communications, are perpetuating a discourse that emerged in early modern Europe as a reaction against the shift from stratified to functional differentiation. In the eighteenth and nineteenth centuries, more or less utopian visions of a future world society built upon rationalism, reasonable social contracts, and common goals emerged. In the United States in particular, images and symbols connected with such visions are still greatly esteemed, as are related rhetorics celebrating freedom and individuality. This is an example of how this semantic reservoir is still highly useful for constructing social self-descriptions. Even North American opponents of globalization use the same semantics and decry the lack of freedom and democracy in world society, which on principle should be democratic and free. The discourse of freedom and democracy, of reason and human rights, may thus well be considered as the one particular self-assertion discourse that has managed to triumph over all others, or, in the words of Kenichi Mishima, as the "inverted self-assertion discourse" of early modern Europe.[8]

On the side of the losers, non-Western self-assertion discourses – in particular those of Arab/Islamic provenance – seem to have become increasingly aware of the communicative dilemma they are in and to be shifting towards different strategies for opposing universalisms. Some of these so-called fundamentalists have become terrorists. Older self-assertion discourses communicated militantly at times but often lacked the means to indeed *act* militarily. They were often merely friendly and enjoyable, but not highly relevant as debating partners for the universalists.[9] Perhaps it is insight into their tragic fate that has turned some self-asserters into suicide bombers. If one necessarily destroys oneself communicatively when asserting oneself against global functionalism, why should one not destroy oneself physically and thereby at least destroy some of one's opponents as well?

The most radicalized transformation of a self-assertion discourse, along with its internal paradoxes, is the terrorist act. The most spectacular terrorist act ever was undoubtedly the attack of 9/11. This monumental act of self-destructive self-assertion has sent shockwaves through the global functional systems of the economy, the law, politics, and the mass media, but other systems, such as religion and education, have been affected as well. Precisely those shocks that the terror initiated fed back into it. Terror cannot escape the exclusive inclusion into global society any more than its peaceful counterpart. Demonstrations of the absolute will to exclusion are systemically met with inclusion – indeed, that is the only way they *can* be met. By irritating global systems, terror becomes systemically utilizable. The mass media feed on terror as a major source for information, and the political system can use it for its own autopoiesis as much as the military or the economy. In this way, terrorism shares the fate of the self-assertion discourses. Like them, it cannot be perceived outside of the global communication systems, and thus it cannot escape the fate of contributing to the perpetuation and proliferation of the systemic functioning against which it intended to assert itself.

NOTES

1 This alludes to the title of a programmatic essay by Rolf Trauzetel: "Denken die Chinesen anders?" *Saeculum* 41, no. 2 (1990): 79–99.

2 See Iwo Amelung et al., eds., *Selbstbehauptungsdiskurse in Asien: China–Japan–Korea* (Munich: Iudicium, 2003).

3 See Kenichi Mishima, "Menschenrechte und kulturelles Selbstverständnis," in Gregor Paul et al., eds., *Humanität, Interkulturalität und Menschenrecht* (Frankfurt am Main: Peter Lang, 2001), 50–81.

4 Niklas Luhmann, *Die Gesellschaft der Gesellschaft* (Frankfurt am Main: Suhrkamp, 1997), 1022.

5 Luhmann writes: "To the surprise of the well-meaning it has to be ascertained that exclusion still exists, and it exists on a massive scale and in such forms of misery that are beyond description. Anybody who dares a visit to the *favelas* of South American cities and escapes alive can talk about this. But even a visit to the settlements that were left behind after the closing of the coal mines in Wales can assure one of it. To this effect, no empirical research is needed. Who trusts his eyes can see it, and can see it so impressively that all explanations at hand will fail." Luhmann, "Beyond Barbarism," in Hans-Georg Moeller, *Luhmann Explained: From Souls to Systems* (Chicago: Open Court, 2006), 269.

6 Moeller, *Luhmann Explained*, 138.

7 See in particular section 4 of Luhmann's essay "European Rationality" in Luhmann, *Observations on Modernity* (Stanford: Stanford University Press, 1998), 22–43.

8 See Mishima, "Menschenrechte."

9 See Michael Lackner, "Philosophie, Theologie oder Kulturwissenschaft? Legitimationen des Modernen Neokonfuzianismus," in Amelung, *Selbstbehauptungsdiskurse*, 275–90.

Chapter Nine

Reconciling the Tension between Similarity and Difference in Critical Hermeneutics

DAVID B. WONG

Practising critical hermeneutics throws us into the tension between two requirements: first, to construe others as being like us; and second, to open ourselves to ways they may differ fundamentally from us and pose challenges to our cherished truths. In this essay I analyse these tensions and propose a way to reconcile them. I will argue that the embrace of difference is necessary if we are to interpret others as being like us. To plausibly interpret others as being like us, we need sufficient diversity within the "us." Furthermore, I will argue that whom we decide to include in the "us" depends on relations of power. Throughout this argument, I will draw from the relationship between China and the West. I will refer to what it takes for "us" in the West to understand some central features of Confucian ethics. I will also refer to efforts by contemporary Chinese thinkers to "translate" the concept of rights from the West.

1. Why Others Must Be Like Us

Making others intelligible to us requires that we interpret them as being like us and that we assume they are navigating the same world as us. This is not to assume that they have the same beliefs about the world as we do, but it *is* to say that whatever beliefs they have about the world, we must be able to see those beliefs as arising from their interaction with the same world that has given rise to our own. For example, however they conceive the stone in their path that they trip over (perhaps they conceive it as a bit of condensed energy-stuff or *qi*, as in traditional Chinese ontology), I must assume it is a stone that I too could trip over if I travelled to where they live.

Moreover, we must interpret these others as beings who hold beliefs, which they combine with desires and values to form intentions and thereby navigate the world. For us to attribute all of this to them, we must draw from our own experience of what it is to believe, to want, to strive, and to measure what we have, want, and strive for against conceptions of worth. We further our understanding of others when we are able to draw analogies between the patterns of behaviour and speech we find them displaying and the patterns we ourselves display in similar circumstances. Then, by analogy, we impute to these others certain beliefs, values, and intentions, as well as relations between these things that would in our own case explain the patterns of behaviour and speech that are observed in us. This is one way in which we must make others resemble us as we try to make them intelligible.

A model of human rationality operates in combination with analogies when we use those analogies to explain others and make them intelligible to us. We understand ourselves to be creatures striving to make sense of the world and to act in ways that make sense to ourselves. We reflect on the adequacy of the beliefs, desires, and values by which we navigate through the world, and we attempt to correct our course when we find those things to be inadequate. It is part of our understanding of what it is to be human that we strive to make sense in these ways. Of course, to *strive* to make sense is not to *succeed*. We need to develop a keen appreciation of how often and how deeply we fail to make sense in spite of our efforts. When we fail to make sense, it is in characteristically human ways – for example, by ignoring evidence that conflicts with our currently held beliefs and by focusing on other evidence that confirms those beliefs. We tend to be disproportionately influenced in our decision making by dramatic though statistically infrequent risks (hearing of a plane crash, we may decide to drive to our destination, thereby multiplying our risk of having a fatal accident). We apply this model of the ways human beings try to make sense of their world and of their actions, in conjunction with analogies, to make others intelligible to us. Consider this case: we observe another person trip over a stone, look down, pick up the stone, study it carefully, and put it in his pocket. By analogy to similar things we have done and from our model of human rationality, we might infer from this pattern of behaviour that he has thought of a use for this stone.

The reasoning I have laid out here forms the basis of Donald Davidson's philosophy of radical interpretation, the intent of which is to elucidate the preconditions for understanding the speaker of a language that is completely unknown to the interpreter. Davidson summarized his philosophy of radical interpretation as the "principle of charity." In his earliest writings, he tended to state the principle as requiring that we maximize agreement in belief, desire, value, and intention. We should make them "right, as far we can tell, as often as possible."[1] What is possible is constrained by "considerations of simplicity, hunches about the effects of social conditioning, and of course our common-sense, or scientific, knowledge of explicable error."[2]

Later on, Davidson wrote that a clearer expression of what he meant is that agreement in beliefs should be "optimized."[3] Rather than the "most" agreement, we need the "right sort" of agreement – one that enables understanding of others. Charity, Davidson explained, may require us to attribute intelligible error. As we form our interpretations of others, we might find that it makes more sense to attribute errors to them, given our emerging conception of how they are interacting with the objects of their beliefs. But there is a limit to such attribution. To attribute massive error to them would be to undermine a crucial assumption of interpretation: that they are forming beliefs about the world we inhabit as well. For us to attribute to the ancients the belief that the earth is flat, but virtually none of the other beliefs we have about the earth, would be to undermine the assumption that they have beliefs at all about the earth.[4]

Still later, Davidson stated the requirements of charity in an even more modest fashion: we should interpret others in such a way that their thought possesses a "modicum" of logical consistency and a "degree of true belief" about the world.[5] Davidson also introduced the productive model of triangulation:

> Each of two people is reacting differentially to sensory stimuli streaming from a certain direction. If we project the incoming lines outward, their intersection is the common cause. If the two people now note each others' reactions (in the case of language, verbal reactions), each can correlate these observed reactions with his or her stimuli from the world. The common cause can now determine the contents of an utterance and a thought. The triangle which gives content to thought and speech is complete. But it takes two to triangulate. Two, or, of course, more.[6]

The model of triangulation points to a greater complexity of interpretation than is suggested by the earlier formulation of maximizing agreement with the other. The interpreter must take into account the differing locations occupied by the other and herself with respect to potentially common objects or events. The differing locations of the two people could be the source of differing beliefs about the third corner of the triangle. "Locations" here should be taken as largely metaphorical. Consider again the Chinese example of belief about physical objects as condensed energy-stuff. Beliefs about common objects and events can be parts of networks of beliefs rooted in traditions of thought about the world. The interpreter may indeed share with the other the stone as the third corner of the triangle, and this satisfies the precondition of understanding that she be able to see the other as inhabiting the same world she does. Furthermore, as she sees the other acting on the stone he had earlier picked up and carried with him – perhaps sliding a thin, pointed object across its surface in repeated motions that she might herself use to sharpen a knife – she has a basis for imputing human rationality to the other. None of this, however, prevents her from understanding the other as having very different beliefs about what *kind* of thing a stone is and its relation to water and air (which are, perhaps, successively thinner and rarefied versions of the same energy-stuff, not an inanimate object, but – like the famous mountains of Chinese landscape painting – something dynamic and changing, although perhaps moving and changing a bit more slowly than water, air, and animals, birds, and insects).

Furthermore, the model of triangulation allows the two people to interact with each other with respect to common objects and events (and as Davidson notes, more than two can triangulate). Out of many such triangulations over time, we can imagine two people coming to understand each other as navigating through a common world, and as possessing human rationality yet also possessing significantly different beliefs about the world; indeed, they may understand that those different beliefs are rooted in long-standing traditions of substantial complexity and continual adaptation to changing circumstances. In his earlier characterizations of the sort of difference that charity might allow, Davidson wrote of explicable error, which is produced by the experience of common objects and events under conditions different from the conditions in which the interpreter experiences them. But if the belief in material objects as condensations of *qi* is an error (albeit in some respects, it may actually be closer to the truth than a Newtonian conception of matter), it is very far from an obvious error.

Davidson is well known for applying his principle of charity as an argument against the possibility of alternative conceptual schemes. There can be no such schemes that are radically different from our own.[7] Different points of view make sense only if there is a common system of coordinates on which to plot them, but the existence of a common system negates claims to dramatic incomparability. The problem with Davidson's argument is that it identifies alternative conceptual schemes with ones that can have no common points of contact with our own. Given this identification, it would make sense to say we cannot understand any such reputed scheme to be a scheme at all – that is, as having any intelligible content. However, those who really do believe in the possibility of alternative conceptual schemes usually point to schemes that have enough overlap with our own that we know they contain some very different claims about a *common* world. Recognition of such alternative schemes could emerge from just the sort of triangulation that Davidson describes in his later writings. After all, an alternative scheme can challenge our own only by shaking our confidence in the singular correctness of our understanding of the world, and such a scheme can do so only by presenting itself as an alternative understanding of that *same* world. Conceptual schemes must have a subject in common in order to be alternatives to each other. Perhaps such considerations are why, in Davidson's later writings, he speaks much more mutedly about charity, whose requirements take a much more modest form that implicitly allows for significant difference.

Even in his later writings, Davidson's philosophy of interpretation is too heavily influenced by the earlier framework of one person who is taking up a neutral observer's perspective and interpreting the other from within a metaphorical glass booth. From within that booth, the interpreter must rely on her own beliefs to reveal what is true and on her own values to reveal what is of value. There is no alternative to such an assumption as long as she cannot interact with the other and is confined to the observer's booth. This is why, even in his later formulations of charity, Davidson allows that we need only attribute a "degree of true belief" to the other person we interpret, as if the only alternative to making others largely resemble us is to attribute a good dose of error to them.

Error is always a possibility, and in Davidson's interpretive philosophy, the reason it must always fall on the side of the other is the interpreter's isolation within the glass booth. If she ventures outside and engages in serious interaction with the other person, if she allows herself to *be* interpreted, for her questions to be *answered* by the other and for the other to question *her*, she must allow for her beliefs, wants, and values to be challenged, and for the possibility that her confidence in their correctness and singular humanness will be shaken. She is no longer entitled to the assumption that her own beliefs, desires, and values constitute the norm by which truth and humanity are to be measured.

2. Why Others Need Not Be So Much like Us

We are now on the other horn of the dilemma. To understand others, we must find points of contact with them: a common world, and some common responses to that world that indicate human rationality at work in the other. But at the same time, we must not treat the other as a purely passive object of interpretation. The other must be allowed to talk back, in the interest of correcting and deepening our understanding not only of the other but also of the world and of the range of possibilities for being human.

This takes us beyond Davidson towards genuine conversation and the possibility of fusing horizons as these appear in Hans-Georg Gadamer's hermeneutics. Gadamer observes that a genuine conversation "is never the one that we wanted to conduct," because the more genuine it is, "the less its conduct lies within the will of either partner"[8] (385). A conversation, Gadamer writes, is a process of coming to an understanding such that "each person opens himself to the other, truly accepts his point of view as valid and transposes himself into the other to such an extent that he understands not the particular individual but what he says. What is to be grasped is the substantive rightness of his opinion, so that he can be at one with each other on the subject."[9] This is not a Davidsonian charitable assimilation of the other's beliefs, desires, and values so that we make them identical with our own "as far as possible" or "as often as possible." Rather, it is a way of seeing how the other could be right about a common subject matter in such a manner that one's original perspectives might be transformed in unpredictable ways.

This is what Gadamer means, I take it, when he suggests that understanding between two persons involves a "fusion" of their "horizons," where a horizon is a "range of vision that includes everything that can be seen from a particular vantage point" and within which one can see the relative significance of everything.[10] As Gadamer stresses, horizons are not fixed; they move as the people who possess them move. When two people engage in genuine understanding of each other, they open themselves to finding a common subject that makes further engagement possible and also to the challenges that each poses to the other's horizon when each opens her- or him-self to the "substantive rightness" of the other's opinion. To understand the other's horizon is to a significant degree to incorporate it into an expanded horizon of one's own: it is to fuse horizons with the other.

3. Interpretation of Confucianism through Analogy and the Model of Human Rationality

To illustrate the points made so far, and to suggest how difference and sameness are interwoven in interpretation, I will discuss how analogy and the attribution of human rationality apply in the interpretation of Chinese thought and culture from an American perspective. To make others intelligible by likening them to us often involves accepting that the analogies we use are extended and approximate, consistent with accepting significant differences between them and us. This is often good enough, and investigating why this is good enough leads to the question of who "we" are when we interpret others as having beliefs, desires, and values similar to ours. I argue that the "we" and the "ours" harbour significant diversity and that any plausible interpretive approach must presuppose a diversity in beliefs and desires across human culture, in particular with regard to the range of values that are central to particular cultures.

Let me begin by identifying three significant and distinct features of the Confucian ethic as it is represented in classical works of Chinese philosophy, primarily the *Analects*.[11] We understand these features by noting their similarity to themes that are familiar in our own culture. But as with all analogies, the similarities coexist with significant differences. Regarding all three cases, I will claim that we have little reluctance to accept the differences.

The first feature is the centrality of *xiao*, usually translated as "filial piety." It is not difficult to find analogies to this within American society about honouring one's mother and father. That said, the Confucian tradition is unusually strict regarding one's duties to parents. The *Analects* 2.7 identifies the requirements of *xiao* as going beyond providing parents with material support when they are elderly, to include *jing*. *Jing* originally applied to the attitude one should have when sacrificing to ancestors, an attitude of devotion to carrying out great responsibilities to one's ancestral spirits. The scope of duties to parents includes taking care of what they alone could have given one – one's body. Cengzi, one of Confucius's students, is portrayed in 8.3 of the *Analects* as gravely ill and near death. He bids his students to look at his hands and feet, and quotes lines from the *Book of Poetry* to convey the idea that all his life he has been keeping his body intact as part of his duty to his parents. It is only now, near death, he says, that he can be sure that he has fulfilled this duty to parents. This idea, that one must keep one's body intact as a duty of gratitude to one's parents, has remained central in Chinese culture.

Why is *xiao* so central a virtue in the Confucian ethic? One reason seems to be that it is so central to the development of ethical character. In *Analects* 1.2, one of Confucius's most prominent students, Youzi, says that being good as a son and obedient to one's elder brothers is the root of character, the basis of respect for authority outside the family. One learns respect for others first by learning it for those within the family. A related reason is that the family is the model for larger social groupings, including the entire country. Just as members of a family are bound together by a common good, so are members of a country. To learn how to be a member of a family is to start to learn how to be a member of a village, a clan, and a country. Still another reason for the centrality given to filial piety is the requirement to express gratitude to those who have given one life and nurture. In *Analects* 17.21, Zaiwo objects to the traditional length of mourning for one's deceased parents. He says that one year is enough to disrupt one's normal life in those ways, and that the traditional period of three years is too long. Confucius comments that all children are completely dependent on their parents for the first three years of life. Did not Zaiwo receive three years worth of love from his parents?

The virtue of *xiao* is visible in American culture, as are its rationales. We can certainly recognize the need for gratitude, and for some sort of reciprocation for great gifts received, and the notion that family relationships are pivotal to the development of both social cohesion and individual character. But this downplays the centrality of filial piety and the stringency of its duties in Confucianism and in the broader traditional culture. While we recognize such rationales for filial piety, we generally do not accord it nearly as prominent a place in the catalogue of moral virtues, nor do we conceive its duties as so stringent. And the theme that one owes one's body to one's parents and that it is deep ingratitude not to take care of such a great gift is something that can be understood from an American perspective but is not generally accepted. We have come to accept such differences as part of the normal range of human possibilities. And indeed, taking the Confucian perspective, an American might come to have the strange feeling that that perspective makes at least as much sense as her own. A kind of fusion of horizons has taken place.

A second feature of Confucian ethics is that it emphasizes harmonious relationships as a central part of the ethical life. Note that in 1.2, the crucial dimension of moral development that begins in the family is respect for authority. The strong Chinese preference for harmony emerges in 2.6, where the Master says to give parents no cause for anxiety except for illness. Consider 4.18, where Confucius considers occasions on which one's own opinions as to what is right or best can conflict with one's parents' wishes. One should remonstrate with one's parents gently, he says. As 4.18 indicates, the value placed on harmony does not require silence in the face of real disagreement with one's superiors. Indeed, the Confucian tradition celebrates the scholar-intellectual who says what he thinks about the ruler's methods and ends, often to the ruler's face. However, the ends served by such moral courage include the end of harmony. Rulers who fail to govern for the good of the community, the state, and the nation must be called to account precisely for the good of all.

Someone must have the authority to settle conflicts, if only in the sense of deciding whose view is to prevail in the present instance. Human beings have yet to invent a society that does not designate such an authority and inculcate some degree of respect for it. The reasons for preferring harmony are quite self-evident, but here again, those reasons downplay the strong preference for harmony manifested in Chinese culture. For example, informal negotiation involving interaction and reconciliation between the contending parties is still the traditional way of resolving business disputes in China; informal mediation committees operate to resolve disputes at the grassroots rural village and urban neighbourhood levels; and Chinese courts encourage mediation between contending parties even after litigation proceedings have begun.

That Chinese culture so strongly prefers harmony does not seem to threaten its intelligibility to those on the outside. Some preference for harmony exists on the American side of the comparison. The *American* side, after all, encompasses a range of subcultures that show a strong preference for harmony. These subcultures include, of course, Chinese American and other Asian American subcultures, as well as Latino and Mexican American subcultures. Moreover, the various

European-descended subcultures of American society have in the past demonstrated a stronger preference for family harmony and cooperation within various levels of community than they do nowadays, when values of individual autonomy and independence have risen to pre-eminence. In part, this internal diversity is what helps make Confucian values intelligible as a path we ourselves could take and in some cases have taken.

Consider another significant feature of Confucian ethics: its inclusion of an aesthetic dimension in its conception of a good and worthwhile life. In Confucian ethics, right action is fitting action. Such action expresses appropriate care and respect for others in a manner that reflects the nature of one's social relationship to them and to other, more particular features of their situation and one's own. There are often conventional forms for expressing these ethical attitudes, ritual forms called the *li*. Among the most important rituals are sacrifice to honour ancestors and the burial of and mourning of deceased parents. Another example of ritual, this one discussed by the Confucian philosopher Mencius (the Latinized form of Mengzi or Master Meng), is a village drinking ceremony in which all drink from a common wine cup and in which the eldest villagers are served first.[12] To fashion oneself into a better person is to become practised in the performance of *li* such that *li* become second nature and express appropriate attitudes through graceful, effortless, and spontaneous actions. The rightness of actions in these contexts encompasses their aesthetic qualities.

In explaining the Confucian view, Antonio Cua draws analogies to the perception of qualities in works of art. He likens the grace or joy that is evident in accomplished ritual activity to the grace of a curve in a painting or the joy in a piece of music.[13] David Hall and Roger Ames observe that the Confucian notion of the "right" action has much in common with the artist's choice of the "right" brush or the "right" colour in the execution of a painting. For the Confucian, doing the right thing means doing one's duty for the right reason, with the right feeling, and with grace and elegance that is an aesthetic end in itself but also bespeaks the ease and contentment of one who has attained the virtues and realized one's humanity.[14]

A close analogy to what the Confucians have in mind in terms of the beauty of ritual practice is the waltz. There is a prescribed form for that dance: one must move the body in certain patterns. But within the waltz form, there is a great deal of space for personal expression and style and for the expression of feeling. Complete mastery of a form allows one to adjust the details of what one does to the particularities of the situation, and to the particular identities of the other participants, and to focus on the expression of one's feelings. This analogy and the others mentioned help make intelligible the aesthetic dimension of Confucian ethics; they also illustrate how analogy can assist in this. They take what is familiar to us in one context (in this case, painting or music or dance) and point to its occurrence in a different context. Analogies illuminate how we can conceive of the familiar taking place in a different context.

There is a connection in Confucian ethics between the importance of ritual and the importance of harmony. Sacrifice to ancestors and the burial of parents train and focus attitudes of reverence, gratitude, and grief. They also foster a common bond between the living participants, a sense of community that is rooted in the past and that stretches into the future.

The role of ritual in fostering harmony is something that Americans can understand by analogy to funeral and memorial services for those who have contributed greatly to their families and communities. In the memorial service for Senator Edward Kennedy, who died in 2009, members of the opposing Republican Party spoke of their Democratic colleague with great warmth and a sense of deep loss.[15] Kennedy was one of the few figures in the Senate who was able to take very clear and unambiguous stands on the left side of the American political spectrum yet was able to work with colleagues far to the right on that spectrum. Such rituals, and their use in affirming the value of harmony even in the context of bitter partisanship, serve as resources for Americans who seek to understand the place of harmony in Confucian ethics and the role of ritual in fostering it.

We have, I suggest, excellent analogical bases for understanding these central features of Confucian ethics. We can understand Confucians without making them exactly the same as us, and we do not need to see them as being in error in order to see them as different. Some of us may make that further judgment, but others of us may see a challenge to our own way of life. Mario Cuomo, then Governor of New York, gave the keynote address at the Democratic National Convention in 1984.[16] He criticized then President Ronald Reagan for characterizing the country as a "shining city on a hill" without acknowledging parts of that city that were in despair. Cuomo invoked the image of a family making its way along the wagon trail through the American frontier when he appealed for the old and the young and the weak not to be left behind on the side of trail, but for the whole family to make it all the way. The image of the country as family has faded in importance since then, yet it remains part of the American political tradition. Indeed, some of us may lament how much that image has faded, with the result that many of the old, the young, and the weak have been left behind.

Daniel A. Bell has argued that rituals in East Asian societies serve the function of acknowledging differences between the vulnerable and the powerful and affirming the responsibilities of the latter to the former. One example Bell gives of the protective effects of ritual is teacher–student social rituals. In such rituals in China and other East Asian countries, students express deference to their teachers through, for example, serving them drinks first and not drinking until their teachers have taken a drink. The benefit for the students in such ritual is that teachers are more likely to recognize that their duties to students include concern for their emotional and moral well-being, having interacted in that social context.

Another example that Bell gives of the protective effects of ritual is the ritual governing meals, where communal dishes are placed in the centre of the table from which everyone takes portions. The healthy adults in their prime defer to the young and the old when it comes to who takes portions first and who finishes up. This is significant in that in times of famine it is the very young and the old who are the most vulnerable. Adults in their prime, who have been trained to restrain their appetites out of respect and concern for others, might be better able to share in times of emergency. A third example Bell gives is the boss–worker relationship. In Japan, bosses commonly eat with workers in the company canteen, sing company songs with them, and go on group vacations with them. This fosters a sense of loyalty in the workers, but that loyalty goes the other way too, which may partly explain, Bell suggests, the practice of lifetime employment in Japanese companies.

There is another argument Bell makes for hierarchical social distinctions of the sort Confucians advocated. The premise of this argument is that people are likely to try to distinguish themselves from others in some way, if not through the set of distinctions embodied in Xunzian rituals. Americans think of their society as socially egalitarian. But Bell suggests that the impulse for distinguishing oneself comes out in the pursuit of wealth and conspicuous consumption.[17] Becoming rich is the American way of achieving distinction. And Bell wonders whether this doesn't have something to do with the high degree of inequality that exists in the United States (economist Emmanuel Saez calculates that in 2007 the top decile of American wage earners pulled in 49.7

percent of total wages, a level higher than any other year since 1917).[18] In Asian societies, which place more importance on the kind of social status that is not linked to wealth, there is significantly less income and wealth inequality. (Didier Jacobs argues that lower income inequality in the Asian countries as compared to the United Kingdom is due not to public policy redistribution of income but rather to inter-household transfers within multi-generational families, such as contributions of younger working adults to their aging parents.)[19]

Interpreting others so that we see something of us in them, therefore, leaves room for ways in which they are significantly different from us, not just by being in error, but also by challenging the adequacy of our own ways of life. It must be stressed that the challenge does not come purely from the way these others are different, but also from the ways they are both similar and different. We can understand very well the value of not leaving behind the old, the young, and the weak, and also the human rationality of using ritual to reinforce a sense of responsibility to others. That is why we can be challenged by the differences we come to understand.

4. Finding Difference within Sameness, but in the Context of Power

So far, I have been assuming that the relevant reference point for understanding Confucianism is the contemporary American perspective and that this perspective is more or less unified. It is not, of course. In reality, we treat such perspectives as unified only for the sake of certain comparisons, for example, in the context of striving to understand a presumably distant culture that is more difficult to comprehend. The "us" in such a comparison is actually diverse, and as shown earlier, such diversity provides some of the analogies we use to make sense of "them." This raises the question of how a diverse group became "us" in the first place.

If we are limited to beginning from our individual selves as models for understanding others, it seems quite unlikely that we can acquire the range of beliefs, desires, and values we take for granted even within relatively small circles. I accept that some people are attracted to holding power and exercising it over others, even though my own psychology does not bear much resemblance to theirs in this respect. I accept that some of my students believe in the libertarianism of Ayn Rand, even though there is an inevitable point where I fail to follow their thought processes when they explain them to me. Yet I accept that they and I occupy points within the range of the fully human, the normal and acceptable; and that insofar as I act in ways they perceive to adversely affect them, I have reason to explain myself to them in Gadamerian conversation. And if I find through analogy that others resemble them in relevant ways, I bear a similar responsibility to those others.

I suggest that we comprehend significant diversity because the very concepts we use to interpret both ourselves and others *embody* diversity. Human beings show a variety of psychological drives and temperaments, and this variety can prove useful to the group. The more differentiated social roles become, the more useful it is to have different kinds of people who are suited for different roles through their distinctive abilities, preferences, and styles of social interaction. Our conceptions of the normal and acceptably human may be deeply influenced by the pragmatic need to include within the scope of the normal and acceptable the variety of people who can make social cooperation flourish.

Another way to make this point is that to classify another as fully human, within the range of the acceptable and normal, is to lay the groundwork for cooperation with her. This can be a powerful force for making the concept of "we" and "us" significantly diverse. The other, darker side of the coin is that when we perceive less need for the cooperation of others, we are not as motivated to count them as one of us, or as similar enough to us. In such cases, we may brutalize them, exploit them, or simply ignore them, and our justification may be that they are less than fully human. We are more likely to include within the circle of the fully human those whom we need, and this brings us to the Foucauldian point that relations of power are not simply repressive but also productive. Those who are needed can enter the circle of the fully human; those who are not needed are vulnerable to selection and exclusion. Knowledge of who counts as fully human, or what we count as such knowledge, is shaped by whom we need to count as fully human.

It is sometimes possible to criticize the way we exclude others from the circle of the fully human by pointing out inconsistencies: we exclude this group because it is different in way X, yet we include some other group that is also different in way X. We humans can be quite ingenious when it comes to finding specific ways to differentiate between groups we want to include and groups we want to exclude. This perverse ingenuity may have been what Freud was getting at when he referred to the human capacity to engage in the "narcissism of minor differences."[20] Thus even if the desire for consistency were a powerful motive for changing belief and behaviour – which it often isn't – it is not clear that consistency alone will help us draw the correct lines around the fully human, the normal and the acceptable. In the end, there may be no way to avoid recognizing that how we draw those lines depends on whom we may happen to need at a given time.

In this light, it is worth examining the history of the way the Chinese understood and incorporated the concept of rights from the West. In the nineteenth century, the British East India Company conducted a very profitable opium trade with China. Alarmed by the number of drug addicts created by the availability of opium, the Chinese imperial government outlawed opium trafficking, but British and other (including American) traders bribed local Chinese officials in order to keep the trade flowing. Stephen Angle describes the efforts of the Imperial Commissioner of Canton, Lin Zexu, to halt the opium trade.[21] Wanting to justify his actions to England and other Western nations, Lin studied with the help of a missionary a textbook on international law, in which it was written that every state had a right to prohibit the entry of foreign merchandise. The missionary who helped Lin understand the text used a Chinese word to translate "right." Lin's efforts were to no avail: the British waged war against China and imposed on her the opium trade as well as other forms of free trade that the East India Company greatly desired.

Other contexts in which the concept of rights drew the attention of the Chinese were similar. Their original goal was to express their right to regulate the actions of foreigners on Chinese soil. The word *quanli* was coined to talk about the rights of nations, with "*quan*" connoting power in a normative sense (the power a nation ought to have) and "*li*" connoting benefit or profit. The Chinese concept of rights arose, then, in a context of power. Western nations had become so powerful that they had to be addressed on their own terms. Eventually, rights in Chinese thought were attributed not only to nation-states but also to individuals.

But in the process, the concept the Chinese took from the West underwent a transmutation. A multitude of concepts of rights were articulated by Chinese thinkers, and these tended to show influences from the West, from Chinese trends in contemporary thought, and from long-standing traditions such as Confucianism. Ideas in China about the legitimacy of individual desires, and about the need for and desirability of self-assertion, fed into evolving thought about individual rights. But so did a number of other ideas: that individuals needed to flourish in order for society to flourish; that individuals depended for their flourishing on society; that individual and social interests could be made compatible (i.e., the legitimate interests of individuals do not necessarily conflict with those of society); and that rights are not intrinsically valuable but are means to the development of personality and the advancement of the nation.

More recently, Xia Yong has expressed views that reflect engagement with the West but also a rootedness in the Confucian tradition. The value of harmony, he has written, is properly interpreted as a balance between separation and connection. He believes that the West has overdeveloped separation in the form of competition and conflict, whereas China has erred in the direction of too much connection. When there is too much connection, harmony is confused with unity.[22] To illustrate the kind of harmony that is different from unity and compatible with the recognition and acceptance of a degree of separation, Angle uses an analogy that draws from an increasingly familiar scenario of contemporary Western life. He asks us to imagine a married couple, each partner with a career.[23] What they need to do to succeed in their respective careers puts a strain on their family life. The ideal of unity might require something like the entire family placing a priority on either the husband's or the wife's career. When the husband gets a good job offer in another city, for example, there is no question as to what ought to be done. By contrast, the ideal of harmony would rely less on the idea of there being a fixed priority upon which everyone agrees in advance, and more on balancing, negotiation, tweaking, and cajoling. Suppose the wife gets an especially compelling offer. Instead of simply deciding to move the family solely on the grounds of her career, the couple may work very hard to find him a good opportunity in the new city, and decide to move only after they find such an opportunity. (Another result of such negotiations may be to "take turns.")

This interpretation of the ideal of harmony fits with the Confucian theme that human beings are profoundly social. It means that our identities, our senses of who we are, are bound up with our social roles and our relationships with particular people. It also means that our sense of what our legitimate interests are is bound up with our judgments about what is needed to sustain our most important relationships. The husband and wife in Angle's example have interests in their own respective careers, but they also have interests in the flourishing of each other's careers, and they have interests in their relationship and their family life that influence their sense of how far their career interests can go and still be legitimate. The "harmonizing" of each partner's interest in a career would involve weaving it into the nexus of all the other interests that matter to the family members.

On the Chinese side of the conversation, we see that engagement begins in the need to engage with those who cannot be ignored, who must be addressed in their language of rights. Once that language enters the Chinese vocabulary, it is transformed in the hands of those who see some "substantive rightness" in Western ideas connected with individual rights. However, that substantive rightness is interpreted within a framework, a horizon, within which Confucian ideas about the relationality and sociality of the individual still assume a prominent place. From both sides of the conversation, then, we have some fusion of horizons. What is interesting, however, is that what each side gets from such a fusion is not necessarily the same.

China and the United States today are in the curious position of having reason to look to relational and social views of human life – of which Confucianism is a prominent representative – to compensate for the increasing isolation, fragmentation, and corrosive inequality growing within both nations, the result of enormously powerful and seductive forms of global capitalism. The prospects for such views are uncertain, and we have no reason to expect that the outcome will be the same for the two nations.

From my point of view, this is as it should be. The various moral traditions are ongoing attempts to structure human cooperative life and the wide array of motivations within the individual. There is enough common subject matter in these different attempts that conversations across these traditions are possible – indeed, various fusions of horizons are possible and have taken place – but there can be no expectation that the results will be or should be the same.[24]

NOTES

1 Donald Davidson, "Radical Interpretation," in Davidson, *Inquiries into Truth and Interpretation*, 2nd ed. (Oxford: Clarendon, 2001), 125–40.

2 Davidson, "On the Very Idea of a Conceptual Scheme," in Davidson, *Inquiries*, 196.

3 Davidson, "Introduction," in *Inquiries*, xix.

4 Davidson, "Thought and Talk," in *Inquiries*, 168.

5 Davidson, "Three Varieties of Knowledge," in *A.J. Ayer Memorial Essays: Royal Institute of Philosophy Supplement* 30, ed. A. Phillips Griffiths (Cambridge: Cambridge University Press, 1991), 158.
6 Ibid., 159–60. For an excellent discussion of Davidsonian triangulation, see Jeff Malpus, "Gadamer, Davidson, and the Ground of Understanding," in *Gadamer's Century: Essays in Honor of Hans-George Gadamer*, ed. Jeff Malpus, Ulrich Arnswald, and Jens Kertscher (Cambridge, MA: MIT Press, 2002), 195–216.
7 Davidson, "On the Very Idea of a Conceptual Scheme."
8 Hans-Georg Gadamer, *Truth and Method*, 2nd rev. ed., trans. Joel Weinsheimer and Donald G. Marshall (London: Continuum, 2004), 385.
9 Ibid., 387. For an especially illuminating discussion of the dialogical dimension of Gadamer's hermeneutics, see Charles Taylor, "Understanding the Other: A Gadamerian View on Conceptual Schemes," in *Gadamer's Century*, 279–97.
10 Gadamer, *Truth and Method*, 301.
11 Confucius (Kongzi), *The Analects of Confucius: A Philosophical Translation*, trans. Roger T. Ames and Henry Rosemont, Jr (New York: Ballantine, 1999).
12 Mencius (Mengzi), *Mencius*, trans. Irene Bloom (New York: Columbia University Press, 2009), 6A5.
13 Antonio Cua, "The Ethical and Religious Dimensions of *Li*," *Review of Metaphysics* 55, no. 3 (2002): 485.
14 David L. Hall and Roger T. Ames, "Chinese Philosophy," in *Routledge Encyclopedia of Philosophy*, ed. Edward Craig (London: Routledge, 2003). Web. 27 August 2012.
15 Republican senators John McCain and Orrin Hatch spoke at the memorial service. See "Transcript of Memorial Service for Ted Kennedy," *Real Clear Politics*, 28 August 2009. Web. 26 August 2012.
16 Mario M. Cuomo, "1984 Democratic National Convention Keynote Address," delivered 16 July 1984, *American Rhetoric: Top 100 Speeches*. Web. 26 August 2012.
17 Daniel A. Bell, *China's New Confucianism: Politics and Everyday Life in a Changing Society* (Princeton: Princeton University Press, 2008), 38–55.
18 Emmanuel Saez, "Striking It Richer: The Evolution of Top Incomes in the United States (Update with 2007 estimates)," 17 July 2010. Web. 2 January 2011.
19 Didier Jacobs, "Low Inequality with Low Redistribution? An Analysis of Income Distribution in Japan, South Korea and Taiwan compared to Britain," CASE paper #33, London School of Economics, Centre for Analysis of Social Exclusion, January 2000. Web. 2 January 2011.

20 Sigmund Freud, *Civilization and Its Discontents* (New York: W.W. Norton, 2005), 108.

21 Stephen C. Angle, *Human Rights and Chinese Thought* (Cambridge: Cambridge University Press, 2002), 104–7.

22 Yong Xia, *Renquan gainian qiyuan* [*The Origin of the Concept of Human Rights: A Chinese Interpretation*] (Beijing: Zhongguo Zhengfa daxue chubanshe, 1992). A translated excerpt is found in *The Chinese Human Rights Reader: Documents and Commentary 1900–2000*, ed. Stephen C. Angle and Marina Svensson (Armonk: M.E. Sharpe, 2001), under the title "Human Rights and Chinese Tradition," 372–89.

23 Angle, *Human Rights and Chinese Thought*, 231–2.

24 For amplification of these themes, see David B. Wong, *Natural Moralities: A Defense of Pluralistic Relativism* (New York: Oxford University Press, 2006). Some parts of this chapter on Davidsonian interpretation overlap with Wong, "Where Charity Begins," in *Davidson's Philosophy and Chinese Philosophy: Constructive Engagement*, ed. Bo Mou (Leiden: Brill, 2006), 103–16.

PART THREE

Expanding Horizons: Empathy, Dialogue, Critique, Wisdom

Chapter Ten

Some Observations on the Prospects of Intercultural Hermeneutics in a Global Framework

MIHAI I. SPARIOSU

This essay starts from three basic premises: (1) that hermeneutics, as it stands now, is a science or, rather, an *art* of interpretation proper to the Western mentality and that it needs to undergo substantial remapping and readjustment in an intercultural and global context; (2) that Critical Theory – understood as a Marxian type of thinking, instituted by Adorno and Horkheimer, and continued today, most notably by Habermas – may, again, be appropriate in a Western reference framework, but not in a global one; and (3) that because of (1) and (2), intercultural hermeneutics would lose rather than gain from associating itself with Critical Theory, if it wishes to go global. In what follows, I briefly elaborate on my premises, using as a point of departure the well-publicized and much-debated exchange on Reason and Religion between Cardinal Joseph Ratzinger (now Pope Benedict XVI) and Professor Jürgen Habermas; I then outline some of the basic principles that I believe ought to guide intercultural hermeneutics – understood not as a "philosophical" or a "scientific" enterprise, but as the art of interpretation – within a global framework. Needless to say, one should constantly keep in mind the *emergent* nature of my proposed guidelines, which necessarily remain tentative and subject to continuous readjustment and enrichment through intercultural research, dialogue, and negotiation.

The exchange between Cardinal Ratzinger and Professor Habermas took place on 19 January 2004 at the Catholic Academy of Bavaria and was later published under the title *The Dialectics of Secularization* (2005).[1] In his intervention "Pre-Political Foundations of the Democratic Constitutional State?," Habermas attempts to answer several essential questions: What is the common foundation that can hold together a pluralistic society with divergent or even conflicting systems of values and beliefs? Are democratic political principles and the rule of law sufficient to ensure the solidarity of the citizens in the modern European state and, by extension, in the European Union? And if not, what factors might ensure such solidarity? All of these are hermeneutically relevant questions, because each can be answered in a number of ways that involve, in turn, a number of interpretive decisions, according to the interpreter's *Weltanschauung*.

For Habermas, however, the main concern seems to be whether and how his theory of communicative reason and action is still relevant and may apply to the current European state of affairs. What has changed since he published this theory in the 1980s is that the social balance seemingly achieved at that time by the liberal democratic constitutional state is now at risk, "because the markets and the power of the bureaucracy are expelling social solidarity (that is, a coordination of action based on values, norms and a vocabulary intended to promote mutual understanding) from more and more spheres of life."[2] Furthermore, "law" in the context of the current European democracies – and, by extension, of the European Union – has lost its traditional meanings, becoming a "straightforward matter of de facto legislation – and nothing else." Thus, Habermas wonders if it were "still possible in any way to provide a secular justification of political rule, that is, a justification that is nonreligious or postmetaphysical."[3]

In an elaborate, roundabout way laden with a cumbersome and occasionally obfuscating sociological vocabulary – which is characteristic of his writing in general (e.g., by "postmetaphysical" he largely means his own materialist, Marxian philosophy) – Habermas answers this question in the affirmative, but with a number of qualifiers concerning the "religious" and the "metaphysical." He concludes that, given the current social imbalance, "it is in the interest of the constitutional state to deal carefully with all the cultural resources that nourish its citizens' consciousness of norms and their solidarity." For him, religion can be just such a "cultural resource" – that is, a powerful instrument, employed by the democratic state to counteract the egregious inequalities of a market economy gone wild and the ever-increasing power of the state bureaucracies at the expense of civil society.

Yet, because earlier in his career the secularization of the European society appeared – at least to Habermas – to be all but a *fait accompli*, he now feels the need to justify his turnabout by referring to a "dialectics of secularization" in which religion becomes a more or less willing social partner of the secular democratic constitutional state. As he puts it, "I myself think it better not to push too far the question whether an ambivalent modern age will stabilize itself exclusively on the basis of the secular forces of a communicative reason,"[4] which is, of course, what he advocated in his earlier work. Instead, he adopts the modernist, fashionable term "postsecular society," even though he is somewhat uneasy about it, since it appears to him to reflect a "conservative" attitude rather than a liberal one.[5] Habermas explains the term as follows:

> The expression "postsecular" does more than give public recognition to religious fellowships in view of the functional contribution they make to the reproduction of motivations and attitudes that are societally desirable. The public awareness of a postsecular society also reflects a normative insight that has consequences for the political dealings of unbelieving citizens with believing citizens. In the postsecular society, there is an increasing consensus that certain phases of the "modernization of the public consciousness" involve the assimilation and the reflexive transformation of both religious and secular mentalities. If both sides agree to understand the secularization of society as a complementary learning process, then they will also have cognitive reasons to take seriously each other's contributions to controversial subjects in the public debate.[6]

Then Habermas asks a question that is of great importance not only in an intracultural but also in an intercultural context: How should believing and unbelieving citizens treat one another? He points out that, under the pressure of the "secularization" of knowledge, religion was compelled to abandon its claim to a monopoly on interpretation and to a comprehensive structuring of human life. At the same time, the neutrality of the liberal state with regard to world views guarantees the same moral and religious freedom to every citizen. This position, of course, conflicts with "the political universalization of a secularist world view" by the modern democratic constitutional state. Notwithstanding this, in a liberal state, the secularized citizens "must not deny in principle that religious images of the world have the potential to express truth."[7] Nor can they deny their believing fellow citizens the right to participate in public debates, based on their faith. Indeed, according to Habermas, a democratic political culture should expect the secularized citizens to "play their part in endeavors to translate relevant contributions from the religious language into a language that is accessible to the public as a whole."[8]

Habermas's arguments reveal the tensions that arise in the modern democratic state that guarantees freedom of expression to every citizen and, at the same time, promotes its secular scientific-materialist agenda. Indeed, Habermas still regards the old dispute between science and religion as the main cultural divide to be bridged in modern Western culture. He takes the viewpoint of a "neutral" European bureaucrat who needs to reconcile the "secularized" with the religious citizens of his state by finding a common, "rational" ground between them, not only through legalistic means but also through a common system of values that will ensure their solidarity. This task is to be accomplished by "communicative reason" – that is, by rational intercultural dialogue that involves "translation" (read: self-serving interpretation) of one another's perspectives. This is a thankless task, because Habermas, no less than any other EU bureaucrat, is caught between the universalist drive of "secularization" and the relativist demands of liberal neutrality *vis-à-vis* all other equally universalist world views. Also, it is not clear that the term "postsecular" has any cogency beyond serving as philosophical cover for those who have been proclaiming "the death of God" and the demise of religion for more than a century now. For better or worse, religion seems to be alive and well in most parts of the world, including large sections of Europe.

Another tension arises from the fact that the modern European state is not bicultural, but multicultural. Although Habermas gives the impression that the main cultural divide is between secularism and Christianity, he is fully aware that a much more urgent and complex question is that of the cultural divides between the Western world and other worlds, particularly the Islamic one. He refers indirectly to this when he recounts the anecdote of a Teheran colleague who once said to him that "the comparative study of cultures and religious sociology surely suggested that *European secularization* was the odd one out among the various developments – and that it ought to be corrected."[9] Overall, however, Habermas's comments are mostly limited to a (Western) European context and largely reflect his desire to update his theory of communicative reason.

While Habermas's perspective in this exchange remains rather "parochial" (not unlike that of a local parish priest, if one may use the simile without offending the German philosopher's secular sensibilities), Cardinal Ratzinger takes the bull by the horns and places the issues within a global framework, not least because the Catholic Church is a multinational organization with complex global concerns and interests. He does pick up on the Teheran anecdote in the course of his argument,[10] but first he points out that present global circumstances demand a reframing of the issues well beyond European liberal secularism. He goes right to the heart of the matter: through the development of new technologies, our mentality of power has reached highly dangerous levels. What is to be done in a situation in which humanity's power has become self-destructive? This, in turn, "lends great urgency to the question of how cultures that encounter one another can find ethical bases to guide their relationship along the right path, thus permitting them to build up a common structure that tames power and imposes a legally responsible order on the exercise of power."[11]

According to Ratzinger, the Western world has formulated a number of such normative elements in the declaration of human rights, and in Hans Küng's principles of the "world ethos." But the obviousness of these values, he adds, "is by no means acknowledged in every culture. Islam has defined its own catalogue of human rights, which differs from the Western catalogue. And if my information is correct, although it is true that today's China is defined by a cultural form, namely Marxism, that arose in the West, it is asking whether 'human rights' are merely a typically Western invention – and one that must be looked at critically."[12]

Of course, there is no uniformity within these individual cultural spheres either; all are marked by profound tensions deriving from conflicting world views within their own traditions. With respect to the tensions within the Western world, Ratzinger's perspective is similar to that of Habermas: the major conflict is the one between the secular rationalist tradition and Christianity. Furthermore, the future Pope notes, both of these traditions regard themselves as universal, and they "may perhaps be universal *de iure*." But *de facto*, he adds, they "are obliged to acknowledge that they are accepted only by parts of mankind, and that they are comprehensible only in parts of mankind – although the number of competitors is of course much smaller than an initial glance might suggest."[13] Even though this tension cannot in principle be resolved, Ratzinger agrees with Habermas that the two traditions should learn from each other through dialogue and translation/interpretation. But he emphasizes again that such dialogue and translation must be intercultural, for "if we are to discuss the basic questions of human existence today, the intercultural dimension seems to me essential."[14]

Ratzinger further observes that there are "pathologies" of a religious nature, which are very dangerous and which must be controlled by reason. By the same token, there are equally dangerous "pathologies of reason." This is why "reason, too, must be warned to keep within its proper limits, and it must learn a willingness to listen to the great religious traditions of mankind." He concludes that there is a "necessary relatedness between reason and faith and between reason and religion, which are called to purify and help each other. They need each other, and they must acknowledge this need."[15]

Once Ratzinger establishes the complementarity of Christianity and liberal secular rationalism within the contemporary Western world, he reframes the issue in global terms. In a global framework, the two become allies and are the main representatives of the Western civilization in the dialogue with other civilizations: "There can be no doubt that the two main partners in this mutual relatedness are the Christian faith and Western secular rationality; one can and must affirm this, without thereby succumbing to a false Eurocentrism. These two determine the situation of the world to an extent not matched by another cultural force."

Nevertheless, one can hardly dismiss the other cultures as insignificant partners in the global dialogue. "For a western hubris of that kind," Ratzinger says, "there would be a high price to pay – and, indeed, we are already paying a part of it. It is important that both great components of the Western culture learn to *listen* and to accept a genuine relatedness to these other cultures, too."[16] But then, Ratzinger concludes on a rather ambiguous note:

> It is important to include the other cultures in the attempt at a polyphonic relatedness, in which they themselves are receptive to the essential complementarity of reason and faith, so that a universal process of purifications (in the plural!) can proceed. Ultimately, the essential values and norms that are in some way known or sensed by all men will take on a new brightness in such a process, so that that which holds the world together can once again become an effective force in mankind.[17]

"That Which Holds the World Together" is also the title of his essay, and echoes Colossians 1:17: "And He is before all things and in Him all things hold together." Thus the implication seems to be that the entire planet might be converted to Christianity, including the latter's main ally in the global intercultural dialogue, Western secular rationality. A less controversial, if more ambiguous, meaning would result if "That which holds the world together" would refer to "Love" – a word that each of the global "partners" may interpret/translate in their own fashion.

In any case, the exchange between these two thinkers constitutes a good example of the kind of problems hermeneutics may encounter not only within an intercultural but also within an intracultural reference frame. In a peculiar yet not uncommon way, the two men speak past each other, at the same time that they appear to agree. The game, again, is one of power, because each of them continues to see the other's tradition as the "junior" partner in their alliance. It is highly significant that Ratzinger speaks openly about power and the limits one might place on it, but avoids discussing the mentality of power itself. For example, he states: "When we are speaking of the relationship between power and law and about the sources of law, we must look at the phenomenon of power itself." But then he immediately adds: "I do not propose to define the essence of 'power' as such. Instead, I should like to sketch the challenges that emerge from the new forms of power that have developed in the last fifty years."

But the issue, especially in a global framework, is precisely the "essence" or nature of power itself, which obstructs a genuine intercultural (and one may add intracultural) dialogue. Perhaps the outcome of their dialogue might have been different had the two thinkers tackled this issue. In proposing the principles that I consider essential for effective intercultural (and intracultural) dialogue/communication and interpretation/translation, let me then state from the outset that the only thing that would work in the end would be for all the partners involved to give up, entirely and unconditionally, their mentality of power and reorient themselves towards a mentality of peace. I am fully aware that this is an enormous task that would involve very long and complex learning processes, because it would mean abandoning all of the major assumptions on which we humans have built our social, economic, political, cultural and personal relations with one another over the centuries, if not millennia. I will return to this point at the end of my essay, but now let me outline some of the principles and practices that ought to inform intercultural hermeneutics, understood, again, as the art of (intercultural) interpretation.[18]

1. Intercultural Hermeneutics Should Continuously Move Back and Forth between Local and Global Reference Frames, Exploring Their Relatedness and Interdependence

As Cardinal Ratzinger points out, intercultural hermeneutics needs to adopt the kinds of principles and practices that would best work within a global reference frame. Before I proceed any further, however, let me clarify what I mean by global and local reference frames. In defining these terms, I start from the assumption – present in contemporary Western general systems theory, but also in early Buddhist thinking in India, early Taoist thinking in China, and, more recently, in Islamic Sufism – that we are an integral part of an infinite, complex, and dynamic network of embedded and/or interconnected levels of organized energy that we call reality. Each of these levels of reality has its own reference frame, with its specific "logic" and operating principles. In this respect, any global frame can be local, and in turn, any local frame can be global, depending on the more or less complex levels of organization that encompass or are encompassed by it.

Furthermore, these levels may be perceived as interconnected either in a chainlike fashion – according to what one calls "linear causality" in philosophy and science – or in a loop-like, interdependent fashion, mutually nourishing one another, that is, according to mutual or reciprocal causality. Because we not only are part of this complex network but also are able to project ourselves outside it, as it were, in order to explore or gain knowledge about it, we humans seem to be in a position, at least within our time-space continuum, both to intervene and to modify it. Therefore, our methods of approaching and exploring reality matter a great deal and will yield positive or negative results according to how appropriate they are for the level of organization or reference framework they are operating in.

2. Intercultural Hermeneutics Ought to Adopt Non-Linear Cognitive Models and Methods

Generally speaking, the age-old traditions of wisdom, such as Buddhism and Daoism, have shown that the best cognitive methods are the non-linear ones, which stem from an integrative, holistic frame of mind and which resonate best with the way in which reality seems to work. Unfortunately, most of our prevalent methods for approaching reality are of the linear–causal kind and have only a limited cognitive reach. These methods belong to what one may call a disciplinary mentality, which organizes our cognitive and learning activities, as well as all other human transactions and indeed reality itself, in terms of linear power relations that are engaged in a continuous struggle to achieve and/or preserve hegemony.

A good example of a disciplinary mentality is mainstream contemporary science (also mentioned by Cardinal Ratzinger in his exchange with Professor Habermas), which prides itself on being largely secular, materialist, and democratic. It involves a strictly regulated protocol of experiment and critical (dis)proof, which continually approximates, although it may never reach, universal and eternal truth, valid in all places and at all times. Those claiming to be in possession of such truth are veritable gatekeepers, as jealous of their treasure as the legendary dragons lying on their pots of gold. What I have just described, in metaphorical form, is the famous equation of knowledge and power – an equation that, despite numerous critiques and challenges from various philosophical and scientific quarters, has long been an explicit or implicit model of scientific thinking and practice in academic and non-academic circles throughout the world. Within this model, the traditional concept of reason itself becomes Reason and loses its traditional etymological meaning of "reasonableness" or the "middle way" – indeed, as Cardinal Ratzinger equally suggests, it becomes *unreasonable* in its relentless insistence on pure Rationality. In this regard, modern philosophy itself has also lost its original meaning of "love of wisdom" and has been mostly preoccupied, ever since the so-called Age of Enlightenment, with Reason.

Within a planetary framework, we need to transcend the equation of knowledge and power that underlies the disciplinary paradigm. We need to set aside all dogmatic beliefs and ideologies and begin to embrace our differences, instead of fighting with one another over their validity. Now more than ever we need a global community of intercultural cooperation and mutual respect. Perhaps, during the "age of the dragons," when we had only bows and arrows to settle our differences, it was fine to be hostile, destructive, and irresponsible. However, in the age of nuclear power and other harmful technologies and ideologies, we cannot continue this line of behaviour without devastating consequences for all involved, as Cardinal Ratzinger also points out. We need not only to become educated about the consequences of our decisions, but also to begin to understand the complicated interrelations and hidden dependencies of global reality. This complex, fast-moving reality, however, requires a much more committed approach and willingness to investigate and understand the issues at hand across all ideologies, philosophies, societies, and nations. The task of intercultural hermeneutics is to enable us to become cognizant of this new reality and to help us navigate its complex levels with adequately reframed interpretive tools.

At the same time, philosophical hermeneutics, especially in its phenomenological version, has traditionally eschewed issues of power. This is perhaps one reason why it has been subjected to criticism by, among others, Critical Theory, and why some scholars have felt the need to introduce the concept of critical hermeneutics. But the latter concept will only perpetuate our agonistic mentality; thus, intercultural hermeneutics might be much better off without it. This does not mean that intercultural hermeneutics ought to ignore issues of power; rather, it should place those issues in their proper reference frames.

3. Intercultural Hermeneutics Ought to Help Remap Existing Knowledge and Create New Cognitive Forms from a Global Perspective

In this regard, an approach to knowledge and learning within a planetary reference frame will require philosophical and scientific presuppositions entirely different from those of a disciplinary mentality. It will not presuppose that knowledge is power, only that power produces certain forms of knowledge, which may become irrelevant or transfigured in other, non–power-oriented reference frames. It will involve not only remapping traditional knowledge as it is acquired, accumulated, and transmitted by various academic disciplines, be they scientific or humanistic, but also generating new kinds of knowledge from an intercultural, global perspective. Intercultural hermeneutics can help this process along by remapping its own concepts of the fusion of interpretive horizons in a planetary framework, as some of the contributors to the present collection are already doing.

4. Intercultural Hermeneutics Ought to Draw from the Mutually Nourishing Interplay of Local and Global Knowledge

In turn, such a planetary framework presupposes a mutually enriching interplay of what various cultures perceive as universal or global and what they perceive as particular or local. Although these perceptions may vary widely from culture to culture, many cultures explicitly or implicitly employ this kind of distinction, be it in a positive or a negative manner. If some cultures – or at least some of their members – appear to perceive the global and the local as mutually exclusive or antagonistic, it is because they basically operate within the reference frame of a disciplinary mentality. When this reference frame is left behind, the two notions become complementary and mutually supportive rather than antagonistic and reciprocally destructive.

The mutually nourishing interplay of globality and locality finds its academic equivalent in the interplay between transdisciplinary or integrative knowledge and specialized or compartmentalized knowledge. It presupposes a holistic mode of thinking that looks beyond constituted academic fields and their divisions of knowledge, although it does not deny their usefulness. Yet a global mode of thinking takes into consideration that knowledge is "local" not only in terms of proper limits or confines (which should, however, remain flexible and open to redefinition), but also in terms of its historicity. Knowledge is always bound to a specific time and place, to a specific culture or system of values and beliefs, or indeed to a specific lifestyle. A global hermeneutic approach would attempt to identify the cultural specificities of knowledge, explore commonalities and differences among them, and negotiate, if need be, among such specificities. It also presupposes that, as we explore cultural commonalities and differences in the ways we acquire and utilize knowledge, new kinds of cross-cultural knowledge will emerge through intercultural research, dialogue, and cooperation, and new kinds of integrative cognitive and learning processes will become possible.

As we move from disciplinary to interdisciplinary and then to transdisciplinary reference frames, and from monocultural to intercultural to transcultural or global ones, new levels of reality emerge, as well as new kinds of knowledge. Intercultural hermeneutics, through its interpretive tools, should also explore and make us aware of these embedded realities, and show us how to access and navigate them.

5. Intercultural Hermeneutics Ought to Be Informed by and Cultivate Global Intelligence

Within the broadest reference frame, intercultural hermeneutics should be informed by global or planetary intelligence, which can be defined as the ability to understand, respond to, and work towards what is in the best interest of not only all human beings but also all other life on our planet. At the same time, this kind of responsive understanding and action can only emerge from ongoing intercultural research, dialogue, negotiation, and mutual cooperation; in other words, global intelligence is interactive, and no single national or supranational body or authority can predetermine its outcome. Thus, intercultural hermeneutics defined as a form of interpretation grounded in intercultural responsive understanding and action would equally be what contemporary non-linear science calls an emergent phenomenon involving lifelong learning.

Intercultural hermeneutics should transcend the current ideological and political impasse of Western-style cultural studies; it should also preserve some of those studies' valuable insights and reorient them towards global intelligence. In doing so, it would be placing itself in the vanguard of a comprehensive and much-needed study of and sustained dialogue among world cultures, not only from a local, national, or regional perspective, but also from a global one.

6. Intercultural Hermeneutics Ought to Help Establish a Common Core of Values for Our Global Communities to Use in Their Interactions with One Another

At the same time, intercultural hermeneutics, in conjunction with other cognitive fields, should explore and seek to define a common core of values on the basis of which the various world communities can work together towards a common purpose – namely, global intelligence. In doing so, intercultural hermeneutics would be aiding in the search for and expansion of the values, institutions, and practices that are common to all cultures. This does not mean, of course, that cultural differences are not real and that intercultural hermeneutics should ignore them. On the contrary, it must thoroughly explore and understand them, both within and outside their specific cultural frameworks. But, intercultural hermeneutics must at all times promote a mentality of peace and show how cultural differences can constitute a source of learning and delight, rather than one of discord and violent conflict.

7. Intercultural Hermeneutics Ought to Adopt, Develop, and Refine the Concept of Responsive Understanding as a Useful Interpretive Tool in a Global, Intercultural Environment

The term "responsive understanding" was coined by Russian thinker Mikhail Bakhtin to describe Dostoevsky's approach to his fictional world. Bakhtin characterizes this understanding as "active," "creative," and "dialogical." Significantly, he attributes it to literary discourse and distinguishes it from the monologic understanding of other types of discourse, such as the scientific and the political. Responsive understanding involves watchful listening and empathetic, interactive participation in an ongoing dialogue, in which each participant carefully and lovingly preserves the integrity of the other. Here, Hans-Georg Gadamer's concept of the "fusion of horizons" may be helpful in cultivating self-awareness and awareness of prejudices related to one's own historical context and world view, together with awareness of the other. To these elements, one may add awareness of the complex affective dimensions of our emotional intelligence, which motivates our actions and can be explored through a behavioural dialogic approach.

Finally, I should note that responsive understanding also conveys the idea of responsibility, understood not as the thou-shalts and thou-shalt-nots of conventional morality, but rather as a free and generous response to the calling of the other, interpreted as a principle of (self-) transcendence, such as God, Nature, the Universe, the global human community, or another human being. It is not enough to put oneself in other people's shoes and understand or sympathize with their views; one must also get involved in an effective manner. Therefore, responsive understanding can never be separated from the willingness and capacity to take positive, responsive action, the causally reciprocal effects of which will then propagate by amplifying feedback loops through the entire social system.

Even from this very brief discussion of responsive understanding, it ought to be clear that Bakhtin's term carries relevance far beyond the realm of literature and can be used very productively in an intercultural hermeneutical context as well. At the same time, it highlights the value that literature and literary studies – indeed a literary or an artistic mode of thinking in general – may have for intercultural hermeneutics.

8. Intercultural Hermeneutics Ought to Become an Art Form

Many of the issues facing the contemporary world are questions of intercultural interpretation, translation, and communication, and our arts and humanities have been addressing these questions for a long time. Artistic ways of understanding and dealing with the world may, therefore, prove to be equally useful in a hermeneutical context. In future global and cross-cultural interchanges, traditional cognitive fields and boundaries will increasingly be challenged and reconfigured. Intercultural hermeneutics could help this process along by contributing to the development of specific blueprints for future reconceptualizations of knowledge. But such blueprints might well need to display the kinds of ontological flexibility and epistemological inventiveness that have always been the mark of literary or fictional discourse in general. To that end, intercultural hermeneutics should abandon its disciplinary ways of thinking and doing things and cease regarding itself as a traditional body of rigid rules and methods. In other words, within a global framework, hermeneutics should drop its scientific claims and become an *art*, that is, a form of liminal activity that can generate new cognitive associations and interactions.

9. To Access and Gain Understanding of New Realities, Intercultural Hermeneutics Ought to Place Itself at the Intersection between Cultures and Become a Ludic–Liminal Activity

Given the complex levels of reality embedded in the global reference frame, intercultural hermeneutics would need to raise and satisfactorily answer the basic questions of how these levels of reality communicate among themselves, how they interact, and how we can have access to and move among them. Here the anthropological concept of "culture contact" may prove equally helpful for intercultural hermeneutics, once it is redefined as *intercultural contact* and is emancipated from the confrontational meanings that North American "culture warriors," both on the right and on the left of the political spectrum, have attributed to it, invoking Samuel Huntington's influential theory of the "clash of civilizations."

Intercultural hermeneutics would, however, do well to stay away from such agonistic notions, which are highly counterproductive in a global environment. It should certainly explore and find appropriate solutions to alleviate tensions in the troubled zones of intercultural contact, but it should also study those zones in which people from various cultures are currently living – or used to live – side-by-side in peace and harmony. These studies, if conducted in a thoroughly cross-disciplinary and cross-cultural manner, and in their proper historical contexts, may reveal unexpected, non-linear causes of conflict, as well as models of peaceful coexistence that might be useful in other parts of the world. Indeed, it might well turn out that the no man's lands between cultures, the empty spaces between borders, or the grey areas in which nothing is quite settled and in which new patterns of organization can gradually or suddenly emerge, may constitute privileged sites for intercultural dialogue and negotiation, rather than privileged sites of conflict.

In this regard, intercultural hermeneutics may have much to gain by linking the notion of intercultural contact with the notions of liminality and emergence. The word "liminal" comes from the Greek/Hebrew *limen*, meaning "harbour" or the place between land and sea, but also "threshold" or even "gateway." It is at, and through, the points of contact between various structured realities that new realities emerge. Ludic time-spaces are also liminal events. It follows that intercultural hermeneutics can best position itself within those spaces where new cultural realities may emerge through intercultural dialogue, negotiation, and mediation.

10. Cultural Critique or Global (Self-)Awareness?

When operating within a global reference frame, intercultural hermeneutics ought to develop alternative concepts to those of "cultural critique" and "critical thinking" – two of the most cherished notions of modern Western thought and the methodological cornerstones of current Western-style cultural studies. Precisely because they are sacred cows, intercultural hermeneutics should submit them to extensive cultural anthropological study and thorough self-analysis, rather than adopting them automatically, as if they were obvious and universally shared values. It should explore the ways in which the idea of critique has always contributed to a perpetuation of various disciplinary mentalities not only in the Western world but in other worlds as well. In this respect, even notions of cultural resistance, opposition, subversion, and survival are part of the arsenal of power that perpetuates politics as usual, be it in a "colonized" or "decolonized" environment, a local or a global one.

Intercultural hermeneutics ought to start from the realization that cultural critique and critical thinking are local notions that might do well in certain Western intellectual circles but not so well in other, non-Western milieux. In the latter milieux, as Cardinal Ratzinger would undoubtedly agree, they are often perceived as needlessly and counterproductively confrontational and aggressive, if not as "soft power" instruments of furthering "imperialist" designs on other cultures. For these reasons, Western hermeneuticians who wish to operate in a global environment should employ such newly coined terms as "critical intercultural hermeneutics" only with great care. We Westerners would have a hard time abandoning these "critical" terms altogether, because they are too deeply engrained in our mentality, but we should at least become aware of them and use them only in their proper, local, cultural contexts.

Even more important, intercultural hermeneutics should consider replacing "cultural critique" and "critical thinking" as conceptual tools in a global learning environment. Possibilities for this in English might be "global awareness" (and "self-awareness") and "global attentiveness." These and other terms should, however, preserve the connotations of reflection and self-reflection that are necessary for any creative thinking and action that seeks human (self-)development. Such terms, however, should remain free of the oppositional or agonistic connotations of "critique," as well as of its etymological link to "crisis," another pet concept of Western modernity. They would thus be less easily co-opted as instruments of power by any warring Western or other ideological factions in a global environment.

11. Intercultural Hermeneutics Should Employ Careful, Well-Informed Intercultural Comparative Analysis

Global (self-)awareness or attentiveness should not only replace cultural critique as the cornerstone methodology in a global milieu but also inform intercultural comparative analysis. Such analysis, however, would need to be much refined and attuned to this milieu. We should consider the impact that reductive approaches in intercultural comparative analysis – and their symmetrical opposites, pluralistic or relativistic approaches – may have within a global reference frame. Both types of approaches can be counterproductive in an intercultural environment: the former, by amplifying cultural conflict and violence; the latter, by impeding and eventually leading to a breakdown in intercultural dialogue.

Intercultural comparative analyses should start from a secure, non-mimetic sense of cultural identity rather than an insecure, mimetic one. It is from the same secure sense of identity, moreover, that members of diverse cultures should engage in intercultural dialogue and negotiation, which otherwise would be stalled by mimetic conflict and violence. An intercultural approach oriented towards global intelligence would obviously not require denying or repressing one's cultural position and identity, as extreme, North American and Western European, liberal forms of political correctness ask Westerners to do, playing on their sense of collective guilt – as if this such denial and repression were desirable or even possible.

Yet one must not trumpet one's own civilization's superiority over all the others, doing so, moreover, from the perspective of one's own standard of evaluation rather than from that of a commonly accepted universal standard. Incidentally, this universal standard simply does not exist today, and if it is ever achieved, it will be only after a long process of intercultural learning, research, dialogue, and negotiation; in other words, it is no less of an emergent phenomenon than global intelligence or any other system of values and beliefs we may put forward as a candidate for such a standard.

Furthermore, such an intercultural standard would require that humans develop a universal language, common to all humankind. This would be re-enacting the myth of the linguistic paradise before the Tower of Babel and would most likely turn our planet into an utterly boring place. (Incidentally, the intercultural project of the Tower of Babel can be studied as an instructive paradigm for an endless series of unsuccessful human attempts at globalization.) Instead, the next step of intercultural hermeneutics should be to thoroughly explore, in a dialogical, non-conflictive manner, the actual and imagined differences that exist among the diverse human languages, cultures, value systems, and beliefs, which in turn determine the ways of thinking, feeling, and acting of various people. It may very well turn out that many of the clichés that various members of one culture circulate, automatically or intentionally, about other cultures and their members are based on incomplete knowledge or received opinion.

12. Intercultural Hermeneutics Should Contribute to the Emergence of an Ethics of Global Intelligence, Based on an Irenic Mentality

Much has been written in recent decades about peace and non-violence, especially in a political context. These ideas are usually seen as going hand in hand with, and are often subsumed to, the concepts of liberal democracy, human rights, social and gender equality, and the rule of law. Peace is generally seen as either "a mere absence of war" or "a lack of war often enriched by further elements and guarantees which make peace constructive, just and democratic."[19] Accordingly, a "peace culture" ought to be based on "the universal values of respect for life, liberty, justice, solidarity, tolerance, human rights and equality between women and men." Additions to this list include, as a rule, "democracy, development, burden-sharing and responsibility as well as non-violence and peaceful resolution and transformation of conflicts."[20]

There is also the praiseworthy initiative of Hans Küng and his colleagues (mentioned by Cardinal Ratzinger as well) to develop a "planetary code of ethics," which would be based on four "irrevocable" commitments: a culture of non-violence and respect for life; a culture of solidarity and a just economic order; a culture of tolerance and a life of truthfulness; and a culture of equal rights and partnership between men and women."[21] Furthermore, most contemporary political scientists share the view that liberal democracy, more than any other system of government, is conducive to peace and non-violence, and that these concepts thrive best in a democratic political system. This view is rather widespread in the West and has been promoted by Francis Fukuyama, David Held, and many other advocates of cosmopolitan democracy (Held's term).[22] It is equally shared, as we have seen, by Cardinal Ratzinger and Professor Habermas.

Such a view, however, refers us back to the dilemma that liberal democracy finds itself in when it pushes its own standards on the rest of the world while proclaiming, at the same time, its neutrality *vis-à-vis* all systems of values and beliefs – a neutrality that seems to be based on philosophical and political relativism. Incidentally, this type of relativism is discussed in another exchange that Cardinal Ratzinger has, this time with philosophy professor and former president of the Italian senate, Marcello Pera, and published under the title *Without Roots: The West, Relativism, Christianity, Islam*.[23] While Professor Pera is right to decry the kind of political correctness that emanates from the EU bureaucracy in particular, he fails to distinguish between relativism and relativity, thus confusing local and global reference frames. Pera sets up a binary opposition between "relativism" as a philosophical and political position that gives equal onto-epistemological value to all other positions, and "universalism," where one position – say, the Christian or Islamic one – is objectively closer to eternal and objective truth than all the others.

Yet within a global framework, the point is precisely to go beyond the opposition between relativism and universalism, and binary oppositional thinking in general. To this end, it would be helpful, for instance, to distinguish between "relativism" and "relativity." "Relativism" is a philosophical and/or political position that makes specific assumptions with practical consequences for public policy. Relativity is a fact of life. I don't think, for example, that Professor Pera would oppose Einstein's theory of relativity, especially since it came out of the Western mainstream scientific tradition. It all boils down to a question of reference frames: in a liberal democracy, as Pera himself points out, one should generally abide by the ideals, principles, and practices of that system of government or, indeed, form of life. These have been worked out very well in theory but are yet to be applied consistently in our daily practice.

At the same time, Pera seems to discount or at least misconstrue the global reference frame (despite his claims to the contrary),[24] within which different conditions ought to apply and humanity as a whole has yet to work out the ideals, principles, and practices that should guide a planetary society, not to mention its daily activities and interactions. Of course, Pera is not the only one to misconstrue this reference frame. Indeed, at the present time each major civilization would like its own system of values and beliefs to become "universal." Consequently, it engages in an improper, unproductive, and futile competition with all the others, and all the while, each proclaims its own superiority over the rest. As we have seen from the positions of both Cardinal Ratzinger and Professor Habermas, to whom we can now add that of Professor Pera, universalism is far from being understood as an emergent reality based on continuous intercultural learning processes, dialogue, and negotiation; on the contrary, it is regarded as a triumph – through persuasion or any other means – of one system of values and beliefs over all the others. The problem resides, again, in the mentality of power that is almost "universally" shared by most human communities.

As to liberal democracy, historical experience seems to prove not that democracies are more peaceful and non-violent than other systems of government, but that all such systems promote and perpetuate themselves by whatever means they can muster, including (state-organized) violence. All existing political systems, including liberal democracy, are based on various mentalities of power and resort to violence whenever they perceive that their core values, beliefs, and interests are seriously threatened. This is obvious, for example, in the very common, unexamined political distinction between "legitimate" and "illegitimate force," equally invoked by Professor Pera in his distinction between "just" and "unjust" wars.[25] Such distinctions sound rather hollow, if not self-serving, considering that throughout history, most governments, democratic or not, have routinely invoked principles of legitimacy and justice in order to perpetrate the worst kinds of violent acts against one another.

Conversely, it will take a radical shift in mentality to change the power politics that dominate the present-day global environment. Until we give up our present mentality, collectively and unconditionally, we humans are doomed to repeat the same horrific historical mistakes over and over again. We will never be able to build a planetary society, no matter how reasonable and fair we claim our own principles to be. Within a global reference frame, intercultural hermeneutics ought to explore ideals, principles, and practices that are appropriate for that frame. And the chances are that these principles and practices will not be found, in their entirety, in any of the large or small civilizations or cultures; rather, they will be found, partially and sporadically, in all of them. The task of intercultural hermeneutics, as well as that of all other cognitive fields, therefore, is to work peacefully and cooperatively towards identifying precisely such principles and practices, finding those which hold the *entire* world together, beyond those which hold any particular culture or civilization together.

In view of this transformative global task, intercultural hermeneutics should seriously consider, and possibly act on, the counter-intuitive assumption that a mentality of peace and local or global cultures of non-violence might be built on principles *other than* human rights, tolerance, non-discrimination, and social, racial, and gender equality, notwithstanding how attractive and incontrovertible these democratic principles appear at first sight. These principles might seem obvious to a Westerner, but they are not necessarily shared by other cultures, as Cardinal Ratzinger has well pointed out. In addition to this, as Ratzinger has equally shown,[26] we should draw up a catalogue of human responsibilities, that is, of proper ways of engaging in intercultural contact and approaching other human beings and the natural environment.

Yet an intercultural hermeneutics should be wary of imposing such abstract catalogues on the global community. Outside the Western world, such catalogues are often perceived, rightly or not, as yet another ploy by Western "imperialists" to impose their own systems of values and beliefs on the rest of the world; and they have often produced exactly the opposite effects from what was intended – that is, more conflict and violence. Instead, we should submit these catalogues to a thorough process of intercultural dialogue and negotiation, in the hope that they will emerge from this process as living practices, not as abstract dogma.

To be sure, within the present Western local and regional contexts, democratic principles should continue to be regarded as valuable and praiseworthy and as constituting proper political ideals for liberal democracy – and one may stress, again, that in these contexts as well, they have not so far progressed much beyond the ideal stage. At the same time, if some societies around the world have now begun to invent their own forms of democracy, it is not because these forms have been imposed or adopted from outside or because they are demonstrably better than others; rather, it is because certain democratic principles resonate with their current inner aspirations. Clearly, there is no single formula for a successful democratic society, within or outside the Western world, that can be imported and replicated throughout the globe. Instead, each country will eventually find its proper social, economic, and political frameworks, should it choose to take a democratic path.

Nor should we content ourselves, if we wish to build genuine cultures of peace, with the lesser-of-two-evils arguments advanced in support of liberal democracy in relation to various forms of authoritarianism (see, for example, Professor Pera's arguments).[27] Democratic principles, no less than authoritarian ones, are agonistic political principles and as such they will always perpetuate the very mentality they claim to oppose. As long as peace and non-violence remain political instruments of power – for instance, in pacifism or in the "soft power" of Western-styled liberal democracy – they cannot achieve anything but the goals of Western-styled liberal democracies.

What one needs to change in the first place is precisely the rather widespread practice of subordinating all values and beliefs to political, utilitarian goals. In the end, intercultural hermeneutics should join other cognitive fields in working towards a global ethics grounded in a mentality of peace, defined not in opposition to war, but as an alternative mode of being, feeling, and acting in the world, with its own reference frames and systems of values and beliefs. This ethics can be called "emergent" because it depends on continuous intercultural research, learning, dialogue, and cooperation. It involves a determined and truly unprecedented effort on the part of the collective imagination of humans all over the planet and can hardly be accomplished overnight or by a single world culture, no matter how well intentioned and globally oriented that culture might be. Meanwhile, intercultural hermeneutics should by no means give up imagining such irenic principles and proposing them, in turn, for sustained, transdisciplinary, and intercultural research and dialogue.

Intercultural hermeneutics should start by exploring and further developing sound mechanisms and practices that will ensure mutually beneficial outcomes for local, regional, and global intercultural encounters. Intercultural dialogue, mediation, negotiation, and conflict management/resolution may be listed among such mechanisms, which should not be regarded simply as tools for achieving one's narrowly conceived political or economic objectives, but also as genuine learning processes conducive to global intelligence. Intercultural hermeneutics should analyse these mechanisms in detail and develop new ways in which they can be used in order to achieve maximum effectiveness in intercultural communication and understanding by reorienting all of the participants in the dialogue towards a mentality of peace.

Finally, within a global reference frame, intercultural hermeneutics should avoid such concepts as "knowledge society," "developed and developing societies," and "cosmopolitan democracy." Rather, it should start from the premise that, from the perspective of human development, there are no "developed" but only developing countries, all of which can bring valuable contributions to the planetary community. Indeed, the deciding factor in human development is not so much how effective a technology or political system may be, but our daily ethos or practice. We might possess, as Professor Pera claims, the "best" scientific theories, the "best" religion, the "best" information and communication technologies, or the "best" political system, such as liberal democracy. Yet we may end up putting all of them to inappropriate and counterproductive uses, as we have seen happen repeatedly throughout the history of scientific and technological development, as well as the history of world politics. Consequently, at the global level, intercultural hermeneutics, together with all the other arts and sciences, should help our planetary communities make the transition from "knowledge societies" to "wisdom societies," grounded in a mentality of peace.

NOTES

1 Jürgen Habermas and Joseph Ratzinger, *The Dialectics of Secularization: On Reason and Religion*, ed. Florian Schuller, trans. Brian McNeil (San Francisco: Ignatius, 2006).
2 Habermas, "Pre-Political Foundations of the Democratic Constitutional State?," in ibid., 45.
3 Ibid., 22.
4 Ibid., 38.
5 Ibid., 46.
6 Ibid., 46.
7 Ibid., 51.
8 Ibid., 52.
9 Ibid., 37f.; italics in the original text.

10 See Ratzinger, "That Which Holds the World Together: The Pre-Political Moral Foundations of a Free State," in Habermas and Ratzinger, *The Dialectics of Secularization*, 75f.

11 Ibid., 55.

12 Ibid., 61.

13 Ibid., 73.

14 Ibid., 73.

15 Ibid., 78.

16 Ibid., 79.

17 Ibid., 80.

18 Some of these principles I have already discussed, in other contexts, in *Global Intelligence and Human Development: Toward an Ecology of Global Learning* (Cambridge, MA: MIT Press, 2005) and *Remapping Knowledge. Intercultural Studies for a Global Age* (New York and Oxford: Berghahn, 2006), but here I am modifying and adapting them to the specific context of intercultural hermeneutics.

19 Janusz Symonides and Kishore Singh et al., *From a Culture of Violence to a Culture of Peace* (Paris: UNESCO, 1996), 15.

20 Ibid., 15.

21 Ibid., 19–20.

22 Francis Fukuyama, *The End of History and the Last Man* (London: Penguin, 1992); David Held, *Democracy and the Global Order: From the Modern State to Cosmopolitan Governance* (Cambridge: Polity, 1995).

23 Joseph Ratzinger and Marcello Pera, *Without Roots: The West, Relativism, Christianity, Islam*, foreword by George Weigel, trans. Michael F. Moore (New York: Basic, 2006).

24 See ibid., 11f.

25 Ibid., 91f.

26 Ratzinger, "That Which Holds the World Together," 71f.

27 See Ratzinger and Pera, *Without Roots*, 7f.

Chapter Eleven

Intercultural Understanding in Philosophical Hermeneutics

LAWRENCE K. SCHMIDT

Instant Coffee, but No Hot Water

In the summer of 2009 I was on an express train from Changchun to Harbin, China. I had just delivered a lecture on Gadamer's philosophical hermeneutics at Jilin University. My gracious hosts made sure I got on the correct train. After a while the snack cart was moving through the aisle. I decided to have some coffee. I asked for "coffee?" – literally, in English, since I do not speak a word of Chinese. Fortunately, "coffee?" was enough for intercultural communication. I was served a cup, a packet of instant coffee, a stirrer, sugar, and creamer. I was quite pleased, but then she moved on to the next person. I guess I had expected her to fill my cup up with hot water. What to do? I had to ask in English where the hot water was. I may have gestured, pointing to my cup. Again, this sufficed to communicate my desire, but the response was in Chinese. Several other helpful travellers also chimed in, to no avail for my ear. The server must have gestured or something, which I interpreted to mean: "Be patient, I will return." So I did and she did, picking up my cup and returning with hot water in it. Now I could mix my drink; by then I was used to instant coffee. After sipping coffee and watching the landscape race past, I decided to dispose of my now empty cup. I guessed there was some sort of trash receptacle at the end of the train car. I got up, walked down the aisle, found the trash bin, and then I saw it. There was a hot water dispenser built into the wall! Now everything made sense.

The Hermeneutic Situation

According to Hans-Georg Gadamer, the hermeneutic situation is fundamentally constituted by the set of prejudgments one has. A prejudgment,

Vorurteil,[1] is a conscious or often unconscious meaning, in the broadest sense, held by an interpreter at the beginning of an interpretive experience. Gadamer accepts Martin Heidegger's analysis of the hermeneutic circle and the conditioning effect one's preunderstanding has in each act of understanding. Both argue that there can be no case of direct understanding that avoids the effects of one's preunderstanding. So in order to understand, one must discover the legitimate prejudgments by which one correctly understands and avoid illegitimate ones that lead to misunderstanding. Gadamer formulates the fundamental epistemological question for hermeneutics: "What is the ground of the legitimacy of prejudgments?"[2] We acquire our prejudgments through acculturation, a major part of which is learning a language. The set of prejudgments one has constitutes one's horizon of possible meanings.

In the coffee example, my set of prejudgments included many legitimate prejudgments such as that the cart being pushed down the isle had refreshments and that the toilet and trash bin were at the end of the train car. These prejudgments were used when I needed them to understand the situation. Most of my prejudgments – for example, all that I judged about trains and train travel – were unconsciously held. I also had the illegitimate prejudgment that there were no hot water dispensers in train cars. My experience on the train permitted me to correct this illegitimate prejudgment and adopt a new legitimate judgment about hot water dispensers and Chinese express trains. This is a simple example of how an illegitimate prejudgment is replaced by a new judgment that will function as a legitimate prejudgment in future acts of understanding. Through this experience my set of prejudgments changed.

Before one begins to think critically, one has inherited in primarily a passive manner the whole set of prejudgments that allow one to experience the world as one does. Each generation passes on a relatively stable set of prejudgments to the next generation. This relatively stable inheritance establishes a culture and its tradition. Of course, each generation slightly modifies its inheritance, so cultures and traditions change while maintaining their basic identities. In a similar manner we identify different languages and their histories. By means of critique and further experience, traditions and languages change. The question is: When is such change justified? "In the end it [language] itself must give way when the use of language is not supported by sufficient experience."[3] Gadamer's example is the change from saying "*Walfisch*" (literally: whale-fish) to only saying *Wal* (whale) in German.

In *Truth and Method,* Gadamer does argue for the authority of tradition against the Enlightenment critique of all tradition. The preservation of questioned prejudgments in tradition is an act of reason.[4] He presents two reasons why temporal distance can solve the problem of legitimate prejudgments. First, some prejudgments that have survived in a tradition have been questioned and found to be legitimate by those in that tradition. Illegitimate prejudgments, if tested, would have been rejected. Second, because of the changes in the historical context of a tradition, a prejudgment can be found to have new significance in the contemporary hermeneutic situation. In the first edition of *Truth and Method,* Gadamer wrote that *only* temporal distance can solve the critical question of how to distinguish legitimate prejudgments from illegitimate ones. In the *Gesammelte Werke* edition of 1986, he changes "only" to "often" and remarks in the footnote that it is distance and not just temporal distance that can solve this hermeneutic task.[5] Distance means otherness.[6] Thus intercultural dialogue is likely to embody greater distance.

But Gadamer has *not* argued that inherited prejudgments are always legitimate, as many interpreters, including Habermas,[7] have claimed. Gadamer rejects both the Enlightenment position that tradition should always be questioned and the Romantic position that tradition is always correct. "Primeval wisdom is only the opposite image of 'primeval stupidity.'"[8] The authority of tradition is not absolute. Gadamer argues, *contra* Habermas, that the recognition of an authority is itself a rational process. Tradition "needs to be affirmed, embraced, cultivated. It is, essentially, preservation ... Preservation is an act of reason though an inconspicuous one."[9] The loss of authority occurs when one judges that the former authority does not have superior knowledge or insight.[10] The example of the classical in *Truth and Method* does not imply that tradition is always correct; rather, it illustrates a mode of historical being – that is, that some texts (prejudgments) have been rationally judged worthwhile (legitimate) and passed on from one generation to the next. In an interview, Gadamer says, "I never defended particular traditions, only that there is a horizon of tradition, which always constitutes the background for change."[11] However, this transmission has also included criticism, change, and reinterpretation. In *Moral Consciousness and Communicative Action,* Habermas reconsiders his critique of philosophical hermeneutics. He admits that "the hermeneutic circle is closed only on the metatheoretical level,"[12] which means that the indeterminacy and conditioning of the preunderstanding is effective on this level. "All rational reconstructions, like other types of knowledge, have only hypothetical status."[13] However, on the object level Habermas allows only testable empirical theories to support an interpretive reconstruction, whereas Gadamer, as will be argued, admits other types of evidence to justify an interpretation.[14]

Due to the role of inherited prejudgments in understanding, everyone has an effective historical consciousness in the broad sense – a consciousness that has been shaped by the inherited prejudgments that constitute one's horizon of meaning. This consciousness "determines in advance both what seems to us worth inquiring about and what will appear as an object of investigation."[15] It also determines what methods are appropriate.[16] So Gadamer concludes: "*That is why the prejudgments of the individual, far more than his judgments, constitute the historical reality of his being.*"[17] Only those who are reflectively aware of the role of inherited prejudgments in understanding have an effective historical consciousness in the narrow sense.[18] Understanding that one has inherited both legitimate and illegitimate prejudices, one is more likely to be self-critical and willing to learn from others.

Reading Confucius in Journeys Class

At Hendrix College we have a multicultural, interdisciplinary, required first-semester course called Journeys. We begin with six class days on what we call Confucian Journeys. Most students have never read *The Analects* (*Lunyu*) of Confucius, and the aphoristic style of the text, not to mention its contents, is foreign to them. Since they are familiar with reading stories, essays, or arguments, the first task is to get them to think that there is something said in such a text. I suggest that it is like a puzzle where they need to collect similar pieces and bring them together to build a picture of the whole. We begin with a few analects about *xiao* (filial piety). Of course we are reading *The Analects* in English and depend on the translator to bring the text to speak to us in English. We read that "filial piety and respect for elders constitute the root of Goodness (*ren*)."[19] One thing that appears to be meant is that one's moral education begins in the family. This idea calls the students' own ideas (prejudgments) into the conversation. Some agree, some are tentative, and others are sceptical. We read in 4.18 that a child can politely disagree with her parents but that if her proposal is not accepted then she should do what the parents say. Here there is more protest: the Confucian prejudgment of proper filial piety challenges the students' prejudgment of using their own reason. Students tend to defend their own prejudgment; we try to make the Confucian position more acceptable. There are certainly some cases, the students concede, where the parents know best; the age, knowledge, and experience of the child enter into consideration. Okay, I hear, but there are clear cases on the other side. What if the parents are bad parents, or just behind the times, too conservative, or just stubborn and clearly wrong? I mention the Confucian theory of the rectification of names, glossing 12.11: a parent is a parent only if he is behaving correctly as a parent and only then is he due filial piety. This helps a little, but there is no mass conversion to Confucian ideals. Of course, this is but an introduction: adjudication between these prejudgments is not the aim; the beginning of an understanding of the other is being sought.

Listening to the Other

Distance or otherness allows differing prejudgments to appear. "It is the other, who breaks my I-centredness, by presenting me with something to understand."[20] The other presents me with a prejudgment that conflicts with one of my own. This is possible only if I presuppose the preconception of completion[21] that Gadamer identifies as "an axiom of all hermeneutics."[22] The preconception of completion is the *initial* assumption on the part of the interpreter that the text is both coherent and truthful – that is, that it has something to say. One begins reading a text from one's inherited set of prejudgments. If, while reading, the interpreter encounters an inconsistency in the text, the presupposition of coherence makes one search for another interpretation that does not produce this inconsistency in the text. It thereby calls into question one's own prejudgments, which produced the inconsistency, and opposes them to other prejudgments (another interpretation) that do not lead to an inconsistency. "The Master said, 'I should just give up! I have yet to meet someone who is able to perceive his own faults and then take himself to task inwardly.'"[23] One could interpret this statement literally to mean that Confucius had never met anyone who was able to change his behaviour. This reading would, however, contradict the importance and success Confucius finds in learning and self-critique. To avoid this inconsistency, the preconception of completion asks the reader to find another interpretation that does not produce an inconsistency. One might follow Zhu Xi's comment that this passage is to be read as a warning to his students about how hard it is to be self-critical and change one's prejudgments.[24] Similarly, the presupposition of truthfulness in the text prevents the interpreter from declaring the text wrong on the basis of her own prejudgments. This permits the text to challenge the interpreter's prejudgments with another prejudgment allowing the text to present another truth. Many students find Confucius's concept of filial piety to be just wrong and are ready to stop reading. However, to begin to understand Confucius they need to call their own prejudgment into question and try to read Confucius as if he is saying something worthwhile. Only then can they develop a clearer concept of what Confucius means by filial piety. If the interpreter does not assume the preconception of completion, he will just declare the text incoherent or untruthful and have no reason to question his own prejudgments that lead to his interpretation.

Intercultural encounters are advantageous because there is likely to be a greater distance, a greater otherness, between the interpreter and the text or other person. The horizons of meaning or sets of prejudgments differ more, and using the preconception of completion, there may be more prejudgments in the interpreter that are called into question. In a conversation each person would make this presupposition. The greater distance increases the chances of a true experience where one learns that what one thought was the case is not the case. Reading a text from a contemporary, like-minded author in one's own tradition is less likely to challenge any prejudgments in the reader; the horizons of meaning are too similar.

Using the preconception of completion initiates the process of listening to the other. Gadamer emphasizes the importance of listening to the other in order to open the possibility of self-critique. The truth of experience is openness to new experience.[25] It is the recognition of one's own fallibility and finitude. "Openness to the other, then, involves recognizing that I myself must accept some things that are against me, even though no one else forces me to do so."[26] One must have what Gadamer called a *good will* towards the other. This is not a form of a metaphysics of the will, as Derrida charges Gadamer; rather, as Gadamer responds, a good will refers to Plato's *eumeneis elenchoi*, a friendly questioning, where one listens to and learns from the other.[27] Gadamer argues that listening to the other and being willing to learn from the other is the soul of hermeneutics or the hermeneutic virtue.[28] "That is the essence, the soul of my hermeneutics: To understand someone else is to see the justice, the truth, of their position. And this is what transforms us."[29] Of course the interpreter need not listen to the other.

The interpreter could naively just apply his inherited prejudgments to the text. One could force the meaning of a text into one's preconceived categories. In a conversation one could pretend to listen while actually not.

So the first critical moment in hermeneutic experience is an openness to self-critique. Justified critique requires an openness to self-critique in order to have considered the position of the other. Travelling in another culture, one is confronted with difference, and this often allows one to become aware of one's own customary behaviours and prejudgments, which may then be questioned.

Intercultural dialogue usually encounters the problem of different languages. There is a continuum here between a bilingual interpreter and one who must rely completely on a translator. Gadamer argues that interpretation in one language is like the case of translation. "The translator's task of translation differs in degree only, not in kind, from the general hermeneutical task that any text presents."[30] The translator must take what is said in one language and transpose it into the other language. He or she must be almost bilingual for there to be much success. However, since each language differs from every other language, translation cannot be a one-to-one correspondence. The humour of one-to-one literal translations indicates the futility of this idea. The translator must take his understanding of what the text has to say, the first interpretation, and express it in another language as best as possible. He knows choices are required that highlight one aspect but diminish another, both of which were heard in the original. The subject matter constrains the translation, since the translator must bring "into language the subject matter that the text points to; but this means finding a language that is not only his but is also appropriate to the original."[31] The reader of a translation performs a second interpretation of the translator's text. If the translation has succeeded the original text will be able to speak to the reader.

My students and I were completely dependent on the translator of *The Analects*. The translation was appropriate to the original, but that still left us the major task of discovering what Confucius was saying. With the translator's assistance we examined some of the key concepts and problems of translation. Concerning *ren*, Goodness, we could follow that it is made of the Chinese character for person plus the number two, so it probably referred to people in general. We noted other translations of *ren*, such as benevolence, humanity, humanheartedness, and authoritative conduct. The best we could do was remember these various possibilities while reading and thinking. "Goodness" is clearly a choice that favours a particular interpretation. When one does not understand the original language and depends on translations, one must be more humble in interpreting and one's critique more tentative.

To bring the language of the text to speak to the interpreter is part of the central task of hermeneutics – namely, application. Heidegger insisted that all understanding is interpretation; to this, Gadamer adds that understanding is interpretation but that application is required as well. Application means applying what the text or an other has to say to the interpreter's horizon of meaning. It entails, so to speak, translating the text into the interpreter's horizon using the preconception of completion. Application is integral to the process of understanding; it is not, as many have thought, the application of what is already understood to some situation. Gadamer clearly states: "Application does not mean first understanding a given universal in itself and then afterward applying it to a concrete case. It is the very understanding of the universal – the text itself."[32] Of course, once we understand a text where we have corrected a prejudgment – even one as simple as the location of hot water dispensers on Chinese trains – this new understanding may well influence the way we act.

The Adjudication of Prejudgments

The adjudication of prejudgments takes place in the fusion of horizons where the hermeneutic event of truth may occur. The interpreter projects a meaning for the text (or other person) using the preconception of completion, one's understanding of the language used, and the appropriate interpretive processes. This projected horizon of meaning is the so-called horizon of the text (or other). Projecting this horizon is the central task of application. "Understanding always involves something like applying the text to be understood to the interpreter's present situation."[33] In fact, this projected horizon exists within and in contradistinction to the horizon the interpreter brings to this process of understanding. There is, therefore, according to Gadamer, actually only one horizon, which contains the differences in prejudgments between the interpreter's original horizon and the projected horizon of the text. "In truth there is, therefore, a single horizon that includes everything that historical consciousness contains in itself."[34]

For example, when reading Mencius and Xunzi on human nature (*xing*) – in translation, of course – I must apply, that is, translate, what is written into my own horizon of meaning. Confucius had not been definitive concerning human nature.[35] About two centuries later, Mencius argued: "If you let people follow their original feelings, they will be able to do good. This is what is meant by saying that human nature is good. If man does evil, it is not the fault of his natural endowment."[36] According to Mencius, our natural endowment includes four basic feelings (*duan*, sprouts or beginnings) that lead to four basic Confucian virtues. Xunzi, on the other hand, claimed that "the nature of man is evil; his goodness is the result of his activity."[37] For humans to counter their inborn nature, "the civilizing influence of teachers and laws and the guidance of propriety [*li*] and righteousness [*yi*]" are required.[38] I may well think of the states of nature in Locke and Hobbes when understanding human nature in Mencius and Xunzi. However, Ames argues that the common translation of "*xing*" as "nature" is misleading, since it incorrectly suggests an essential nature as found in Western metaphysics. *Xing* for him is a dynamic concept indicating "the propensity for growth, cultivation, and refinement."[39] Goldin, on the other hand, argues that Mencius and Xunzi meant different things by *xing*. Xunzi meant "what we have from birth – in other words different forms of desires," while Mencius meant "the unique characteristics of human beings" as opposed to other species.[40] So in my expanded horizon I have these various voices or conflicting prejudgments.

Within this enlarged horizon the adjudication of prejudgments occurs – "*understanding is always the fusion of these horizons supposedly existing by themselves*."[41] The adjudication of prejudgments is the hermeneutic event of truth. The questioned prejudgments concern some subject matter that has been called into question. In the discussion of Mencius and Xunzi, the subject matter is human nature. As Heidegger states and Gadamer agrees, the justification of a prejudgment occurs when it is grounded in the subject matter and is not based on fancies or popular conceptions.[42] In his habilitation, *Plato's Dialectical Ethics*, Gadamer discusses the role of justification in the friendly questioning of a proper conversation. The care for justification is *Redestehen* (a standing for something in discourse). *Redestehen* is the "task of justifying by the presentation of the reason."[43] The reasons or arguments provided in justification of one prejudgment as opposed to another claim to be *einsichtig*, able to be seen and understood. The other conversant is called upon to agree or disagree with the proffered reason. "The other is free to respond to it [the reason], i.e. not only in the manner of agreeing but also in that of disagreeing."[44] An acceptable reason, Gadamer continues, must also be grounded in the subject matter, and it must entail or ground the proffered reason.[45] If the other disagrees, she must herself offer her position and reasons. In interpreting Mencius and Xunzi, I consider the arguments each presents as well as the arguments presented by the commentators. The productivity of the conversation in coming to understand the subject matter at hand comes from this back and forth of the discussion.[46] The aim of a conversation is to reach "agreement concerning the subject matter."[47]

In *Truth and Method*, Gadamer reiterates this process of coming to be in agreement in a conversation. He emphasizes that it is not just the "preponderance of reasons for the one and against the other possibility" that decides a question. "The thing itself [*Sache selbst*] is known only when the counterinstances are dissolved, only when the counterarguments are seen to be incorrect."[48] In dialogue one needs also to strengthen the arguments of the other in order to possibly learn from them. Importantly, Gadamer also argues that "to conduct a conversation means to allow oneself to be conducted by the subject matter to which the partners in the dialogue are oriented."[49] To seek to uncover the subject matter and not just defend one's own position opens up the possibility that during a conversation a new prejudgment that was initially not held by either of the conversation partners could come into the discussion. This movement in conversation indicates the event character of understanding or the hermeneutic event of truth.

In understanding a text from one's own tradition the reader cannot claim she is "discovering" by the application of method what actually was intended. However, this situation does motivate secondarily "the indispensible methodological discipline one has towards oneself."[50] Gadamer is here considering the case where the inherited text has something truthful to say.[51] It is the "coming into language of what has been said in tradition ... Thus here it really is true to say that this event is not our action upon the thing, but the act of the thing itself [*Sache selbst*]."[52] What comes to be understood in this hermeneutic event of truth is not the thing in itself but only "an 'aspect' of the thing itself [*eine Ansicht der Sache selbst*]."[53] This limitation arises because one must understand using a particular language. Agreeing with Humboldt, Gadamer argues that each language can only present an aspect of the world, a world view, and not the world in itself.[54]

In the last pages of *Truth and Method*, by means of a discussion of Plato's concept of the beautiful, Gadamer solves the epistemological question of how to ground legitimate prejudgments. "Obviously what distinguishes the beautiful from the good is that the beautiful makes itself immediately evident [*einleuchtend*]."[55] Understanding correctly "is a genuine experience [*Erfahrung*] – i.e., an encounter with something that asserts itself as truth."[56] Truth for Gadamer, following Heidegger, is alethetic, an uncovering of an aspect of the subject matter. The aspect of the subject matter that is uncovered in the hermeneutic conversation is, according to Gadamer, enlightening. "Like everything meaningful, the beautiful is enlightening [*einleuchtend*]."[57] Gadamer relates the term enlightening to a series of terms in the rhetorical tradition. "The *eikos*, the *verisimile*, the true-shining [*Wahr-Scheinliche*], the enlightening [*Einleuchtende*] belong in a series that defends their own correctness in opposition to the true and certain of the proven and known."[58] The meaning of enlightening (*einleuchtend*) here must be understood from the common German expression "*Es leuchtet mir ein*," which can be translated as "That makes sense to me" or "That convinces me." As Gadamer states: "What is enlightening is always something said – a proposal, a plan, a conjecture, an argument or something similar."[59] It is, so to speak, the ingenuity of the proposal, the congeniality of the plan, or the strength of the argument that convinces the conversation partners of the correctness of this result. It is why they come to be in agreement. The poetic word shines forth, enlightening the reader so that she can say, quoting Gadamer quoting Goethe, "so true, so full of being [*so wahr, so seined*]."[60]

In the hermeneutic conversation various plans, arguments, or interpretations are considered and defended in the back and forth of the discussion. At some point one proposal, one answer to the question posed, shines forth and elicits agreement from the conversation partners. The prejudgment has been grounded in or legitimated by the aspect of the subject matter. The conversation has reached its completion, and the legitimated prejudgment becomes the judgment of that conversation. Gadamer speaks of the event of hermeneutic truth for several reasons: one cannot predict the agreement that a conversation will reach at the beginning of the conversation; new and previously unconsidered answers may come to be discussed within the movement of a conversation; the conversation occurs within the limitations of a particular language and horizon of meaning of the conversation partners; and, in the end, one answer enlightens the conversation partners as being the aspect of the subject matter under discussion. The conversation partners are taken up into the play of conversation, into the search for legitimate prejudgments, for the uncovering of truth. When agreement has been found the conversation reaches its completion. This is the reason Gadamer writes, "In understanding we are drawn into an event of truth and arrive, as it were, too late, if we want to know what we are supposed to believe."[61] Once the conversation has come to agreement, it makes no sense to ask what one should believe since one has just come to be in agreement about the legitimacy of the answer to the question. At the beginning as well as during a conversation, one cannot predict which answer will be legitimated, so again, it makes no sense to ask what one should believe, for that is still unknown. At most one can say that when agreement has been reached then one knows what one believes, what has enlightened, what aspect of the *Sache selbst* has been uncovered.

In considering the sense of human nature in Mencius and Xunzi, I arrive at a provisional agreement or conclusion to this conversation. I do not find Goldin's arguments decisive. It makes sense to me that Mencius and Xunzi were disagreeing with each other about the same sense of human nature. Xunzi criticizes Mencius, so at least he thought they were speaking about the same idea. I take Ames's worry seriously that I may well be reading Western metaphysical connotations into the idea of human nature. I agree with Fung Yu-lan that Mencius and Xunzi agree that heaven (*tian*) is not partial, awarding some humans good natures and others bad ones.[62] I bracket and leave unanswered the exact metaphysical status of human nature. What appears correct to me, what makes sense, what is enlightening to me at this point is that Mencius and Xunzi represent two opposing views about how humans would behave if left to their own devices. Xunzi, like Hobbes, contends that humans by nature would follow their appetitive, egocentric desires for the most part, leading to disorder and chaos. Mencius thinks that humans begin with the four original feelings or sprouts, which if nurtured will lead to harmonious behaviour similar to what Locke posits. Although one can say that the conversation has ended for the moment, I realize all too well that another conversation concerning this subject matter could easily begin.

Possibilities of Intercultural Critique

In many intercultural exchanges the preconditions for a hermeneutic conversation are not met. Exposing the lack of such preconditions constitutes a form of justified critique that questions any agreement that may have occurred. Such a critique would itself have to follow from a legitimate hermeneutic conversation that achieved agreement.

One general case of failure occurs when one of the conversation partners or the interpreter presumes to already know the truth about the subject matter. The interpreter simply reads a text using his own prejudgments. Not using the preconception of completion, he naively declares the text or the other incoherent or wrong if this is what his reading presents. Here, the other is treated as an object, objectified into preaccepted categories. Encountering foreign customs, the traveller has already presupposed that her own customs are the better ones. One's own way of life and beliefs are unquestionably correct. One who claims to know does not really enter into a conversation, but rather gives a speech.[63] In general the speaker is not open to the possibility of self-critique. Gadamer writes: "I completely disagree with the desired goal of a single language either for Europe or for humanity ... We may perhaps survive as humanity if we would be able to learn that we may not simply exploit our means of power and effective possibilities, but must learn to stop and respect the other as an other, whether it is nature or the grown cultures of peoples and nations."[64]

Another case of failing to meet the prerequisites for a hermeneutic conversation is to aim only to win the argument. One does not really listen to the other; rather, one employs whatever means one can muster to defeat the other. Gadamer characterizes this position in reference to Plato's discussion as *phthonos,* which means "concern about being ahead of others and not being left behind by others."[65] One uses whatever rhetorical tricks one has to win the argument. One avoids being led by the subject matter under discussion and reformulates the other's counter-arguments into a weaker version that can be defeated easily. The speaker recognizes the other as a person but claims to have superior knowledge about the other, to know the other better then he does himself. "The claim to understand the other person in advance functions to keep the other person's claim at a distance."[66] When the aim is to win, position and power may be used to browbeat the other into agreement. That other may agree simply in order to escape the situation.[67] In this way, one avoids the need for justification and simply uses one's power; one is authoritarian but not a true authority.[68]

A proper hermeneutic conversation requires that one enter it with goodwill towards the other – that is, with a willingness to listen to and learn from another. To not listen to the other's proposals and justifications is to ignore the possibility of learning from the other. In a proper conversation one should even help the other person improve his justification. A conversation begins with a question that frames the subject matter to be investigated. A slanted question, Gadamer states, is not a false one; rather, it is one that makes presuppositions that lead in the wrong direction so that the question cannot be correctly answered.[69] As Gadamer responded to Habermas, one cannot presuppose that following a particular method will automatically lead to truth. The choice of method itself must occur within a conversation and must be called for by the subject matter. Finally, one should not just consider the initial proposals in a conversation, but follow the lead of the subject matter as it directs the conversation.

Assuming that the preconditions for a hermeneutic conversation have been met, what possible results of an intercultural conversation exist? And where can one speak of justified critique?

In one case, the interpreter or initiator of a conversation may in fact have the correct position and be able to convince the other of this. The interpreter's reasoning and justifications are acceptable. The other has been acknowledged and listened to, and her arguments have been strengthened. Nevertheless, the interpreter's prejudgment is legitimate and agreed to by the other. Gadamer rarely considers this case.[70] One reason might be that here, the interpreter does not have a true experience of discovering he was wrong, but rather discovers he is right. Another reason might be that in *Truth and Method*, Gadamer is discussing how correct understanding of a text from one's tradition occurs without presupposing the scientific method. Yet at the same time, Gadamer is certainly critical of the traditional assessment of the scientific method as the sole means to attain truth. He also criticizes the traditional interpretation of Plato. Although I would not agree with Kögler's analysis of Gadamer in *The Power of Dialogue*, Kögler's final position requires the agent's consent to the theorist.[71] However, his analysis is in danger of presupposing that the theorist has the correct methodology or superior position. On the other hand, he allows that in a critical dialogue "each subject in dialogue finds herself in a position to reconstruct the other's background."[72]

The opposite case would be where the text or the other is discovered to have the legitimate prejudgment. The text challenges a prejudgment of the interpreter, and in applying the preconception of completion and bringing the text to speak, the interpreter realizes he was mistaken. The text had something truthful to say to the interpreter. In *Truth and*

Method, Gadamer is generally concerned with this case – with coming to understand the truth of what a text has to say. In a conversation the other disagrees with my thesis and with my proffered reasons. She presents another position and her justification. I am able to listen to her and her arguments or justification, am open to self-criticism, and come to agree that she is correct. One has the genuine experience of learning from the other. The environment can also correct an illegitimate prejudgment, as in my discovery of the hot water dispenser. Travelling in another culture helps one learn about one's own cultural presuppositions, which can then be questioned. Similarly, in reading Mencius from a previous understanding of Locke, one might not have considered the possibility that the endowment in human nature could be just the beginning stages of goodness. Mencius's theory of the four original feelings or sprouts shined forth and was convincing. Mencius's case of the child about to fall into a well appears correct. Most people would be concerned, and the few who might not be could be accounted for by negative environmental factors that prevent one natural sprout from growing into the full virtue of *ren*.

Another case of coming to be in agreement is a hermeneutic conversation where a new legitimate prejudgment is uncovered in the back and forth of the conversation. This possibility is the most productive result. In this case neither the prejudgment of the one nor the prejudgment of the other is found to be adequate. Neither is enlightening. However, during the give and take in a conversation where different possible prejudgments or answers are explored, a new prejudgment comes to be explored and justified. This new prejudgment is enlightening and answers the original question about the subject matter. A new perspective of the subject matter is found to be legitimate and is agreed upon by the conversation partners. It is primarily in this sense that Gadamer can argue that the conversation is being led by the subject matter. There is an event of truth that could not have been predicted at the beginning of the conversation. Both you and I have learned something new.

In intercultural conversations neither culture had the correct answer, but each learned a new answer that was more correct than the one they had before. Gadamer writes: "I do not know what answers humanity will one day finally arrive at concerning how people will live together, either in relation to the rights of the individual versus the rights of the collective, or in relation to the violence that comes from the family or from the state … I do venture to say, however, that if we do not acquire the hermeneutic virtue – that is, if we do not realize that it is essential first of all to *understand* the other person ... then we will never be able to accomplish the essential tasks of humanity, whether on a small or large scale."[73]

Of course a conversation, even under the prerequisites of a proper hermeneutic conversation, may fail in that neither can come to agree with the other. Each has listened to the other and has even tried to make the other's arguments stronger. Nevertheless, each conversation partner finds her own position to be more convincing. On both sides an impasse occurs. Neither of the conflicting prejudgments is enlightening to everyone. The conversation has failed to attain agreement. There is no event of hermeneutic truth. Gadamer notes in this case that the inability to agree is not really a result but rather an incomplete conversation that, in a sense, requests that it be taken up anew.[74] Intercultural conversations often encounter this type of incompleteness. Perhaps such is the case concerning the question of whether humans are to be understood as primarily individuals or as primarily constituted by their relations to others, as Ames and Rosemont argue is the case for the Confucian world view.[75]

In another, yet similar, case of a failed conversation, Gadamer writes that the inability to reach agreement is due to "undiscussable [*undiskutierbaren*] presuppositions" held by each concerning the subject matter under discussion.[76] These presuppositions are undiscussable in this conversation in that they are presupposed in the question of horizon that framed this conversation. If these presuppositions are acknowledged, then another conversation can engage this difference as its subject matter. If agreement could be reached in this second conversation, then the original one could be resumed.

Such a situation is often encountered in intercultural conversations where more fundamental differences concerning some subject matter prevent an agreement in a conversation that presupposes these differences. The nature of human nature could be a presupposed prejudgment in my thinking about Mencius and Xunzi. From a Western metaphysical perspective one has presupposed that humans do have an essential nature that individuates them. However, if Ames is correct, the proper understanding of human nature in the debate between Mencius and Xunzi concerns a dynamic sense of human being. Before deciding on an interpretation of Mencius and Xunzi, one would have to open another questioning about the concept of human nature in general.

Another possible result of a hermeneutic conversation I would term an agreement to disagree. This differs from the previous case of an incomplete or failed conversation where each conversation partner thought his or her own prejudgment was correct. In agreeing to disagree each person acknowledges that the justification proffered by the other is equally as strong or convincing as their own, but sees no way at the moment to decide between these positions. There may be two or more equally appropriate ways to answer the question concerning the subject matter being discussed. We may not, at the time, have enough evidence to support one prejudgment and refute the other. However, the conversation does reach an amicable agreement. Here one can say that one is truly respecting difference.

In an intercultural conversation we could conclude that there is more than one possible correct answer concerning the subject matter. Each culture may have its particular manner of greeting a stranger. One may bow or shake hands to greet the other. Both manners are equally justified, and one can respect the custom of the other. In special circumstances, such as a viral epidemic, one could come to agree on which practice is more hygienic, without claiming that it is better in all cases. Concerning the meaning of human nature in Mencius and Xunzi, the arguments for the different interpretations appear to me at the moment to be equally justified.

The foregoing analysis of the hermeneutic situation – listening to the other, the legitimization of prejudgments, and possible results of hermeneutic conversations – demonstrates how justified critique in intercultural conversations is possible within Gadamer's philosophical hermeneutics. The question that brings various prejudgments into contention receives its answer when the conversation partners can come to agree on the correctness, the enlightening aspect of the subject matter, of one prejudgment. The agreed judgment is a justified critique of the other contending prejudgments. What is enlightening – the ingenuity of the proposal, the congeniality of the plan, the strength of the argument, or the saying of the artwork – is the truth that has come forth in that conversation. However, since there is no last word, no final truth, the agreement can always be questioned in a later conversation. Another form of justified critique concerns the situation of the conversation itself. If the prerequisites of a proper hermeneutic conversation have not been met, the justified critical stance is to demonstrate this failure and gain agreement on this circumstance. Critical theory as ideology critique is most concerned with the situation where an inherited and reigning prejudgment is the result of "systematically distorted communication."[77] To expose the illegitimate genesis and propagation of this prejudgment would be to attain agreement on the failure of the previous conversations to meet the prerequisites for a true hermeneutic conversation, thereby invalidating the previous agreement.

If, on the other hand, the prerequisites of a hermeneutic conversation have been met, then the agreement of the conversation partners represents the temporary but critical stance. Of course, an agreement may not be attained. Each conversation partner may remain convinced that his or her position is the stronger one. The conversation is at best incomplete. However, the lack of agreement may be due to as yet undiscussed presuppositions that could be brought to light. Habermas claims that "there is a sense in which any interpretation is a *rational* interpretation."[78] Since the interpreter must reconstruct the reasons the author could have had, and since he must use his own reasoning to project and evaluate these reasons, the interpreter must appeal to "standards of rationality and hence to standards that he himself considers binding on all parties."[79] Importantly, Habermas recognizes that this appeal to "presumably universal standards of rationality" does not, in fact, prove these to be "truly rational."[80] Habermas's concept of rationality appears to require an empirically testable, supporting theory. For Gadamer what is enlightening could be the strength of the arguments, including empirical data, but it could also include the saying of the artwork or the ingenuity of the plan, depending on what convinces in the conversation. There might be different concepts of rationality in intercultural conversations that require examination before agreement can be reached. Alternatively, one may come to agree to disagree, respecting the other to have an equally justified position. There are many areas of human conduct where there is no finally correct answer, but rather several modes of equally appropriate ways of acting. Difference, including cultural difference, may be celebrated. This, of course, does not imply that all ways are equally good.

One could also come to agreement in a conversation. The other could be correct and I could come to understand. Knowing I have an effective historical consciousness in the narrow sense, that I have inherited many untested prejudgments, I am open to self-critique. I am willing to listen to the other, exemplifying the hermeneutic virtue. I realize that I can only learn that what I thought was the case is not the case, if I allow the other to speak to me. On the other hand, I could be correct and justified in my criticism. I convince the other and he agrees with me. Here we need to be more careful since we tend to think we are correct and so are in "danger of appropriating the otherness of the other."[81] The most fruitful hermeneutic conversation is the one where each conversation partner discovers that his or her original position was not correct, and in the back and forth of the conversation a new prejudgment, a new idea, is discovered to which all agree. Everyone has learned something. Beyond the mere critique of the other, the value of intercultural conversations is when both learn from the other and learn something new that neither had known before.

NOTES

The following abbreviations are used for Gadamer's *Gesammelte Werke*:

GW Hans-Georg Gadamer, *Gesammelte Werke*, vols. 1–10 (Tübingen: J.C.B. Mohr [Paul Siebeck], 1985–95), which includes:

GW1 Bd. 1: *Hermeneutik I: Wahrheit und Methode. Grundzüge einer philosophischen Hermeneutik* (1960), 1986. English: *Truth and Method*.

GW2 Bd. 2: *Hermeneutik II: Wahrheit und Methode. Ergänzungen, Register*, 1986. "Zwischen Phänomenologie und Dialektik – Versuch einer Selbstkritik." 3–23. "Rhetorik, Hermeneutik und Ideologiekritik." 232–50. English: "Scope."

GW5 Bd. 5: *Griechische Philosophie I*, 1985. *Platos dialektische Ethik*. 3–163. English: *Plato's Dialectical Ethics*.

GW7 Bd. 7: *Griechische Philosophie III: Plato im Dialog*, 1990. "Natur und Welt." 418–42.

GW8 Bd. 8: *Ästhetik und Poetik I: Kunst als Aussage*, 1993. "Wort und Bild – 'so war, so seiend.'" 373–99. English: "Artwork."

1 *Truth and Method* translates "*Vorurteil*" as "prejudice," which is quite correct. I will use "prejudgment" here to avoid the usual negative connotations of "prejudice." I have modified other translations of *Truth and Method*. See Hans-Georg Gadamer, *Truth and Method*, 2nd rev. ed., trans. Joel Weinsheimer and Donald G. Marshall (New York: Crossroad, 1991).
2 GW1, 281; Gadamer, *Truth and Method*, 277.
3 GW7, 436.
4 GW1, 286; Gadamer, *Truth and Method*, 281.
5 GW1, 304; Gadamer, *Truth and Method*, 298.
6 See Gadamer's discussion of the importance of otherness with reference to temporal distance in GW2, 8–9. Gadamer also notes that there is in this situation the continual danger of appropriating the otherness of the other and so not recognizing this otherness (n230, GW1, 305; Gadamer, *Truth and Method*, 299).

7 Jürgen Habermas, "A Review of Gadamer's Truth and Method," in *The Hermeneutic Tradition: From Ast to Ricoeur*, ed. Gayle Ormiston and Alan Schrift, trans. Fred R. Dallmayr and Thomas McCarthy (Albany: SUNY Press, 1990), 213–45, 236.

8 GW1, 278; Gadamer, *Truth and Method*, 274.

9 GW1, 286; Gadamer, *Truth and Method*, 281.

10 GW2, 244; Gadamer, "On the Scope and Function of Hermeneutical Reflection," in *Hermeneutics and Modern Philosophy*, ed. Brice Wachterhauser, trans. G.B. Hess and R.E. Palmer (Albany: SUNY Press, 1986), 277–300 at 290.

11 Gadamer, "Interview: The 1920s, 1930s, and the Present: National Socialism, German History, and German Culture," in *Hans-Georg Gadamer on Education, Poetry, and History*, ed. Dieter Misgeld and Graeme Nicholson, trans. Lawrence Schmidt and Monika Reuss (Albany: SUNY Press, 1992), 150.

12 Habermas, *Moral Consciousness and Communicative Action*, trans. Christian Lenhardt and Shierry Weber Nicholsen (Cambridge, MA: MIT Press, 1990), 31.

13 Habermas, *Moral Consciousness*, 31.

14 See my "Critique: The Heart of Philosophical Hermeneutics," *Consequences of Hermeneutics: Fifty Years after Gadamer's* Truth and Method (Evanston: Northwestern University Press, 2010), 202–17.

15 GW1, 305–6; Gadamer, *Truth and Method*, 300.

16 See GW2, 439; Gadamer, *Truth and Method*, xxix. See also Gadamer's discussion of the importance of both ways of investigating in "Vom Wort zum Begriff," in *Gadamer Lesebuch*, ed. Jean Grondin (Tübingen: J.C.B. Mohr [Paul Siebeck], 1997) 100–11 at 104f.; and Gadamer, "From Word to Concept: The Task of Hermeneutics as Philosophy," in *The Gadamer Reader: A Bouquet of the Later Writings*, ed. and trans. Richard Palmer (Evanston: Northwestern University Press, 2007), 108–20 at 114f.

17 GW1, 281; Gadamer, *Truth and Method*, 276–7; original emphasis.

18 GW2, 444; Gadamer, *Truth and Method*, xxxiv.

19 Confucius, *The Essential Analects: Selected Passages with Traditional Commentary*, trans. Edward Slingerland (Indianapolis: Hackett, 2006), 1.2.

20 GW2, 9.

21 The English translation uses "fore-conception of completeness." The preconception of completion is similar to the principle of charity.

22 GW1, 376; Gadamer, *Truth and Method*, 370.

23 Confucius, *The Essential Analects*, 5.27.

24 Qtd in Confucius, *The Essential Analects*, 76.

25 GW1, 361; Gadamer, *Truth and Method*, 355.

26 GW1, 367; Gadamer, *Truth and Method*, 361.

27 Gadamer, "Reply to My Critics," in *The Hermeneutic Tradition*, 273–98, 55.

28 Gadamer, "Wort," 109; Gadamer, "Word," 119. See note 16 above.
29 Gadamer, "Interview," 152.
30 GW1, 391; Gadamer, *Truth and Method*, 387.
31 GW1, 390; Gadamer, *Truth and Method*, 387.
32 GW1, 346; Gadamer, *Truth and Method*, 341. In *Truth and Method*, Gadamer discusses Aristotle's analysis of *phronesis* (ethical knowledge) as a model for understanding application. Three points are made. First, the universal, what the text has to say, is more a "guiding image" than a universal law, so that application may involve modification to achieve the spirit as opposed to the letter of the law. Application is not the deductive subsumption of a case under the universal. Second, application requires deliberation and is not predictable. Third, application asks for sympathetic understanding.
33 GW1, 313; Gadamer, *Truth and Method*, 308.
34 GW1, 309; Gadamer, *Truth and Method*, 304.
35 Confucius, *The Essential Analects*, 17.2.
36 Mencius, "Idealistic Confucianism: Mencius," in *A Source Book in Chinese Philosophy*, ed. and trans. Wing-Tsit Chan (Princeton: Princeton University Press, 1963), 49–83 at 66.
37 Xunzi (Hsün Tzu), "Naturalistic Confucianism: Hsün Tzu," in *A Source Book in Chinese Philosophy*, 115–35 at 128.
38 Xunzi, "Naturalistic Confucianism: Hsün Tzu," 128.
39 Roger T. Ames, "The Mencian Conception of *Ren xing*: Does It Mean 'Human Nature'?," in *Chinese Texts and Philosophical Contexts: Essays Dedicated to Angus C. Graham*, ed. Henry Rosemont, Jr (La Salle: Open Court, 1991), 152.
40 Paul Rakita Goldin, *Rituals of the Way: The Philosophy of Xunzi* (Chicago: Open Court, 1999), 12, 13.
41 GW1, 311; Gadamer, *Truth and Method*, 306; original emphasis.
42 See *Sein und Zeit*, 153; qtd in GW1, 271; Gadamer, *Truth and Method*, 266, as "our first, last, and constant task in interpreting is never to allow our fore-having, fore-sight, and fore-conception to be presented to us by fancies and popular conceptions, but rather to make the scientific theme secure by working out these fore-structures in terms of the things themselves [*Sachen selbst*]."
43 GW5, 22; Gadamer, *Plato's Dialectical Ethics*, ed. and trans. Robbert M. Wallace (New Haven: Yale University Press, 1998), 27.
44 GW5, 28; Gadamer, *Plato's Dialectical Ethics*, 36.
45 GW5, 28; Gadamer, *Plato's Dialectical Ethics*, 36.
46 GW5, 30; Gadamer, *Plato's Dialectical Ethics*, 39.
47 GW5, 29; Gadamer, *Plato's Dialectical Ethics*, 38–9.

48 GW1, 370; Gadamer, *Truth and Method*, 364.
49 GW1, 373; Gadamer, *Truth and Method*, 367.
50 GW1, 465; Gadamer, *Truth and Method*, 461.
51 In the case of understanding a truth in an inherited text, Gadamer writes: "the content of tradition is the sole criterion and it expresses itself in language" (GW1, 476; Gadamer, *Truth and Method*, 472–3). This does not mean, as many have thought, that what the tradition says is always true and so critique of tradition is not possible. In this context Gadamer is comparing the hermeneutic dialectic of question and answer that has no final end to Hegel's dialectic that does end in absolute knowledge. Gadamer is considering a case where tradition has something to say to the interpreter. The interpreter recognizes "the absolute openness of the event of meaning" (GW1, 476; Gadamer, *Truth and Method*, 472). This does not mean that the interpreter can read anything into the text; rather, there is a standard that limits this openness. This standard is the content of tradition. The German word "*maßgeblich*" has been translated here as "criterion." In this context "*maßgeblich*" might rather have been translated as "standard." The content of tradition is the sole standard that limits possible interpretations. See Jean Grondin's discussion of this point in Grondin, *Hermeneutische Wahrheit?: Zum Wahrheitsbegriff Hans-Georg Gadamer* (Königstein/Ts.: Verlag Anton Hain Meisenheim, 1982), 179.
52 GW1, 467; Gadamer, *Truth and Method*, 463.
53 GW1, 477; Gadamer, *Truth and Method*, 473.
54 GW1, 446; Gadamer, *Truth and Method*, 442.
55 GW1, 485; Gadamer, *Truth and Method*, 481.
56 GW1, 493; Gadamer, *Truth and Method*, 489.
57 GW1, 488; Gadamer, *Truth and Method*, 485.
58 GW1, 488; Gadamer, *Truth and Method*, 485.
59 GW1, 489; Gadamer, *Truth and Method*, 485.
60 GW8, 383; Gadamer, "The Artwork in Word and Image: 'So True, So Full of Being!'" in *The Gadamer Reader: A Bouquet of the Later Writings*, ed. and trans. Richard Palmer (Evanston: Northwestern University Press, 2007), 192–224 at 207.
61 GW1, 494; Gadamer, *Truth and Method*, 490.
62 Fung Yu-lan, *A History of Chinese Philosophy*, 2 vols. (Princeton: Princeton University Press, 1952), I:284–6.
63 GW5, 36; Gadamer, *Plato's Dialectical Ethics*, 48.
64 Gadamer, "Die Vielfalt Europas: Erbe und Zukunft," *Das Erbe Europas* (Frankfurt am Main: Suhrkamp, 1989), 7–34, 31, 33–4; Gadamer, "The Diversity of Europe: Inheritance and Future," in *Hans-Georg Gadamer on Education, Poetry, and History*, 221–36, 234–6.

65 GW5, 34; Gadamer, *Plato's Dialectical Ethics*, 44–5.
66 GW1, 366; Gadamer, *Truth and Method*, 360.
67 GW5, 30; Gadamer, *Plato's Dialectical Ethics*, 40.
68 See Gadamer's essay "Autorität und Kritische Freiheit," in *Über die Verborgenheit der Gesundheit* (Frankfurt am Main: Suhrkamp, 1993), 149–58.
69 GW1, 370; Gadamer, *Truth and Method*, 364.
70 "His [the other's] substantive agreement is the only sufficient standard for the adequacy of the logos to the facts of the matter" (GW5, 31; Gadamer, *Plato's Dialectical Ethics*, 40).
71 Hans Herbert Kögler, *The Power of Dialogue*, trans. Paul Hendrickson (Cambridge, MA: MIT Press, 1996), 263.
72 Kögler, *The Power of Dialogue*, 311n1.
73 Gadamer, "Wort," 109; Gadamer, "Word," 119. See note 16 above.
74 GW5, 30; Gadamer, *Plato's Dialectical Ethics*, 39.
75 Roger T. Ames and Henry Rosemont, Jr, trans., *The Analects of Confucius: A Philosophical Translation* (New York: Ballantine, 1998), 24.
76 GW5, 30; Gadamer, *Plato's Dialectical Ethics*, 39.
77 Habermas, "The Hermeneutic Claim to Universality," in *The Hermeneutic Tradition*, 245–72 at 252.
78 Habermas, *Moral Consciousness*, 31.
79 Ibid., 31.
80 Ibid., 31.
81 GW1, 305; Gadamer, *Truth and Method*, 299.

Chapter Twelve

Making Sense of Critical Hermeneutics: Pragmatist Reflections

RICHARD SHUSTERMAN
AND WOJCIECH MAŁECKI[1]

I

In recent years, many scholars have pointed to various convergences between philosophical hermeneutics and pragmatism – for example, between the thought of Hans-Georg Gadamer on the one hand and John Dewey and Stanley Fish on the other,[2] or between the work of Richard Rorty and so-called radical hermeneutics.[3] Contemporary pragmatists such as Rorty and Richard Shusterman, in turn, have explicitly drawn from the work of Gadamer and Heidegger,[4] with Rorty's sympathy towards the hermeneutical tradition being further confirmed by his common publications with Gianni Vattimo.[5] Yet the relation between the two movements is far from completely harmonious, as evidenced, for instance, by Rorty's and Shusterman's criticisms of Heidegger and Gadamer, and by Heidegger's rejection of pragmatism in general, something that obviously complicates the whole picture (especially when we consider that Heidegger himself has been declared a pragmatist by some).[6]

As pragmatists invited to this hermeneutically oriented volume, we are interested in exploring how the relation between pragmatism and hermeneutics (which are culturally embedded, respectively, in Continental Europe – Germany in particular – and America) provides an interesting case study for a theory of intercultural interpretation. However, we shall address this relation only in the last part of the essay, as first we would like to lay out our views on interpretation in general and address the question of the (inherent) criticality of intercultural hermeneutics or interpretation.

II

From our pragmatist perspective, meaning is not a separate object but merely the correlate of understanding. And understanding something does not entail the mirroring correspondence or hermeneutic capturing or reproduction of some fixed semantic content. It is fundamentally an ability to handle or respond to that thing in certain accepted ways that are consensually shared, sanctioned, and inculcated by the community but that are nonetheless flexible and open to (divergent) interpretation and emendation. What counts as the proper response of true understanding not only depends on the normative practices of the given society but also varies with respect to different contexts within that society and its subcultures. We should expect, for example, different responses to be manifested in the ordinary, the literary, and the psychoanalytic understandings of an utterance. Interpretive knowledge may also be seen in this fashion as a performed ability to respond to an artwork, an utterance, or a person in ways conforming to the range of culturally appropriate responses, ways already accepted or ways that are able to win acceptance. On this account, our aims in interpretation are not always and essentially to excavate and describe the meaning already carefully buried in the text by its author (or in an action by its agent), but rather to develop and transmit a richly meaningful response to the text (or action). The project is not to describe the text's given and definitive sense but rather to *make sense* of the text. Our sense-making activity is not enslaved to mirroring or capturing a fixed antecedent meaning, but neither is it totally free, nor is it condemned to arbitrary, deviant "misreading." Consider the example of literary texts. We are initially constrained by our cultural training to interpret them in certain ways that highlight their coherence, depth, and reflection on life's problems; we are also driven to continue this practice out of fear that so much beauty and meaning will be lost if we interpret them differently. Our most established and respected practices of literary interpretation seem informed by a twofold principle that could be called "coherent comprehensiveness of understanding." For it aims at connectively constituting a greater wealth of meaningful features into a more coherent whole, a coherent understanding that exceeds the limits of the work itself and that we can indeed construct on the apparent inconsistencies of the work by explaining and placing them in a larger context.

However, from this general hermeneutic direction no strict uniformity of interpretive aims is implied, since there are a vast variety of socially entrenched, aesthetically proven, yet mutually competing interpretive strategies for making sense of texts, for rendering them coherent (even in their incoherence) to our understanding. Among the most deeply entrenched and richly meaningful interpretive strategies is the quest for authorial intention. Yet to affirm the value of this interpretive strategy is not to demand that the text's meaning be limited to the author's intention or even that the author's intention take the form of a single, determinate, unchanging semantic content. Authorial intentions can be vague and elusive; they also require an act of interpretation (even by the author herself) to render them determinate enough to provide a standard for acceptable interpretation. And even within a single sense-making strategy (such as authorial intention), the precise aims and consequent standards of interpretive validity will vary with the context, which always determines the whole in which understanding takes place. What is adequate for the Sunday paper may not do for the lecture hall or for academic journals, whose standards, again, are hardly uniform.

Three other points contribute to the variety of textual sense making. First, not all interpretive responses are dominated by cognitive purposes; the goal of enhanced aesthetic experience (such as in creative interpretive performance) can override the aim of trying to be "true" in some other than aesthetic sense. Knowledge, we scholars need reminding, is not the only worthy reason for reading and interpreting. Second, sense making is not always a matter of constructing some articulate verbal response to represent the text's content or form. Indeed, some ways of sense making can be so direct, immediate, and unthinking that they are better described as simply reading or understanding rather than interpretation.

For pragmatism, interpretation or making sense often renders changes in what is understood. But if these changes are sufficiently underpinned by continuities, we continue to identify and refer to the object of understanding as the same text. Textual objects are cultural entities that are constituted and reconstituted as individual objects by the social and linguistic practices and traditions of the culture they serve. Their individuation and identity (referential and substantive) rest on nothing beyond such practices; thus, they are as open to change as these practices are. Recognizing this, we can easily explain how the text's substantive identity of properties and meaning can change significantly over time even though the text has already been written or "completed" by its author and even though we continue to identify it as the same text. Nor do we need to agonize about whether, given such change, it *really* is the same text, assuming the question must have a definite answer, as indeed it should if we assume the work exists as an antecedently determinate and independent object of reified meaning.

Instead, on the pragmatist account we have been sketching, the text turns out to be a continuous and contested construction of efforts to understand and interpret it – that is, of efforts to determine how and what the text will be taken to be, which amounts, pragmatically speaking, to how and what it actually is. Although such efforts to determine understanding can perhaps be said to begin with the author (if we forget that literary and linguistic traditions already determine her determining efforts), the intentions that guide and shape understanding extend far beyond her authorial control. In speaking about interpretation as making sense, we have focused on texts, but we believe that this general approach can be extended to the interpretation of actions and characters, so that even one's own self-interpretation is more a matter of making sense of one's (changing, developing) self rather than the revelation of a fixed essence of the self that always was and always will be the self's true meaning.[7]

III

Now that we have presented our views on the nature of interpretive processes, we turn to the question of the criticality of intercultural hermeneutics. One might ask, how can there be intercultural understanding if understanding depends on ways of making sense that are consensually practised in a given cultural community and if different cultures are, by definition, different communities with different languages, values, and norms – and thus ways of making sense? The apparent problem of transcultural understanding disappears, however, when we recognize that along with differences between cultures there are an extraordinary variety of similarities and overlaps in norms, values, and ways of life. All cultures share the basic needs to eat, sleep, excrete waste, reproduce, and deal with death and with the education of children. There is also the obvious fact that almost every culture has been significantly shaped by processes of globalization and cultural interaction – processes that have been going on since ancient times through trade and warfare. It is not surprising that as a result of shared needs and common practices and our long history of transcultural interaction, various cultures have come to share some common interpretive strategies, among them authorial intention. Commonalities of understanding have been greatly accelerated in recent times through new communication technologies and the hegemony of Western culture.

The authors of this essay can be viewed as an example of cultural overlap despite deep differences. Shusterman is a Jew who was born in America, spent many of his teen and young adult years in Israel, and for a few years served in that country's military intelligence service; he then earned his PhD at Oxford University and now lives again in the United States. Małecki was born in Poland to ethnically Polish parents and has lived in that country all of his life, except for several research stays abroad that were no longer than a few months. We are surely different (note here that Shusterman's identity has been formed in several cultural contexts), and this, theoretically speaking, may hinder our ability to understand each other, let alone write an essay together. But to begin with trivialities, both of us belong to so-called Western civilization and are part of the same international academic system. Moreover, Małecki has been saturated with American culture for his entire life, given that its span has coincided with the time of America's global expansion, while Shusterman lived in Israel for several years with a family of Polish Jews.

But even if the convergence or overlap between cultures allows for their understanding of what they have in common, how can they understand what is *different* between them? If understanding involves making sense in *shared* ways, how are we to understand what is different or *not* shared with another culture? At the most basic level, however, we understand another culture simply as different, as not fitting into our usual ways of making sense, of resisting in some way those habitual ways we have of making sense. This can stimulate us to look for new ways of making sense of the foreign material, since we have a *prima facie* presupposition that the cultures of others do make sense to the members of those cultures even if they do not yet make sense to us. We project the idea that these foreign modes are understandable and can make sense, even if we do not yet understand them or as yet fail to understand them properly or fully. There are partial understandings that, while they are in some sense misunderstandings, can be corrected by further, better ways of making sense, and that in any case are better than no understanding at all.

Take, for instance, Jean-Paul Sartre's well-known essay "Black Orpheus," which begins by telling the (white) reader that if she expected to find, in Léopold Sédar Senghor's anthology[8] of black poets, praise of white culture, then she is in for a disappointment, and that another feeling that she is likely to experience while reading those texts is one of shock, a shock of "being seen":

> For three thousand years, the white man has enjoyed the privilege of seeing without being seen; he was only a look – the light from his eyes drew each thing out of the shadow of its birth; the whiteness of his skin was another look, condensed light. The white man – white because he was man, white like daylight, white like truth, white like virtue – lighted up the creation like a torch and unveiled the secret white essence of beings. Today, these black men are looking at us, and our gaze comes back to our own eyes; in their turn, black torches light up the world and our white heads are no more than Chinese lanterns swinging in the wind.[9]

It does not take much hermeneutic sensitivity to recognize that Sartre's vision (the word has been used purposively here) of black poetry is mediated through a certain philosophical paradigm – one that we might identify as phenomenological but that can be also described more generally as ocularocentrism – which is a Western invention or at least (has) primarily characterized Occidental thought.[10] In other words, what Sartre does here is filter poems written by black non-philosophers through the alembic of white philosophy and its peculiar obsessions,[11] including its penchant for using visual metaphors to denote epistemic processes. Needless to say, this move makes just as much sense as imposing on the same anthology an interpretive grid of class struggle, something that Sartre also does and that would be protested by Frantz Fanon,[12] who also accused Sartre of the "intellectualization of black existence" and, if that was not enough, of forgetting "that the Negro suffers in his body quite differently than the White."[13] Yet notwithstanding Sartre's particular interpretive inflection – or indeed because of it – the poems that Senghor anthologized (poems that included phrases such as "At times, we will haunt Montparnasse and Paris, / Europe and its endless torments, like memories / or like malaises [...]"[14]) generated in him a sense of shock (the shock of his own culture beginning to "seem exotic in [his] eyes" and of his "dignity beginning to crumble under" the look of black people),[15] and they may generate the same reaction in contemporary white readers who have been inspired by Sartre's essay to adopt a certain approach to the poems in question, which in turn may lead them to a critical interrogation of their attitude towards black people.

To give an even more extreme example, in the sense of not even being an instance of intercultural hermeneutics, but rather an interspecies one, and also in the sense of not dealing with a genuine text produced by the other, but merely with a fictional representation of such a text, consider Leo Tolstoy's story "Kholstomer." Its fictional narrator is a horse, who is also an acute observer of the human world, for whom many aspects of that world seem, however, puzzling. The concept of property is one example, but let the horse speak:

> I understand well what they said about whipping and Christianity. But then I was absolutely in the dark. What's the meaning of "his own," "his colt"? From these phrases I saw that people thought there was some sort of connection between me and the stable. At the time I simply could not understand the connection. Only much later, when they separated me from the other horses, did I begin to understand. But even then I simply could not see what it meant when they called me "man's property." The words "my horse" referred to me, a living horse, and seemed as strange to me as the words "my land," "my air," "my water."
>
> But the words made a strong impression on me. I thought about them constantly, and only after the most diverse experiences with people did I understand, finally, what they meant. They meant this: In life people are guided by words, not by deeds. It's not so much that they love the possibility of doing or not doing something as it is the possibility of speaking with words, agreed on among themselves, about various topics. Such are the words "my" and "mine," which they apply to different things, creatures, objects, and even to land, people, and horses. They agree that only one may say "mine" about this, that, or the other thing. And the one who says "mine" about the greatest number of things is, according to the game which they're agreed to among themselves, the one they consider the most happy. I don't know the point of all this, but it's true. For a long time I tried to explain it to myself in terms of some kind of real gain, but I had to reject that explanation because it was wrong.
>
> Many of those, for instance, who called me their own never rode on me – although others did. And so with those who fed me. Then again, the coachman, the veterinarians, and the outsiders in general treated me kindly, yet those who called me their own did not. In due time, having widened the scope of my observations, I satisfied myself that the notion "my," not only in relation to horses, has no other basis than a narrow

> human instinct which is called a sense of or right to private property. A man says "this house is mine" and never lives in it; he only worries about its construction and upkeep. A merchant says "my shop," "my dry goods shop," for instance, and does not even wear clothes made from the better cloth he keeps in his own shop.[16]

Of course, the horse's perspective is a projection of Tolstoy's own radical Christian outlook, so it could be argued that we have not left the anthropocentric domain even for a moment. Yet it seems equally clear that for some of us the horse's (or Tolstoy's) culturally alien perspective on property can promote a more critical understanding of that deeply structural dimension of our culture that we take for granted. The Russian formalist Viktor Shklovsky, in his seminal essay "Art as Technique," argues that the horse monologue induces a powerful feeling of *ostranenie* (defamiliarization), which can inspire one to ponder, critically indeed, on many things – for instance, on why humans should believe that the more things they will be able to label "mine" the happier they will become.

These two examples suggest a general point we would like to make: that criticality does not demand an *absolutely* detached perspective – pulling ourselves up by our bootstraps, so to speak – so even if the other's perspective that we are trying to adopt is to some extent coloured by our perspective, this does not annul its critical potential. For instead of necessitating being entirely outside the examined situation, criticality, we contend, requires merely a reflective perspective on it that is not wholly absorbed in the immediacy of our ordinary world view – a perspective better described as positionally eccentric (or decentred) rather than as external. And such perspectives can indeed be achieved through experiences of dissonance where unreflective perception is disrupted, which thus stimulates a decentred, reflective critical attention to what is going on.[17]

Now if our argumentation is right, so far we have shown that intercultural hermeneutics is possible (albeit fallible, as all understanding is), and that it *can* be critical (albeit with limitations). Intercultural understanding and criticism can take different forms. An encounter with the cultural other may prod one into critically examining the presuppositions of her culture (which she may have taken for granted and never reflected upon at all), but it can also leave one even more firmly entrenched in one's own cultural beliefs. Consider again our two examples. Suppose that we recommended Tolstoy's story to a staunch capitalist whose vision of achieving happiness is inextricably related to the idea of accumulating all sorts of goods. That person may read and enjoy the story and even experience a certain dissonance that transforms or at least diminishes her lust for possessions. But it may lead her to confirm her initial approach because of the very strangeness of the narrator's perspective. The person in question may simply say to herself: "That's indeed really strange what is being said here, no wonder that these words come from a horse. He just can't have any clue as to what property is all about." In other words, an alternative perspective may be rejected for the very reason that it is another's perspective, and some others are more likely to provoke such a reaction than other others.

The same logic could apply to the Sartre example. In reaction to the idea that the "wild and free looks [of colonized African and Caribbean peoples] ... judge our world,"[18] a racist white person might come to cast a new critical regard on her cultural prejudice; but conversely, it might lead her to stronger resentment against such blacks for their ingratitude towards the European culture that she believes has generously tried to educate them.[19]

The reaction that actually occurs depends, of course, on all sorts of contingencies, such as one's birth, one's socialization, and one's mood in a given moment. But at least the introduction of the different perspective can create the possibility of change, of weakening cultural prejudice. Thus even if there is no guarantee that the change is possible, the very presence of change of consciousness (and of heightened consciousness) has a positive potentiality. Moreover, if we look more closely into the actual concrete context of our question – the context of this particular essay collection and the wider academic context in which it is situated – the matter becomes at once more manageable and more positive. Most people who discuss intercultural hermeneutics are academics in the humanities who are saturated (regardless of their ethnicity and primary cultural background) with the same set of ideological presumptions (largely associated with the Western tradition of progress through enlightenment), and thus who look at critical intercultural hermeneutics with the tentative hope that it will allow them to approach critically the unquestioned presumptions and prejudices they harbour against cultural others.

For us pragmatists, critical intercultural hermeneutics is not an infallible method that always has happy results. Just as our desire to understand the culturally other can lead to an exoticism of accentuating and cherishing differences where we fail to see our connections and convergences with those other cultures in terms of shared histories and influences, so the idea of using foreign cultures to criticize our own perspectives can lead (often through the same simplistic exotic idealization of the other culture) to a simplistic misunderstanding of the diverse roots and complexities of our own culture. American country music might be seen by both its fans and detractors as pure, white American music (and be respectively celebrated or rejected for its chauvinistic purism), yet the roots of this music extend into Africa, Hawaii, and Europe.[20] In the same way, one often tends to idealize Asian traditions of spirituality in contrast to American pragmatic materialism, forgetting that key figures in the latter tradition (such as Emerson and Thoreau) sought to absorb and renew those spiritual traditions. This sort of simplifying critical misunderstanding can generate an unhelpful cultural self-loathing that blinds us to the resources our own culture, leading us away from pragmatic piecemeal meliorism towards a wholesale rejection of the culture that has made us and that continues to shape even our critical perspectives.

Our conclusion, in short, is that critical intercultural hermeneutics, like any method or instrument, has its limitations. It can be useful in some contexts but clumsy or even dangerous in others. If our emphasis on the question of usefulness reflects the basic orientation of pragmatism, and if that pragmatic orientation is in turn an expression of the American culture from which pragmatism emerged, then it could be enlightening in terms of critical intercultural hermeneutics to close our essay by examining the reception of American pragmatism in other cultural traditions. That reception has been understandably uneven, varying with the different sorts of affinities and divergences between pragmatism and the dominant tendencies of the receiving cultures.[21] We confine ourselves to European and East Asian cultures, focusing on the most important philosophical traditions (Germany and France in Europe, and China in East Asia) and giving particular attention to how their differences have played out with respect to Richard Shusterman's philosophy, since we have first-hand experience of this reception.

IV

To begin with Germany, we should note that rather than deploying pragmatist philosophy as a defamiliarizing perspective through which they could critically examine themselves, German philosophers often chose instead to criticize it from a perspective reflecting the worst kinds of cultural prejudice – a proclivity that prompted Hans Joas (himself a German scholar) to call the German reception of pragmatism a "history of misunderstandings."[22]

This history, as Joas tells it, begins in 1908 with the almost unanimously hostile reaction of German scholars to William James's *Pragmatism: A New Name for Some Old Ways of Thinking*, whose first German translation was published that year. The criticism was so intense that it made pragmatism "the main subject of debate at the 1908 World Philosophical Congress, which was held in Heidelberg, and the topic spawned a mass of essays in German journals in the years that followed."[23] However, as Joas argues, the vehemence of the critique presented in those works stands in gross disproportion to the quality and accuracy of their interpretation of pragmatist authors. That interpretation included the following errors: "accusing James of propagating a theory of truth which espoused the simplistic equation of truth with [subjective] utility" (something that can be seen even much later in Max Horkheimer's *Eclipse of Reason*);[24] the "failure to make the effort to consult Peirce's work," whose influence on James and Dewey was crucial (and whose understanding remains crucial for understanding these latter); and the wrongheaded association of pragmatism with the philosophy of Ernst Mach, or "its interpretation as a crass version" of Nietzsche ("Georg Simmel is said to have called pragmatism 'the part of Nietzsche which Americans adopted'")[25] or as merely a "philosophy of life."[26]

The early German adversaries of pragmatism absurdly misrepresented its positions. They not only failed to read the texts carefully but failed to take the complex "background of pragmatism into account."[27] "The reason for this," writes Joas, "lies presumably in some self-confident assumption of the traditional superiority of German philosophy: the opponent was to be recognized, but should not, of course, be overestimated."[28] Moreover, they reduced the culture of the new philosophy to a flat caricature of mercenary capitalism. Consider the following quotation from the German philosopher Gutberlet, whose opinion was typical among his contemporaries:

> We are encountering a new fad in philosophy, this time brought to us from across the ocean, from the land of the dollar which must be regarded as the ideal of this philosophy [the land where people are "degraded to the status of slaves of materialism, of industry"]. This philosophy degrades

> the truth to the level of expediency, just as in days gone by, a similar way of thinking was imported to us from the land of the shopkeepers [i.e., Britain] preaching the reduction of morality to utility.[29]

Joas's account of how German thinkers misrepresent pragmatism goes on to include such luminaries as Heidegger, Max Scheler, Ernst Bloch, and Max Horkheimer. But turning to more recent times, let us examine Shusterman's controversial reception in Germany.

On the one hand, four of his books and many of his articles have appeared in German, and he has enjoyed appointments in Germany. On the other hand, his work has often been treated as mere American pop-culture provocation rather than a nuanced philosophical position of meliorism, even when it is warmly received in some popular media precisely for going against the philosophical tradition. The Berlin entertainment weekly *Zitty Magazine* published an article on the German translation of *Pragmatist Aesthetics* whose headline screamed "Kant was no fan of rap," while the *Tagezeitung*'s headline for discussing the book was "Rap und Pragmatismus," as if all that pragmatist aesthetics had to offer was an American interpretation of African American hip hop culture, formulated by a Jew (the analogue of being black in German history). When Shusterman first introduced the notion of somaesthetics in his German book *Vor der Interpretation*, it caught the attention of a reviewer for *Frankfurter Allgemeine Zeitung*. But that philosopher completely ignored somaesthetics' central ideas and tried to make it look ridiculous as a form of reading gymnastics, telling his readers "to imagine [somaesthetics] as something like whipping oneself while reading Kant, mountain-climbing while reading Nietzsche, and doing breathing exercises while reading Heidegger."[30]

The history of the French reception of pragmatism displays similar problems of cultural prejudice that still need to be overcome. Here again, despite William James's strong friendship with Charles Renouvier and Henri Bergson, pragmatism was caricatured and condemned as the expression of the mercenary vulgarity of American culture. But pragmatism also suffered because its few French advocates deployed its appreciation of affect and the vague in order to oppose the philosophies of rationalism and science that dominated French academic, sociocultural, and political life at the time. Thus Durkheim warned against pragmatism as "an *attack on reason*" (reason being the hallmark of France's Cartesian and Enlightenment philosophical tradition), which in France "chiefly appears in the neo-religious movement."[31] Part of the French interest in James's pragmatism came from thinkers who interpreted and used it as an anti-intellectualist philosophy of faith, feeling, and action (sometimes in politically reactionary contexts), although they failed to give voice to its appreciation of scientific thinking and of the progressive values of enlightenment and democracy.

This problematic image of pragmatism also hampered the French reception of Dewey's works, which found even less resonance than James's. In more recent times, the French reception of pragmatism continues to be haunted by its identification with an anti-rational impulse and with French philosophies critical of traditional French rationalism or logocentrism. Richard Rorty, a past master of philosophical analysis whose pragmatist conversion inspired Shusterman to follow him from analytic philosophy to pragmatism, provides a good example. Although his works have been widely translated into French, their impact has been greatly diminished by his praise of imaginative poetry and fiction over philosophical reason and by his close association with Derrida and deconstruction. These French philosophical "negativities" are in Rorty's case greatly exacerbated by his defence of "postmodern bourgeois liberalism" – a political *bête noire* in French philosophical circles, which are predominantly left-leaning. With their own Nietzschean postmoderns like Derrida, Lyotard, and Foucault, French thinkers felt they did not need Rorty's pragmatism, whose Nietzscheanism seemed more superficial and politically suspect.

Richard Shusterman's pragmatism, although sometimes mistaken as a defence of superficial American culture, has nonetheless had a much easier time in France, partly perhaps because of its leftist political leanings and its championing of African American culture (a traditional focus of French intellectual passion). On the one hand, mass media discussion of his *Pragmatist Aesthetics* (under its French title, *L'art a l'etat vif*) neglected much of its philosophical import and concentrated almost entirely on the book's single chapter on rap (*Le Monde*: "Une esthetique du Hip Hop"; *Libération*: "L'or du rap"; *Le Nouvel Observateur*: "Le Champ du Rap").[32] Moreover, in certain academic circles, his interest in the 1980s hip hop scene was sometimes seen as reflecting American naivety and as a lack of appropriate scientific distance. But on the other hand, the politically left-oriented French intellectual scene typically welcomed and commended Shusterman for being progressive, useful, and cool largely because of his risqué pioneer study and advocacy of rap. Newspapers and magazines discussed his work, and he even made an appearance on national network TV's program on rap music. Shusterman's affirmation of early hip hop for its democratic potential and emancipatory message, for its cultural freshness, and for its challenge to the American socio-political and cultural mainstream, appealed to left-leaning French intellectual culture (note that his book was not reviewed in the conservative *Le Figaro*). Moreover, the book's publication by the avant-garde publisher Minuit in a series edited by the respected left-wing intellectual Pierre Bourdieu confirmed Shusterman's status as a serious but "hip" philosopher with the requisite political orientations. Another factor, we believe, in the different French reception of Shusterman's work is that the cultural field of philosophy in France is largely defined by radical figures who are often either outside the academy or critically divergent from it. In contemporary times, think of Sartre, Camus, de Beauvoir, Bataille, or (among academics) Foucault or Deleuze. But this tradition of radical philosophy stretches back to Diderot, Rousseau, and de Sade. In contrast, the German philosophical field is culturally defined in terms of the university professor, a bourgeois civil servant or *Beamter*. Again, since France is a very body-conscious country, the French cultural and philosophical world has been much more receptive than the German one to Shusterman's project of somaesthetics. This burgeoning interest has resulted in the publication of eight books by Shusterman in French, some of which have no English counterparts, and in a published collection on somaesthetics.[33]

Turning now from European to East Asian culture, we can see again how different cultural fields create different critical receptions and understandings. Japan was the first Asian country to translate a book by Shusterman, and it is where he has spent the most time. But his reception there has been rather narrow, essentially confined to the circle of aesthetics, which is a separate academic discipline from philosophy in Japan and one that lacks wide visibility. Orienting itself principally in terms of traditionalism (mostly Western aesthetic traditions rather than its own), Japanese academic aesthetics has hesitated to embrace pragmatist aesthetics' emphasis on novelty, earthiness, and emancipatory political dimension. In China, however, where Dewey was once a great philosophical figure and where today's post-Mao dynamism has created a very forward-looking albeit in many respects politically limited cultural curiosity, introducing pragmatism has been much easier. Rorty has had a very strong reception there, and there has been increasing interest in Shusterman's work. Since 2002, four of his books have been published there, and his research has been widely discussed both in academic journals and in daily newspapers such as the *Beijing Morning Post* and the *Guangming Daily*. His work, we believe, is well appreciated there because of its similarities to classical Chinese philosophy; thus, Shusterman's philosophy seems intriguing and helpful to the Chinese because it helps them understand their own tradition in a positive, productive way. Five themes seem central in this convergence between the very different philosophical cultures of (Shusterman's) pragmatism and classical Chinese philosophy (especially Confucianism but also, to some extent, Daoism).

First, there is the priority of practice (especially meliorative practice) over the sort of metaphysical inquiry that is crucial to the pragmatist and Confucian traditions. Philosophy's primary aim is to improve understanding so as to improve lives, character, behaviour, society, and culture. The goal is not to define reality in an absolute, universal, metaphysical sense but rather to understand the real in its context, which can help us improve the concrete situations and realities we face. Similarly, in the field of aesthetics, the goal of theory is not to define art for its own sake but rather to formulate general principles that can help us improve our understanding of art and our creating of art in practice, and where high among the arts is the ethical art of living.

A second fundamental principle that classical Chinese philosophy shares with pragmatism is pluralism and contextualism, an appreciation of complementarities and how oppositions can work together in productive alternation or productive tension. One does not choose absolutely between yin and yang; one needs both in different measures at different times to address different circumstances. Connected with this pluralism is the further principle of the importance of change; because our world is an essentially changing world, our theories must be flexible to absorb new forms of life and to address new conditions and new forms of artistic expression. As Chinese philosophy is significantly grounded in the *Book of Changes*, so pragmatism rests on Darwin's view of the world as the scene of evolutionary change. [34]

Beyond these three general principles of convergence, Shusterman's particular brand of pragmatism has special resonance with Chinese thought for two other reasons. His advocacy of popular art (and particularly the politically engaged genre of hip hop) resonates strongly with the democratic aesthetic advocated by contemporary Maoism, traces of which can also be found in classical Chinese philosophy's respect for popular art. Finally, Shusterman's emphasis on somaesthetics converges with the centrality of the body and the need for its meliorative cultivation – something that is advocated, albeit in different ways, by Confucianism and Daoism as well.

Recently, Shusterman has more explicitly introduced classical Chinese philosophy into his writings on aesthetics and somaesthetics. This has only increased the interest that Chinese philosophers are taking in his work, an interest that is sometimes critical when, for example, it notes how the Chinese tradition of somaesthetics differs from what he is offering. Critical differences remain, of course. But they are more productive, for they are based on a wider understanding and trust, and such a basis, needless to say, is necessary for the success of any attempt at intercultural hermeneutics.

NOTES

1 Wojciech Małecki wishes to acknowledge that he worked on the final version of this chapter during his research stay in Germany as an Alexander von Humboldt Foundation Fellow.

2 See, for example, Steven J. Mailloux, *Reception Histories: Rhetoric, Pragmatism, and American Cultural Politics* (Ithaca: Cornell University Press, 1998), 7–8; and Thomas M. Jeannot, "A Propaedeutic to the Philosophical Hermeneutics of John Dewey: *Art as Experience* and *Truth and Method*," *Journal of Speculative Philosophy* 15, no. 1 (2001), 1–13.

3 See, for example, John D. Caputo, *More Radical Hermeneutics: On Not Knowing Who We Are* (Bloomington: Indiana University Press, 2000), 84–124.

4 See, for example, Richard Rorty, *Essays on Heidegger and Others* (Cambridge: Cambridge University Press, 1991); Rorty, *Philosophy and the Mirror of Nature* (Princeton: Princeton University Press, 1981), 357–64; Richard Shusterman, *Pragmatist Aesthetics: Living Beauty, Rethinking Art*, 2nd ed. (New York: Rowman and Littlefield, 2000); and Shusterman, *T.S. Eliot and Philosophy of Criticism* (London: Duckworth, 1988).

5 See, for example, Rorty and Gianni Vattimo, *The Future of Religion*, ed. Santiago Zabala (New York: Columbia University Press, 2005). Cf. Rorty, *An Ethics for Today: Finding Common Ground between Philosophy and Religion*, intro. by Vattimo (New York: Columbia University Press, 2011).

6 See, for example, Mark Okrent, *Heidegger's Pragmatism: Understanding, Being, and the Critique of Metaphysics* (Ithaca: Cornell University Press, 1988).

7 For more detailed discussion of interpretation as sense making, see Shusterman, *Pragmatist Aesthetics*, chapter 4; and for the extension of this approach into the interpretation of actions and persons, including one's self-identity, see Shusterman, *Practicing Philosophy: Pragmatism and the Philosophical Life* (London: Routledge, 1997), chapter 7.

8 Leopold Sédar-Senghor, *Anthologie de la nouvelle poésie nègre et malgache de langue française* (Paris: Presses universitaires de France, 1948).

9 Jean-Paul Sartre, "Black Orpheus," *Massachusetts Review* 6, no. 1 (1964–5), 13.

10 For an account of contemporary philosophical criticisms of ocularocentricism, see Martin Jay, *Downcast Eyes: The Denigration of Vision in Twentieth-Century French Thought* (Berkeley: University of California Press, 1993).

11 Indeed, reading Sartre's essay, one is amazed at how almost every line he interprets raises in him philosophical associations, for instance with Bataille, Heidegger (36), Bergson (38), Lucretius (41), Nietzsche (42), Pascal (44), Plato (48), and Jaspers (49).

12 As Robert Bernasconi underscores, Sartre "did so on his own initiative, but on the basis of the contents of Senghor's Anthologie," yet he "had no right to privilege the Marxist voices in the Negritude movement over the other voices," or at least this is what Fanon thought. Robert Bernasconi, "The European Knows and Does Not Know: Fanon's Response to Sartre," in *Frantz Fanon's Black Skin, White Masks: New Interdisciplinary Essays*, ed. Max Silverman (Manchester: Manchester University Press, 2005), 107.

13 Frantz Fanon, *Black Skin, White Masks*, trans. Richard Philcox (New York: Grove, 2008), 112, 113. Cf. Bernasconi, "On Needing Not to Know and Forgetting What One Never Knew: The Epistemology of Ignorance in Fanon's Critique of Sartre," in *Race and Epistemologies of Ignorance*, ed. Shannon Sullivan and Nancy Tuana (Albany: SUNY Press, 2007), 231–8.

14 Cited in Sartre, "Black Orpheus," 15.

15 Ibid., 14, 15.

16 Cited after Viktor Shklovsky, "Art as Technique," trans. Lee T. Lemon and Marion J. Reis, in *Literary Theory: An Anthology*, 2nd ed., ed. Julie Rivkin and Michael Ryan (Malden: Blackwell, 2004), 16–17.

17 For more detailed discussion of this idea of the decentring or distance of reflection and the possibilities it gives for what is often described as immanent critique, see Shusterman, "Somaesthetics and Architecture: A Critical Option," in *Thinking through the Body: Essays in Somaesthetics* (Cambridge: Cambridge University Press, 2012), 219–38.

18 Sartre, "Black Orpheus," 14.

19 See Sartre's following remark: "If these poems shame us however, they were not intended to: they were not written for us; and they will not

shame any colonists or their accomplices who open this book, for these latter will think they are reading letters over someone's shoulder, letters not meant for them." Ibid., 15–16.

20 See, for example, Shusterman, "Affect and Authenticity in Country Musicals," in *Performing Live: Aesthetic Alternatives for the Ends of Art* (Ithaca: Cornell University Press, 2000).

21 For more discussion of the limits of pragmatism's international reception, see Shusterman, ed., *The Range of Pragmatism and the Limits of Philosophy* (Oxford: Blackwell, 2004).

22 See Hans Joas, *Pragmatism and Social Theory* (Chicago: University of Chicago Press, 1993). In the following section on the German reception of pragmatism, we draw exclusively on this study.

23 Ibid., p. 96.

24 See, for example, Max Horkheimer, *Eclipse of Reason* (New York: Continuum, 1974), 65.

25 Joas, *Pragmatism and Social Theory*, 99.

26 Ibid., p. 102.

27 "What immediately strikes one about most of the pronouncements forthcoming in the framework of the controversy is that they show no willingness even to take James's arguments … into account. James's own statement of his intentions and the replies he penned to critics of pragmatism are largely ignored, although they were already included in the book *Pragmatism*, which contained the lectures of the same name. In fact, the commentators do not even make the effort to consult Peirce's work, despite the fact that James so clearly refers to it. Various spellings of the name Peirce (usually Pierce, though also Pearce) – are to be encountered in articles at this time, suggesting that the critics lacked firsthand knowledge of his essays. A little detective work would undoubtedly soon reveal who copied from whom instead of referring back to the original source." Ibid., 96.

28 Ibid., 98. "Any better understanding of [pragmatism] was … impaired by the fact that these false interpretations wee linked to a distinct tendency to be culturally condescending toward America, and by the reference to national stereotypes to express philosophical divergences," 102.

29 C. Gutberlet, "Der Pragmatismus," *Philosophisches Jahrbuch* 21 (1908): 437, 445, qtd after ibid., 98.

30 These articles can be found on http://www.fau.edu/humanitieschair/Media_Commentary_in_German.php.

31 Emile Durkheim, *Pragmatism and Sociology*, trans. J.C. Whitehouse (Cambridge: Cambridge University Press, 1983), 1, 9.

32 Christian Delacampagne, "Une esthétique du Hip Hop," *Le Monde,* 31 January 1992, 26; Daniel Soutif, "L'or du rap," *Libération*, 23 April 1992, 29; Bernard Loupias, "Le champ du rap," *Le nouvel observateur*, 28 March 1992, 117.

33 The books are *L'art à l'état vif: la pensée pragmatiste et l'esthétique populaire* (Paris: Minuit, 1992); *Sous l'interprétation* (Paris: Éditions de l'éclat, 1994); *La fin de l'experience esthetique* (Pau: Presse Universitaire de Pau, 1999); *Vivre la philosophie* (Paris: Klincksiek, 2001); *Conscience du corps: Pour une soma-esthétique* (Paris: l'éclat, 2007); *L' Objet de la critique littéraire* (Paris: Questions Théoriques, 2009); *Soma-esthétique et architecture: une alternative critique* (Geneva: HEAD, 2010); and *Le style à l'état vif* (Paris: Questions Théoriques, 2012). The collection on somaesthetics is Barbara Formis, ed., *Penser en Corps: Soma-esthétique, art et philosophie* (Paris: L'Harmattan, 2009).

34 See, for example, the following essays by Richard Shusterman: "Pragmatism and East-Asian Thought," in *The Range of Pragmatism and the Limits of Philosophy*, 13–42; "Body Consciousness and Performance: Somaesthetics East and West," *Journal of Aesthetics and Art Criticism* 67, no. 2 (2009): 133–45; "Pragmatist Aesthetics and Confucianism," *Journal of Aesthetic Education* 43, no. 1 (2009): 25–7. Cf. Satoshi Higuchi, "Eastern Mind–Body Theory and Somaesthetics," in *Concepts of Aesthetics Education: Japanese and European Perspectives*, ed. Yasuo Imai and Christopher Wulf (Münster: Waxmann, 2007), 88–96. For more discussion of interrelations between pragmatism and Chinese thought, see also Yong Huang, ed., *Rorty, Pragmatism, and Confucianism: With Responses by Richard Rorty* (Albany: SUNY Press, 2009); and David Hall and Roger Ames, *The Democracy of the Dead: Dewey, Confucius, and the Hope for Democracy in China* (Chicago: Open Court, 1999).

Chapter Thirteen

Critical Interventions: Towards a Hermeneutical Rejoinder

LORENZO C. SIMPSON

One of the difficulties facing global, multicultural societies is how to negotiate judiciously the criteria that will guide us in determining what should command our recognition as participants in cultural and political communities. The dilemma lies in discerning how to pursue such a negotiation in a way that does not beg questions against the yet-to-be-included or against what is taken to have established its credentials for recognition. Central among the questions facing democratic and democratizing societies the world over is how to find principled ways to acknowledge the claims of the distinct cultural groups comprising them. Forging a language for such a negotiation seems to me one of the central challenges facing us now.

Any conception of intercultural understanding that will be politically credible at our current juncture must then also be a *critical* conception. As hermeneutically informed conceptions exhort us to fuse horizons, to pursue an open-minded and non-parochial inclusiveness – in a sense, to expand the circle of the "we" – they must also have the resources to challenge those practices and social formations that thwart or undermine human flourishing. Accordingly, in this essay I seek to outline what can be characterized as a critical hermeneutics. I do so by way of an elaboration of what I have elsewhere referred to as a dialogical or postmetaphysical humanism.[1] Humanism, properly conceived for our times, must be informed by a conception of *critical* pluralism, a non-relativistic but hermeneutic version of critical rationality.

I have elsewhere pursued at length the potential for self-critique and self-estrangement that is inherent in an adequate conception of hermeneutic understanding, and I do not wish to downplay its importance (indeed, as I have argued, because of the symmetry inherent in mutual understanding, any fully adequate understanding of another will place the informing assumptions of both self and other at risk).[2] Here, however, I wish to train my focus in a more sustained way on highlighting this understanding's potential for non-parochial questioning of the other.

The form that my argument takes is in part a response to a still-influential conception of the nature and scope of intersubjective or mutual understanding. This conception has been pithily articulated by the distinguished German Levinasian, Bernhard Waldenfels, who claims that thinkers who promote and privilege the virtues of mutual understanding ineluctably presuppose a "third person position," a standpoint that, in allowing for comparability, is itself a moment of convergence, stability, and universality that effaces difference and alterity.[3] In my view, this conception holds out unjustifiably limited prospects for mutual understanding – it is one that locates the very idea of reciprocal understanding somewhere between chimeric illusion and imperialist gesture. This dichotomy between Enlightenment universalism and postmodernist fragmentation and relativism – a dichotomy that informs much of our social and political discourse about difference and identity – is a false one. In addition to underestimating the potential for edifying and self-transformative encounters with cultural others, this "postmodern consensus" has profound implications for our understanding of the nature and scope of practical deliberation. That is, it has profound consequences for our confidence in our ability to frame non-question-begging, critical responses to the manifold cultural practices that populate global society – for our response to the treatment of women under Islamic law, for instance – and for our understanding of the scope of community, given the salience of matters of "difference" in multicultural societies.

However, while taking issue with the "postmodernist" position, it is important to remain informed by postmodernism's salutary critique of essentialism as well as by its sensitivity to matters of social and cultural difference. So my conception of mutual understanding arises directly from two concerns: on the one hand, to acknowledge social and cultural difference, and on the other, to counter both the claims to the effect that persons and cultures are thereby ineliminably opaque to one another and the related relativistic claims that are typically taken to follow from this mutual opacity. Accordingly, the position for which I offer a brief here implies that non-question-begging critical perspectives on cultural formations need not entail an objectionable universalism or essentialism, just as an appreciation of matters of difference need not entail a simplistic relativism. And the premium on our capacity to take up such critical yet sympathetic perspectives is at an all-time high as contemporary events around the globe suggest that "the idea of a common international humanity appears as remote as ever."[4]

I

In light of these concerns, I here pursue the social-epistemological problem of determining how genuine – that is, non-invidious – understanding of cultural formations not our own is possible, of determining what the conditions and limits of such understanding are. What then are the conditions of possibility of such a critical hermeneutics? In general, I take the perspicuous intelligibility of the other to be a criterial property of an adequate hermeneutic understanding. This will involve the production of a perspicuous account of what the other takes her life to be about, that is, of her distinctive and fundamental aims, of the ways those aims are pursued, and of the assumptions she holds about the situation (structures or institutions) that provides the context for those pursuits. Adequate attention to these facets of intercultural hermeneutic understanding will demonstrate that the potential for meaningful critique is an ineliminable *internal* feature of such understanding.

As an alternative to Enlightenment universalist and postmodernist responses to matters of difference, I propose a third approach – one inspired by the evident possibility of an always provisional mutual understanding effected through dialogical interaction on the part of participants who bring their differences with them to the negotiation. This allows us to see how to give difference its due without abandoning critical standards; it also provides a basis for distinguishing between a progressive expansion of our intellectual horizons and an indiscriminate relativism.[5]

My approach to these issues is articulated in terms of a model of critical, hermeneutic dialogue, that is, of a critical dialogue oriented to the achievement of mutual understanding. This dialogue, as I conceive it, is enabled by ongoing practices of forging commensurable or mutually enriched vocabularies for identifying and discussing differences, vocabularies that enable, among persons differently situated, a mutually critical and respectful dialogue about matters of common concern.

I understand the vocabularies that can emerge from intercultural encounter to be "situated metalanguages." Each distinct cultural vocabulary embodies a distinctive set of responses to the full range of human concerns, and it is the distinctiveness of the responses that distinguishes one culturally indexed vocabulary from another. Put somewhat differently, the criteria of individuation for such vocabularies are furnished by the distinctive classes of shared points of appeal or of shared matrices of intelligibility that provide common reference points for those who are said to share a culture, allowing for the mutual intelligibility of agreement and disagreement within a culture.[6] Dialogue between such communities of intelligibility is enabled by the forging of situated metalanguages that facilitate linguistically mediated community formation, a process that can produce a new community of consensus on terms for negotiating and adjudicating differences by expanding the scope of what is mutually intelligible, even if it only yields mutual acknowledgment and acceptance of the terms in which disagreement or difference is expressed. Such an emergent common language will be the source of an ever-expanding shared vocabulary for discussing and representing, though *not* for standardizing, moral and cultural identity. This negotiated metalanguage – marking an emergent moment of common humanity as it enables the articulation of difference – is a situated metalanguage that is reflexively constituted by difference.

Dialogue between or across communities of intelligibility requires the identification of the *topic* that is being addressed in contrasting ways by the communities in dialogue. Here I believe we must consider the hermeneutic problem from a somewhat different angle of vision than Gadamer was wont to adopt. His tendency was to focus on the tradition that both text and interpreter share, a focus that tends to occlude the problematic and deeply contested nature of *Sache* identification – that is, the identification of the topic that will allow us to maximize the conspicuous intelligibility of a given response – in cases where one cannot rely upon the commonality provided by a shared tradition. My concern here is to "rotate" the relationship with which Gadamer is preoccupied, namely, the vertical relationship of an authoritative tradition to an interpreter, so that it becomes a horizontal relationship between interlocutors. This will mean that, in general, we will be unable to take for granted a shared tradition and the advantage it gives us of already being "in" on the cultural conversation and the topics being addressed. In cross-cultural conversation, we may often be able to rely upon only the expressive potential of language in general (on the fact of what John

Searle calls the "principle of expressibility," that anything that can be meant can be articulated in language[7]), our hermeneutic talents, and, crucially, the free response of intercultural interlocutors to our proposals. Accordingly, the presumption of authority that Gadamer accords tradition, I want to locate in the reciprocal recognition of interlocutors, though we must of course remain sensitive to real asymmetries between dominating and dominated languages.[8]

This approach entails that I view the perspective of another culture as having a *claim* on me, as in fact being something like a validity claim about something that is of concern, a *Sache*, to me. Finding the appropriate topic of concern and consequently discerning just what claim is being made on me will require both my interpretive powers, which will by themselves yield only hypotheses, and the confirmational resources of dialogue. In dialogue, both self and other can challenge where they are located on the spectrum of responses to a given concern, they can challenge the way in which the spectrum is articulated, and they can challenge the spectrum itself, that is, the logical space or dimension of experience that we took to be best for perspicuously representing our differences. The aim of dialogical understanding is to produce an "ordered pair" – consisting of topic and response – that displays the most *compelling connection* between the two.[9]

The *telos* of this mode of understanding is thus not agreement – though on occasion this may occur; rather, it is to *achieve* systems of contrast for all the various horizons that allow for the perspicuous representation of the other. Such a dialogue will initiate symmetrical learning processes that expand, *on both sides of the dialogue*, notions of the kinds of games people play (the kinds of concern that are humanly addressed) as well as notions of the different, and sometimes better, ways of playing them.

In so highlighting the symmetrical nature of these encounters, I am not claiming that, for any two cultures, it will turn out that both sides occupy positions of equal merit with respect to every topic of human concern. *Ultimately*, there may turn out to be asymmetries between them with regard to specific topics, for example, with regard to rendering a reliable and technologically pregnant account of natural processes, or with regard to coming to terms with the inevitable. For if we take seriously the very idea of learning, with its ineliminable implications of progressive development, we must certainly allow that, for a given and sufficiently narrowly defined concern, some positions are more likely to be fruitful than others. So by "symmetry," I do not refer so much to the *outcome* of such an encounter as I do to the mutual dispositions of participants in dialogue to proceed as if they could learn from, and be challenged by, the other.

There are additional methodological constraints that condition our access to the fundamental concerns of others. It is in light of what are concerns and issues for us that we are able to understand a form of life other than our own. (In order to do so, we invoke *Sachen* or dimensions of *our* experience such as love, sexuality, religion, power, natality, and an awareness of our mortality.) That is, unless we can identify the dimensions of experience that are addressed by the practices distinctive of the form of life we seek to understand – and we can do this only through modelling upon what can be logical spaces or dimensions of experience *for us* – then we cannot understand it.

I would argue that analogy plays a crucial role here. When we seek to identify the topic in question and to make the best case for a response to it, we ask such questions as, "What category of phenomena, or what topics, do *we* treat similarly, or address in the way – or in *some* way that can be intelligibly connected by us to the way – that *they're* addressing X?" And, guided by such questions, when we adduce such a category that we then *hypothetically* project upon them – say, the category of "art" – we shall ask, "*Is* there, *for them*, a category of objects that they treat (both linguistically and non-linguistically) in the way – or in a way that can be intelligibly connected by us to the way – that *we* treat things we call 'art'?" In both cases – in both the generation of a topic and in its justification – we are relying on analogy. In the first case, we are asking, "Which of the topics with which we are familiar is analogous to what they're addressing, such that the best case can be made for what they're doing?" In the second case, we are asking more generally, "*Is* there for them something analogous to our X?"[10]

There is thus a sense in which some degree of ethnocentrism is epistemologically unavoidable. To see others as engaged in, say, argumentative practices or in morally relevant practices requires *our* experience with those kinds of practice as a touchstone. And we can be sure – to pick morality – that if another culture's criteria for the application of moral terms demonstrated *no* overlap with ours, we would have no reason to think they were engaged in moral discourse at all. The interpretation that yields a *Sache* and contrasting approaches to it is, in the last analysis, ours. But I take this to be relatively harmless, for two reasons. First, we can distinguish, on the one hand, what I would call the "transcendentally" necessary ethnocentrism of our unavoidable appeal to our notions of rationality and cogency, or to what we deem can be intelligibly related to them, from, on the other, the residue of a contingent, empirical, and possibly invidious ethnocentrism. We can combat the latter by acknowledging the crucial importance of dialogue (with cultural others) aimed at mutually acceptable descriptions of the *Sache* and of its correlative contrasting practices.

Second, who "we" are is always subject to revision, for our identities are best viewed as being open to non-fatal contestation in that certain elements of the set of features that collectively constitute one's social identity may be revised as a result of critical reflection without resulting in the loss of identity. The conversational practices of redescription and fusion that I advocate can broaden our sense of human possibilities without fatally threatening identities. The threat to cultural distinctiveness need not be feared if we acknowledge that identity is a cluster concept in that few if any beliefs or professions of value, taken singly, are essential to an identity. Our identities, it follows, need not be construed as being *identical* to our *prevailing* purposes, goals, and projects. What counts as the proper description of the self is, then, open to contestable interpretation. Thus, the modification of one's matrix of intelligibility in response to an interpretive/dialogical challenge need not entail the risk of losing oneself.

So, a hermeneutically self-aware ethnocentrist, one who is aware of her transcendental ethnocentrism, would interpret others in accordance with the criteria that her lights reveal but not in a way that dogmatically precludes the possibility (or desirability) that her standards may change – that is, that she could learn from others. Conversely, the relativist's refusal to judge can betray a refusal *to be judged*, a refusal both to make claims *on* others and to be claimed *by* those others. Our openness to the claims of the other places our identities in relief. And the critical renegotiation of identity can take place on both sides of the conversation table.

Here is but one example: as Akeel Bilgrami has argued forcefully, to be a Muslim is not necessarily to accept the strategic framing of one's identity put forward by some of one's fundamentalist co-religionists[11]; such an identity can be critically reconfigured. He points out that Muslim communities are defined by competing values, of which Islam is one, and that furthermore, Islamic identity is itself negotiable.[12] As the political theorist Yael Tamir has argued, "although cultural choices are neither easy nor limitless, cultural memberships and moral identity are not beyond choice," and they can be made the subject matter for a politicized discussion oriented towards bringing these emotional processes to discursive consciousness.[13] Like humanity itself and the vocabularies for expressing it, cultural identities are as much forged as found. They are fields of contestation and negotiation, often of struggles to expand existing and socially acknowledged logical spaces in order to accommodate the intelligibility of styles of group membership that were previously marginalized.[14]

Because I have placed such great stress upon conversational practices that can expand our sense of human possibilities without fatally threatening identities, I also refer to the position I describe here as a form of "situated cosmopolitanism." Situated cosmopolitanism refers to the demand – to use Hannah Arendt's suggestive phrase – that we "enlarge our mentalities," while recognizing that this expansion will always be situated, will always take place on and depart from, the plurality of grounds on which we actually stand. While acknowledging our finitude – that is, the situation-bound character of our understanding – I reject pluralism in that I do not see the territories from which we begin our narratives of understanding and edification as being isolated, self-enclosed monads, impenetrable to critique and emendation from the outside. So, here I advocate a cosmopolitan humanism and a corresponding form of hermeneutic understanding that call neither for a pledge to an already existing universal notion of humanity nor for a "static respect for each other's integrity, ... but [rather] for a dynamic of mutual [understanding] and transformation."[15] Humanity, in its terms, is then the unfinished project of learning to treat others as equals in our conversations without, on the one hand, losing ourselves or our identities or, on the other, retreating into a rigid conception of self that is impervious to change.

II

Given the hermeneutic account of intercultural understanding outlined above, what resources does it offer for critical responses to differently cultured others? Or, to invoke a formulation recently used by Habermas, with what success can it mediate between, on the one hand, a "politics of identity" with its tendency to make *collective* rights of different social groups sacrosanct and, on the other, an "Enlightenment fundamentalism" that would in an invidious fashion abstract individuals from their identity-informing socio-cultural milieux? To address this challenge, I discuss, briefly, my account's implications for human rights; then I turn to a form of immanent critique that it licenses; and last I consider a conversational modality that takes advantage of the fact that – as my earlier remarks on identity suggest – cultures are not monolithic, homogeneous wholes but rather are sites of contested interpretations, of competing interpretational narratives.

The assumption I adopt – that others have distinctive takes on the world that I can learn to respect and from which I can perhaps learn – is a methodological one that in my view underlies cross-cultural understanding. But it is not an indefeasible claim with respect to any particular case; in fact, I would insist there are practices that *defeat* such a presumption. In the final section of my book *The Unfinished Project*, I briefly consider practices that fall under the sign "human rights violation." I say there that

> we would fail to learn from the latter sorts of practice because they arguably violate an "un-get-over-able" criterial property of the good life. I take the recognition of the centrality of the freedom of individuals to assent to or ... reject propositions put forward by others [propositions purporting genuinely to represent what those individuals endorse as important in their lives] to define the minimalist core of any set of criterial properties of the good life that would meet with reciprocal acknowledgment and survive the test of the conversation of humanity.[16]

So, in this minimalist sense, something like an "ethics of human rights" – in the sense of the centrality to my conception of the freedom of individuals to accept or reject descriptions of themselves or the languages within which those descriptions are couched – is built in and can be viewed as such either on proceduralist grounds as a presupposition for participation or as a claim about the minimalist core of any product of such a conversation.

There is a second sense in which the model of understanding I am proposing, emphasizing as it does hermeneutic charity, does not leave us powerless to respond critically to the forms of life we wish to understand. That this model does not promote or even countenance a promiscuous relativism can be demonstrated by way of a brief counterargument to a claim that Richard Rorty was wont to make – namely, that the only way to take seriously the distinction between the merely socially or culturally sanctioned, on the one hand, and the valid, on the other, is to adopt a discredited Platonic commitment to metaphysically grounded essentialist structures.

Pace Rorty, I believe that we can understand the appearance/reality distinction as marking a distinction between what even *everyone* in a culture happens to think – and indeed, thinks honestly and after considerable reflection – and what is *true* for them. And such a distinction does not require that we appeal to anything beyond the standards of rationality and/or the central vocabulary of a particular group. Rather, it depends simply upon our recognizing that we can sometimes be brought to see that practices of justification that we may have heretofore relied upon may prove to be untrustworthy. And there is no reason to think that others cannot be brought to see this as well. To *convince* someone of the untrustworthiness of their practices is *ipso facto* to provide them with a *reason* to consider alternatives. I refer here to justificatory practices as being untrustworthy in the sense that they turn out not to be truth-tracking or sensitive to warranted assertibility in the way that members of a given community thought they were, or in the way in which they previously had no reason to disbelieve that they were. By this, I mean that there are cases when persons can be brought to see that there is (to them) no *intelligible* connection between, on the one hand, the reasonableness of their holding a particular claim or of holding it to be true, and, on the other hand, the outcome of what they take to be procedures for evaluating it and other such claims. For they might be brought to see that those procedures are "loaded" in such a way that their outcome is prejudiced. By "loaded," I mean that the procedures, because of a flaw in their design, may yield an outcome that would support (or disconfirm) a claim even if the claim were false (or true) and such a flaw could be detected and assessed from *within* the purview of the standards of rationality and/or central vocabulary of the group in question. These are cases, such as the discovery of an unbalanced scale in an economic transaction, where the outcome of a justificatory procedure will have been *exposed* as an artefact of the procedure and not of the procedure's truth-tracking sensitivity, and is therefore not to be taken (by those who relied upon the procedure) as a reflection of the truth or falsity of what the claim asserts.

This is obviously the sort of thing that occurs when an experimental design in the sciences is criticized, but it can also happen when a sacred text or a political constitution is being interpreted. The form of rationality that is implicit in my account here is a form of rationality that I take to have transcultural, or cross-cultural, or culturally invariant, standing. It is what I would call a "second-order rationality" that we are entitled to impute to everyone – that is, an inclination to reform one's practices in the direction of more rationality when one's lack of rationality is pointed out to one in terms with which one is conversant.

Accordingly, we can – without appealing to anything beyond the matrices of intelligibility, standards of rationality, and/or central vocabulary of any particular epistemic community or cultural group – intelligibly mark a distinction between what even everyone in a particular epistemic community *happens* to believe and what is, by their *own* lights, *reasonable* for them to believe, a distinction, moreover, that should command *their* attention. To *convince* someone of the questionability of their practices is *ipso facto* to provide them with a *reason* to consider alternatives.

This cross-cultural commitment to second-order rationality implies that social agents must, even if only pre-reflectively or implicitly, *anticipate* relationships among their aims, beliefs, and practices whose rational coherence differently situated others (including cultural "outsiders") could also appreciate. (I should emphasize, however, that this exploitation of the transcultural presumption of second-order rationality depends on a prior hermeneutic *understanding* of the cultural context in which the disputed practices are situated; we would need to know what the aims of the disputed practices are, which topics they are addressing. Only such an understanding would allow the sort of critical representation that I have elaborated here.) In thus providing members of a particular cultural tradition with an optic for recognizing and acknowledging what could be problems *for them*, the unavoidable presumption of this modality of reason fully entitles critical outsiders to view "insiders" as eligible – and in a way that begs no questions – to accept the burden of rational critique. In this sense, social agents, however implicitly, anticipate a dialogical confirmation of their rationality, thus granting an opening to potential critics.

In my view, humanism entails, among other things, a disposition to genuinely respect differently situated others. And this, I would argue, transcendentally demands that we treat differently cultured others as being like us in that they, too, operate with an *ideal* of themselves wherein their actions can, if challenged in ways that are understandable to them, be held accountable to *reasons* that have a non-parochial purchase. Now, given its identity, every culture implicitly makes the claim that its practices provide the best avenue for its flourishing, that they represent the best way for *it* to address the *Sachen*. Even the most insular forms of life can be understood implicitly as claiming that their practices are the best way for *them* to flourish. (Of course, cultures do not make *only* this sort of claim; they also make aesthetic-expressive claims about who they are, although, as I have suggested, even these identity claims are subject to critical renegotiation.) This sort of culturally rooted validity claim about optimal modalities for flourishing provides the occasion or basis, then, for a non-question-begging cultural critique informed by the presumption of second-order rationality.

I close this essay by sketching a third way in which hermeneutically informed approaches to intercultural understanding can allow us to navigate successfully between the Scylla of arrogant cultural imperialism and the Charybdis of impotent cultural relativism. I wish to make a case for a particular sort of conversational practice that can claim to be a genuine "development practice." This would be a conversational practice whose *internal* normative pressure would do the critical work that the "imposition of normative standards developed in the West" would otherwise do.[17] I will illustrate this conversational modality primarily with reference to the practice of female genital cutting or excision, a practice that is pursued – often with the apparent consent of women themselves – in parts of Africa, the Middle East, and Southeast Asia. To be sure, although the existence of such a practice is clearly a matter of concern in and of itself, I am not here claiming that the fact of its existence is the main problem these societies face. Focusing on it, however, is useful for illustrating how resources for critique can be unearthed when careful attention is paid to the *autonomously* voiced preferences and concerns of those local cultural agents who are affected by such a practice – that is, how the critical potential of these resources can be redeemed independently of any one-sided imposition of "Western" standards.

We begin by reminding ourselves that cultures are not seamless wholes – that in the words of one observer, "since a culture's system of beliefs and practices, the locus of its identity, is constantly contested, subject to change, and does not form a coherent whole, its identity is never settled, static and free of ambiguity."[18] And furthermore, as a UN report on justice and gender indicates, "the history of internal contestation reinforces [the premise] that cultures are not monolithic, are always in the process of *interpretation* and *re-interpretation*, and never immune to change."[19] These statements confirm what I earlier referred to as the conception of culture as a *cluster* as well as the idea that cultures are in general sites of conflicting interpretations. If we further concede – as I have argued elsewhere we must – that the distinction between *intra*-cultural hermeneutic dialogue and *inter*cultural hermeneutic dialogue is a matter of degree, not of kind, then we should expect to find *within* many cultures traces of the tensions that we are more accustomed to noticing *between* them.[20] Consistent with this, it can be argued that many intercultural normative disagreements can be productively analysed as *intracultural* conflicts.[21]

Consider in this regard some of the conversations about genital cutting that have recently begun to take place in a number of societies where it has been traditionally practised. In the African country of Mali, for example, they are pursued under the indigenous auspices of the COFESFA Women's Association and other NGOs. These conversations highlight the physical and emotional consequences of the ritual, the plurivocity of the cultural narratives deployed to justify the practice, and the patriarchal interests that it serves. Of course there are no guarantees; given, however, that these conversations seek to engage opinion leaders and that they take place among both men and women in local communities, they may give rise to proposals that will be candidates for the sort of general social recognition – or what I have called semantic authority – that can foster cultural reinterpretation. It is useful to think of these conversations as a component of the within-group struggle to expand the moral imaginary by persuading members of dominant social groups to acknowledge the semantic authority of claims put forth by others. Indeed, such community-based discussion, sponsored by an NGO in Kenya (the Maendeleo Ya Wanawake Organization), has in some cases led to the implementation of alternative non-invasive rituals marking female rites of passage in local communities (visit Maendeleo Ya Wanawake, http://mywokenya.org/index.php). And similar developments are occurring in Senegal. It is worth noting that in the Senegalese case, where the issue of genital cutting was explicitly raised by Senegalese women themselves, care was taken in the discussion of this issue to avoid descriptors such as "barbaric" and other potentially question-begging cognates that would invidiously prejudge the issue ("Senegal Curbs a Bloody Rite for Girls and Women," http://www.nytimes.com/2011/10/16/world/africa/movement-to-end-genital-cutting-spreads-in-senegal.html?src=me&ref=world&_r=0&pagewanted=all).

What lessons can we draw from these examples, highlighting as they do the conversationally underwritten and enhanced agency of local groups? Hermeneutics' emphasis on the conversational negotiation and expansion of interpretive frameworks enables a distinctively illuminating analysis of the pragmatics and intelligibility of such conversational situations. Given that cultures are not monolithic, homogeneous wholes such that none of their component parts – be they beliefs or practices – can be altered without loss of integrity, we must be wary of taking at face value any *single* narrative that purports to capture definitively a culture's identity. This suggests that we be attentive to ways in which cultural identity claims may be reified products. Categorically asserted cultural identity claims can be understood as reified products in at least two ways: they may disingenuously veil strategic orientations, and they may belie conflicting interpretations of a culture's identity-defining structures, that is, the fact that cultural identity is best seen as a cluster concept.[22] Cultural identity claims should not then be given *carte blanche* to function in such a way as to quarantine intracultural practices from discursive view so as to immunize them from critical examination.

The operating assumption behind the conversational practice that I am here endorsing, "counterfactual narrative critique," is that cultural agents can be encouraged to consider social possibilities that, while currently unrealized, might actually be preferred by them, social possibilities whose realization is suppressed not because such realization would offend against all intelligible interpretations of cultural identity, but rather primarily because it would offend against particular vested interests. For this reason, then, we should be on the lookout for interpretations of cultural identity that operate as cloaks or ideological veils concealing concerns that are interest-based.[23]

The interests that occasion such strategic representations are unlikely to be distributed *uniformly* among individuals and groups within a culture. The *representativeness* of such strategic self-images can then be interrogated through dialogue with a representative variety of such individuals, acknowledging of course that what counts as a representative variety may itself be a matter for interpretive contestation. Nevertheless, it would be reasonable to start with representations parsed out in terms of standard demographic categories such as class, ethnicity, and gender.

Furthermore, one should be on the lookout for signs that would trigger a "hermeneutics of suspicion," signs such as observed conflicts between speech and behaviour, conflicts of interest within the culture, and observed indices of perceived or actual power asymmetries between interlocutors within the culture.[24] But what if, as is not infrequently the case with female excision, there is no overt contestation of what seem to us problematic cultural practices? The *appearance* of asymmetrical or invidious treatment of identifiable demographic groups can trigger hypotheses about the *real* interests that are being implicated and about whether or not the interests of all cultural members converge in the way that prevailing cultural identity claims implicitly assert that they do.

It is useful here to consider a suggestion made by Habermas – indeed, one that I myself have criticized in another context:[25]

> I make the methodological assumption that it is meaningful and possible to reconstruct (even for the normal case of norms recognized without conflict) the *hidden* interest positions of involved individuals or groups by counterfactually imagining the limit case of a conflict between the involved parties in which they would be forced to consciously perceive their interests and strategically assert them, instead of satisfying basic interests simply by actualizing institutional values as is normally the case.[26] (italics mine)

My suggestion here is that we treat Habermas's comments as pertaining to what philosophy of science was wont to call the context of generation, the context in which hypotheses are proposed. Central now is the question, "How are we to 'test' these hypotheses concerning suppressed interests?" Habermas makes reference to the possibility of indirect *empirical* confirmation based on predictions about conflict motivations.[27] However, I want here to emphasize the extent to which the suspicion of potential dissensus can also be *hermeneutically* redeemed (or, for that matter, falsified). We need not restrict ourselves to the social theorist's monologically produced picture of a counterfactually imagined conflict. The reasoning behind the ascription of a potentially hidden interest can and indeed should be collaborative and dialogical, involving those whose interests are in question. With regard to female excision, this means the affected and potentially affected women, whose perspective would be articulated under conditions I describe below.

As an explicit *stylization* of the sorts of question that might, implicitly or not, underlie such a dialogical engagement, capture its critical intent, and perhaps thereby prompt some of the processes of cultural self-reinterpretation alluded to above, I offer the following. When encountering some form of the practice of excision or genital cutting, a witness, whether sharing cultural membership with the affected women or not – one who failed to find the "general" acquiescence to the practice on the part of women to be perspicuously intelligible – might initiate conversations of a particular sort with them, conversations guided by two basic questions: "Armed with the knowledge of the all too likely physical and emotional consequences of the procedure, if the connection between undergoing the procedure (or the procedure in the concrete form that it now assumes) and your chances for flourishing in your society were virtualized, if that connection could be severed, would you still choose to undergo the procedure?"[28] And, "What might your response be if it were not constrained by your fears?" – particularly in cases where there are reasons to believe there to be a connection between fear of reprisal and truthful self-representation. Such sorts of question could be raised in the conversational modality that I refer to as counterfactual narrative critique, a modality that, if practised within a society, illustrates the plausibility of non-question-begging, non-invidiously ethnocentric, critical perspectives on practices within cultural formations that are not our own.[29]

Non-question-begging conversations with affected social agents could be initiated in "safe" spaces providing immunity from the threat of reprisal. These would be aimed at eliciting fundamental or overriding interests – interests that, for the agent herself, might not be readily apparent and might require varying degrees of introspection.[30] Woven into such conversations might well be discussions in which the agent is encouraged to imagine a variety of possible conditions for realizing those interests; these would be the virtualizations of counterfactual narrative critique. This would entail considering scenarios in which the links are gradually severed between succumbing to the procedure of excision in the form it currently assumes and being able to realize those interests. These counterfactual narrative scenarios might range from replacing clitoridectomy with lesser forms of mutilation, to a ritualized symbolic circumcision consisting of a small cut on the external genitalia performed under medical supervision and hygienic conditions, all the way to nothing at all.[31] If the agent, upon reflection, expressed a genuine *preference* for situations in which her interests – chances for marriage and other important forms of social recognition, for example – and *forgoing* the procedure were jointly realizable, then this would count as her opting out of the putative "consensus." At the very least, a discussion informed by these alternatives is more autonomously pursued – and a life led in an awareness of them is more lucidly lived – than one that is not. In any case, the agent would be conversationally interrogating the reasonableness of socio-cultural configurations wherein women are faced with the forced choice between flourishing and bodily integrity and are confronted with the demand to choose between "mutilation" and "social death." My aim here is to try to capture some of our intuitions about the criterial conditions for exercising genuine autonomous agency. And minimally, that involves the agent's *informed endorsement* of what she does.

It might be objected that this conception of autonomy is too demanding to be of critical use, for none of us choose all of our choices. Many choices are "thrust" upon us by the very nature of things or in situations we uncontroversially regard as "normal." Everyone faces disjunctive situations not of their choosing. But some face situations of this sort that others do not, and do so for reasons that are more contingent than necessary, more "contrived" than "natural." The critical purchase of the concept of the restriction of autonomy takes as its background, then, what someone would otherwise – absent arbitrary constraint – be capable of doing. The asymmetrical arrangement wherein one determinate group of mature agents must exercise a choice within a dichotomous or disjunctive framework – that is, one structured by the alternatives of flourish or retain bodily integrity, but not both – while others are exempt from facing such a dilemma may well serve the interests of those who are exempt. This is sufficient to question the rational warrant of this arrangement and to suspect the arbitrary (i.e., *unreasonably* limited and, hence, *criticizable*) nature of the framework for choice for those who are constrained by it.

It is important to note that this dialogical method of critique requires no *wholesale* opposition to the actual options and choices of action available to, and sustained by, a given culture. It is attuned more to the *distribution* of those social options and choices. And what about those cases where, even after such a conversation, some persist in their view that a ritualized procedure such as this has an identity-constitutive character that is itself of overriding value? Consistent with the dialogical nature of the enterprise I am here proposing, this response may ultimately have to be acknowledged as a "falsifying" event. Prior to such acknowledgment, however, and given the heterogeneous constitution of culture, our questioning can be broadened to ask, "Given the likely physical and emotional harms of undergoing such a procedure, whose interest is served by the perpetuation of the practice?" "Given the newly conceived alternatives that our discussion has brought to mind, and in light of the hypothesis that the restricted alternatives were promulgated in the interest, or implicitly served the interests, of some as opposed to others, would you now *endorse*, in the sense of voluntarily choose, what you would have chosen before?"

The evaluative stance is I believe an inescapable aspect of intercultural understanding. The symmetry requirement that is presupposed by my model of cross-cultural conversation – a requirement that demands equality of respect for the other's practices and claims as *candidates* for acceptability – does not *ipso facto* deem such practices and claims as equal in their *ultimate* acceptability. And this underscores the status of my proposal as a model for mutually *critical* conversation.

NOTES

1 See my *The Unfinished Project: Toward a Postmetaphysical Humanism* (New York and London: Routledge, 2001).
2 Ibid., 78ff.
3 Bernhard Waldenfels, "Der Andere und Der Dritte im interkultureller sicht," in R.A. Mall and N. Schneider, eds., *Ethik und Politik aus interkultureller Sicht* (Amsterdam: Rodopi, 1996), 71–83.
4 Philip Gourevitch, "Just Watching," *The New Yorker*, 12 June 2006, 50.
5 In keeping with this, I have elaborated an argument for what I call "humanity as an unfinished project," an argument that suggests that humanity is to be understood in a postmetaphysical fashion, is to be understood as *forged* rather than *found*. This position was developed in part to propose an alternative, in discussions of community and difference, to liberal appeals to an overlapping consensus; to the communitarian failure to do justice to difference; and to postmodern tendencies to valorize fragmentation.
6 *Unfinished Project*, 83.
7 John Searle, *Speech Acts: An Essay in the Philosophy of Language* (Cambridge: Cambridge University Press, 1969), 19–20.
8 On the obstacles posed to intercultural translation by asymmetrical power relations, see Talal Asad, "The Concept of Cultural Translation in British Social Anthropology," in *Writing Culture: The Poetics and Politics of Ethnography*, ed. James Clifford and George E. Marcus (Berkeley: University of California Press, 1986).
9 See *Unfinished Project*, 87.
10 There are two constraints on the metalinguistic predicates that are invoked in a situated metalanguage. On the one hand, we have to avoid vacuity; the predicates must have sharp enough boundaries to be meaningfully applied. On the other, we need capaciousness; the predicates must be flexible and expansive enough to subsume competing conceptions. So, the *Sache* or topic that we dialogically adduce in the analogical process I discuss

here must be fashioned at a sufficiently "low altitude" to have adequately concrete criteria of application to *exclude* some candidates for inclusion. Yet such a topic must have purchase at a sufficiently high altitude or level of generality to embrace or fuse conceptions on both sides of an intercultural dialogue. There has been a great deal of discussion among cultural anthropologists, art historians, and philosophers of art, regarding the transcultural status of aesthetic judgment, that usefully illuminates these issues. Participants in that discussion have demonstrated, for instance, that judgments of aesthetic merit have *meaning* on both sides of cultural divides. The social anthropologist Howard Morphy has argued, for example, that, when "aesthetic" is taken to name the dimension within which *formal* properties are apprehended independently of function, the "aesthetic" meets the criteria I have adduced for a viable cross-cultural predicate. In this way he offers an illuminating account of the cross-cultural purchase of the concept of the aesthetic (Howard Morphy et al., "Aesthetics Is a Cross Cultural Category," in *Key Debates in Anthropology*, ed. Tim Ingold [London: Routledge, 1996], 258). And, to illustrate the point, many experts claim that, despite differences in what counts as aesthetically satisfying, many African societies, for example, seem to acknowledge a meaningful if not absolute distinction between aesthetic value and functional sufficiency (see Robert Ferris Thompson, "Esthetics in Traditional Africa," *Art News* 66 [1968]: 44–5, 63–6; and the summary discussion in Frank Willett, *African Art* [New York: Thames and Hudson, 1971], 208–22). And, as H. Gene Blocker implies in his *The Aesthetics of Primitive Art* (Lanham: University Press of America, 1994), 147–8, even if members of the culture in question do not have anything in their vocabulary corresponding to our word "art," they may well have practices that overlap saliently with those that we associate with art. That is, they may treat a class of objects in their world in ways that are *analogous* to the ways we treat art objects.

11 Akeel Bilgrami, "What Is a Muslim? Fundamental Commitment and Cultural Identity," *Critical Inquiry* 18 (1992): 821–42.

12 Ibid., 823. When we think of a fairly recent controversy, the so-called Rushdie affair, we should note that, given the highly charged and contested nature of intracultural struggles to articulate and systematize expressions of cultural identity, the Muslim reaction to Salman Rushdie's *The Satanic Verses*, and to the *fatwah* that followed its publication calling for his death, was hardly uniform (see Sadik J. Al-Azm, "The Importance of Being Earnest about Salmon Rushdie," *Die Welt des Islams* 31 [1991]:1–49, esp. 34). An evaluation of the charges and countercharges made in the course of this episode would take me beyond the scope of this chapter,

but a brief comment informed by the spirit of this chapter would be in order. This affair amply illustrates, for me, the importance to intercultural understanding of attempting to strike a delicate balance between critical discrimination and hermeneutic modesty. On the one hand, on the hand of hermeneutic modesty, we should acknowledge that the understandable "Western" defence of Rushdie was deployed in terms of sets of contrasts that may have little or no purchase in Islamic cultural contexts and in terms of liberal commitments with unacknowledged Christian roots – both historical and normative – that beg important questions within Islamic traditions. Accordingly, as Charles Taylor wisely avers, "to live in this difficult world, the western liberal mind will have to learn to reach out more" (see Taylor, "The Rushdie Controversy," *Public Culture* 2 [Fall 1989]: 118–22; L.A. Siedentop, "Liberalism: the Christian Connection," *Times Literary Supplement*, 24–30 March 1989, 308; and, of course, Hegel's comments throughout the corpus of his writings claiming the Western conception of individualism to be a secularized version of the Christian notion of the equality of all before God). On the other hand, on the hand of critical discrimination, we cannot avoid believing that critical pressure must be brought to bear on a regime that believes itself entitled to sentence a person to death for exercising his creative freedom. And the point that a writer like Bilgrami would like to make here is that, given the spectrum of positions actually occupied by members of Muslim communities, such pressure need not be viewed as an ethnocentric, imperialistic imposition from the outside; rather, it can be applied from the inside, where there are indigenous resources and aspirations that can fuel *internal* processes of critical response (see Akeel Bilgrami, "Rushdie, Islam, and Postcolonial Defensiveness," *Yale Journal of Criticism* 4 [1990]: 301–11).

13 Yael Tamir, "Liberal Nationalism," *Philosophy and Public Policy* (Winter–Spring 1993): 4.

14 I have discussed the within-group struggle to expand the moral imaginary in terms of persuading members of dominant social groups to acknowledge the semantic authority of claims put forth by others (on the concept of semantic authority, see my *Unfinished Project*, 110–11; and my "Humanism and Cosmopolitanism after '68," *New Formations* 65 [2008]: 57–8, 64–5). By this I mean to highlight the importance of ensuring that a claim made by a particular social group has a claim on all, that it be recognized as a general claim. This would compel interlocutors both to make perspicuous the hermeneutic and social contexts implicated in such a claim *and* to make a genuine and open-minded effort to assess the extent to which such a claim is generally compelling, that is, the extent to which it has purchase

beyond the specific socio-cultural context of its generation. Such a general claim would be one that *addresses* everyone, one that ultimately invites reply. It is a claim that is to be taken seriously by *all* as a *candidate* for a perspicuous description of the world, one that renders salient features that should command respectful attention. Such an acknowledgment involves treating the other's claim as making a claim on all, not by demanding acknowledgment or accession by force, but by getting each to recognize that it is addressed to them as a possible way for all to view the world that they share. And it might be discovered that mutual efforts to understand the heretofore marginalized or newly emergent descriptions may initiate social learning processes whereby what was previously seen as (merely) private becomes a matter of right and in need of public recognition and regulation.

To treat a claim as general in this way is to treat it as a speech act that imposes a mutual burden: the "addressee" assumes the obligation of taking the claim seriously enough to enter, along with the sender, a dialogically constituted space of reasons and reasoning in considering its general applicability; the "sender" assumes an obligation to justify the claim or a particular application of a term or to persuade the addressee, again in a mutually forged justificatory language, of the usefulness of so applying the term. To treat a claim as general in this way is to take it up in such a way that we are willing genuinely to risk having our view of things challenged, without of course there being any *guarantee* that we will be so persuaded. General claims remain defeasible, criticizable claims. But to fail to seek to understand, and to take such claims seriously *as claims*, is to fail to give the other her due. To take examples from our society, to treat, say, sexual harassment and police brutality as merely descriptions of social interaction from the points of view of women and blacks, respectively, with no presumption that these descriptions will have *general semantic authority*, is to enact a restriction that would allow these issues to be understood as simply idiosyncratic matters of "their perception," where *their* perception has unfortunately become *our* collective problem, a problem to be handled perhaps strategically, rather than to be understood as a matter of what their perception *reveals* about our *common* social reality.

15 See David A. Hollinger, "Not Universalists, Not Pluralists: The New Cosmopolitans Find Their Own Way," *Constellations* 8 (June 2001): 240.

16 See *Unfinished Project*, 139–40.

17 See, for example, Thomas McCarthy, *Race, Empire, and the Idea of Human Development* (Cambridge: Cambridge University Press, 2009), 243.

18 Bhikhu Parekh, *Rethinking Multiculturalism: Cultural Diversity and Political Theory* (Cambridge, MA: Harvard University Press, 2000), 148.

19 "Gender, Justice, Development, and Rights," Report of the UN Research Institute for Social Development Workshop (2000), cited in Monique Deveaux, "A Deliberative Approach to Conflicts of Culture," *Political Theory* 31 (December 2003): 780–807; emphasis mine.
20 See my *Unfinished Project*, 105, 109–10, 112.
21 See, for example, Deveaux, "A Deliberative Approach."
22 On the latter, see my *Unfinished Project*, 91–2.
23 Devaux, "A Deliberative Approach," 788.
24 On the occasion of a seminar that he offered at the Humanities Institute at SUNY Stony Brook on 9 September 1999, I understood Renato Rosaldo to offer the following methodological advice in response to a question that I put to him concerning strategic representation: one should in the first instance take what is said at face value, but be prepared to question it when, for instance, conversations with others seem to contradict it or when the respondent's own behaviour seems to belie what s/he has said. Then go on to hazard interpretive projections of the form, "what would be the case if what the 'informant' has said is true? or false?" Then, making the process recursive, return to engage the interlocutor in a confirmatory or disconfirmatory dialogue informed by what one has learned.
25 See my "On Habermas and Particularity: Is There Room for Race and Gender on the Glassy Plains of Ideal Discourse?," *Praxis International* 6 (1986): 338.
26 Jürgen Habermas, *Legitimation Crisis*, trans. Thomas McCarthy (Boston: Beacon, 1975), 114.
27 Ibid.
28 The health implications of female genital cutting have been well documented. See, for example, UN, *Human Rights Fact Sheet 23: Harmful Traditional Practices Affecting the Health of Women and Children* (Geneva: 1995) (cited in Sally Sheldon and Stephen Wilkinson, "Female Genital Mutilation and Cosmetic Surgery: Regulating Non-Therapeutic Body Modification," *Bioethics* 12 [1998]: 263–85).
29 Here I am not concerned to address the putative inconsistency or hypocrisy of Western objections to such practices while apparently tolerating potentially dangerous forms of cosmetic surgery aimed at increasing sexual desirability (see Sheldon and Wilkinson, "Female Genital Mutilation and Cosmetic Surgery"). I am concerned to elaborate mechanisms for critical responses to such practices that are untethered to "Western" views.
30 The idealization implied in the notion of "safe" spaces is deployed in the defence of the meta-ethical claim that non-question-begging, critical cross-cultural conversations can be meaningfully held. It does not address the equally important political question of how such spaces are to be created,

maintained, and respected as sources of proposals that are treated as candidates for semantic authority – that is, as candidates for general social recognition and acknowledgment.

31 On this spectrum of procedures, see Anna Elisabetta Galeotti, "Relativism, Universalism, and Applied Ethics: The Case of Female Circumcision," *Constellations* 14 (March 2007): 91–111.

Chapter Fourteen

Empathy, Dialogue, Critique: How Should We *Understand* (Inter)Cultural Violence?

HANS-HERBERT KÖGLER

The question of how an adequate understanding of human agents is possible aims at the heart of the human and social sciences, especially if the agents express unfamiliar and seemingly bizarre beliefs, attitudes, or values. For a long time, it was taken for granted that the task of the skilled interpreter was to render the other "intelligible" by making his or her beliefs and practices look as "rational" as possible. Since making someone look rational must always mean making him or her look rational *to us*, the rationality attribution seems to imply making the agent as familiar to us as possible. This, however, involves first the danger of a too hasty assimilation of the other's views to our own beliefs and assumptions. If the agents orient themselves to rules and standards different from our own, assimilating their views to our own rationality will miss the mark of their meaning. Second, if beliefs and practices are interpreted with the aim of reaching consensus, the potential of the defamiliarizing effects of intercultural encounters is left unexplored. Understanding thus misses its opportunity to unfold the challenge that intercultural encounters pose to our own truth-based accounts, and we thereby lose the opportunity for a different perspective on ourselves.

One could immediately ask: Why would we even *want* an interpretation that has the potential to estrange us from ourselves? For an understanding to designate a mental state in which an intentional and symbolically mediated phenomenon – such as a text, speech act, action, picture, event, or practice – makes sense to us, must it not be compatible with many of our beliefs and assumptions, perhaps as many as of them as possible? How can the aim of estranging ourselves from our beliefs and assumptions, especially if these provide the ground on which understanding is possible, even make sense as an objective of critical interpretation? The answer to this question will come at the end of the essay. Yet the starting point in favour of such a defamiliarizing, disruptive, challenging stance (i.e., of a self-critical practice of understanding) can be gleaned from a more sceptical, socially informed sense of one's own cultural situatedness. Today, all hermeneutics agrees that the interpreter's background is a necessary, constitutive, and historically shaped resource of interpretation. But if we now consider – and this much should be plausible *prima facie* – that the interpreter's background not only consists of true beliefs and normatively impeccable standards, but also is infused with complex assumptions, attitudes, and dispositions, the project of gaining reflexive self-distance from one's own self-understanding should become more viable as a normative project. Moreover, a critical and self-challenging hermeneutics makes sense if we consider that intentional agency relies on a hermeneutic background of beliefs and assumptions that are embedded in a context of cultural and social practices entailing power relations. If the influence of power on meaning goes undetected, as indeed it often does, a hermeneutics that displaces our common ways of understanding fulfils an important cognitive function.

The core idea of such a "critical hermeneutics of self-displacement" can be expressed in conceptual contrast to the principle of rational assimilation that I sketched above. If it were possible to understand differently situated agents without assimilating their views to ours, we could then employ the hermeneutic understanding of such views to look at ourselves from their perspective and thereby achieve a relative outsider position *vis-á-vis* our own taken-for-granted interpretive schemes. Inasmuch as many of our usual beliefs and assumptions are intertwined with power relations, such a hermeneutics would, by displacing our interpretive schemes, contribute to a *reflexive self-distanciation* from our power-shaped social agency. This hermeneutic project would thus allow for the reflexive reassessment of our situation in order to achieve a higher degree of self-empowered agency and autonomy. Also, interpretive practices in the human and social sciences would support the normative project of reflexive self-determination.

In what follows I suggest that *reflexive self-distanciation* should be the central focus of the methodological grounding for critical interpretation. Yet when we examine the dominant perspectives in hermeneutics, we find that a clear articulation of this objective is missing. Hermeneutics as it is paradigmatically conceived is still dominated by three frameworks: empathy, dialogue, ideology-critique.[1] I will be subjecting all three to immanent critique with regard to the project of a self-distanciating intercultural hermeneutics. Of particular interest will be these two interpretive mediations: (a) approaching the other's meaning and self-understanding in a manner that does not assimilate different perspectives and standards to one's own; and (b) reconstructing the structuring effects of social contexts that entail power practices. The task is to develop a non-ethnocentric hermeneutics that is still capable of a power-critical bite. At stake is a practice of dialogical understanding that does not merely accept or fuse beliefs into acceptable truth, but makes explicit the underlying mechanisms of constraint and oppression, of exclusion and domination, without employing entirely context-foreign and therefore symbolically violent means. The task of a critical intercultural hermeneutics is realized in the successful balancing act between the avoidance of symbolic power exercised through the act of interpretation and an analysis of the power relations found and reconstructed in the meaning contexts at stake.

I focus the following discussion on a concrete hermeneutic encounter with an unfamiliar practice in order to show how this phenomenon may entail the methodological potential to trigger a self-distanciation from one's taken-for-granted assumptions. The cultural practice I discuss is "female excision/genital mutilation," that is, the act of cutting a girl's or woman's genitals in a ritualistic and culturally meaningful way.[2] "Female excision/genital mutilation" has acquired a central place in debates about cultural and intercultural violence, and rightly so. The challenge this phenomenon poses is largely a consequence of its normatively ambiguous status, which is well expressed by the fact that the terms for characterizing it are themselves contested. The issue of *understanding* female excision/genital mutilation is taken to involve either (a) *symbolic violence committed by the interpreter* (if she fails to understand the perspective of the agents themselves and merely imposes a Western and ethnocentric perspective of moral rejection *vis-à-vis* the phenomenon), or (b) *social violence committed by the agents* (if we consider the practice itself to be a violent act, i.e., one of genital mutilation committed against girls and women as victims of an oppressive society).[3] The phenomenon thus raises in an exemplary fashion the issue of how to mediate the cultural self-understanding of agents and the power-laden construction of self-identity in the course of a concretely enacted interpretive practice. By reconstructing how an empathic, dialogical, or ideology-critical perspective would have to approach the practice, we will eventually see how a self-distanciating orientation would enable a reflexive insight into one's own as well as the other's embeddedness in social power relations. The critical-hermeneutic approach that instantiates a reflexive mediating of one's self-understanding with power relations thereby preserves the situated autonomy of agents within a power-defined social context on both sides of the hermeneutic dialogue.

1. Empathy and the Symbolic Scope of Meaning

According to the idea of empathetic understanding, our hermeneutic efforts are geared towards recapturing the authentic subjective experiences of other selves. The interpreter's goal is taken to consist in the re-experience (*Nacherleben*) of the true intentions, the experiential scope and feelings that constitute the other's self-understanding. With regard to female excision, empathetic interpretation implies that we learn to put ourselves in the place of the African woman herself. Yet what exactly does this mean? Would we then try to re-experience her pain, her fears, her expectations, her sense of the meaning and significance of the practice? Certainly some form of simulated re-experience is assumed, yet this list of desiderata also shows that to reduce empathetic understanding to the experience of mere emotions would in this case fail to do justice to the agent's self-understanding. To re-experience this event from the agent's perspective also implies to understand how a woman may take this practice to be indispensable to her female identity – how she sees this interference into her bodily integrity as a gratifying and honouring act, and how she can approve or even desire what strikes us as a painful and harmful procedure. Hermeneutic understanding is conceived as a process through which we approach the other as co-subject, as another concrete individual self; thus, we cannot be satisfied with a formal or abstract reconstruction of social rules, cultural habits, or conceptual schemes. It seems that in order to understand, we have to attain a *state of mind* similar to that of the subject herself, a first-person condition of feeling, experience, or existence by means of which we can truly capture the *intentional meaning of the other*. In empathetic hermeneutics, this re-experience is taken to be the only way in which the other's self-understanding can truly emerge as a unique and alternative form of life, as a meaning that makes sense to the other as well as to us.[4]

But clearly, in order to achieve such a re-experience of the other's self-understanding, we must reconstruct the "symbolic scope" within which the other's intentional states are embedded. This is because it is the *symbolic* context that conveys the specific meanings of that event for the other. Only by reconstructing the holistic context in which female excision is embedded can we hope to gain a sense of the "authentic meaning" this event has for a particular African woman. "Authentic meaning" designates here the cognitive content that the woman herself takes to be real, that she understands as defining the objective context in which she moves and in which she makes her decisions. Precisely because this practice is utterly foreign to our beliefs and assumptions, we are forced to re-create the cultural context in which such behaviour can make sense. We have to explicitly articulate and reconstruct those beliefs and value-assumptions that stand behind the (usually unquestioned) wish to have this procedure performed on oneself or one's daughters. We similarly need to know why this ritual plays the role of an important event in the life of, say, a Malian woman, and why the associated pain and resulting mutilation so often do not lead to resistance or openly articulated criticism. Only be reconstructing these background assumptions can we hope to attain a sense of the meaning this event has for the other.

In the case of female excision, we would then find (thereby coming closer to hermeneutic understanding) that this practice is generally a major factor in the crucial transition from being-a-girl to being-a-woman in the culture at hand.[5] We will also see that the self-conception of the Malian woman – her "female self-identity" – is ritually and institutionally linked to having this procedure performed on herself and that this act carries the meaning of purification. All of this adds to our emerging understanding of how this particular phenomenon is embedded in a whole network of assumptions concerning female identity, social status, bodily purity, and *cultural self-identity* more generally. In this way, we are able to make sense of the *accepting* stance of African women towards "female excision." Thus, making sense involves articulating a network of basic conceptions of identity and reality that together define the symbolic scope of a particular hermeneutically challenging event or practice.

Let us now consider this process methodologically. The interpretive orientation at an intentional re-experience forces us, by its own logic, to take into account the broader symbolic, cultural, and social context.[6] Interpreting "female excision" thus involves making explicit the underlying beliefs and practices that form the symbolic context of this act of "bodily mutilation." We can only approach a radically other event *hermeneutically* if we embed it in a symbolic order. That being so, however, Gadamer seems justified when he argues that the process of interpreting the other *must fail* if it is rendered in terms of a psychological reproduction of the other's authentic intentional meaning "within" ourselves.[7] It is inconceivable that such an empathetic transposition of ourselves "into the other" would allow us to fully experience that event *in the same way* as the other experiences it. Turning to our concrete example, the act of "bodily mutilation" is *as such* too foreign, "cruel," and arbitrary for us to truly immerse ourselves in an accepting and endorsing mental state. Any uncompromised first-personal re-experience of the other's mental and emotional states is thereby excluded, without further symbolically mediating (and thus also distancing) steps and concepts. The empathy model seems to reach its limit with a phenomenon like female excision, since (a) we cannot (and possibly should not!) avoid perceiving this procedure as mutilating, harmful, and painful, and (b) we are nonetheless well aware that it is experienced and accepted by the other as a highly significant and important event. The "interpretive bridgehead" into the other's experiential world thus cannot consist in an act of psychological re-experience; rather, it must rely on the reconstruction of the symbolic scope that makes that event meaningful for the other self.[8]

2. Dialogue and the Epistemic Potential of the Interpretive Outsider

Should we, then, interpret "female excision/genital mutilation" in terms of Gadamer's model of a dialogic "fusion of (cultural or historical) horizons," whereby we define the logic of interpretation as aiming at a mutual understanding of a certain subject matter, with "understanding" defined as a shared consensus regarding what to believe? We would thus (correctly, I suggest) assume that we cannot surpass our own beliefs and convictions regarding the other phenomenon, since we must bring our own prejudices into play to even take part of the interpretative process. To understand another's beliefs or assumptions, we must be able to see them as meaningful and intelligible, which is only possible if we conceive them (literally!) in terms that can make them meaningful and intelligible by our own (admittedly culturally and historically situated) standards and assumptions.

So it is not enough to reconstruct the other's symbolic order as such, but it is crucial – indeed unavoidable, if understanding is to occur – that the other's horizon be productively related ("fused") with our own way of understanding. For a hermeneutically productive dialogue to take place, the background understandings of both sides must come into play. For the interpreter must *be aware* of his or her own beliefs in order to acknowledge the perspective induced *vis-á-vis* the meaning by her own context, and still *be open* to the specific perspective of the other in order to reconstruct the other's meaning as a distinct voice in the dialogue. Put this way, the difference of both horizons as cognitive-intentional perspectives onto a shared subject matter is methodologically acknowledged, and the other is thereby hermeneutically recognized.[9]

To be sure, Gadamer's particular conception of the *dialogic attitude* conceives of interpretation as a truth-oriented conversation in which both partners attempt to reach an *understanding* – by which he means a substantive agreement – about some shared question or subject matter.[10] With regard to "female excision/genital mutilation," this would mean that our different visions are taken to be capable, in the course of the interpretive encounter, of fusing into a *shared view* regarding the meaning and "truth" of this practice. But what can this possibly mean in our case? It could mean either that we could come to see this particular form of bodily mutilation as an adequate mode of self-realization for ourselves, or, in a weaker and context-relative perspective, that we accept it as an adequate practice in its own symbolic and cultural context. Or it could imply that the deeper truth of "female excision" is found in its symbolic and ritual function, which might in turn lead to a rejection of particular features of this practice – such as the concrete bodily mutilation – as dispensable and unnecessary. In this vein, other non-violent "symbolic" means of marking the transition from girlhood to womanhood may take the place of the supposedly purifying cutting of genitals. But in the latter case, the phenomenon of "female excision," which presents its radical challenge as the practical embodiment of a (gendered) self-identity, has already been transformed and overcome, and thus has not been recognized in its concrete truth.

We should thus acknowledge that a *shared understanding of the truth* of "female excision," where this practice retains its current cultural identity as an act of severe genital cutting, is highly unlikely to occur. Nor does it necessarily seem that an accepting endorsement is an adequate response to this practice. It appears to be hermeneutically far-fetched to assume that we as interpreters will come to see this form of "bodily mutilation" as a serious candidate for our own life context. Indeed, the claim that we *should or could possibly accept* this practice as part of *another* context poses a serious challenge to our sense of justified or justifiable cultural practices. It may well be that the Western experience of the African practice of clitoridectomy cannot help perceiving it as a mode of violence and domination, as an ultimately arbitrary form of self-castration in which women participate in order to gain social and cultural recognition. It is doubtful whether even the most thorough understanding of the symbolic scope of female excision will make this practice appear "rational" and "morally good" in our eyes.

It is, moreover, questionable whether we should even desire such a state of sympathetic understanding, given that our perception of this practice *from the outside* does in fact reveal its harmful and violent side concerning the agents involved. It may well be an error to ask the interpreter to forget or to overcome his or her initial negative reaction.[11] This is not to say that we should stop short at such a normative dismissal. On the contrary, the project of critical intercultural interpretation implies that we get hermeneutically acquainted with others' perspectives in order to see ourselves from their perspectives as well. Rather, I am suggesting that once we engage in a hermeneutic process of localizing phenomena and practices in their cultural contexts, the Gadamerian fusion of horizons, understood as the substantive agreement about the value of a phenomenon or practice, is unlikely to occur for a good reason.

Indeed, an interpretive attitude that is solely oriented towards a shared understanding of the truth of a phenomenon too quickly dismisses the *epistemic potential* that is opened up by the role of the *interpretive outsider*. According to the dialogic attitude, the interpreter does not simply attempt to re-experience the other meaning authentically from within – a process bound to fail due to the intrinsic connection between authentic meaning and cultural expression. Rather, the interpreter relates to the coherence and rationality of the other symbolic context from the perspective of her own background understanding. Yet because it conceives interpretation in terms of a dialogue that renders the other's perspective intelligible and plausible, this approach idealizes both the hermeneutic encounter as such and the hermeneutic experience of concrete phenomena like female excision. The dialogic goodwill aimed at a truth-based fusion epistemically denies the challenge that such a practice poses to our self-conception.

The arbitrariness of female excision that is revealed to the non-African observer may indeed point to its deeper truth and should therefore not be absorbed by a reconstruction of the intentional and accepting attitudes of the agents involved. Indeed, looked at "from the hermeneutic outside," *we* can see that this practice enforces a rigid and oppressive conception of female identity, one that is constructed as devoid of autonomous sexual desire and pleasure. *We* can also see that this rite of passage, connected to immense pain and suffering and possibly even to death, is *in itself* a highly arbitrary practice that only from within its cultural context seems inevitable and essential to the self. *We* can furthermore detect that both the act and its supporting context imply a highly enforced and power-laden mode of self, since participation in it seems to be a largely non-negotiable requirement for a strictly gendered membership in a given African culture.[12]

Now I am well aware that by describing this practice as "rigid," as "oppressive," as "implying a highly enforced and power-laden sense of self," we as critical interpreters are on the verge of falling back into the trap of a completely "un-hermeneutic," ethnocentric outsider's perspective, one that completely misses what this practice means for the agents themselves. I fully agree that we do have to avoid any simple ethnocentric misconstruction of meaning derived from our own assumptions. Still, we similarly cannot and should not deny the distance and estrangement that we experience with regard to that practice as an *epistemic source of insight*. It is just such an unfamiliar gaze upon the other that allows us to see aspects and facets of the other's being that are usually too well hidden for his or her own self-understanding. The position of the interpretive outsider thus offers a special *epistemic opportunity*. By the same token, I wish to emphasize that this opportunity involves the danger of a moral criticism combined with an analysis of the constraints of the other's perspective such that our own standards come again to define what can be "rationally acceptable," what is to be understood as right or wrong about a particular event or phenomenon. How can the epistemic potential of the interpretive outsider be unleashed in such a way that an ethnocentric assimilation of the other's meaning to our standards can nevertheless be avoided?

3. Critique of Ideology and the Illusion of Methodological Superiority

Given our critical analysis of female excision as a power-induced contextual practice, it may seem to follow naturally to adopt the perspective of the "critique of ideology." Rationally unacceptable beliefs or practices are an opportunity for us to switch to an *explanatory* mode of analysis. If we fail *to make sense* of the other by reconstructing her good reasons and true beliefs, then we now have *to explain* what *causes* the other to hold her false and rationally misguided assumptions. This points to a two-step method. The interpreter always starts out trying *to understand* the other human agent by attributing rational beliefs and desires; only if this attempt fails will she have to switch to a "causal" explanation of meaning that accounts for the lack of rationality – and thus intelligibility – in terms of various empirical factors. She thus has to adopt a third-person perspective *vis-à-vis* social practices that explains how the other is made to accept apparently oppressive, irrational, or plain false beliefs and assumptions.[13]

Strictly speaking, this mode does not really constitute a new interpretive effort, inasmuch as it uses the same *hermeneutic knowledge* with regard to female excision that we discussed in the previous empathetic and dialogic perspectives. Rather, it recontextualizes the other's beliefs and assumptions within a theoretical frame that introduces some general assumptions regarding social agency and power. In our case, this would take the form of treating *belief systems* about purity, female identity, or the necessity of female excision/genital mutilation as elements of "ideologies" that are acquired in a social context – a context, moreover, that pre-constructs the agent's identity according to structural or functional imperatives and demands. For instance, introducing the theoretical claim that social agents depend on *social recognition* in order to maintain their sense of self, we can argue that the self is forced to participate in practices that establish its identity through other agents' cultural identification.[14] The female rite of passage that defines the self-identity of a woman would precisely constitute such a practice of identification. *We* do not accept the intrinsic connection between womanhood and excision, so in order to explain the meanings of the other, we switch to an objectifying theoretical framework regarding the function and structure of socialization. The purpose of this frame is to explain why misguided beliefs regarding bodily and mental identity are held and practised by the other.

We have thus left behind the idealized dialogic model according to which two situated interpreters meet in order to mutually understand and learn from each other. For a traditional critical theorist, a phenomenon such as female excision seems to justify, if not demand, the attitude change towards an explanatory mode *vis-á-vis* the other agent. As critical theorists, *we* now have to explain *her* beliefs and behaviour in objective terms. The epistemic relation between interpreter and interpretee is now between subject and object, or, in the analogy suggested by the early Habermas, between analyst and patient.[15] Note that the explanatory switch here follows from the (in fact implausible) assumption that we are generally capable of achieving a truth-based fusion of perspectives leading to a shared view. The explanatory attitude *vis-à-vis* the other follows from this because the idealized fusion model allows only two options: *either* a truth-based fusion *or* an explanation of the other's lack of reason. Because these two modes become the only available *modi operandi,* the lack and failure of fusion leaves us with explanation. And as we saw, "female excision" is a case of the failure of a truth-based fusion. What this case now poses as a question is whether the only options in critical interpretation are a truth-based fusion of opinions or an explanatory account of the other's false beliefs. I submit that they are not. Let us return to Gadamer's dialogical hermeneutics to see why not.

With regard to the problem of interpreting meaning in symbolic expressions such as texts, documents, artworks, or actions, Gadamer's hermeneutics shows that interpretation is not to be confused with the interpreter's "transposition" into the other's inwardness.[16] It is not the actual re-experience of the other's intentional states that defines the process of understanding another. Instead, since intentional states can only be inferred from symbolic objectifications, we must *interpret* the text from the very start. Since the interpretation of symbolic expressions, in turn, has to address the subject matter (*die Sache selbst*), we must invest our own (taken to be true) conceptions regarding the issue at hand in order to understand. Thus, to relate to the content of what is said, we must bring our "fore-conceptions" to bear on the issue as presented by the other or the text. Because our own as well as the other's context-knowledge have to be employed in order to make sense of the topic at hand, interpretation reveals itself to be constituted as an engaged conversation about a shared subject matter.

By conceiving of interpretation thus – in terms of a dialogue about something – this model of understanding draws together the interpreter's dependency on pre-understanding with his or her necessary openness towards any meaning and truth-claim of the other. Gadamer characterizes the logic of understanding as a "dialectic of question and answer."[17] This means that statements or symbolic expressions are seen as performative responses to questions that both conversation partners are taken to be asking, rather than being reified as in a Platonic model of propositional content, where the meaning is considered to be fixed and determined in advance. Furthermore, the pre-conceptions of interpreters are linguistically mediated and embedded in an implicit-holistic context of beliefs and assumptions, thus reaching beyond the representational content of the interpreter's consciousness. Insofar as the interpreter can never know beforehand what background assumption will be challenged and transformed, interpretation must be seen as a *dialogic happening* that is never fully anticipated or controlled by the partners in the process. In the course of dialogic exchange, different hermeneutic standpoints relate to one another in a "fusion of horizons" that brings into play the background knowledge of both sides in order to create new meaning. The meaning of texts is thereby permanently deepened and transformed by an ongoing dialogic process in which multiple viewpoints concerning the subject matter merge into new understandings.

However, the particular way in which Gadamer defines the nature of such a dialogic disclosure of meaning entails some problematic conceptual moves. Given the overwhelming ontological designation of language as the holistic ground of interpretation, the agent's self-understanding is now seen as deeply shaped by language, which in turn is understood as the cultural-linguistic background of the tradition. For Gadamer, this means that the self should be viewed as fully integrated into the general meaning of an "effective history" (*Wirkungsgeschichte*) from which there is practically no escape.[18] Gadamer broadly acknowledges the reflexive nature of hermeneutic understanding; nonetheless, he conceives *the self* as fully embedded in the coherent whole of tradition. This means that *reflexivity* is ultimately conceived as a process that is related to the *tradition as a whole*, and not to the concrete epistemic competences of the culturally and socially situated agent. Different interpretations emerge within time in a given hermeneutic situation, yet the underlying ground of a traditional pre-understanding will always be encompassing and consistent enough to finally sustain an orienting and grounding function. Therefore, the goal of interpretation cannot be the reflexive break with tradition (by whom anyway, if all agency is pre-constituted and encompassed by traditional understanding?); rather, it must be the ever-renewed rediscovery of its deeper truth and significance. The normative function of dialogue is thus the *deepened reintegration* into a traditional truth that has always already shaped the interpreter's pre-understanding and that provides an inescapable ground for her interpretive practice. Interpretation, that is, the disclosure of meaning that is both true and significant, can only succeed by returning to this underlying consensus.

This model of interpretation as tradition-based, truth-oriented dialogue entails at least three questionable assumptions. First, the dialectic between a reflexive interpreter and the historical background is dramatically shifted towards the overwhelming and encompassing power of tradition. Tradition is seen here in too undifferentiated a manner – as an overly holistic unit that allows for interpretive differentiations of its "own" self-understanding (such as different and even conflicting accounts of biblical, Aristotelian, Platonic readings) but that never allows such interpretations to transcend or break from the basic traditional tenets. This, it seems, leaves unexplained the hermeneutic potential to transcend one's own background by relating to different cultural and social paradigms, by creating a reflexive distance that deepens and reiterates or perhaps even challenges and rejects deeply held beliefs, assumptions, and practices of any concrete tradition.[19]

Second, the smooth integration of subjectivity into the communal-traditional whole is problematic if we cannot assume that the traditional background is morally exemplary and rationally justified. Since for Gadamer we have no alternative but to rely on our traditional beliefs and assumptions when it comes to making sense of something, he identifies the idea of what is in principle true and right with substantive conceptions that we entertain regarding some subject matter. It is indeed a questionable practice to raise some transcendental standard against which one then hopes to overcome one's own cultural limitations; but it is equally problematic to infer from the unavoidability of our background knowledge that those concrete beliefs and assumptions are to be identified with truth and reason per se.

Third, this account leaves out the structural influence that social practices can have on the form and content of our linguistic practices. Here, it has especially been Habermas's critique of Gadamer that has brought to light this lack of an adequate thematization of objective power structures (including economic and bureaucratic systems) in philosophical hermeneutics.[20] Habermas sees correctly that for Gadamer, language has the quasi-transcendental power of world-disclosure and that as such, it constitutes a self-sufficient source of meaning. Hermeneutics thus only captures the relation between intentional meaning and its cultural-linguistic background; it cannot approach objective social influences on beliefs and assumptions in an equally articulate and focused manner.[21]

It is important for us to remind ourselves of these criticisms, since they do *not* imply – even though they show that philosophical hermeneutics is insufficiently aware of the critical nature of reflexivity, normativity, and power – that we should move towards an un-hermeneutic "critique of ideology."[22] What they actually suggest, I contend, is that we develop a critical hermeneutics that takes those criticisms into account while preserving important insights of Gadamer's dialogical hermeneutics. The ideology-critique falsely assumes that the encounter between incompatible or "wrong" standards justifies a methodological attitude switch towards the other. Yet the experience of disagreement and incompatibility of evaluative standards does not amount as such to evidence for the *methodological superiority of one's own perspective*. This is because that experience does not exempt the interpreter from relying on context-dependent background knowledge, which is itself historically and culturally shaped.

But this is not to suggest a relativistic position in the sense that all value-judgments are now considered context-relative, or that there can never be a rational judgment concerning normative issues. It merely makes the methodological point that within a hermeneutic process of understanding another, the encounter with his or her practice as seemingly wrong compared to one's own does not *as such* justify moral rejection without further analysis and understanding. Such a move would make one's own prejudgments the uncontestable arbiter of any alien cultural expression, thereby insulating one's own value-basis from any critical assessment from the viewpoint of the other. The hermeneutic openness towards learning from the other, towards critically assessing oneself in light of another's perspective, would clearly be violated here, and without good reason. The goal is not to defend an ultimately relativistic position – shared values and good reasons should indeed emerge in the dialogical encounter; rather, what is rejected is an unhermeneutic dogmatism that proceeds via a normatively condemning judgment towards the explanation for the other's moral monstrosity.

We thus face two interrelated methodological gaps in a classic "critique of ideology" approach. On the one hand, the idea of an "objective" social theory downplays or ignores the dependency on language and cultural situatedness that interpretation faces, including interpretation with critical intent. It falsely assumes that critical reflexivity or normative judgment can bypass, as it were, one's traditional and cultural beliefs and assumptions in order to assess other beliefs, assumptions, or practices, as it were, from a "view from nowhere."[23] On the other hand, the unavoidable situatedness of the interpreter undermines the assumption that the critical theorist is entitled to exercise therapeutic criticism with regard to other culturally, historically, or socially situated selves. Habermas uses the relation between psychoanalyst and patient to illustrate the relation between critical theorist and social agent. However, in the social context of historical and intercultural interpretation, agents and cultures with different values and perspectives encounter one another in such a way that the attitude of reconstructing distorted or pathological behaviour can easily amount to an unjustified and presumptuous claim of superiority on the theorist's side.

Let us now consider the methodological upshot of this debate. We have reached the following ground on which to build. Interpretation is necessarily embedded in a structured whole of background beliefs and assumptions. This compels the interpreter to take an open-minded and dialogic attitude towards the other. Since every reflexive agent, in his or her self-understanding, depends on pre-reflexive traditional background assumptions, the interpreter is never justified to claim normative or epistemic superiority over another cultural, social, or historical agent. Yet we also have to account for the justified concern that a hermeneutics grounded solely on linguistic world-disclosure lacks a coherent approach to the question of social power. Therefore, the situatedness of the interpretive social theorist should not lead her to abstain from an analysis of how power relations shape and construct the epistemic and ethical perspectives of situated agents – an analysis that could show how critical reflexivity and normative judgment can be undermined by certain modes of social and cultural existence. While philosophical hermeneutics is thus right to emphasize the situatedness and partiality of every interpretive starting point, critical theory's aim to analyse the structuring influence of power on meaning seems equally legitimate. Put constructively, what now emerges is the need for a methodological position that allows for the fusion of situated hermeneutic dialogue with an interpretive approach that gets at the hidden and underlying impact of power.

4. Dialogic Self-Distanciation and the Assertion of Agency against Power

Let us now return to the hermeneutic phenomenon of female excision/genital mutilation. We are on the verge of reaching a more satisfactory stage of understanding, one that will do justice to the complexity of the hermeneutic experience involved in this practice. We have seen that the realization of this ritual's ethical status and implications in social power-relations *does not involve* abandoning the dialogic attitude *vis-à-vis* the other. While the interpretive outsider has at his or her disposal the epistemic opportunity to understand arbitrary practices *as arbitrary and power-laden*, her specific theoretical assumptions and premises cannot lay claim to ungrounded moral objectivity or methodological superiority *vis-à-vis* the other. As our has discussion brought out, the critical interpreter is not, owing to the encounter of unacceptable and apparently violent social practices, suddenly exempt from his or her own cultural situatedness. The general framework of a theory of socialization and social recognition makes basic insights possible concerning the acceptance of modes of identity and a sense of self. However, these general assumptions do not in themselves justify rejecting any particular manifestation or practice as power-laden or wrong.[24]

Indeed, given the universality implied in such a framework of recognition and power, we ourselves face the need for social recognition and identity formation, which may take forms in our culture that appear equally arbitrary or violent from another's point of view. Moreover, the specific disclosure of "female excision/genital mutilation" as violent or "unnatural" simply assumes that we are in a position to define what may count as an acceptable or "natural" human practice. Yet all we can do is compare and contrast our own situated experience of female identity with that of another culture. The claim that this practice is "objectively" violent cannot be grounded in the epistemic position of the hermeneutic outsider as such, since this outsider position is itself situated in a concrete cultural context. Nor is a universal moral judgment as such supported by the assumptions attached to socialization theory and identity formation, since this framework of social recognition allows for multiple modes of realization, the value of which cannot be deduced from a general social theory.

The problem with a hermeneutically unreformed "critique of ideology" – or, respectively, moral criticism – is that it inscribes a *hierarchical mode of analysis* onto an interpretive encounter that otherwise would have the potential to reveal new insights on the side of the interpreter as well. If we instead hold on to the *basic reciprocity* posited by the dialogic attitude, we have to attempt to disclose ourselves from their perspective as well, in order to understand arbitrary and constraining influences on our own understanding. Relating critically to ourselves from the other's viewpoint does not imply giving up our critique regarding the forced and constraining nature of certain of *their* beliefs and practices, but it does avoid limiting the interpretive dialogue to a one-way channel of the explanation of *their* meaning in terms of social power. Interpretive understanding in its fullest dialogic sense attempts to utilize the perspective of the other *vis-á-vis* ourselves in order to reveal and reconstruct constraining aspects of *our* beliefs and practices *as well as theirs*. Interpretation that is sensitive to both self-understanding *and* social power has to be *dialogic all the way down*. The successful execution of this process will reveal that agents on both sides of the interpretive dialogue are faced with the contextual mediation of their own agency with socially induced power practices, as much as this process helps articulate for these agents how they are situated in their contexts.[25]

Next we sketch how such a methodological attitude of *dialogic perspective taking* may look with regard to a new hermeneutic understanding of "female excision/genital mutilation." We realize that we are dealing with a form of severe bodily mutilation with lasting and highly problematic consequences for the women as far as their experience of sexual pleasure and satisfaction is concerned.[26] Also, we have noted that the social consequences of not participating in this practice can be grave, such that abstention from it may amount to "social death" and might even be unimaginable from the agent's point of view. There is thus no doubt that interpretations of "female excision" can and must be supplemented by a critical outsider's perspective that acknowledges their power-based dimensions. Yet it is also clear that (a) this in no way eliminates the basic capacity for agency and choice from the other's context, and (b) it also invites and demands that such a power-based analysis be undertaken with regard to ourselves. The challenge of a critical interpretation that draws on the epistemic potential of dialogical turn taking is thus to emphasize the power in one's own context, as much as the agency in the other's.

Accordingly, in order to set this process on its path, we must consider whether we find structurally similar practices implying bodily mutilation in our own culture. While we assumed the outsider's perspective with regard to their practices and reconstructed how their self-understanding is intertwined with social power, we now take the stand imaginatively from within their context "to look back" in a similar way on our own, usually taken-for-granted assumptions and practices. The encounter with female excision/genital mutilation thus challenges us to search for social practices and rituals defining self-identity based on social recognition in our own culture. The productive outcome of this stance would be the critical and reciprocal comparison of modes of power-laden social integration in their culture as well as our own. The proposed procedure involves a dialogic approach that reconstructs the other's symbolic order and social practices in order to gain a reflexive distance from one's own taken-for-granted assumptions and institutions, and then moves back and forth between the two. Dialogic self-distanciation, which involves both sides equally, thus captures the productive dialogic insight of hermeneutics without losing sight of social power. While hermeneutics without power analysis is idealistic, social criticism devoid of true reciprocity is ethnocentric. Critical hermeneutics, by placing dialogic perspective taking at the core of understanding, combines insights of both sides into a new model.

To show that "female excision/genital mutilation" entails the potential for innovative interpretive experiences requires some stage setting. So far we have seen that neither the empathetic nor the fusion-of-horizons model of understanding captures our hermeneutic dispositions with regard to this cultural phenomenon; the switch to a critical-explanatory approach contained equally unacceptable assumptions. How, then, can we transform these negative findings into a positive interpretive attitude? How can we conceptualize the issue of "female excision/genital mutilation" so as to trigger a fully reciprocal yet critical process of understanding? One way is by examining the French context in which the legal assessment of female excision became a pressing issue.[27] French courts defined female excision as a criminal practice falling under the French penal code (Article 312, 3), one intent of which is to protect minors against *violence*. Accordingly, an established cultural practice of African immigrants was now to be treated as a criminal activity within the boundaries of the French state. Today, then, the social violence exercised by adults against minors stands against the cultural violence exercised by the French legal system against Malian immigrants. The intercultural clash of beliefs and practices raises issues ranging from the incommensurability of different conceptions of individual freedom and self-realization, to the equality of legal practices regarding different practices of bodily mutilation, to the integrity or value of social customs and practices over against the rights of the individual.

One concrete and illuminating argument raised in this context is that "female excision" has been declared a *violent* bodily mutilation, even though other forms of bodily mutilation, such as male circumcision and abortion, are legal and protected by the state. The fact that other forms of bodily mutilation such as male circumcision and abortion go unpenalized, while female excision is now severely punished, has drawn attention to the unequal standards of prosecution as well as to the problematic and highly counterproductive consequences for the very subjects the law supposedly protects.[28] This is not to say there is no strong difference between "female circumcision" and "male circumcision," or that excision and abortion could be seen as equivalent acts of bodily mutilation. Yet as I will try to show, the seemingly constructed and artificial comparison between "female excision" and "abortion" can illuminate some structural features of the practice of abortion. The illuminating contrast appears less with regard to the fact of bodily mutilation as such, granting that both practices involve a rather severe act of physical intervention in one's body. More important is what the act of such an intervention *means* in the symbolic economy of a woman's self-identity.

Let us, then, assume an epistemic outsider perspective, similar to our natural attitude regarding "female excision/genital mutilation," with regard to our own cultural practice of abortion. The analogous comparison is grounded in the admittedly weak identity of both practices. The major difference between the two may be that one mode involves the possible life of another human being, at least as suggested by one strong fraction of the anti-abortion wing. However, for our purposes, the difference between the act of genital mutilation and the act of an "aborting mutilation" (as an act cutting "something"/"someone" growing in one's uterus) must not be overstated, especially if we orient ourselves to the view of defenders of the "right to choose," for whom abortion does not directly affect another human being. From this perspective, we are therefore not dealing with a relation between two (full) persons, but rather with a self-relation of the woman to her body in which she herself decides whether to undergo the procedure.[29]

Now in this context it is indeed our Western, liberal, taken-for-granted assumption that this practice, if granted as a right, recognizes that the woman *in the West* has the *freedom* to choose. Yet if we now take our comparison to the practice of female excision seriously, we recall that we saw this practice *in the other's context* as strongly induced by forms of pervasive social power and constraint. For us, it seemed obvious that a Malian women's "decision" to choose "female excision/genital mutilation" was consensual, if at all, as a socially induced mode of "accepting an established mode of self-identity," one that a more liberal society would likely abandon. With this view, which we easily adopt with regard to the socially situated other, let us now turn to our own social practices. Does this new perspective affect our view of what it means to choose an abortion? If we now conceive of abortion in the same light – that is, of embedding it in a context of possibly *socially enforced standards of self-identity* – we may come to this practice differently. In our view, it is usually and often solely connected with the issue of the free decision and choice of the individual woman, yet we may now see that it is nonetheless embedded in a power-shaped constellation of social practices of recognition. We may immediately question this analogy by arguing that the right to an abortion is an intrinsic part of *the individual right* for self-definition, that the argument in favour of abortion must be normatively understood. Yet the issue at stake is precisely whether the normative level at which this discourse operates does justice to the hermeneutic phenomenon in its full social situatedness, regardless of how justified it is to claim "the right to choose" at the normative level.

Recall that the idea of the freedom to choose an abortion is understood as a true realization of autonomy, of one's own self-determined identity as a woman. The idea of choice in such a fundamental matter is thus opposed, by its very concept, to any socially induced schemata of female identity that seem to stand behind practices such as female excision. And the right to have an abortion is indeed a right that resists the usual social demand that women be defined solely as mothers, that pregnancy means motherhood. However, if we apply the same theoretical framework of social recognition and power that we employed to explain the other in the context of female excision, it becomes clear that while the right to abortion is generating a certain realm of choice, the social context of choice is far from constituting a sphere of autonomous deliberation. What can now come into view are social practices and value assumptions that induce women towards abortion as a (doubtlessly very particular) bodily-intervening practice. It becomes obvious how the social context provides a horizon of (power-shaped) intelligibility that constraints the allegedly "free choice." As long as women are socially punished and ostracized for being single mothers, having a child might amount to a social death similar in kind to the one experienced by a non-excised Malian woman. Single women with children from previous relationships often express fear of being unable to find a new and enduring partner; there is a deep sense of being undesirable, or of not fulfilling the future vision of a man, by bringing "excess baggage" into the new relationship. As long as women feel that they have to choose between motherhood and career, and as long as single female parents are stigmatized as "unwed mothers," the decision to abort is structurally shaped and influenced by similar forces of social recognition and anxiety that drive a Malian woman to accept female excision. Just as female excision/genital mutilation is embedded in a context of social recognition that enforces standards of identity and self, so is abortion: the Western woman is equally forced to choose in light of highly demanding and often irreconcilable expectations and conceptions of herself.

The need to be recognized as acceptable in order to avoid social exclusion prevails and shapes the self-understanding *in both contexts*. The need for a socially recognized self-identity that is both accepted and understood by others puts women in a position to choose abortion because symbolic and social acceptance seems otherwise unattainable. To be sure, we should not therefore ignore crucial differences between female excision and abortion, one of which is that *the right* to choose *does create a normative space of self-definition* that in this form is absent for female excision, especially when we are dealing with a closed context in the form of an unquestioned and culturally well-established practice. Yet we also saw that the existence of this space of normative options remains nevertheless situated in a context of structurally defined tracks and expectations that restrict and dominate the agent. Here, the reapplication of an interpretive perspective that we projected onto the other in order to illuminate hidden power-laden conceptions of the other's self, can now help *us* recontexualize and reconceptualize *our own* taken-for-granted assumptions and practices. It can thus reveal superficial assumptions of freedom and self-realization on our part, and point to the fact that both of our background contexts are subject to subtle forms of social and symbolic power. It is in light of those that agency, in our own as much as in the other's context, must find and define its multiple modes of self-assertion.

To end, it may be good to sum up the methodological structure of this mode of hermeneutic experience. In this orientation, we do not empathetically transpose ourselves into the other in order to re-experience his or her intentional states, nor do we fuse our beliefs so as to gain a new and shared vision of life. Equally, we do not simply objectify the other as an ideologically distorted subject in a one-sided manner by assuming a privileged position *vis-á-vis* his or her power-laden world. Rather, we place a radically challenging practice such as "female excision/genital mutilation" within a symbolic-practical order without losing sight of the implied power relations, and then apply the same perspective to ourselves. Our specific beliefs and assumptions, when combined with general theorems concerning the acceptance of identity-images and the need for social recognition, thus allow insights into how power shapes and constructs reality by establishing taken-for-granted interpretive schemes in both contexts. Power reveals itself as a symbolically enforced feature of social life, operating in subtle ways by instilling self-conceptions in subjects that are reproduced in the context of social practices.[30]

Due to our *epistemic outsider position*, we can easily adopt this perspective with regard to the other. Having reconstructed the other's symbolic scope, we are then in a position to apply this perspective to our own beliefs and practices. There are no clear methods or rules for arriving at the relevant phenomena in both contexts, but we can reconstruct the process in terms of *dialogic perspective taking*. We must look for phenomena in our own context that compare to those of the other (such as "female excision" and "abortion") and then imaginatively conceive how arbitrary and imposed these beliefs, assumptions, and practices must look from the perspective of the other. Here, in order to reunderstand abortion, we had to locate it in our general social context of beliefs and practices. Inasmuch as we perceive female excision as situated in a context of enforced conceptions of identity, we must search for similar features in our own taken-for-granted practices. The general path of this dialogic self-distanciation entails (a) approaching an unfamiliar event, belief, or practice of the other, (b) recontextualizing that phenomenon in order to make sense in a symbolic-practical context, and (c) determining points of possible analogy in order to trigger a similar process of symbolic recontextualization with regard to our own cultural context. In the emerging assessment of phenomena and their contextual meaning, we engage in a truly reciprocal to-and-fro movement that displaces our familiar assumptions as we become more familiar with the other. This presents us with a form of the hermeneutic circle that, even though it begins with our own pre-understanding, clearly transcends the uncritical acceptance of inherited traditions and customs. Instead of reconciling us with the cultural contexts and traditions we come from, it defines the constant struggle and revolt with regard to the specific contexts of beliefs and practices that pre-define our existence.

NOTES

1 This is no doubt a gross oversimplification, but makes sense as a typological orientation for the following discussion. Roughly, the three models succeeded each other in thinkers like Schleiermacher and early Dilthey (empathy), Gadamer (dialogue), and early Habermas (critique of ideology). Versions of all three orientations are still predominant today, as the later

discussion will show. For a good overview regarding the classic roots, see G. Ormiston and A. Schrift, *The Hermeneutic Tradition* (Albany: SUNY Press, 1990); and J. Grondin, *Introduction to Philosophical Hermeneutics* (New Haven: Yale University Press, 1994).

2 I am much indebted to Francoise Lionnet's analysis in "The Limits of Universalism: Identity, Sexuality, and Criminality," in *Postcolonial Representations: Women, Literature, Identity* (Ithaca: Cornell University Press, 1995), 154–66, and in "Woman's Rights, Bodies, and Identities: The Limits of Universalism and the Legal Debate around Excision in France," in *Female Circumcision and the Politics of Knowledge: African Women in Imperialist Discourses*, ed. Obioma Nnaemeka (Westport: Praeger, 2005), 97–111. For an excellent overview of the issue from an anthropological perspective, see B. Shell-Duncan and Y. Hernlund, eds., *Female "Circumcision" in Africa: Culture, Controversy, and Change* (Boulder: Lynn Rienner, 2001). See also Chantal Zabus, *Between Rites and Rights: Excision in Women's Experiential Texts and Human Contexts* (Stanford: Stanford University Press, 2007).

3 "Female excision/genital mutilation" is usually considered either as a culturally specific form of expressing and acquiring a female identity (as in "female circumcision" and thus seen in similar light as male circumcision), or as a violent form of mutilating a woman's capacity for natural development and sexual self-expression (as when named "genital mutilation"). See William G. Moseley, *Taking Sides: Clashing Views on African Issues*, 3rd ed. (Dubuque: McGraw-Hill, 2008), which includes an instructive presentation of opposing views regarding the question "Should Female Genital Cutting Be Accepted as a Cultural Practice?" Fuambai Ahmadu argues in favour of it in an essay initially published as "Rites and Wrongs: Excision and Power among Kono Women of Sierra Leone," in Shell-Duncan and Hernlund, *Female "Circumcision" in Africa;* and Liz Creel and colleagues argue against it in "Abandoning Female Genital Cutting: Prevalence, Attitudes, and Efforts to End the Practice," in *A Report of the Population Reference Bureau* (August 2001). www.prb.org/pdf/AbandoningFGC_Eng.pdf. I thank Rosa de Jorio for her helpful suggestions and discussion.

4 For an analysis and critique of recent attempts to reactivate a psychological conception of intersubjective understanding based on empathy as "simulation," see H.H. Kögler and K. Stueber, eds., *Empathy and Agency: The Problem of Understanding in the Human Sciences* (Boulder: Westview, 2000). A sophisticated overview and concrete application is provided by Hans Alma and Adri Smaling, "The Meaning of Empathy and Imagination in Health Care and Health Studies," *International Journal of Qualitative Studies on Health and Well-being* 1 (2006): 195–211.

5 See Shell-Duncan and Hernlund, *Female "Circumcision" in Africa*; and Zabus, *Between Rites and Rights*.

6 See also Rudolf Makreel, "From Simulation to Structural Transposition: A Diltheyan Critique of Empathy and Defense of *Verstehen*," in Kögler and Stueber, *Empathy and Agency*, 181–93; and chapters 6 and 7 in the same volume.

7 See Hans-Georg Gadamer, *Truth and Method* (New York: Crossroads, 1989), esp. 184 ff. See Kögler and Stueber, *Empathy and Agency*, for proposals to avoid a psychologistic understanding of "empathy."

8 To be sure, the "self" itself remains, so to speak, beyond our comprehension. It would be worth clarifying more thoroughly what that "hermeneutic ineffability of the self" means for a theory of social situatedness. In particular, we have to ask how the self comes to "attach" itself to specific symbolic assumptions and practices, in a way that transforms those assumptions into core facets of his or her personal identity. The general metaphor of "socialization" as an answer can only be taken as the marker of the problem, a marker that often is invoked as already providing its solution.

9 Drawing out the methodological grounds of this example, we see that as an interpretive premise, we have to assume that the other agent *accepts* the symbolic assumptions and practices as correct and meaningful, and that she views the practice of "female excision" in light of her own generally accepted beliefs and assumptions. Now, because of the discursive mediation of her positive stance, it appears rather than attempting to gain access to the other self's "pure intentions," we have to gain access to the *convictions* on which the other situated self relies. If we thus hold on to the hermeneutic attitude by approaching the other as co-subject, whom we take to identify with and accept the beliefs and practices of her cultural context, we have to *take seriously* the symbolically mediated beliefs and practices of the other. Instead of attempting to empathically enter into the other's inner core, we now have to approach the other's symbolically mediated self-understanding as *alternative discursive claims* about a certain subject matter – that is, in our case the specific ways and practices to define our identity that we ought to take seriously as answers or challenges for ourselves.

10 Gadamer, *Truth and Method*, 265ff.

11 One can indeed argue that by assuming that we should come to *accept* a particular practice as justified simply because it is embedded in a surrounding horizon of assumptions and practices, we are falsely identifying understanding an event or practice in its symbolic scope with the agreement that such a practice is in principle justified and good. It thus

limits the role of the interpretive understanding to a reconstruction of (assumedly) self-subsisting and internally justified worlds without considering the perspective that is open to someone not already initiated in the context at hand.

12 As the women themselves state, the abstention from this practice would result in exclusion and ostracism, if not in complete "social death." See Shell-Duncan and Hernlund, *Female "Circumcision" in Africa*. In this regard, Ahmadu's freely endorsing attitude (in Moseley, *Taking Sides*, see n3) is significantly different, since she does not live and belong to those societies, but is engaged in this practice as a guest from the outside based on her individual decision.

13 The methodological ambiguity of such an approach has been pointed out by the "strong program" in the sociology of knowledge defended by Barnes and Bloor. While I agree with the critical intent of such a program, inasmuch as it tries to avoid applying the causal method only to the other, I disagree with the conclusion that we should therefore become methodological relativists. The uniform application of the causal method is no solution, for it ignores the normative and intentional dimension of meaning-attribution that the two-step model – however inadequately and one-sidedly – correctly acknowledges.

14 Elements of such a theory can be found, for instance, in George Herbert Mead, *Mind, Self, and Society* (Chicago: University of Chicago Press, 1934); Pierre Bourdieu, *Distinction* (Cambridge, MA: Harvard University Press, 1988); and Axel Honneth, *Struggle for Recognition* (Cambridge, MA: MIT Press, 1995).

15 See J. Habermas, *Knowledge and Human Interest* (Boston: Beacon, 1972); see also Habermas, "The Hermeneutic Claim to Universality," in Ormiston and Schrift, *The Hermeneutic Tradition*, 245–72.

16 Gadamer, *Truth and Method*, 177ff.

17 Ibid., 369–79.

18 See especially Gadamer's critique of Schleiermacher in this context, in *Truth and Method*, 184ff.

19 I have developed this immanent criticism of Gadamer in *The Power of Dialogue: Critical Hermeneutics after Gadamer and Foucault* (Cambridge, MA: MIT Press, 1999).

20 Habermas, *The Logic of the Social Sciences* (Cambridge, MA: MIT Press, 1989). See also Habermas, "The Hermeneutic Claim to Universality," in Ormiston and Schrift, *The Hermeneutic Tradition*, 245–72.

21 The fact that Gadamer grants a unique status to authority seems to underscore the conservative and problematic features of that hermeneutic

approach. While authority in Gadamer is in fact not to be identified with blind obedience, but rather with an informed reconstructive judgment that opened itself to the truth claim of a traditional text, Gadamer's designation of the encompassing tradition as the possible ground of any validity of such a judgment does devalue the force of critical reflexivity. See Gadamer, "Reply to my Critics," in Ormiston and Schrift, *The Hermeneutic Tradition*, 273–97.

22 I am referring here to Habermas's early conception of critical theory as developed in *Knowledge and Human Interest*. The later "theory of communicative action" is much more influenced by Gadamer's dialogic model insofar as it reconstructs reason as dialogic and truth-oriented in nature. However, even this conception retains a combination of (a) quasi-transcendental claims to transcend cultural limits via the reconstruction of universal presuppositions of communication, and (b) a social-theoretical analysis of objective, anti-communicative media like power and money. See Habermas, *Theory of Communicative Action*, vols. I and II (Boston: Beacon, 1984 and 1987).

23 See Gadamer, "Reply to my Critics," in Ormiston and Schrift, *The Hermeneutic Tradition*, 273–97.

24 In addition, it should be emphasized that our hermeneutic version of a theory of social recognition would always involve an objective and a subjective side of phenomena, in the sense that the formal need to be recognized, and the socially inculcated schemes that allow selves to identify themselves, are nevertheless subject to the situated reflexive interpretations of agents, and thus allow for multiple instantiations and applications. Just as rules do not prescribe their application, but rely on a contextual sense of how they are "to be understood," so forms of identity do not determine their social realization in concrete cultural contexts.

25 For a parallel discussion of the issue of agency, see Lois McNay, "Feminism and Post-Identity Politics: The Problem of Agency," *Constellations* 17 (2000): 512–25. For a position that convincingly challenges the limits of a solely "cultural" view of the other, in favour of situating cultural practices in a context of power and global interconnectedness, see Lila Abu-Lughod, "Do Muslim Women Really Need Saving? Anthropological Reflections on Cultural Relativism and its Others," *American Anthropologist* 104, no. 3 (2002): 783–90.

26 This claim, it should be emphasized, is not based on an outsider's perspective, but draws rather on the reports and accounts of African women themselves. But see also Ahmadu, "Rites and Wrongs," in Shell-Duncan and Hernlund, *Female "Circumcision" in Africa*, 283–312.

27 See Lionnet, "The Limits of Universalism."

28 See ibid.

29 Notwithstanding the strong disagreements between, say, Catholic critics of abortion and defenders of "women's right to choose," almost everyone agrees that there are two difficulties deeply associated with "abortion," namely, (a) to determine the exact beginning of human life as emerging from the act of conception, and (b) to end a process that involves the beginning of a human being.

30 For further elaboration of the relation between symbolic worlds and power practices in the process of an interpretive dialogue, see my *Power of Dialogue*, chapters 3, 5 and 6.

Afterword: Contesting the Real

MING XIE

[I]n every contestation of the real, which is the way in which a value surges forth into the world, an affirmation of being is included.

Paul Ricoeur[1]

In this afterword, I offer further reflections on the relations among the key terms in this book, especially *agon* and *critical*, so as to bring them into sharper focus and more explicit articulation. The main objectives of a critical hermeneutics may be seen as threefold: (1) to question the central assumptions of hermeneutics, (2) to make explicit the conditions of interpretation and understanding, and (3) to articulate alternative possibilities of interpretation and understanding.

Critical hermeneutics is not just epistemological but also ontological. Reality itself is fundamentally contingent and thus could be otherwise than it is. It is not just a question of our inability to know things adequately, or a question of how things can be and are inaccessible or unknowable. The radical contingency of reality itself, of things themselves, should also be the focus of a critical hermeneutic understanding. This radical contingency of the real is directly linked to the function of *agon*. *Agon* is usually evoked for a sense of disagreement and contestation between cultures and peoples. But what we need to realize is that *agon* pertains only to views and interpretations, not to cultures and peoples. *Agon* is not antagonism between cultures and peoples. In this sense, an agonistic world view entails epistemological humility. But *agon* needs to be taken as epistemological for another reason, that is, due to the difficulty of reality, or the recalcitrance of reality. In this sense, symbolic reality alone is not adequate: the real refuses to be reduced to what is interpreted of it by different cultures. Reality may reside in the gaps among the different symbolic orders of the real as they have been organized by different cultures. Or rather, the meaningfulness of *agon* pertains to what remains contingent and inaccessible. This conception of *agon* has a built-in ontological radicality. Critique certainly pertains to that which, in our experience of the world, is capable of being judged and evaluated. But more importantly, critique is transformative self-awareness, for it is not an objective standard by which something being critiqued is measured or judged. It is rather the process of experiencing the gap between the world and our concepts and practices, and hence the process of trying to achieving a self-awareness of how we experience the world and how we can experience it differently.

Agon can have at least three implications for a critical intercultural hermeneutics: (1) openness, (2) equality, and (3) normativity. Critical agonism means contrapuntal juxtaposition of two or more perspectives in a productive and creative tension. This is precisely what *agon* is about: to ensure the equality of all cultures. The ethical comes into being in the *agon* between cultures in their critical mutual engagement as equals. Being (self-)critical means being open to a plurality of modes of thinking and being. Critical distance is not opposition, nor mere detachment, but is vital to a dialogical and dialectical engagement with different perspectives and interpretations. *Critical* also means that no interpretation or representation of a thing is that thing, since there is always a discrepancy between them. Thus *critical* pertains to our awareness of the partiality and incompletion of our representation and interpretation of the world. *Critical* means not being content with, but being willing and even aspiring continually to go beyond, one's current horizon of understanding. Contrary to the conventional view that it implies or entails a sense of superiority, critique is in fact a form of engagement and thus respect for the equality of those with whom we may not (totally) agree. Critique does not just occur at the level of *doxa* or opinions or viewpoints, but pertains to *epistemes* or different systems of assumptions and presuppositions.

We may draw on Chantal Mouffe to clarify this point further: "By 'the political' I mean the dimension of antagonism which I take to be constitutive of human societies, while by 'politics' I mean the set of practices and institutions through which an order is created, organizing human coexistence in the context of conflictuality provided by the political."[2] Yet antagonism is not necessarily inevitable in constituting "the political"; much depends on how politics is conceived, recognized, and played out, or on our ways of approaching it. So without endorsing Mouffe's Schmittian concept of the antagonism of the political, we may develop her notion of *agon* or agonistic pluralism. To extend Mouffe's point, I would argue that agonism is necessitated by reality's radical contingency as well as by its elusiveness and complexity, and by the inadequacy and partiality of our epistemological grasp of reality.

While the very notion of critique has come to be called into question,[3] critique need not by any means be confined to the sense of superior stance or ideological purity that it is often supposed to assume. Critique is not negative criticism. Nor does it mean criticizing from a vantage point of secure knowledge and superior mastery. Critique is a mode of inquiry that does not aim for mastery, that does not culminate in secure identity or certain knowledge. Being critical does not imply that there is a standpoint or vantage point outside one's contingencies and embeddedness, or a standpoint of unconditioned objectivity and rationality. Critique has often been misconstrued but needs to be reconceptualized. Critique is not a form of thought, and neither is it a method; rather, it is a mode of inquiry, a way of engaging the world and of engaging ourselves in the world. In particular, it can engage in the disclosing of assumptions that underlie views and interpretations. While critique aims to disclose these assumptions, it does not necessarily invalidate them. Critique therefore does not have to mean that the one who critiques is always right, since she is also implicated in the critique. Critique doesn't necessarily mean superiority of distancing and detachment, aggressive unmasking, debunking, or exposure, or privileged access to truth. In other words, critique doesn't have to be a hermeneutics of suspicion; it is not one-upmanship. In this sense, the idea of critique should be rehabilitated and recognized for its epistemological function as well.

It is in this redefined sense of "critique" and by extension "the critical" that we can reconsider the significance of a new critical intercultural hermeneutics. Such hermeneutics has much to do with self-knowledge and self-awareness, both of which include a recognition of one's own historicity and contingency. Thus criticism, as Foucault has pointed out, "is no longer going to be practiced in the search for formal structures with universal values, but rather as a historical investigation into the events that have led us to constitute ourselves and to recognize ourselves as subjects of what we are doing, thinking, saying."[4] Recognition of contingency ties critique to crisis, the two notions being connected etymologically through *krinein*. This criticality of crisis also forces one to step outside of the framework of one's own cultural and intellectual presuppositions. The critical thus implies distance and (self-)distancing, but critical distance is not a negative stance.

There are at least three main modes of critique: Kantian critical philosophy, Frankfurt School critical theory, and Foucault's genealogical approach.[5] For the purpose of this collection of essays, Foucault's genealogical critique seems the most productive approach. It is necessary to get away from the idea of "ideology critique," since ideology critique presupposes an impossible standpoint beyond ideology. In contrast, genealogical critique is both critical hermeneutics and hermeneutic critique. Critique is not to negate other existing beliefs but to become aware of other beliefs and to discover new beliefs, new grounds and reasons for beliefs. Critique does not require all-knowingness, or a superior knowledge of the larger determining structures of which one cannot be fully conscious or over which one doesn't have control. Hermeneutics is by definition concerned with revealing or making explicit what remains hidden or obscured, what is hard of access or even inaccessible. Hermeneutics cannot by itself delineate the larger context of its own interpretive activities. Hermeneutic interpretation is always partial and incomplete. There are always things or dimensions that are not and cannot be captured by interpretation. In this sense, critique can only be self-critique. A genuinely critical hermeneutics would be self-critical, because it would be aware of its own preconceptions, limitations, and therefore its openness and true potentiality.

A critical hermeneutics in the Foucauldian mode would regard (self-) critique as a matter of imagining the present "otherwise than it is, and transform[ing] it not by destroying it but by grasping it in what it is."[6] For Foucault, critique is "the endeavor to know how and to what extent it might be possible to think differently, instead of legitimating what is already known … to explore what might be changed, in its own thought, through the practice of a knowledge that is foreign to it."[7] If Kant had shown the limits of the thinkable, Foucault historicizes the limits of thinking by showing how to test the possibility of going beyond our present limits through genealogical critique. Thus, Foucault's conception of critique is a "critical ontology of ourselves." This is not a purely theoretical project, but a practical one of transforming the present and ourselves:

> The critical ontology of ourselves has to be considered not, certainly, as a theory, a doctrine, nor even a permanent body of knowledge that is

> accumulating; it has to be considered an attitude, an ethos, a philosophical life in which the critique of what we are is at one and the same time the historical analysis of the limits that are imposed on us and an experiment with the possibility of going beyond them.[8]

Thus critical intercultural hermeneutics may even be called "*experimental* intercultural hermeneutics."

Critique as a mode of inquiry presupposes openness and receptivity, as well as recognition of the inadequacy and limits of one's own understanding of the world. Critical reflection promotes a fallibilist awareness of our current conditions of knowledge. *Critical* thus means critical and dialectical self-knowledge in which the inadequacy of one's knowledge is recognized and accounted for. This is one of the meta-dimensions of critique. Critique and hermeneutics are not opposed to each other but are in fact inextricably tied together. Indeed, moving back and forth between critique and hermeneutics is itself a special form of the hermeneutic circle. Critique is not an alternative to interpretation but its deepening and going beyond. Critique as self-reflection is already an explicit thematization of the presuppositions of one's own tradition as well as those of a different tradition. Critical inquiry makes no claims of ideological purity or critical superiority. Rather, it enables an awareness of our own and others' preconceptions that have been unconsciously conditioning us and thus enables us to see the world in a new way. In being reflexive about something or somebody or some aspect of the world, one is also disclosing something about oneself. So critique works in both directions at once.

This intrinsic mode of (self-)reflexivity in critical intercultural hermeneutics will therefore radicalize (Western) hermeneutics for reconceptualizing intercultural reason. This is to say that intercultural hermeneutics is critical because it is normative. Its normativity has to do with a process of becoming of all cultures involved in global exchange and interaction. The normative structure of intercultural hermeneutics is inherent in a process of becoming between the potential and the actual. This process of becoming is normative because what is yet to be realized is, to borrow R.G. Collingwood's formulation, "affecting the process as a goal towards which it is directed."[9] Critical intercultural hermeneutics thus means not taking the given for granted, that is, not taking what has been deemed given for granted. It is to deactualize and thus reactualize what is (deemed) given. Critique is immanent in the very process of deactualizing what is given.

The intercultural potential of critique, as redefined in this volume, has enormous implications and significance for our increasingly globalized world of cultures. Despite its often assumed ostensible and specific origins in the European Enlightenment, critique or the critical impulse or attitude in the broad sense is not a Eurocentric prerogative, but is in fact present in many if not all cultures.[10] It would be unwarranted condescension to think that critical thinking or agonistic thinking is exclusive to the West. This is why, while it has examined some of the most important tools of understanding in the modern Western tradition, the present volume has set out to do more in intercultural terms.[11] The contributions in this collection have brought us much closer to recognizing the necessity and potential of a critical intercultural hermeneutics and have helped clear the ground for further explorations in that direction.

NOTES

1 Paul Ricoeur, *History and Truth*, trans. Charles A. Kelbley (Evanston: Northwestern University Press, 1965), 322.

2 Chantal Mouffe, *On the Political* (London: Routledge, 2005), 9.

3 See, for example, Rita Felski, "Critique and the Hermeneutics of Suspicion," *M/C Journal* 15, no. 1 (2012). Web. 20 October 2012.

4 Foucault, "What Is Enlightenment?," in *The Foucault Reader*, ed. Paul Rabinow (New York: Pantheon, 1984), 45–6.

5 For diverse conceptions of critique in philosophy, see Karin de Boer and Ruth Sonderegger, eds, *Conceptions of Critique in Modern and Contemporary Philosophy* (New York: Palgrave, 2012).

6 Foucault, *Ethics: Subjectivity and Truth*, ed. Paul Rabinow (New York: New Press, 1997), 311.

7 Foucault, *The Use of Pleasure* (New York: Random House, 1985), 8–9.

8 Foucault, "What Is Enlightenment?," 50.

9 R.G. Collingwood, *The Idea of Nature* (Oxford University Press, 1960), 83.

10 For an important example of the Indian tradition of "argumentative" critical reason, see Amartya Sen, *The Argumentative Indian: Writings on Indian History, Culture, and Identity* (New York: Farrar, Straus & Giroux, 2005).

11 For a recent example of dialogue between Western and Eastern thought, see Bret W. Davis, Brian Schroeder, and Jason M. Wirth, eds., *Japanese and Continental Philosophy: Conversations with the Kyoto School* (Bloomington: Indiana University Press, 2011).

Contributors

Suzi Adams, Senior Lecturer, Department of Sociology, Flinders University, Adelaide.

Ian Angus, Professor of Humanities, Department of Humanities, Simon Fraser University, Vancouver.

Jean Grondin, Professor, Département de philosophie, Université de Montréal.

Graham Harman, Distinguished University Professor, American University in Cairo.

Hans-Herbert Kögler, Professor of Philosophy, University of North Florida, Jacksonville, Florida.

Wojciech Małecki, Assistant Professor, Institute of Polish Philology, Wroclaw University.

Hans-Georg Moeller, Senior Lecturer, Department of Philosophy, University College Cork.

R. Radhakrishnan, Chancellor's Professor of English and Comparative Literature, School of Humanities, University of California, Irvine.

Lawrence K. Schmidt, Harold and Lucy Cabe Distinguished Professor of Philosophy, Hendrix College, Conway, Arkansas.

Richard M. Shusterman, Dorothy F. Schmidt Eminent Scholar Chair in the Humanities and Professor of Philosophy, Dorothy F. Schmidt College of Arts and Letters, Florida Atlantic University.

Lorenzo C. Simpson, Professor, Department of Philosophy, State University of New York, Stonybrook.

Mihai I. Spariosu, Distinguished Research Professor, University of Georgia, Athens, Georgia.

Bernhard Waldenfels, Professor of Philosophy, Ruhr-Universität Bochum.

David B. Wong, Susan Fox Beischer and George D. Beischer Professor, Department of Philosophy, Duke University.

Ming Xie, Associate Professor, Department of English, University of Toronto; Siyuan Professor, Nanjing University.

Zhang Longxi, Chair Professor of Comparative Literature and Translation, City University of Hong Kong.

Index

www.ingramcontent.com/pod-product-compliance
Lightning Source LLC
LaVergne TN
LVHW090150080826
844660LV00013B/748/J

* 9 7 8 1 4 4 2 6 4 3 5 3 6 *